The Haldanes of Gleneagles

'Union Jack': John Haldane (laird 1685–1721).

The
Haldanes *of*
Gleneagles
A SCOTTISH
HISTORY
*from the Twelfth Century
to the Present Day*

NEIL STACY

MA, DPhil, FRHistS

BIRLINN

First published in 2017 by
Birlinn Limited
West Newington House
10 Newington Road
Edinburgh
EH9 1QS

www.birlinn.co.uk

Photographs by Anna Blakey.
Plates 6 and 10 are reproduced by kind permission of the
National Portrait Gallery and plate 9 by kind permission of Trinity House, Leith.

ISBN: 978 1 78027 472 0

British Library Cataloguing-in-Publication Data
A catalogue record for this book is available from the British Library

The support of The Strathmartine Trust
towards this publication is gratefully acknowledged.

THE
STRATHMARTINE
TRUST

Typeset by Initial Typesetting Services, Edinburgh
Printed and bound by Gutenberg Press, Malta

Contents

List of Illustrations

Front endpaper: Gleneagles from the north
Back endpaper: The glen from the south, with the house in the middle ground and the hotel in the distance

Plate Section I

1. Margaret Fraser, 1666
2. James Haldane of Airthrey (1728–68)
3. Capt. Robert Haldane, R.N. (*c*.1723–61)
4. Lt Col. James Haldane (1692–1742)
5. Robert Haldane (laird 1760–68)
6. Patrick Haldane (laird 1755–60)
7. Brigadier-General George Haldane, 1755
8. Brigadier-General George Haldane; a caricature
9. Admiral Viscount Duncan, 1798
10. The third earl of Camperdown, 1895
11. Robert Haldane of Airthrey, then of Auchengray, *c.* 1817
12. James A. Haldane, 1801
13. Alexander Haldane, 1878
14. Sir Nicholas Chinnery, 1836
15. Airthrey Castle
16. Auchengray
17. Anna Chinnery-Haldane (1844–1907)
18. Alexander Chinnery-Haldane, bishop of Argyll and the Isles
19. Travelling on diocesan business
20. Alltshellach
21. Dunbeg

Plate Section II

Foreword

Martin Haldane, Twenty-eighth of Gleneagles

The Haldanes have been fortunate in their chroniclers. General Sir Aylmer Haldane's *The Haldanes of Gleneagles*, published in 1929, concluded in the early part of the twentieth century, and was a remarkable achievement considering the author was trained as a soldier rather than a historian. Now, nearly a hundred years later, it seems an appropriate time to take the story forward, and this time the author, Dr Stacy, is an academic historian.

Inevitably, academic rigour has detected elements of the earlier history that require some adjustment. A non-familial eye also brings a somewhat different perspective to events and personalities, some of whom under the benevolent eye of their descendant displayed the plumage of swans rather than the geese they arguably more resembled. Judgement of those who have recently left or indeed are still on the stage may also in due course be changed by the perspective of another eye and of history.

The Haldanes would not be numbered among the greatest families of Scotland, but from earliest times they have demonstrated an ability to survive; in so doing they have played a not insignificant part in Scotland's story, whether in the Bruce war of independence, the political upheavals which accompanied the establishment of the Stewart dynasty, the religious struggles of the sixteenth and seventeenth centuries, the Darien

Scheme and the Act of Union, the Jacobite rebellions, the development of the East India Company, or in the theological controversies of the nineteenth century. In the twentieth century, when the story becomes more domestic, Haldanes are still to be found in the public eye with some influence on matters of national significance, while the domestic story affords a window on how one landed family has attempted to deal with a changing social scene and in so doing teases out personal stories of an amusing and sympathetic nature.

What I think Dr Stacy has done in his work is, through the telling of one family's story and putting it in the context of the history of the times, to shed a light on that history, and to make the family story of interest not only to those who bear the name or have kinship, but hopefully to a wider audience.

Acknowledgements

Above all, I must thank my friends Martin and Petronella Haldane for entrusting me with the task of writing this book, and for their hospitality and collaboration during the many visits to their home which its research happily involved. I am also deeply grateful to Anna Blakey for the photographic expertise which she has devoted to the production of the illustrations. Of the librarians and archivists who have responded with unfailing consideration to my enquiries, I owe particular thanks to those at the National Records of Scotland, the Perth and Kinross District Archive, the Isle of Wight Record Office, and St Mary's School, Calne. I must also record the pleasure it has been to work with Andrew Simmons and the team at Birlinn in preparing the book for the press.

My frequent citation of General Sir Aylmer Haldane's *The Haldanes of Gleneagles* illustrates the extent to which I have benefited from the researches he conducted in the 1920s, and my occasional disagreement with his conclusions in no way detracts from my indebtedness to his work. Moreover, those wanting information about collateral branches of the family should seek it in Sir Aylmer's book, not in this, which concentrates on the owners of Gleneagles and the chiefs of the Haldane name.

July 2017   NS

Abbreviations

Brit. Lib.	London, the British Library
Cal. Stuart Papers	*Calendar of the Stuart Papers . . . at Windsor Castle,* 7 vols (HMSO, 1902–23)
CDS	*Calendar of Documents relating to Scotland,* 5 vols (Edinburgh, 1881–1986)
CSPSc	*Calendar of State Papers relating to Scotland,* 15 vols (Edinburgh, 1898–1969)
Complete Peerage	*The Complete Peerage,* ed. G.E. Cockayne, rev. by V. Gibbs et al., 12 vols in 13 (London, 1910–57)
Exch. Rolls	*Rotuli scaccarii regum Scotorum: the Exchequer Rolls of Scotland,* 23 vols (Edinburgh, 1878–1908)
HG	J.A.L. Haldane, *The Haldanes of Gleneagles* (Edinburgh, 1929)
HMC	Historical Manuscripts Commission
Lib. Kelso	*Liber S. Marie de Calchou,* 2 vols (Bannatyne Club, 1846)
Lib. Melrose	*Liber S. Marie de Melros* (Bannatyne Club, 1837)
Lives	A. Haldane, *The Lives of Robert Haldane of Airthrey and His Brother James Alexander Haldane* (4th edn, Edinburgh, 1855)
'Notes'	'Notes collected for the history of the Haldanes', transcribed by J.A.L. Haldane, 2 vols, typescript (at Gleneagles)

NRS	Edinburgh, National Records of Scotland
ODNB	*Oxford Dictionary of National Biography*
Reg. Privy Seal	*Registrum Secreti Sigilli Regum Scotorum, Register of the Privy Seal of Scotland*, 8 vols (Edinburgh, 1908–82)
RMS	*Registrum Magni Sigilli Regum Scotorum, Register of the Great Seal of Scotland*, 11 vols (Edinburgh, 1882–1914)
RPC	*Register of the Privy Council of Scotland*, 14 vols (Edinburgh, 1877–98)
RPS	Records of Parliaments of Scotland
RRS	*Regesta Regum Scottorum*
Scots Peerage	*The Scots Peerage*, ed. J. Balfour, 9 vols (Edinburgh, 1904–14)
TNA	Kew, The National Archives of the United Kingdom

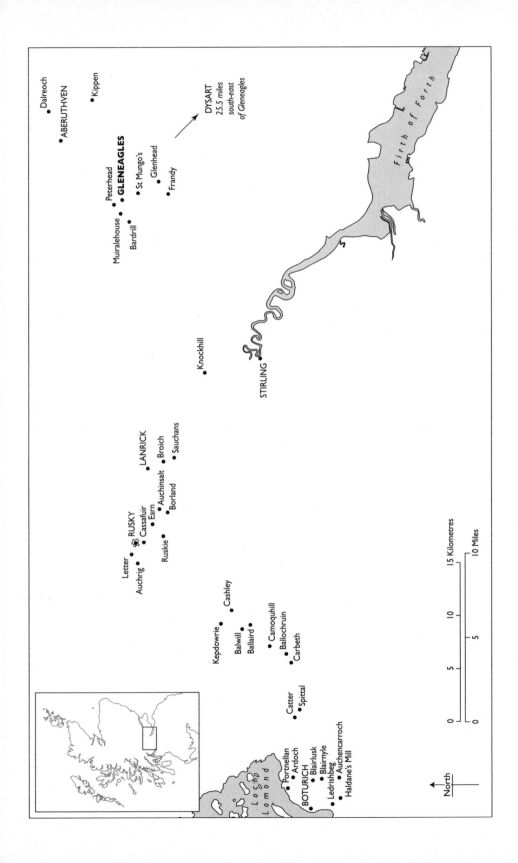

North

Loch Lomond

Portnellan
Ardoch
BOTURICH
Blairlusk
Blairmyle
Ledrishbeg
Auchencarroch
Haldane's Mill

Catter
Spittal

Kepdowrie
Cashley
Balwill
Ballaird
Camoquhill
Ballochruin
Carbeth

Letter
Auchrig
RUSKY
Cassafuir
Earn
Ruskie
Borland
Auchinsalt
Broich
LANRICK
Sauchans

Knockhill

STIRLING

Firth of Forth

Dalreoch
ABERUTHVEN
Kippen

Muiralehouse
Bardrill
Peterhead
GLENEAGLES
St Mungo's
Glenhead
Frandy

DYSART
25.5 miles
south-east
of Gleneagles

0   5   10   15 Kilometres
0   5   10 Miles

I

Arrival

Border barons

In 1165, as King Malcolm IV of Scotland approached the end of his life, a large group of bishops, abbots, earls, and other lay magnates and royal officials, already gathered perhaps in anticipation of their king's death, witnessed a grant of land by one of their number to Melrose Abbey.[1] Eight of the twelve laymen present bore names revealing their Anglo-Norman or Breton origin. Their presence was evidence of a process, which gathered pace as the twelfth century progressed, whereby broad acres of southern Scotland came under the control of such men. Their landed endowment was the response of David I (1124–53) and his successors to the need to modernize the military capacity of their realm with trained mounted knights, and to introduce a Frankish aristocratic milieu with which they had become familiar through time spent in England and Normandy. A ready source of recruits was provided by younger sons who had no expectation of inheritance in the south.[2]

1. *Liber S. Marie de Melros* (Bannatyne Club, 1837), no. 39; cf. *Regesta Regum Scottorum* [hereafter *RRS*], i, *The Acts of Malcolm IV*, ed. G.W.S. Barrow (Edinburgh, 1960), no. 292 note. The date-limits are set by the presence of Richard, bishop of St Andrew's, who was consecrated on 28 March, and by the charter's confirmation by Malcolm IV, who died on 9 December.
2. See G.W.S Barrow, *The Kingdom of the Scots* (2nd edn, Edinburgh, 2003), pp. 250–78; idem, *The Anglo-Norman Era in Scottish History* (Oxford, 1980), *passim*.

Among the last to witness the Melrose charter was Bernard fitz Brian, a man not named in any other surviving document of Malcolm IV's reign (1153–65), but one who was to become a frequent member of the court of that king's brother and successor, William I the Lion (1165– 1214). Bernard's testimony would not have been requested had he been without a landed estate, and, early in William's reign, he is found disposing of ground lying just within Scotland, where the border with England leaves the Tweed as the Redden Burn enters it and strikes south towards the Cheviot. The place was 'Haudene', now Hadden, today a hamlet in Sprouston (Rox.) but in the twelfth century the centre of a 'territory' situated at one of the most sensitive points of the Anglo-Scottish border, and a place of some importance, being the site of meetings between the king of Scots and the bishop of Durham in 1174 and 1181, and its precise boundary being the subject of an Anglo-Scottish dispute which was brought to an inconclusive settlement in 1245.[3] It is from this manor that the family which came to be established at Gleneagles took its name. Its members were 'of Haudene', 'Hawedene', or 'Hawdane' (and briefly 'Holden' and 'Houdene' in documents emanating from the English administration during Scotland's wars of independence), forms which gave way during the 1420s and 1430s to 'Halden' or 'Hadden', which (with 'Haddin') persisted before settling as 'Haldane' in the late eighteenth century, while the preposition 'of' was dropped during the latter part of the fifteenth. Meanwhile, the place name, which had alternated between 'Halden' and 'Hadden' in the seventeenth century, became fixed as 'Hadden'.[4]

3.   Barrow, *Kingdom of the Scots*, pp. 124–5. For march-days at Hawdenstank in the late fourteenth and fifteenth centuries, and truce negotiations there in 1397 and 1399, see *Calendar of Documents relating to Scotland* [hereafter *CDS*], iv, nos. 492, 502, 520, 660, 804, 1030, 1032, 1506; v, nos. 930, 1075.

4.   For varying forms of the place name, see NRS, GD40/1/110, 352, 364, 466; 40/3/40; B59/31/1; CS163/135; E41/17; GD6/823; for the personal name, see NRS, RH9/7/10; GD86/713; GD124/2/16, 27; GD184/1/1/4/1; GD198/2, 35 & *passim*; JC27/30; the English variants are found in *CDS*, ii, no. 291, p.199; iii. 406, 419, 425, 429. Bernard's son John wrote 'Hawdane' in 1472: GD198/18.

Hadden first enters historical record some time in the reign of Malcolm IV (1153–65), when Waltheof ('Waldev') granted to the monks of nearby Kelso a ploughgate of arable (about 100 acres) with a croft and toft at 'Haudena'.[5] The grantor's name tells us that he was a member of the Anglo-Scandinavian population which inhabited this northern part of the old kingdom of Northumbria, and had come under the sway of Scottish rulers in the second half of the tenth century. When next we hear of Hadden, within the first five years of the reign of Malcolm's brother William (1165–1214), its lord was not a representative of the native élite but Bernard fitz Brian. We know that he was a newcomer, because he tells us so. He confirmed the monks of Kelso in their possession of the ploughgate which they had held 'before I had Hadden', with the same boundaries as 'before I came'.[6] Whence had he come?

One clue is his father's name. 'Brian' was of Breton origin, and is usually found on honours belonging to lords with links either to Brittany or to western Normandy. Sir Aylmer Haldane's suggestion that Bernard's father may have been Brian fitz Count, lord of the vast honour of Wallingford, and a natural son of Count Alan IV of Brittany, meets the immediate objection that this Brian died, aged about sixty, without legitimate issue in *c.*1149. There is no record from his well-documented life of any natural son, and, even had there been one, his position as

5. *RRS*, ii, *The Acts of William I*, ed. G.W.S. Barrow & W.W. Scott (Edinburgh, 1971), no. 63, a charter confirming liberties and possessions granted the monks by William's predecessors, based on one issued by Malcolm IV in 1159. Waltheof's grant is, in fact, not to be found in the text of Malcolm's charter, but this should not be taken to imply that it was made after 1159, since this text also omits grants by Roger de Eu and Earl Cospatrick, which are known to have been made before 1152: *RRS*, i, no. 131; *Liber S. Marie de Calchou* [hereafter *Lib. Kelso*], 2 vols (Bannatyne Club, 1846), nos. 71, 138; cf. G.W.S. Barrow, *Anglo-Norman Era*, p. 179. Sensitivity about the inclusion of these omitted grants in Kelso's copy of William I's charter is revealed by the scribe's note, after listing the names of the witnesses, that 'King Malcolm said entirely the same, adding or omitting absolutely nothing': *Lib. Kelso*, no. 12.
6. *Lib. Kelso*, no. 214.

offspring of so great a magnate and, moreover, friend of David I, would have warranted a more extensive benefice than Hadden.[7] It is likely, too, that 'Brian' would have appeared in the nomenclature of Bernard's descendants, had their progenitor been so grand, but it never recurs. Brian's origin is probably to be sought among the lesser members of the Anglo-Norman baronage, and their subtenants.

By great good fortune, at the very time that Brian's son Bernard appeared in Scotland, the names of the holders of most English baronies and their military tenants were listed in letters sent by the barons to King Henry II, in 1166, in response to his demand for information about their services. Although certainty is impossible, the chance that Bernard's father may be found among them is a real one, and the odds on finding him are shortened by the scarcity of his name: no tenant-in-chief bore it, and, of over 3,700 subtenancies, only three were in the hands of anyone called Brian. One was a Lincolnshire tenant of Earl Simon de St Liz and therefore unlikely to have had a son who hoped to find his fortune at the court of Malcolm IV, since Earl Simon and the Scottish king had rival claims to the earldom of Huntingdon.[8] The second, Brian le Chien, held a knight's fee in Norfolk within the barony of the Breton, William fitz Alan of Oswestry (Salop); his candidacy to be Bernard's father may at first seem plausible, for William fitz Alan's uncle, Walter the Stewart, had gone north in the 1130s and found great favour with David I, and firm evidence shows many men from Shropshire and a few from Norfolk with fitz Alan connections becoming established in Scotland during the twelfth century.[9] Bernard, however, did not adopt Brian's byname, a name which today may appear eminently discardable, but, in an age when far less flattering nicknames were jealously preserved, was found perfectly acceptable by his descendants in Norfolk.[10]

7. J.A.L. Haldane, *The Haldanes of Gleneagles* [hereafter *HG*] (Edinburgh, 1929), pp. 2–3; cf. E. King, 'Brian fitz Count', *Oxford Dictionary of National Biography* [hereafter *ODNB*] (2004–14).

8. *Red Book of the Exchequer*, ed. H. Hall, 3 vols (Rolls Ser., 1896), i. 383.

9. Ibid., i. 271; Barrow, *Anglo-Norman Era*, pp. 15, 65–6 & notes.

10. For Hervey Canis in the late twelfth century, see British Library, MS Harley 2110 (Cartulary of Castle Acre Priory), fo. 22; cf. *English Episcopal*

The third Brian to be found in the English baronial documents of 1166 held part of the manor of Tewin (Herts.) for half the service of a knight, which he owed to Robert de Valognes, lord of the large barony of Bennington (Herts.) as well of ancestral lands in western Normandy, and this connection takes us straight back to Bernard's charter which confirmed the possessions of the monks of Kelso in Hadden. Among those witnessing this deed was Robert de Valognes's younger brother Roger. His presence requires explanation, for the Valognes family occupied the highest rungs of Anglo-Norman society, while the widow of Robert's elder brother and predecessor was a niece of the lady Ada de Warenne, mother of Kings Malcolm IV and William the Lion. Since Nicholas the chancellor and Hugh the king's clerk head the charter's witness list, it seems that Bernard was using the facilities of the royal court at Roxburgh, where Roger may have been in attendance, but his base was eighty miles from Hadden at East Kilbride, and so grand an aristocrat would have needed a particular reason to concern himself with the deed of so much lesser a personage as Bernard fitz Brian.[11] Although neither Hertfordshire nor the honour of Bennington, which extended into Essex and East Anglia, has yet been shown to have produced any settlers in Scotland in the twelfth century outside the Valognes family itself, yet the possibility that Brian of Tewin was the father of Bernard

Acta VI, Norwich 1070–1214, ed. C. Harper-Bill (Oxford, 1990), no. 195 note.

11. *Red Book of the Exchequer,* i. 361; *RRS,* ii, no. 249; *Lib. Kelso,* no. 214. The other lay witnesses did not approach de Valognes's status: Hugh de Sartis, probably related to Essex tenants of Earl Warenne; William Dolepen, a Templar or Hospitaller from a family of subtenants in Somerset; and Ulfkell of Hadden, for whom see below: cf. Barrow, *Anglo-Norman Era,* pp. 103, 184; *Cartularium Prioratus de Colne,* ed. J.L. Fisher (Essex Arch. Soc., Occasional Publ., 1, Colchester, 1946, no. 85); *The Cartulary of the Knights of St John of Jerusalem in England: Secunda Camera, Essex,* ed. M. Gervers (Brit. Academy, Records of Social & Econ. Hist., n.s., vi, Oxford, 1982), no. 262. For Ada de Warenne, see *Early Yorkshire Charters,* viii, *The Honour of Warenne,* ed. C.T. Clay (Yorks. Arch. Soc., 1949), pp. 11–12, 28–9; V. Chandler, 'Ada de Warenne (c.1123–1178)', *Scot. Hist. Rev.,* lx (1981), 119–39.

fitz Brian is real. Robert de Valognes's younger brothers, Roger and
Philip, both arrived in Scotland at the very start of William I's reign, at
much the same time as Bernard, the former being given East Kilbride
(Lan.), the latter first Ringwood in Teviothead (Rox.) and later Benvie
and Panmure in Angus.[12] Philip in particular was close to William I,
being appointed his chamberlain in the first year of his reign.[13] Bernard
fitz Brian was not in their league, but, if his father were a tenant of their
elder brother in England, it may be that he owed the grant of his Scottish
estate to their patronage, and that the obligations of lordship brought
Roger to give moral support on the occasion of what was perhaps his
first issue of a charter as lord of Hadden.[14]

The witness list to Bernard's confirmation charter may also contain
a clue to the nature of his takeover at Hadden. Listed last is Ulfkell
('Ulkill') of Hadden, evidently a representative of the old Anglo-
Scandinavian order, now subordinated by the king to an incomer, but not

12.   Barrow, *Anglo-Norman Era*, pp. 23–4.
13.   *RRS*, ii. 33. Bernard's attendance on William at Jedburgh in the last days
      of Malcolm IV's reign may be indicative of a special relationship with
      him; the other witnesses all had links with the honours of Huntingdon or
      Warenne: ibid., no. 5 & cf. p. 6; for the connections of other witnesses see
      W. Farrer, *Honors and Knights' Fees*, 3 vols (London, 1923–25), ii. 316–17,
      342, 370; *Early Yorks. Charters*, viii. 137–40; Barrow, *Anglo-Norman Era*,
      p. 43; idem, *Kingdom of Scots*, p. 289.
14.   If Bernard fitz Brian's origin did indeed lie in Tewin, it would provide the
      nicest of coincidences, for the Valognes' tenant of that manor in 1086 had
      also held it independently before the Norman conquest, and his name
      was 'Aldene': *Domesday Book*, ed. A. Farley & H. Ellis (4 vols, London,
      1783–1816), i. 141bi (Phillimore edn, *Hertfordshire*, 36/19). For many years
      it was believed that the Haldanes derived their name from the Anglo-
      Scandinavian personal name, 'Healfdene' or 'Halfdan', whose latinized
      forms were 'Haldanus', 'Aldenus', and similar variations. The family's
      name, however, was clearly territorial, as General Haldane demonstrated
      in 1929: *HG*, p. 1; above, p. 2, & n. 4; Olof von Feilitzen, *The Pre-Conquest
      Personal Names of Domesday Book* (Nomina Germanica, 3, Uppsala,
      1937), pp. 283–4. Nevertheless, the error is persistent: e.g. G.F. Black, *The
      Surnames of Scotland* (New York, 1946).

completely swept aside.[15] Ulfkell's readiness to move with the prevailing wind is illustrated by his choice of a Norman name for his son: William. Between 1165 and 1177 the presence as witnesses of both father and son was valued by Abbot John of Kelso and William fitz Alan the Stewart.[16] Ulfkell and his family survived, owing services not to the king but to the king's new tenant, Bernard fitz Brian, with whom they evidently found a *modus vivendi*. Some incomers obtained their lordships after marriage to an heiress, but it is unlikely that Bernard's wife, Margaret, was his passport to Hadden. She did not feature in his charter of confirmation to Kelso, and her presence as a witness to his subsequent grant of ten acres of arable to the abbey may be explained if the land included part of her allocated dower.[17] No account of the services owed by Bernard to the king in return for Hadden has come down to us, but there does survive a document from 1223 or 1224, which specifies those owed by his descendant. It describes Hadden as a knight's fee owing garrison duty at Roxburgh castle for forty days a year, which might be commuted to an annual payment of 20s., except in time of war or emergency; should the king command Bernard to go with his army north of the Forth or south of the Border, he was exempted both castle-guard and payment.[18]

We can only guess what propelled Bernard fitz Brian from obscurity to the position of a tenant-in-chief, albeit a minor one, of the Scottish king. Whatever his origin, he must have shown promise of some sort, and the field in which that promise lay is most likely to have been military. William I's enthusiasm for jousting is well attested, while Philip de Valognes was renowned within the international tournament circuit

---

15. *Lib. Kelso*, no. 214.
16. Ibid., nos. 115, 158, 170.
17. Ibid., no. 217.
18. *RRS: Handbook of the Acts of Alexander II 1214–1249*, ed. J.M. Scoular (Edinburgh, 1959), no. 34; G. Neilson, 'Tenure by knight service in Scotland', *Juridical Review*, xi (1899), 173ff., correcting the date given in *Registrum Magni Sigilli Regum Scotorum*, ed. J.M. Thomson et al., 11 vols (Edinburgh, 1882–1914) [hereafter *RMS*], i, App.i, no. 55; cf. A.A.M. Duncan, *Scotland: the Making of the Kingdom* (Edinburgh, 1975), pp. 383–5; Barrow, *Kingdom of Scots*, p. 268.

as one of the finest and best equipped knights of his day.[19] It would be surprising if Bernard were a stranger to the tilt-yard. He certainly fitted readily into the chivalric circle which William I collected around himself, being present to witness the king's transactions not only in the neighbourhood of Hadden and within Lothian, but also at Edinburgh, Stirling, Forfar, Perth, Lanark, and in Fife. Perhaps most tellingly of all, in 1185 he accompanied the king when he travelled south into England, in March being at Kingscliffe in Northamptonshire, where most of his companions were household officers and lords of much larger fiefs than his own.[20]

Bernard's last appearance as a witness is at Stirling between 1187 and 1195.[21] The earliest attestations of his nephew and successor, Bernard II de Haudene, fall between 1189 and 1195.[22] Before 2 February 1196 Bernard II had confirmed to the abbey of Kelso the grants of his uncle, and given it in addition eight acres and one rood of arable in return for consent that he and his heirs might have a chapel in their court.[23] Disputes arising from its establishment were settled by an agreement whereby the abbot and convent accepted that Bernard, his household, and his villeins should hear services in his chapel throughout the year with the three exceptions of Christmas, Easter, and Michaelmas, when they were all to attend the mother church of Sprouston (which belonged to Kelso), while the free tenants of Hadden were always to go to Sprouston. Bernard was to provide the chaplain entirely at his own expense, and the mother church was safeguarded against any loss of obventions and oblations.[24]

19. Ibid., pp. 255–6; *History of William the Marshal*, ed. A.J. Holden & D. Crouch, 3 vols (Anglo-Norman Text Society, 2002–7), i. 68–9 (ll. 1324–9).
20. *RRS*, ii, no. 263 & Index *s.v.* Bernard.
21. Ibid., no. 322.
22. Ibid., nos. 286, 367, 369.
23. *Lib. Kelso*, nos. 205–6; the *terminus ad quem* is given by the witness of Archdeacon Simon of Glasgow and John, dean of Roxburgh: *RRS*, ii. 62, note 36.
24. *Lib. Kelso*, no. 211.

Bernard II de Haudene was accompanied as a witness, probably 1204, by his son, also Bernard.[25] Whether or not the son survived to succeed the father is uncertain, but Alexander II's confirmation of Hadden's terms of service in 1223 or 1224 was possibly occasioned by the succession of a new laird.[26] Bernard II de Haudene's appearance as sheriff of Roxburgh in 1212 or 1213 perhaps came towards the end of his career, and it was probably his son, Bernard III, whose last attestation is found in 1233.[27] By 1236 he had been succeeded by William de Haudene, whom we find as constable of Roxburgh in 1250, but whose exact relationship to his predecessor is not known.[28]

Between 1251 and 1256 William was followed by his brother Aymer,[29] and he before 1278 by Bernard IV. In that year, the boundary dispute which had been unresolved in 1245, and evidently had been simmering ever since, boiled over, and the prior of Kirkham (Yorks.), whose possessions included Carham, Hadden's immediate neighbour across the English border, complained that Aymer, 'son and heir of Bernard de Haudene', had encroached beyond the March and seized over 400 acres.[30] As Bernard was not the direct target of the prior's complant, he was perhaps either absent or in retirement. Between 1278 and 1285 Aymer II had become the unquestioned proprietor of Hadden, since for some

25. *Lib. Melrose*, nos. 113–14; for the date see *RRS*, ii, no. 447 note. Two other fathers witnessed these transactions with their sons; one father (Philip de Valognes) died in 1215, the other (Richard le Naim) was still alive in 1208, so the sons' presence was not indicative of imminent paternal demise: Barrow, *Anglo-Norman Era*, p. 189; idem, *Kingdom of Scots*, p. 294.
26. See above, n. 23.
27. *RRS*, ii, no. 515; *Lib. Kelso*, no. 395.
28. *Lib. Melrose*, no. 343; 'Registrum Domus de Soltre', no. 31, in *Charters of the Hospital of Soltre, of Trinity College, Edinburgh, and other Collegiate Churches in Midlothian* (Bannatyne Club, 1861); *Liber Ecclesie de Scon* (Bannatyne & Maitland Clubs, 1843), no. 77; W. Fraser, *The Scots of Buccleuch* (Edinburgh, 1878), ii, part 2, p. 412.
29. *RRS*, iv, part i, *The Acts of Alexander III, King of Scots, 1249–1286*, ed. C.J. Neville & G.G. Simpson (Edinburgh, 2012), no. 7; *Lib. Kelso*, no. 218.
30. *CDS*, ii, no. 144; *Ancient Petitions relating to Northumberland*, ec. C.M. Fraser (Surtees Soc., clxxvi, 1966 for 1961), pp. 43–4.

time between those limits he was in annual receipt of 22 merks (£14 13s. 4d.), apparently in compensation for loss of land at Hadden.[31] He was still alive in 1305, when he petitioned Edward I of England for payment of this sum, but by then another laird, Ralph, had appeared at Hadden, engaging with enthusiasm in the quarrel with the prior of Kirkham. In 1285 Edward I ordered an inquiry into the boundary dispute which had produced such 'long strife' between the prior and Ralph's ancestors. The following year, the prior asked King Alexander III to restrain Ralph de Haudene, who had seized the monks' lands, cattle, and men.[32] Where was Aymer II? If he were the same Aymer de Haudene who had land at Oxton in Lauderdale and who married a coheiress to four manors in the bishop of Durham's franchise of Norham,[33] he may have lost his appetite for border raids and, settling in one of his new acquisitions, formally resigned his position at Hadden. Before Alexander III's fatal riding accident in March 1286, Ralph was in receipt of £18 p.a. in compensation for damage suffered in his 'border lands'.[34]

In 1291, Edward I of England established himself as direct lord of Scotland during the interregnum following the death of Alexander III's granddaughter and heir, the Maid of Norway, in September 1290. He required an oath of loyalty from his Scottish subjects, and in June 1291 Ralph de Haudene was among 'the knights and barons of the realm of Scotland', who met Edward at Upsettlington to swear fealty.[35] That is the last we hear of him. Further oaths of homage were required by Edward after he had deposed John Balliol in July 1296, and hundreds of names were forwarded to him by the sheriffs. From the shire of Edinburgh came the submission of Aylmer de Haudene and Eymer de Haudene, perhaps the relocated Aymer II and his heir; from the shire of Roxburgh came

31. *RRS*, iv, part i, no. 270.
32. *CDS*, ii, nos. 275, 291; *Cal. Patent Rolls 1281–92*, p. 211.
33. *CDS*, ii, nos. 1481, 1594; iii, nos. 245, 258; iv, no. 171.
34. *RRS*, iv, part i, no. 316.
35. *Edward I and the Throne of Scotland 1290–1296*, ed. E.L.G. Stones & G.G. Simpson, 2 vols (Oxford, 1978), ii. 104; G.W.S. Barrow, *Robert Bruce and the Community of the Realm of Scotland* (4th edn, Edinburgh, 2005), pp. 49–50.

that of Bernard de Haudene, evidently Ralph's successor at Hadden, as well as that of Simon de Holden.[36] Another Simon (de Houden), whose youthful designation 'valet' makes it improbable that his homage had been required, lost two horses in sallies into the town of Roxburgh during the siege of its castle by Wallace in 1298.[37]

Arrival at Gleneagles

No homage at any date came from a Haldane in Perthshire, but an otherwise unknown John de Hauden did homage to Edward I for his lands in the sheriffdom of Stirling in March 1304.[38] Some 150 years later, Knockhill in Lecropt, two miles north of Stirling Castle, appears in Haldane hands, where it remained for centuries, but how it arrived is undocumented.[39] If it had been the base of John de Hauden, which can only be conjectured, its subsequent position within the barony of Gleneagles would raise the possibility that he should be considered the founder of the line. In 1312 a Simon de Houden and his elder brother William were to be found in the English king's garrison at Perth castle.[40] The same year saw an Eymer de Houden mustering at Dundee.[41] Neither Simon nor Eymer can have been identical with the contemporary Border Haldanes of those names. The southern Aymer had joined Bruce in 1310, invaded England 'with banners displayed, burning and plundering', and forfeited his lands in Northumberland;[42] although he had renounced his fealty to the English

---

36. *CDS*, ii, no. 823 (pp. 199–201).
37. Ibid., no. 1007; *Documents illustrative of the History of Scotland, 1286–1306*, ed. J. Stevenson (Edinburgh, 1870), ii. 266–7.
38. *Documents & Records illustrating the History of Scotland*, ed. F. Palgrave (Record Comm., 1837), i. 301; for date, see Barrow, *Robert Bruce*, p. 173.
39. Sasine of Knockhill, just south-east of Keir (grid ref. NS 782983), was granted to lairds of Gleneagles in 1457 and 1769: *Exchequer Rolls of Scotland*, ix. 666; Sasine of George Cockburn-Haldane, p. 3 (original at Gleneagles); cf. GD198/12.
40. Stevenson, *Documents 1286–1306*, ii. 425.
41. Ibid., p. 429.
42. *Cal. Inquisitions Miscellaneous (Chancery)*, iii, nos. 754, 801; *Cal. Patent Rolls 1367–70*, p. 447; above, n. 38.

king once before, and subsequently (in 1304) returned to his peace, his decision in 1310 proved permanent. Meanwhile, given the different localities, it is unlikely that the Simon de Houden mustering at Perth in 1312 was identical with the Simon found in the English king's garrison at Roxburgh in the same year.[43] It is clear that a branch of the family had migrated benorth Forth. That it was kin to the Borderers is suggested by the coincidence of the names 'Simon' and 'Aymer', and virtually confirmed by the recurrence of the far less common Christian name 'Bernard' among their successors based at Gleneagles.[44]

The absence of documentary evidence for the date of the Haldanes' arrival at Gleneagles is a lack common to the charter-chests of many settlers within the earldom of Strathearn.[45] Until the succession of Earl Malise II in 1245, Strathearn had remained strongly Gaelic, a land where neither southern incomers nor the written evidence of landholding which they brought in their wake had taken any hold. Neither the date of Simon and William's arrival nor whether they were the first of their kin to settle in the earldom is known, but members of the Hadden family would have been alert to the earldom's opportunities after Malise's marriage, a couple of years before his succession as earl, to a daughter of Robert de Muschamp. Muschamp held the Northumberland barony of Wooler, whose manor of Branxton was only seven miles across the border east of Hadden, and he already held land of the Scottish king in Berwickshire. On at least three occasions in the 1220s, Bernard (II or III) de Haudene was to be found in his company, attesting deeds in favour of Melrose Abbey.[46]

43. *CDS*, iii. 406, 419.
44. *HG*, pp. 8, 12. Prof. Barrow, whose opinion one does not lightly disregard, seems to have ignored this coincidence when declaring that the family of Haldane of Gleneagles was 'quite distinct and different [from the family] which took its name from Hadden in Roxburghshire': *RRS*, ii, no. 375, note.
45. C.J. Neville, *Native Lordship in Medieval Scotland: The Earldoms of Strathearn and Lennox, c.1140–1365* (Dublin, 2005), pp. 23, 43; eadem, *Land, Law and People in Medieval Scotland* (Edinburgh, 2010), p. 81.
46. *Lib. Melrose*, nos. 279, 283–4; Neville, *Land, Law and People*, pp. 117–20.

No surviving record mentions Gleneagles before 1434, but its very absence from the content of a charter of 1172 or 1173 implies the existence of a territorial unit at that date with broadly similar boundaries. The deed in question is William I's confirmation of Earl Gilbert of Strathearn's infeftment of his nephew Malise with lands including Bardrill and Ogilvy to the west of Gleneagles, Muthill and part of Blackford to the north, and Kincardine to the east.[47] Gleneagles was a significant omission, for its position was of strategic importance, forming as it did the northern half of a pass through the Ochil Hills, giving Strathearn access to western Fife.[48] It may well be that the earls of Strathearn retained it in their demesne, but by 1362 Glendevon, the southern extension of this pass, had been granted by the earl to Murray of Tullibardine.[49] With lands to the north, east, and west, and now to the south granted as feus, it is highly improbable that the enclave of Gleneagles would have stayed under the earls' direct control, but when they released it, and to whom, must remain uncertain. As the Haldanes have left no record of making, or indeed witnessing, any benefactions whatever to Strathearn's religious foundations (in contrast to their record in the Borders), we may suspect that they arrived at Gleneagles, perhaps through marriage, after the era of pious generosity had passed, as it had by 1300. The family tradition current in 1681 was that a representative of 'Hadden of that ilk in the shyre of Roxburgh' married the heiress of Gleneagles 'called Faussyd . . . diverse yeares before King Robert the First'.[50]

47. *RRS*, ii, no. 136; *Charters of Inchaffray Abbey*, ed. W.A. Lindsay, J. Dowden, & J.M. Thomson (Scottish Hist. Soc., lvi, 1908), p. 153; Neville, *Native Lordship*, p. 46. All reverted to the earl, Kincardine and Bardrill forming part of the tocher of Earl Robert's daughter when she married Sir David Graham *c.*1260, and Ogilvy being granted by Malise IV to his son-in-law, Moray of Drumsargard, early in the fourteenth century: ibid., pp. 48, 50n.; *Ch. Inchaffray*, p. 303.

48. cf. A.R.B. Haldane, *The Drove Roads of Scotland* (London, 1952), p. 1. For the probable meaning of 'Gleneagles' as 'glen of the pass', see below, pp. 19–20.

49. *RRS*, vi: *The Acts of David II, King of Scots, 1329–1371*, ed. B. Webster (Edinburgh, 1989), no. 281.

50. W. Drummond, *The Genealogy of the Most Noble and Ancient House of*

The difficulty in establishing the precise antiquity of its lairdship greatly exercised the Gleneagles family in the early eighteenth century, when a boundary dispute with the Morays of Abercairny was exacerbated by social rivalry.[51] Abercairny could trace his family's tenure of the barony of Drumsargard (Cambuslang) from about 1330 at the latest, whereas the earliest deed giving a Haldane the designation 'of Gleneagles' was drawn up some hundred years later.[52] However, in 1745 or thereabouts, Mungo Haldane felt able to trump James Moray's Drumsargard card. Doggerel verse, describing an acrimonious meeting between the two lairds, has Mungo proclaim:

> Altho' you be Drumshargat proud,
> And think yourself a Grandee,
> Cannot I talk and boast as loud?
> Am I not Baron Frandie?[53]

Now, Frandy was not, and never had been, a barony. It was a hill farm in Glendevon, four miles south of Gleneagles Castle. Its name, however, had been used in a clumsy, but effective, piece of forgery, intended originally perhaps in a lighthearted spirit to supply the Perthshire Haldanes with a documented twelfth-century pedigree.[54] The mischief had been perpetrated by 1724, when an inventory of Gleneagles 'Writes and Evidents' was compiled, having as its first item a 'Charter of King William to Rodger of Haldane of the lands of Frandie.'[55] Direct tenure from the king was the basis of a barony, and, if Mungo thought or pretended that he had a royal charter infefting a twelfth-century ancestor with Frandy, that would have underpinned his boast. In fact, the

Drummond, 1681 (Glasgow, 1889), p. 190; for benefactions of the Border Haldanes, see *Liber Kelso*, nos. 205–6, 213–4, 217; *Registrum Domus de Soltre*, ed. D. Laing (Bannatyne Club, 1861), no. 10.

51. See below, pp. 121–2.
52. *Red Book of Menteith*, ed. W. Fraser (Edinburgh, 1880), ii. 230; NRS, GD198/10; below, p. 25.
53. NRS, GD51/10/27 (Melville Castle Papers).
54. See *HG*, pp. 341–4, for a facsimile of the document and H.M. Paton's scholarly analysis of it; cf. *RRS*, ii, no. 375.
55. Now NRS, GD86/1002/28.

charter in its original form was a grant by William the Lion to Roger de Mortimer of the land of Fowlis in Gowrie. The faker did not need to touch 'Rogero', but over a partially erased 'Mortimer' he wrote 'Haden'; 'Foulis' was quite delicately altered to 'Frande', but the conversion of 'Gouerin' to 'Glendin' was blotched. He carelessly forgot to attend to the telltale clerical endorsement: 'carta de Foulis per regem W'.[56]

Nevertheless, the fabrication passed muster, and Roger of Hadden became for over 200 years the accepted founder of the Perthshire Haldanes.[57] His name had been found in the cartulary of Kelso Abbey, where a deed of Bernard fitz Brian (to be dated 1173 or 1178) is witnessed by his nephew (*nepos*) Roger.[58] The cartulary had, since 1704, been in the library of the Faculty of Advocates at Edinburgh, where it may have been brought to the attention of Mungo's brother, Patrick Haldane, who was admitted advocate in 1715.[59] Another possible source of the information was the antiquarian Harry Maule of Kellie, whose library at Brechin Castle had an eighteenth-century copy of the cartulary.[60] He was known to Mungo Haldane, who, in 1732, actually sent him an uncorrupted charter of William I and a thirteenth-century tack, both relating to Fowlis, which had been Maule property before passing via the Mortimers to the Grays of Broxmouth, from whom the documents may have arrived at Gleneagles in 1663 or 1664, when Mungo Haldane's grandfather and namesake married Margaret Gray.[61] The similarity of the witness list in the pristine diploma to that in the Frandy concoction was remarked upon, but, the latter remained at Gleneagles, for, had Harry Maule inspected it, he was too good a scholar to have been fooled.

56. *HG*, p. 344.
57. Cf. A. Nisbet, *A System of Heraldry* (Edinburgh, 1816), i. 138–9; *Burke's Peerage, Baronetage, & Knightage, Clan Chiefs, Scottish Feudal Barons* (107th edn, Delaware, 2003), ii. 1722.
58. *Liber Kelso*, no. 217.
59. Ibid., p. xvii; *HG*, p. 135.
60. G.R.C. Davis, *Medieval Cartularies of Great Britain* (London, 1958), p. 134; *Complete Peerage*, x. 298 n. (b), 304 n. (a).
61. *HG*, pp. 98, 343–4; *Registrum de Panmure*, ed. J. Stuart (Edinburgh, 1874), ii.80, 84–5; *RRS*, ii, no. 302.

While boldly accepting the unreliability of the Frandy evidence, Sir Aylmer Haldane could not quite bring himself to deny Roger of Hadden's place as the Perthshire family's traditional founder.[62] There is, in fact, no evidence of any kind to connect Roger, the nephew of Bernard fitz Brian, with Gleneagles or anywhere near it.[63] General Haldane's family loyalty was further tested by the record of the Perthshire Haldanes in the Scottish wars of independence, and here he allowed himself to be misled into assuming that the Haldane brothers, Simon and William, were supporting Bruce when they and their chargers were listed in the garrison at Perth in 1312. The document recording their presence, however, came from the English secretariat, and the garrison was holding Perth Castle for the English king.[64] He also thought that Simon had withheld his homage in 1296, but, while we cannot say that he was the Simon de Holden of Roxburghshire who did do homage, we cannot be certain that he had in that year any base which would have made his homage required. He may have been too young, like the 'valet', Simon de Houden, who fought in the Roxburgh garrison in 1298 against Wallace.[65] It was, therefore, from an entirely false premise that Sir Aylmer inferred that Simon was 'an adherent of King Robert' and so must have 'fought at Bannockburn'.[66]

King Robert's patriotic status was unquestioned when Sir Aylmer sought to attach his ancestor's wagon to Bruce's star, but in 1312 such clarity was not available to Simon de Hauden. Scotland was in the grip not only of a patriotic but also of a civil war. For many, the legitimate king was John Balliol, and Robert Bruce a usurper, who in 1306 had murdered Balliol's chief supporter, John Comyn of Badenoch. The first document which places Simon de Hauden unequivocally in the neighbourhood of

---

62. *HG*, p. 3; cf. p. 343, where Mr Paton of the Register Office was reluctant to urge his client to abandon the tradition.
63. He may be the Roger de Houeden who pursued a clerical career in the bishopric of Glasgow: *Liber Melrose*, nos. 121–2.
64. *HG*, p. 6; *CDS*, iii. 425. Perth fell to Bruce in January 1313: Barrow, *Robert Bruce*, pp. 250, 254.
65. Above, p. 11.
66. *HG*, pp. 6–7, 345.

Gleneagles also places him within the Comyn faction. The deed, probably to be dated between 1300 and 1306, and certainly before 1313, records a grant to Simon of the eastern third of Bardrill, reserving the succession, should the heirs of Simon's body fail, to his eldest brother, William, followed by brothers David and Gilbert; the grantor was Sir John Logie, who had himself received the land from Earl Malise III of Strathearn.[67] The earl's countess was a Comyn, and both she and Logie were to join a conspiracy against Bruce in 1320, for which Logie was forfeited. Two of the grant's witnesses, William de Muschet and Eustace de Rattray, were with Simon in the Perth garrison in 1312, while another, William de Mortimer, was with Eymer de Hauden at Dundee.[68] Earl Malise himself was also in arms against Bruce in January 1313. He was taken prisoner by his own son, who had been won over by Bruce, and, as Earl Malise IV, remained loyal for the rest of his reign.[69]

A willingness to tack, as demonstrated within the comital family of Strathearn, was a necessary strategy for survival at this testing time for landed families, and Simon de Hauden followed the lead of his new earl. Within a decade or so of the siege of Perth (1312), he had contracted a marriage alliance which now brought him within the orbit of Bruce stalwarts.[70] His bride was the widow Matilda de Arnot, a coheiress of

67. NRS, GD198/2. The earl's grant to Logie was made with the consent of his son, 'the lord Malise' (the future Malise IV), whose consent was unlikely to have been required much before 1300, since he was born 1275–80; Malise III himself was in England between 1306 and 1310, and was deprived of his lands by Bruce in 1313. Among the witnesses, Malcolm of Innerpeffray was perhaps present in his capacity as sheriff of Auchterarder, a position he held until he joined Bruce in 1306; he was confined in the Tower of London in May 1311: *Complete Peerage*, xii/i. 384–5; Neville, *Native Lordship*, pp. 33–4; *CDS*, ii, no. 1858; ibid., iii, no. 218; Barrow, *Robert Bruce*, p. 206.

68. *CDS*, iii. 425–6, 428; J. Barbour, *The Bruce*, ed. A.A.M. Duncan (Edinburgh, 1997), p. 336; M. Penman, *Robert the Bruce, King of the Scots* (New Haven & London, 2014), pp. 221–2.

69. Neville, *Native Lordship*, pp. 33–5.

70. NRS, GD198/3; W. Fraser, *The Lennox* (Edinburgh, 1874), ii. 406. The date of this complex document must be after 1320, when Sir Thomas was dead,

Sir Thomas de Cremannan (in Killearn), who had been forfeited by Edward I for joining Bruce in 1306. Those attending the announcement of a prenuptial agreement formed a very different set from those who had witnessed the infeftment of Simon by Sir John Logie. There were Gilbert de Drummond and his brother Malcolm, who had spent at least four years imprisoned in Kenilworth Castle; Ewan Mackessan, who had endured forfeiture for going with Bruce in 1306; and Sir John Menteith, who had joined Bruce before 1309. The only man present on both occasions (apart from Simon) was Sir William Muschet, who had become a regular member of Bruce's court after surrendering Dundee to him in 1313.[71] All, like Thomas de Cremannan, were prominent men in the Lennox, whose earl, Malcolm II, had never faltered in his support for Bruce.[72] In the same company, and presumably at the same time, Matilda announced that she had granted Simon tenure for life in a quarter of her land of Cashley (near Buchlyvie) 'in consideration of the advice he has given me in my onerous affairs'.[73] Perhaps he had been acting on her behalf in negotiations with the representatives of her two sisters in the division of the Cremannan inheritance.

The marriage apparently went ahead, and produced an heir, for the land in Kepdowrie (near Buchlyvie) and 'Ardas' (also in Lennox), which

but probably not long after: Fraser, *Lennox*, i. 67; *Cartularium Comitatus de Levenax*, ed. J. Dennistoun (Maitland Club, 1833), pp. 81–3. Matilda's toponym 'Arnot' or 'Arnoth' may relate to 'Arnaack' near Cardross, south of Port of Menteith on Pont's map. The seals of David Graham of Cardross and Sir William Muschet of Kincardine-in-Menteith were appended to the charter, because Matilda's was 'too little known'. Sir Aylmer's suggestion (*HG*, p. 7) that Matilda's first husband was an earl of Menteith is unlikely in view of this description of her seal, while his association of her with the Arnots of Kinross was made in ignorance of her Cremannan connection. The name 'de Arnoth', rather than 'de Cremannan', given to Matilda and her sisters suggests that they were not daughters of Sir Thomas (as in Neville, *Native Lordship*, p. 74); nieces would be more likely.

71. *CDS*, ii. 177 & no. 1610; Palgrave, *Documents & Records*, i. 313; Barrow, *Robert Bruce*, pp. 206, 336, 371–2.

72. Neville, *Native Lordship*, pp. 36–7.

73. NRS, GD198/5.

the agreement vested in Simon and his heirs by Matilda, is later found within the Gleneagles barony; so, too, is Cashley, which, like many life-holds, developed permanence in the family of the life tenant.[74] A younger son, who had supported the losing side in a civil war, Simon de Hauden could have looked back on his career at the end of Robert Bruce's reign (1306–29) with a degree of satisfaction. Even though his tenancy of Easter Bardrill may not have survived the crash of Sir John Logie's fortunes in 1320, he had increased his property in Strathearn by obtaining from Adam Thain of Dunning a grant of Upper and Lower Kippen, about 6½ miles north-east of Gleneagles.[75] Moreover, he had acquired a presence in the Lennox, which he was able to pass down within his family. Future lairds of Gleneagles regarded him as an ancestor,[76] and, although certainty is elusive, his own lairdship, perhaps in succession to his elder brother William, may be conjectured with a modicum of confidence. The lack of documentary proof suggests that the Haldanes had obtained Gleneagles through marriage to the heiress of a now unknown family, whose title originated before written evidences became the rule in Strathearn.

Appendix: The name 'Gleneagles'

The name's earliest manifestation is as 'Glenegese' and 'Gleneges' in deeds of 1434;[77] thereafter it appears frequently as 'Glen(n)egas(s)',

74. GD198/22, 118. Matilda's condition, that Simon 'and his heirs' should hold Kepdowrie and 'Ardas' 'of me and my heirs', reads oddly after the clause vesting the land in him 'and his heirs issuing from his body and mine', but it was probably intended to protect the rights of her issue by a previous marriage in the event of her union with Simon proving barren, or even not materializing. The content of GD198/3 & 5 suggests that a good deal of bargaining lay behind them. 'Ardas' was evidently an area between Killearn and Buchlyvie, in which are found the Haldane properties of Balwill, Camoquhill, Ballochruin, and Carbeth.
75. GD198/223, 225; *HG*, pp. 6, 11; for Bardrill, see below, p. 23.
76. For reference to Simon as the ancestor of Sir John Haldane in 1414, and of Sir John Haldane of Gleneagles in 1509, see GD198/223, 225.
77. GD198/10; *Charters of the Abbey of Coupar Angus*, ed. D.E. Easson (Scot. Hist. Soc., xli, 1947), ii. 28.

'Glen(n)egeis', 'Glenegis', and once, in 1577, as 'Glennegnis'.[78] The introduction of a second 'l' is first found alongside 'Glenegas' in 1547, then
twenty-seven years later in a testament of 1574, when 'Glennaglis' accom-
panies 'Glennageis'.[79] By about 1611, when a Haldane kinsman, David
Home, published his book on the Humes of Wedderburn, the idea was
being floated that the name meant 'eagle valley'.[80] Although 'Glenegies',
'Glenageis', and 'Glenhegeis' continue to appear throughout the
seventeenth century, and 'Glenegis' is found in local use *c.*1750,[81] 'Glen-
(n)eglis' becomes common from the 1620s onwards, being replaced by
'Gleneagles' in the early eighteenth century.

   The lack of a second 'l' in the early forms of the name undermines
both the derivation from the bird of prey, and that from the Gaelic
eaglais, 'church', which has found currency in place-name dictionar-
ies.[82] The possibility of a connection with *eigeas*, 'a learned man', has
been proposed,[83] but a more likely origin lies in the glen's strategically
important position as the northern half of a pass through the Ochils.
The Gaelic for a pass, or notch, is *eag*, and that probably is the element
contained in the early forms of 'Gleneagles'.[84]

78.   NRS, B68/25/142 (Stirling Borough Records).
79.   NRS, GD198/231; CC8/8/3 (test. 1575 George Haldane).
80.   'Johanni Haldano Gleneglisio (sive Vallaguilio interpretemur)': D. Hume,
      De Familia Humia Wedderburnensi Liber (Abbotsford Club, 1839), pp. 58,
      68.
81.   NRS, GD51/10/27 (Melville Castle Papers); a notary used 'Glenegies' in
      1753: NRS, CC8/8/114 (test. 1753 Neill McKinnon).
82.   J.B. Johnston, *Place-Names of Scotland* (3rd edn, London, 1934), p. 193;
      M. Darton, *The Dictionary of Place Names in Scotland* (Orpington, 1994),
      p. 136; cf. *HG*, p. 307.
83.   *HG*, p. 307, followed by A. Watson, *The Ochils: Placenames, History,
      Tradition* (Perth, 1995), p. 62.
84.   This possibility was first suggested by J. Christie, *The Lairds and Lands of
      Loch Tayside* (Aberfeldy, 1892), p. 92. Dr Simon Taylor of the Department
      of Celtic Studies, Glasgow University, compares it to Aigais by Beauly,
      'place of the notch': personal communication, 28 January 2014, for which
      I am most grateful.

II

Expansion and Advancement

Losses and gains, c.1330–1456

Simon de Hauden is last recorded in 1337, when the bishop of Dunkeld redeemed from him episcopal land two miles north-west of Stirling at Greenocks, close to Haldane ground at Knockhill.[1] Four years earlier the bishop had crowned Edward, son of John Balliol, as king of Scots, and Scotland was once more torn by the rivalry between Bruce and Balliol, rekindled by the minority of David II, the five-year-old heir left by Robert I on his death in June 1329. Support for Bruce had never been strong in the earldom of Strathearn, and, since Earl Malise V had pledged allegiance to Edward Balliol in 1333, it should occasion no surprise that a Haldane was transacting business with Edward's episcopal stalwart.[2]

The resurgence of factional strife brought in its wake the return of English armies and devastation to the Borders. Although Strathearn saw a good deal of military action, with Balliol's army defeating Bruce forces in August 1332 south-east of Perth on Dupplin Moor, and Perth itself becoming the key Balliol stronghold before falling in 1339, it was not subjected to the ruthless and sustained campaigns of plunder and destruction which afflicted the marches. Few places were more

1. *Rentalia Dunkeldense*, ed. R.K. Hannay (Scot. Hist. Soc., x, 1913–14), p. 336.
2. Cf. M. Brown, *The Wars of Scotland 1214–1371* (Edinburgh, 2004), pp. 234, 236.

vulnerable than the Haldanes' ancestral barony of Hadden. Roxburgh, within whose shire it lay, had been the most regular seat of royal government when Bernard fitz Brian began his family's career in Scotland, but, for eight years after 1334, its sheriffdom in common with five others was incorporated in England, whither it returned after the battle of Neville's Cross, in 1346, and remained for some thirty-five years. Hadden was vulnerable to constant attack from both sides, and, when its laird, the sixth Bernard of Hadden, was forfeited by the English king Edward III in November 1357, its annual value, which in peacetime had been about £43, was now reckoned to be no more than £5, the manor being 'utterly destroyed and wasted' by the Scots, and its tenants fled.[3]

It was instability rather than obliteration that threatened the Haldanes based in Strathearn, with Edward Balliol replacing the last Gaelic earl in 1334 by the English earl of Surrey, whose position was not recognized by the Bruce administration; with David II installing Maurice Moray of Drumsargard in 1344, and Moray being slain two years later at Neville's Cross, where David himself was captured by the English; and with the guardian and heir presumptive, Robert Stewart, seeking to fill the vacuum by strengthening his position in the region. In 1357, when King David returned from captivity, the earldom was, in fact, given to the Stewart, whose predominance in central Scotland, although occasionally challenged by the king, became irresistible, and, after his succession as Robert II on David's death in 1371, he used that predominance to reward and extend his affinity.[4]

Where there are winners there are also losers. The first surviving record since 1337 to illumine the history of the Perthshire Haldanes is a grant made in 1376 by Robert II of lands within the thanage of Alyth (Forfar) to his nephew James Lindsay. The king's protest that the lands had come into his hands 'lawfully' suggests that those who had previously held them may not have agreed. Among them was Bernard de

---

3.   CDS, iv, no. 1; cf. Nicholson, *Scotland: Later Middle Ages*, pp. 148, 162.
4.   Brown, *The Wars of Scotland*, pp. 248–9, 328–9; Neville, *Native Lordship*, pp. 35–6; M. Penman, *David II, 1329–71* (Edinburgh, 2004), pp. 106–8, 200; S. Boardman, *The Early Stewart Kings: Robert II and Robert III, 1371–1406* (East Linton, 1996), pp. 16–17, 24, 71, 88–9.

Hauden.[5] It seems that this abortive eastward expansion had been the result of a marriage alliance between Haldanes and either Rattrays or Bickertons, for associated with Bernard as previous owners of the lands thus transferred were Thomas of Rattray and Richard of Bickerton; a couple of generations later, a Thomas Rattray of Tullymurdoch (north-west of Alyth) referred to Sir Walter of Bickerton as his grandfather and to Sir John Haldane of Gleneagles, son of Bernard, as his kinsman.[6]

Whatever manoeuvrings had brought his part of the thanage of Alyth into Robert II's hands, Bernard de Hauden's relations with the first Stewart king were good enough for him to have received knighthood by 1385.[7] In 1388, he entered a contractual arrangement with the Maxwells of Pollok, who, some time before 1372, had obtained from the earl of Strathearn Easter Bardrill on the western border of Gleneagles, together with its neighbour Easter Banheath and the eastern half of 'Glen Frandy'. The Haldane tenancy of Easter Bardrill under Sir John Logie had evidently terminated with his forfeiture in 1320, when the land must have escheated to the earl as its superior. In order to recover it from the new tenant, Maxwell of Pollok, Sir Bernard exchanged Jackton, near East Kilbride in Renfrewshire, a property some twenty-five miles south of the nearest Haldane ground at Cashley.[8] How Jackton had been acquired is unknown, but, as it lay deep in Maxwell country, with their castles of Calderwood to the east and Pollok itself to the north, and since Maxwell was to owe no service from it after the exchange, it is possible that Haldane was his tenant. Sir Bernard, on the other hand, was to pay one penny blench ferme to Maxwell, as well as perform whatever service Bardrill owed to the earl of Strathearn. In 1414, Sir Bernard's son was confirmed in his possession of Bardrill by Countess Euphemia of Strathearn.[9] Bardrill was back.

---

5. *Registrum Magni Sigilli Regum Scotorum* [hereafter *RMS*], i (1306–1424), ed. J.M. Thomson (Edinburgh, 1912), no. 630.

6. NRS, GD198/10.

7. W. Fraser, *The Douglas Book* (4 vols, Edinburgh, 1885), iii. 32.

8. GD198/8; W. Fraser, *Memoirs of the Maxwells of Pollok* (Edinburgh, 1863), i. 131–2.

9. Ibid., p. 134.

Recovery within Strathearn was soon, however, to be outweighed by a reverse in the Lennox. When Sir Bernard de Hauden died in 1401, Earl Duncan of Lennox declined to accept the homage of his son and heir, John, for Kepdowrie and the ground to the south contained in 'Ardas'. These lands had come to the Haldanes from Matilda de Arnot, as part of her share of the estate of Thomas de Cremannan, an inheritance which had evidently been problematic to secure.[10] Another portion of it passed to the Cunninghams of Drumquhassle, and it seems that in 1401 the Cunninghams had the ear of Earl Duncan, for they supplanted John de Hauden in Kepdowrie and 'Ardas'.[11] Earl Duncan was close to the centre of power in Scotland: the king, Robert III (1390–1406), was an invalid, marginalized by his brother Robert, duke of Albany (d.1420), whose heir, Murdoch, was the earl's son-in-law. Fear for the safety of his own son and heir, James, led the king, shortly before his death in 1406, to send the prince to France, but his ship was intercepted by Norfolk pirates, and James spent the first eighteen years of his reign in captivity in England. In the interim, the Albany Stewarts ruled Scotland, and Sir John de Hauden had to wait until 1425 for the restoration of his property in the Lennox. In April 1424, the released James I returned to his kingdom. In May the following year, he struck at his overmighty Albany cousins, and the ensuing judicial bloodbath engulfed the octogenarian Earl Duncan of Lennox, as well as his son-in-law Murdoch, now duke of Albany, and Murdoch's sons, Walter and Alexander.[12] Four months later, Sir John de Hauden was retoured as heir to his father's lands of Kepdowrie and 'Ardas', which had for twenty-four years been kept in hand by 'the baron of Lennox'.[13] Before the century was out, the politics

---

10. GD198/9; above, p. 18.
11. For Cunningham's succession to 'Aschend' on Endrick Water, see *Cart. Levenax*, pp. 66–7, 81; Croy Cunningham had also been Cremannan property: ibid., pp. 79–81.
12. M. Brown, *James I* (Edinburgh, 1994), pp. 16–17, 54–67; Boardman, *Early Stewart Kings*, pp. 255–97.
13. GD198/9; the Cunningham rights were acknowledged by a nominal payment. General Haldane was mistaken in identifying the 'baron of Lennox' of the retour as the king: *HG*, p. 12.

of the Lennox were to transform the fortunes of the descendants of the Haldane whose rights Earl Duncan had withheld.

Meanwhile, having recovered his family's position in the west, Sir John turned his attention south-eastwards to Edinburgh and its environs, becoming a tenant of John Lindsay of the Byres at Coates, barely half a mile west of Edinburgh Castle, and at Harvieston near North Middleton, some ten miles to the south.[14] Lindsay of the Byres was close kin to the wife of Patrick, Lord Graham, in whose household at Kincardine are found, in 1448, the squires (*scutiferi*) William and John Haldene.[15] William's relationship to Sir John is uncertain, but John was his grandson, son of his heir Bernard, and destined to father the future husband of a granddaughter of Patrick Graham.[16]

Further opportunity for south-eastward expansion led Sir John towards Fife, where in 1434 he was able to use his family's Rattray connection to obtain half the share of Dysart which Thomas Rattray of Tullymurdoch had inherited from his grandfather, Sir Walter de Bickerton (d.1424).[17] The property usefully diversified the Haldane portfolio, bringing salt-workings on the shore of the Firth of Forth as well as 'the coals beneath the earth' inland at Blair.[18] In the charter recording his grant Rattray refers to Sir John not only as his kinsman but also as 'the laird (*dominus*) of Glenegese', thus providing the earliest surviving instance of the appellation which is still borne by the head of the Haldane family.

The Lennox inheritance, 1456–93

Sir John de Hauden's most significant advancement came without his need to exert any effort. The earldom of Strathearn had been forfeited

14. GD198/222.
15. W. Fraser, *The Stirlings of Keir and their Family Papers* (Edinburgh, 1858), pp. 223–4; *Complete Peerage*, iii. 511; vi. 53; viii. 6–7; C.A. McGladderty, 'Lindsay family of the Byres', *ODNB* (2004).
16. See below, p. 37.
17. GD198/10.
18. *RMS*, iii, no. 1368; cf. *Acta Dominorum Concillii, 1478–95*, ed. T. Thomson (Record Comm., 1839), p. 6.

by Walter Stewart on his conviction for regicide in 1437.[19] As a consequence, the laird of Gleneagles became a tenant-in-chief of the king,[20]
and Sir John's heirs entered a higher league in the marriage market than
that occupied by their predecessors. Early in 1456, successful negotiations were proceeding for a marriage between Sir John's grandson and
namesake and Agnes Menteith, the elder of the two sisters and coheirs of
Patrick Menteith of Rusky, who had died in 1439, when his lands fell into
the king's hands and his sisters into the king's gift.[21] Sir John Haldane of
Gleneagles died at an advanced age in November 1456, and three years
later his successor Bernard, perhaps in accordance with the terms of the
marriage contract, resigned the lands of Gleneagles, Bardrill, Dysart, and
Knockhill to his son and daughter-in-law, John and Agnes.[22] Known now
as 'of Rusky', John Haldane had acquired a valuable property between
the rivers Teith and Forth, centred on towers at Lanrick and on a small
island in Loch Rusky,[23] and conveniently situated between Gleneagles
and Kepdowrie; to this would be added, on his mother-in-law's death,
ground straddling Loch Tay, whose liferent formed her jointure. The
bride who brought the land had been the gift of James II, and it was

19. *Complete Peerage*, xii/i. 391–2.
20. Thus Haldane's tenancy within the barony of the Byres fell into the king's
    hand on Sir John's death in 1456: GD198/222.
21. In May 1456 John de Hawdene acted as Agnes Menteith's attorney
    when she received sasine in the lands of 'Thome' (between Lanrick and
    Deanston, south of the Teith: cf. GD198/38; W. Fraser, *The Red Book of
    Menteith* (Edinburgh, 1880), ii. 225–7), Lanrick, and Rusky (Rusky was
    the principal messuage in Loch Rusky; the settlement on Goodie Water
    is Ruskie): GD198/44. Being but the eldest son of Gleneagles's heir
    apparent, his position can only be explained by an impending match with
    Agnes. The marriage of her sister Elizabeth had been given away by the
    king in 1455: NRS, GD430/174 (Napier Papers).
22. GD198/12–15; Bernard reserved his own life interest, and the rights of his
    wife, Elizabeth; Cairnquarter in GD198/13 was another name for Bardrill
    (cf. GD220/1/A/3/6/3). Bernard died between 30 September 1472 and
    1474: GD198/18, 49.
23. Fraser, *Red Book of Menteith*, i. 505–6; J. Riddell, *Tracts, Legal and
    Historical . . . chiefly relative to Scotland* (Edinburgh, 1835), pp. 104–5.

probably as a token of gratitude to his monarch that, at the christening of his son, John introduced the name 'James' to Haldane nomenclature, where it still predominates today.

While Agnes's immediate inheritance lay in Menteith, her potential inheritance was in the Lennox, and to appreciate her significance it is necessary to return to the fall of Earl Duncan in 1425. When he was executed, he left three daughters: Margaret, widow of Robert Menteith of Rusky; Elizabeth, who was married to Sir John Stewart of Darnley; and the eldest, Albany's widow Isabella, upon whom succession to the earldom of Lennox had been settled in 1392. In 1425 James I appropriated the lands of the earldom and incarcerated Isabella. Whether or not he had formally forfeited her father, as he certainly had her husband, is unclear. If he had, neither she nor her sisters would have had any inheritance, in land or status, to transmit. The king's grandson, James III, stated that the Lennox had escheated to the crown, but the chancellor from whom he would have been taking advice was, as we shall see, an interested party.[24] Whatever the facts of the matter, in the administrative confusion which followed the murder of James I in 1437, Isabella recovered her freedom and assumed her rights as countess of Lennox, living on Inchmurrin in Loch Lomond in probably greater state than she gave the pope to understand in 1454, when she described herself to him as 'a countess solitary, lordless, widowed, and most impoverished'.[25] She was being allowed to behave as if there had been no forfeiture, and, were that the case, her sisters and their heirs had an interest in her inheritance.

When she died in 1458, Isabella had outlived both of her sisters, as well as Elizabeth's son Sir Alan Stewart of Darnley, and both Margaret's son Murdoch and grandson Patrick Menteith. Elizabeth's representative, with a claim to half the Lennox, was John Stewart, now Lord Darnley, with the claim to the other half divided equally between Margaret's representatives, Agnes and Elizabeth Menteith. Any claim to the comital

24. Below, pp. 28, 30.
25. M. Brown, 'Earldom and kindred: the Lennox and its earls, 1200–1458', S. Boardman & A. Ross (eds), *The Exercise of Power in Medieval Scotland, c.1200–1500* (Dublin, 2003), pp. 220–1; *Calendar of . . . Papal Letters*, ed. W.H. Bliss et al. (London,1893), x. 623.

title itself was not, of course, divisible and would pass to the senior repre-sentative of whichever of Isabella's sisters had been the elder. This was to become a debatable issue, but in 1451 the countess had made it clear that she considered the seniority to belong to Margaret.[26] Accordingly, while young Elizabeth Menteith had, in 1455, married John, son and heir to Alexander Napier of Merchiston,[27] her elder sister, Agnes, remained in the king's ward for another year; being a matter of greater moment than that of her younger sister, the destiny of her hand, and perhaps with it the Lennox title, was consequently a subject for longer deliberation.

That the king's choice for Agnes's husband fell on John, son and heir of Bernard Haldane of Gleneagles, may have been influenced by Patrick, Lord Graham, in whose household John had served in 1448. Graham's opinion would have been valued, since he was the dominant vassal in the eastern Lennox, and it would have been trusted by the most influential member of the king's intimate circle, Andrew Stewart, Lord Avandale. In him we meet a fourth descendant of Earl Duncan, one whose inter-est in the Lennox was driven by deep personal motives, for his father was Walter of Lennox, Countess Isabella's son, intended by his family to succeed Duncan as earl, but executed with his father and grandfather in 1425. Andrew, however, was illegitimate. If the earldom had not been forfeited, but was held by the crown in ward before delivery to the heirs (during their non-entry, to use the lawyers' term), he had little hope of coming into what he considered his own, but it would be helpful if the husband of Agnes Menteith were to be congenial to him. In such a matter he would have trusted the advice of Lord Graham, since Patrick's predecessor and his father had been firm friends.[28]

Lord Avandale was not the only interested party in the Lennox inheritance to be an intimate of James II. Both he and Lord Darnley had been with the king at Stirling in 1452, when he stabbed the earl of Douglas, and both had used their own blades to make sure that the

26. *Complete Peerage*, vii. 593–4; *HG*, p. 324.
27. NRS, GD430/174 (Napier Papers); M. Napier, *The Partition of the Lennox* (Edinburgh, 1835), p. 153.
28. Brown, 'Earldom and kindred', pp. 210, 216, 220; idem, *James I*, pp. 28–9.

SIMPLIFIED TREE TO ILLUSTRATE THE LENNOX CLAIM.

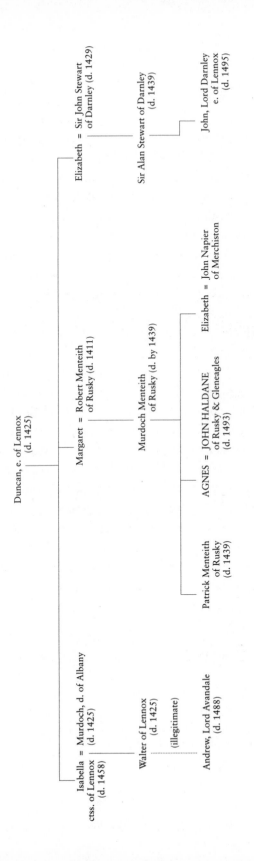

earl was dead.[29] As the sole legitimate male descendant of Earl Duncan (albeit through a female line) and claimant to half the lands of the earl-dom, Darnley persuaded himself that his grandmother was the senior of Countess Isabella's sisters and that his claim to the comital title was irresistible. Without the king's compliance, however, he could make no progress, and he had failed to advance in James's favour as successfully as had Andrew Avandale. Already warden of the west march, in early spring 1460 Avandale became king's guardian, a post entailing regular attend-ance on the monarch, and, on 6 July of the same year, he was appointed chancellor.[30] He was now in an ideal position to mould the king's plans for the Lennox, but in less than a month, at the siege of Roxburgh, James II's infatuation with guns led him fatally close to a piece of artillery which exploded on firing.

That Avandale's position did not similarly disintegrate is testimony to his political skill. The minority of the new king, James III, lasted nine years, during which Avandale remained chancellor, while control of the king passed from the queen mother (1460–63) to the bishop of St Andrews (1463–65), and finally, by kidnap, to the Boyds (1465–69). Grants obtained during royal minorities often proved impermanent, and, rather than seek them, Avandale, perfectly placed in control of the chancery to frustrate the ambitions of others, spent his time establishing a firm relationship with the young king. Darnley was less patient, open-ing the question of the Lennox inheritance as soon as James II was dead. By his own account, he 'daily' sought letters from the chancery recogniz-ing his right to half the earldom, in exasperation petitioning parliament on 12 October 1464 to help him get a settlement.[31] Among the lords of parliament listening to his request was the chancellor, whose office had

29. C. McGladderty, *James II* (Edinburgh, 1990), p. 66.
30. Ibid., pp. 66–7.
31. Records of Parliaments of Scotland [hereafter RPS], A1463/10/1; *HG*, p. 316; S.I. Boardman, 'Stewart, John, tenth or first earl of Lennox', *ODNB* (2004). For James II's annulment of all land grants made during his minority held to be prejudicial to the crown, see McGladderty, *James II*, p. 96.

found itself unable to grant the letters in the first place, and Darnley's petition was predictably ignored. The reaction of John Haldane to Darnley's proceedings was to seek support against the day when the Lennox might be released from the king's hold; he opened negotiations with Colin, earl of Argyll, and in February 1465 signed a contract whereby his eldest son, James (aged about eight years), was to marry the earl's second daughter.[32] Earl Colin was the Lennox's most powerful western neighbour, and, should the comital title come to Haldane, the potential value of his alliance was obvious. The title, however, did not come, and, unsurprisingly, nor did Argyll's daughter.

Lord Avandale saw no profit in revealing his own scheme for the Lennox during the king's minority, but, within eighteen months of James III's assumption of power, the nature of his ambition became clear: in April 1471 he was granted the liferent of the earldom. The next year his birth was legitimized, and the son of Walter of Lennox may with satisfaction have reflected that, for as long as he lived, the profits of the Lennox would flow into his coffers, and all that the representatives of his father's aunts could debate was not immediate possession, but distant inheritance.[33] The premise that the Lennox had been forfeited in 1425 was a prerequisite of the king's grant to Avandale; it had to lie in the king's gift, rather than be in ward against the day that Earl Duncan's heirs would inherit, for Avandale's original illegitimacy debarred him from inclusion among their number. His interests had therefore demanded that their inheritance be considered forfeit, an escheat with which the king might do what he will, and that the king's freedom of action should not be inhibited by a prior grant of the comital title. Once he had achieved his objective, however, and secure in the king's favour, Avandale seems to have advised James III that unnecessary ill will could be avoided if the forfeiture be rescinded and the chancery's doors opened to the claimants.

32. *HG*, p. 21.
33. *Complete Peerage*, xii/i. 271–2; N. Macdougall, *James III: a Poltical Study* (Edinburgh, 1982), pp. 101–2 (where the evidence for the escheat of the Lennox is ignored).

The claims of John Haldane were first addressed. Having entered the royal household perhaps as early as 1456, he was well known to James III, and on 28 March 1473 it was as the king's 'familiar esquire (*armiger*)' that he received, not only recognition of his heritable right to one-quarter of the Lennox, but also acknowledgement as 'the first and principal person of the earldom',[34] and as such entitled to the feudal incidents accruing from free tenancies and presentation to church livings (advowsons). This satisfactory affirmation of the seniority of his wife's grandmother over Darnley's had probably been obtained through the good offices of the chancellor, whose price was paid three days later, when the king gave him Kepdowrie, 'which John de Haldene of Rusky has resigned'; John was to buy it back seven years later.[35] John now left the country on embassies to France and Denmark, having first obtained letters placing his rights under the king's protection against challenge through the courts during his absence.[36]

In watching the lands of Lennox pass to Avandale, and its superiority to Haldane, Darnley's temper must have been tested. In July 1473, he found what he considered to be proof of his grandmother's seniority, and, doubtless in the interests of peaceful coexistence, by the end of the month James III not only acknowledged Darnley's heritable right to half the earldom, but also granted him the comital title.[37] When retoured as heir to her quarter of the Lennox in the autumn of 1473, Agnes's sister, Elizabeth Menteith, compliantly accepted that she was descended from the younger daughter of Earl Duncan.[38] Avandale may have viewed these proceedings as somewhat academic, since his liferent was accepted by all parties, but Haldane, on his return from Denmark,

34. *RMS*, ii, nos. 1116; cf. *HG*, p. 331. For payment to John Haldan in 1456 for German ale bought for the king's use, see *The Exchequer Rolls of Scotland*, ed. J. Stuart et al. (Edinburgh, 1878–1908), vi. 118.
35. *RMS*, ii, nos 1120, 1510; NRS, GD198/20.
36. *HG*, pp. 16, 322, 333; *Acts of the Parliaments of Scotland*, ed. J. Thomson & J. Innes (Edinburgh, 1814–75), ii. 103–4.
37. *RMS*, ii, no. 1136; W. Fraser, *The Lennox* (Edinburgh, 1874), ii. 101–2; *HG*, pp. 323–5.
38. NRS, GD430/78; *HG*, pp. 325–6.

felt no such detachment, insisting before the lords of council in January 1476 that Darnley's actions had invaded his rights of superiority and violated the immunity which the king had guaranteed him during his service overseas. James III's protection could not be seen to be worthless (although it patently was, unless its recipient could look after himself), and Haldane's superiority of the earldom of the Lennox was confirmed; Darnley had to drop his use of the comital title.[39] Within a year Avandale was calling himself 'the lord of Lennox', which accurately reflected the territorial reality.[40]

Darnley did not react calmly to his reverse. In the summer of 1476, he protested that Agnes Menteith was illegitimate. His case had no merit and merely protracted litigation by removing it to the ecclesiastical courts, in whose jurisdiction such questions lay. Darnley failed, and a year later Agnes's right to her quarter of the Lennox was confirmed. She accepted that kings since 1425 had been acting lawfully in treating her share, like the rest of the Lennox, as within their gift, and James III, doubtless following the careful prompting of the chancellor to whom he had given it, reiterated that the earldom had been in crown hands as an escheat.[41] The contradiction inherent in the confirmation of the rights of an heir in an inheritance which had been forfeited was one which Chancellor Avandale could contemplate with equanimity.

During the following decade, John Haldane moved in the corridors of power. He never received knighthood,[42] perhaps through some physical incapacity, since the attribution in Scotland still had military overtones, but by 1477 he had succeeded the earl of Argyll as master of the king's household, a great office of state, and in 1478 he was appointed

39. *HG*, pp. 326–8; *Complete Peerage*, vii. 595.
40. NRS, GD220/1/E/4/4/4 (Montrose Muniments). For earlier instances of lordship of an earldom, see A. Grant, 'The Development of the Scottish Peerage', *Scot. Hist. Rev.*, lvii (1978), 5–6.
41. *HG*, pp. 315, 328–30.
42. *Pace HG*, p. 17, citing a document of 20 July 1485, where John's name, in fact, appears simply as 'Johne of Halden of Glennegas': W. Fraser, *The Douglas Book* (4 vols, Edinburgh, 1885), iii. 436; J. Anderson (ed.), *The Oliphants of Scotland* (Edinburgh, 1879), p. 25.

a general justice north of Forth.[43] In both positions he would have worked closely with the chancellor, Lord Avandale, and it is tempting to speculate whether or not Haldane was his protégé. In 1478, 1481, and in 1485, Haldane sat as one of the barons in parliament; in 1484 he was a lord auditor of causes and complaints, sitting with Lords Glamis and Oliphant.[44]

Groundwork had been laid for the prospects of his son and heir by finding a placement for young James in the royal household in the early 1470s; the lord treasurer's accounts of 1474 refer to the cost of fitting out 'Jame Halden of the kingis chalmire [chamber]' with black hose, a green gown, and white doublet.[45] A generation earlier, John himself had served in the household of Lord Graham at Kincardine.[46] The connection was particularly valuable, since Graham lands centred on Kincardine marched with those of Haldane in Strathearn, while those centred on Mugdock bolstered Haldane's position in the eastern Lennox. By 1481 John Haldane had managed to strengthen the relationship by securing his son's marriage to Christian, sister of William, third Lord Graham and future first earl of Montrose.[47]

In January 1483, John had the lands which he had inherited from his father united to form the barony of Gleneagles. Gleneagles itself and Bardrill were removed from the stewartry of Strathearn; Wester Dysart from the sheriffdom of Fife; and, from the sheriffdom of Stirling, Knockhill (by Keir), together with the lands of Kepdowrie, Ballaird, Balwill, Camoquhill, Carbeth, and 'Ardas' in eastern Lennox: all were combined and erected into a barony within the sheriffdom of Perth.[48] On its ground Haldane now exercised powers of criminal jurisdiction, with authority to inflict capital punishment, as well as conducting the

---

43.	NRS, GD198/52; RPS 1478/6/67; cf. *Accounts of the Lord High Treasurer of Scotland*, i, *A.D. 1473–1498*, ed. T. Dickson (Edinburgh, 1877), p. lviii.
44.	RPS 1478/6/2; 1481/4/1; 1484/2/44; 1485/5/2.
45.	*Treasurer's Accounts*, i. 59, 61–2; cf. ibid., pp. clxviii–clxxviii; *HG*, pp. 22–3.
46.	Above, p. 25.
47.	NRS, GD198/16–17; *HG*, p. 24.
48.	NRS, GD198/22–3.

less dramatic but more profitable business of supervising civil disputes and enforcing official regulations.[49] The grant both enhanced his status and increased his revenue.

The status quo in the Lennox was to be radically altered by two events in the summer of 1488. On 11 June, James III was killed at Sauchieburn near Stirling in a confrontation with rebel forces including both his son, the future James IV, and Lord Darnley.[50] The second event concerned Lord Avandale, who had been edged out of the chancery in the turmoil of James III's last years, but not out of the Lennox: he survived his king for less than a month, and the liferent expired with him. Haldane's sister-in-law, Elizabeth Menteith, a widow since the death of John Napier in 1482, immediately obtained possession of her quarter of the earldom, and two years later, in May 1490, so did his son and heir, James Haldane, obtain that of his.[51]

In the matter of superiority the Haldanes faced a fait accompli: Darnley sat in the October parliament of 1488 as earl of Lennox, and thus did the king address him on his appointment as keeper of Dumbarton on the tenth of that month.[52] His rebellion the following year succeeded in bringing him into the regime which governed during the young king's minority. In May 1490, ever compliant to his wishes, Elizabeth Menteith granted him superiority and advowsons in her quarter of the earldom in return for some fishing rights and an island (Inchmoan) in Loch Lomond.[53] After waiting to gauge the security of Darnley's position, the Haldanes yielded in February 1493, declining to challenge his claim to be descended from the senior of Countess Isabella's sisters.[54] On 11 July in Drymen kirk, three weeks before his death, John Haldane of Gleneagles and his son James signed an agreement with John Stewart,

49. A. Grant, *Independence and Nationhood: Scotland 1306–1469* (London, 1984), pp. 124, 151, 157.
50. Macdougall, *James III*, p. 238.
51. Fraser, *Lennox*, i. 305; NRS, GD198/53–4.
52. Fraser, *Lennox*, i. 305.
53. N. Macdougall, *James IV* (Edinburgh, 1989), pp. 64–76, 80–2; NRS, GD430/92–4 (Napier Papers); GD430/17 for the death of John Napier.
54. GD198/58.

earl of Lennox, whereby they surrendered all claim to superiority of the earldom in return for a grant of lands out of Darnley's half-share, which consolidated the property to the south-east of Loch Lomond which had come as their quarter-share.[55]

Agnes Menteith's quarter of the earldom was based on the principal messuage of Boturich castle on Loch Lomondside. In the loch were the isles of Torrinch, Ellanderroch, and Ross; to the south of Boturich was Ledrishbeg with its profitable mill, remembered on modern maps as the settlements of Haldane's Mill and Mill of Haldane; moving eastward, Shanacles, Blairnyle, Barquhoys, and other lands led towards the Catters, with the ferry on Endrick Water crossing towards Drumakill by Drymen. One can only speculate about the degree to which, on their marriage, John and Agnes had expected this inheritance to materialize. What cannot have originally been envisaged was the compensation received for the surrender of superiority in the earldom, which increased the concentration of Haldane ground by adding Ledrishmuir and Auchencarroch to its south, Blairlusk in its centre, Knockour with its fishing just north of Boturich, and Drumbeg by Drymen towards its eastern extent. The seniority would have proved an untenable asset once the comital title, bolstered by half the lands of the earldom, was securely in Darnley's hands; the Haldanes had no choice but to bargain for its exchange.

John Haldane had never had a realistic chance of becoming earl of Lennox; indeed, he never claimed the title. Darnley's lands in Renfrewshire and Ayrshire, when added to his half-share of the Lennox, gave him far greater substance with which to maintain an earl's dignity than anything Haldane could have aspired to. It may be, in the last weeks of his life, that John Haldane wondered if he had been used by Lord Avandale, but he had enjoyed a distinguished career in the king's service, proved himself a doughty fighter for his rights, saw his patrimony of Gleneagles erected into a free barony, and passed to his son an inheritance about twice the size of the one to which he had succeeded. The game had been worth the candle.

55.   Fraser, *Lennox*, ii. 148; GD198/59.

Consolidation and calamity, 1493–1513

John's son, James, inherited in August 1493, having been an active partner during the last years of his father's life.[56] His position both in Strathearn and in the Lennox was enhanced by the status of his wife, Christian Graham, the lands of whose brother, Lord Graham, either marched with or were close to those of the Haldanes. In 1502, James expanded his family's landholding in Menteith with the purchase of Rusky's north-western neighbour, Auchrig, from the Drummonds.[57] All that is known of his public career after his succession as laird is that, by November 1500, he had been appointed captain of Dunbar Castle, whose recent refortification was a project dear to the heart of King James IV, and, by March 1501, he had been knighted.[58]

In 1503, however, Sir James died, and, since his son and heir, John, was still a minor, the Haldane lands fell into the king's wardship, where they remained for two years, even though John had attained his majority, and received knighthood, by September 1504.[59] Despite the grant of sasine in his inheritance to Sir John between July and October 1505, the exchequer was still drawing income from the land of Gleneagles in 1506.[60] The king had leased the wardship to John Elphinstone of Airth and Master Richard Lawson,[61] and it was not unusual for such lessees to

56. GD198/26; cf. GD198/53–9. In 1487 James had found it worthwhile to take 'a dwelling house' in Edinburgh's Canongate: *Protocol Book of James Young, 1485–1515*, ed. G. Donaldson (Scottish Record Soc., 1952), no. 84. Since the occasion of his marriage in 1481, James had enjoyed the revenue from a group of substantial tacks in Gleneagles (at Bardrill, Common Hill, Frandy, Hawk's Craig, Cairnquarter, and Carrisquarter): GD198/16.

57. *RMS*, ii, no. 2673; *Treasurer's Accounts*, ii. 11; GD198/117.

58. *Acts of Lords in Council in Civil Causes*, p. 496; NRS, GD1/1213/1; cf. N. Macdougall, *James IV* (East Linton, 1997), p. 228.

59. GD198/67; *Fasti Aberdonenses, 1494–1854* (Spalding Club, 1854), pp. 49–50. There was no standard age for receipt of knighthood in Scotland: K. Stevenson, *Chivalry and Knighthood in Scotland 1424–1513* (Woodbridge, 2006), pp. 18–19.

60. GD198/29–32, 67–70; *Treasurer's Accounts*, iii. 27, 241.

61. *Treasurer's Accounts*, iii. 27.

purchase control of the marriage of the minor whose property they were leasing. Master Richard Lawson is known to have bought the marriage of the Tweedy heir in 1506,[62] and, had he done the same at Gleneagles, no further explanation would be required for the appearance of his daughter, Marjorie, as Sir John Haldane's spouse.[63] Some explanation is needed, since the Haldanes at this time were seeking marriage alliances among the daughters of the higher nobility, and Mr Richard Lawson of Humbie did not come into that category. He was, however, a royal servant and lawyer of distinction and wealth, having been one of the lords of council since 1483, thrice provost of Edinburgh, and the king's justice-clerk from 1491 until 1506.[64]

Although Master Richard died in 1507, it may be that observation of his legal expertise encouraged Sir John to initiate the proceedings that culminated in January 1509 in the clarification of the Haldane title to Kippen and, more importantly, in the extension of his rights of free barony by erecting his lands in western and central Lennox, in Menteith, and on Tayside into the barony of Haldane, with its principal messuage specified as the tower of Rusky (now lost on its island beneath the raised water level of Loch Rusky); he was to be answerable for all the

62. Ibid., p. 25.
63. GD198/71; *RMS*, ii, no. 3288, a charter of conjunct fee, the occasion for which was not, as has been assumed, the marriage of John and Marjorie, but the creation of the barony of Haldane (whose constituent lands are the subject of the charter); the date of the marriage is unknown (*pace HG*, p. 31, giving Marjorie as the daughter of 'Sir John Lawson'), but their son James was born in 1503 or 1504 (below, p. 40); D. Laing (ed.), *The Poetical Works of Sir David Lyndsay* (3 vols, Edinburgh, 1879), i. 316, 323. The identification of Marjorie as the daughter of Mr Richard Lawson of Humbie was made by Robert Lindsay of Pitscottie, whose source was probably his kinsman, Sir David Lindsay: *The Historie and Chronicles of Scotland*, ed. A.J.G. Mackay (3 vols, Scottish Text Soc., 1911), i. 260.20; 299.9; ii. 388.
64. Macdougall, *James III*, pp. 200, 303–4; Laing, *Lyndsay's Works*, i. 316. For Master Richard's death in 1507, see M. Livingston (ed.), *Registrum Secreti Sigilli Regum Scotorum*, i, no. 1538.

constituent lands, just as he was for the barony of Gleneagles, solely in the sheriff court of Perth.[65]

Marjorie Lawson enjoyed conjunct rights in the new barony, but, on 11 August 1513, she resigned them, excluding only the lands of Rusky and Lanrick, and also her dower in the lands of eastern Lennox which were within the barony of Gleneagles.[66] Her deed of resignation, unlocking significant revenue for the support of an heir in the event of her widowhood, came two weeks after James IV had summoned the Scottish host, and among it Sir John Haldane, to prepare for an invasion of England. By 24 August, the army had crossed the Tweed, and the king proclaimed the exemption of the heirs of any who died during the expedition from his rights to wardship, marriage, and the succession duty known as relief – a proclamation which was not unusual, and which may have been anticipated by Marjorie Lawson's advisers. The dispensation was to cost the exchequer more than the most pessimistic could have anticipated. When the Scottish and English armies met in battle at Flodden on 9 September, the Scottish losses were catastrophic.[67] Among those slaughtered in the centre of the field, near the royal banner, lay the body of James IV, stripped of its armour and clothing. Surrounding it, 'left naked on the field', were the corpses of 'a number of goodly men, well fed and fat'.[68] One was that of Sir John Haldane of Gleneagles, who had died 'on the field of battle, guarding the person of the king'.[69]

65. *RMS*, ii, no. 3288; GD198/71, 78. It thus became possible to refer to both Gleneagles Haldanes and Hadden Haldanes as 'of that ilk': e.g. GD198/80–1. The superiority of Kippen with its mill was bought from the Thains of Dunning by John Stirling of Keir in 1530, and acquired from Keir by James Haldane in 1545, being incorporated within the barony of Gleneagles in April 1546: *RMS*, iii, nos. 969, 3225; *HG*, p. 39; *Treasurer's Accounts*, viii. 202.
66. GD198/121.
67. Macdougall, *James IV*, pp. 270–6.
68. *Letters & Papers, Foreign & Domestic, of the Reign of Henry VIII*, i, part ii (2nd edn, rev. R.H. Brodie, London, 1920), no. 2283.
69. GD198/122–3.

III

Romance, Reformation, and Revolution

Marjorie Lawson, William Meldrum, and
James (II) Haldane, 1513–47

In the aftermath of Flodden the kingdom of Scotland entered a period of instability, as factions vied for control of the regency during James V's minority. This uncertainty appears to have been mirrored at Gleneagles, where James Haldane cannot have been more than ten years old when granted sasine in January 1514. Common practice was to appoint as a minor's tutor the nearest agnate kinsman over the age of twenty-five, and Sir John had nominated in his will Master Gilbert Haldane, who was almost certainly James's uncle.[1] Thanks to the king's dispensation on the eve of Flodden, there were no rights of wardship over James's inheritance to complicate Master Gilbert's task, but Sir John's widow, Marjorie Lawson, remained at Gleneagles, drawing revenue from her widow's terce (third) in that barony, and from her conjunct fee at Rusky and Lanrick.[2]

Just as the dowager queen's remarriage ignited factional strife, so, at a local level, did that of Lady Gleneagles. It seems that plans had been made for her to marry Luke Stirling, an uncle of the new laird of Keir, but

---

1. NRS, GD128/124: 'tutor testamentar and legal'; cf. K. Brown, *Noble Society in Scotland: Wealth, Family and Culture from the Reformation to the Revolution* (Edinburgh, 2000), p. 173. Sir John's will is now lost.
2. GD198/121, 126.

Marjorie had not emerged from her period of mourning before she was swept off her feet by a young man from Fife, William Meldrum of Cleish and the Binns.[3] Our knowledge of this affair comes from Meldrum's close friend, Sir David Lindsay of the Mount, who composed a poem in 1550 recounting his life.[4] Sir David knew his subject well, and there is little reason to suspect that poetic licence distorted the basic facts of the story he chose to tell.

Before bearing upon the life of Lady Gleneagles, Meldrum's career had been spent at home and abroad as a soldier of fortune, and his facility as a raconteur now made him a welcome house-guest (ll. 849–55). Since he was a kinsman of the late Sir John Haldane (ll. 966–8), Meldrum would not have been a total stranger when, one evening in May 1514, he appeared at Gleneagles Castle, 'this triumphant plesand place', whose mistress ('ane lustie ladie') provided a supper of venison, sweetmeats, brawn, and jelly, accompanied by whisky, wine, and ale (ll. 863–4, 883–7). After a board-game, he retired to his 'well-arrayit' chamber, where, next morning, he was 'quyetlie' joined by his hostess, 'hir golden traisses hingand doun; … hir pappis … hard, round and quhyte, quhome to behald was greit delyte' (ll. 942–6). The following days and weeks were filled with games of chess, cards, and dice, with hawking, hunting, and riding, while William also demonstrated his prowess at the butts, in the tilt-yard, and at 'the futeball' (ll. 1042–7). The lovers planned to marry, but, because of Meldrum's consanguinity with Marjorie's late husband, papal dispensation was required and would take time to obtain (ll. 981–2). A daughter was born (l. 1162), and Meldrum's position at Gleneagles was sufficiently established for him to command a company of Haldane tenantry in rebuffing the Macfarlanes of Arrochar, who were seeking to take advantage of near anarchy in the Lennox (ll. 1053–96). During this period, when the general assumption

3. Binn now represents the Binns, three miles east by south of Cleish in Kinross-shire.
4. 'The Historie of William Meldrum, umquhyle laird of Cleische and Bynnis' in *The Poetical Works of Sir David Lyndsay*, ed. D. Laing (3 vols, Edinburgh, 1879), i. 159–220. I have given line references within brackets in the main text.

was that the duke of Albany's regency would be weak and that possession, however violently obtained, would be ten points of the law,[5] the Macfarlanes had descended from the north of Loch Lomond to seize a Haldane castle (presumably Boturich) and harry the surrounding land. Meldrum recovered the castle and drove off the Macfarlanes (ll. 1097–1141). On his return to Gleneagles, he formed a company of thirty gentlemen, arrayed in a livery of scarlet and green, and contracted to him by a bond of mutual protection (ll. 1165–70). During 1515, William's second year at Gleneagles, life was lived pleasantly 'with musick and with menstralie' (l. 1174).

Meanwhile, the Stirlings of Keir had not abandoned their plan for Luke Stirling's marriage to the lady of Gleneagles, a plan which evidently had the approval of her paternal family, the Lawsons. Their attempts to separate her from Meldrum seem to have culminated in an accusation that he had kidnapped her and resulted in an ordinance of the Lords of Council on 20 June 1515, commanding that 'the lady of Glennegas be put at freedom and have hir free will to pass quher scho plesis best, and that William Meldrum, allegit to be hir spous, Maister James nor Maister Patrik Lausone mak hir na truble nor impediment tharintill, as thai will answer to my lordis regentis and consell tharapon.'[6] The regent had left for France earlier in the year, nominating as his deputy Antoine d'Arces, seigneur de la Bastie. Since the deputy was in Meldrum's debt, the Scot having saved his life in 1513 in a skirmish with the English in Picardy (ll. 1396–1401), it is a safe assumption that the ordinance guaranteeing Marjorie's freedom of action was issued after consultation with Meldrum, who was probably confident about the choice she would make. If so, he was correct, and the pair set out from Edinburgh with eight companions (including George Haldane) to return to Gleneagles through Fife via the ferry from Leith (ll. 1211–26). They were ambushed outside Holyrood by the laird of Keir together with Patrick Lawson and

5. See W.K. Emond, 'The Minority of King James V, 1513–1528', Ph.D. thesis (St Andrews, 1989), p. 49.
6. *Acta Dominorum Concilii*, xxx. 31; for a different interpretation of this ordinance, see *HG*, p. 33.

a large body of armed men.[7] Meldrum called on Keir to engage him in single combat, but he declined. Marjorie had to watch her soi-disant husband, laying about him with his two-handed sword and doing great damage, but hopelessly outnumbered, eventually cut down, savagely maimed, and left for dead (ll. 1230–1308, 1343–64). Her friends advised her to go back to Gleneagles, 'because scho micht do him no gude' (l. 1460), and the pair never met again.[8]

Marjorie Lawson continued to be subjected to pressure from her father's family; finally, she succumbed and married Luke Stirling.[9] A new regime had been installed at Gleneagles, with James Haldane's uncle Gilbert being replaced as tutor before the end of 1518 by his great-uncle, George Haldane of Kippen. James had evidently now reached the age of fourteen, when a minor was allowed to choose 'curators' from the circle of family friends to advise his tutor in guiding his affairs.[10] Supported by the family's most important neighbours, the earl of Montrose and Sir William Murray of Tullibardine, who led this group of the young laird's 'principal friends', George negotiated a marriage contract, sealed on 14 December 1518, between James and Margaret, sister of John, Lord Erskine. George's position was not a strong one, since much of the Haldane estate which remained outside Marjorie Lawson's control was apparently mortgaged. Lord Erskine and his mother agreed to pay

7. Lindsay says 'sixty', which was probably a synonym for 'a lot'. Patrick Lawson was amerced in £80 for the mutilation of William Meldrum, George Haldane, and their companions: *Lord High Treasurer's Accounts*, v. 108.

8. Meldrum, in fact, recovered and entered the household of Lord Lindsay of the Byres, serving as controller and marshal, and as sheriff-depute in Fife; he seems to have died in the mid 1530s: *Lyndsay's Poetical Works*, i. 327, 329, 331. Keir was pursued by de la Bastie to Linlithgow, captured, and imprisoned, but was released shortly after the deputy regent's murder by Home of Wedderburn on 17 September 1517; Keir himself was murdered in 1539: ibid., p. 322; 'William Meldrum', l. 1490.

9. GD198/126, a deed of 9 December 1526, in which Marjorie appears as 'relict of John Haldene of Glenneges and of Luke Striviling'. Lindsay says: 'Scho aganis hir will wes maryit': 'William Meldrum', l. 1458.

10. Brown, *Noble Society in Scotland*, p. 175.

their proposed in-law 1,000 merks, of which 900 were to be used to redeem land and 100 to be spent on repairs to Barkis, an Erskine house in Aberdeenshire, which had been allotted to the couple. Until the redemption was complete, the reversion of the lands would be retained by the Erskines, and, should James not solemnize the marriage on coming of age, the lands would remain with them until the 1,000 merks had been repaid. James was to endow his bride with a £20-land of old extent in his barony of Haldane. The young couple being related in the fourth degree, Lord and Lady Erskine were to obtain the necessary papal dispensation.[11]

James Haldane probably came of age in 1524.[12] The required redemption of mortgaged lands may have left him in straitened circumstances, and in September 1526 he sold the superiority over his tenants on the north side of Loch Tay to Campbell of Lawers.[13] Three months later his position was eased by his mother's resignation in his favour of her widow's third part of the barony of Gleneagles.[14] Nevertheless, it seems that he was unable to attend to his obligation to infeft his wife with a £20 land until 1533, when Margaret Erskine was granted conjunct rights, not in the Lennox as stipulated in the marriage contract, but in Dysart, Haldane's valuable property in Fife.[15]

Meanwhile, the career of his brother-in-law was flourishing. In 1522, Lord Erskine had been entrusted with the safekeeping of the ten-year-old king at Stirling Castle, whose hereditary keepership was granted to

11. GD124/3/4; HMC, *Earl of Mar & Kellie* (1904), i. 9; for the use of Barkis in a marriage settlement in the fourteenth century, see ibid., p. 2; for the consanguinity, see *HG*, p. 43.

12. Letters were issued in June 1524 restricting distraint against James Haldane to the sheriff court of Perth: GD198/80–1; cf. *HG*, p. 39.

13. GD112/1/829, where James is seen still to be using his father's seal; *Reg. Secreti Sigilli*, i, no. 3537.

14. GD198/126; she also assigned him an annual render of one chalder of wheat from lands in the earldom of Lennox, and her third part of Blairequhois in the parish of Kilmaronock; she reserved to herself Eastside and Wester Hillkitty in Gleneagles.

15. *RMS*, iii, no. 1368.

him three years later.[16] The queen mother described him as a 'familiar daly resident with oure derrest son, and of his secrate counsall, and ane gude reasonable man'.[17] In July 1535, he was able to place opportunity in the path of the laird of Gleneagles by including him in his embassy to France to treat on James V's behalf for the hand of the daughter of the duke of Vendôme, travelling via England in order to allay Henry VIII's suspicions of a French alliance.[18] On his return, James Haldane thought it worthwhile to buy two tenements in Stirling, in St Mary's Wynd.[19] Between 1537 and 1539, he received payment for his services as captain-depute of Dunbar Castle,[20] but this is the only public office he is known to have held, and he never received knighthood.[21] In August 1537, a letter was issued to distrain 'the lairde of Glennegas and his complices' for £200. It may be that this was the result of proceedings initiated by the abbot of Cambuskenneth in relation to teinds (tithes) withheld by Haldane and his tenants in the parish of Kilmaronock since 1528,[22] but four years later, he 'and his colleagues' paid 1,000 merks (£666 13s. 4d.) for a remission in respect of 'certain crimes'. It was not difficult to fall foul of the royal administration in the 1530s and early 1540s, but the laird of Gleneagles was being mulcted in significant sums.[23] Whatever lay

16. Emond, 'Minority of James V', p. 305.
17. *The Hamilton Papers*, ed. J. Bain (Edinburgh, 1890), i, no. 21.
18. *The Register of the Privy Seal of Scotland*, ii, no. 1732
19. NRS, B66/25/100 (2 November 1535), the vendor being a kinsman, Bernard Haldane, burgess of Edinburgh. The property was still in Haldane hands in 1588: B66/25/158.
20. *The Exchequer Rolls of Scotland*, xii. 119, 163–4, 171, 259
21. As evidence for James's knighthood, Haldane cites the register of Cambuskenneth Abbey, where a copyist has attached '*miles*' to his name in a list of witnesses to a dedication in July 1521: *Registrum Monasterii Sancte Marie de Cambuskenneth* (Grampian Club, 1872), pp. 122–3; *HG*, p. 38. The attribution was, however, a scribal error: no government record and no deed issued in his name ever referred to James as a knight: cf. GD198/80–1, 127, 231; GD47/21; GD112/1/829.
22. *Reg. Cambuskenneth*, pp. 218–22.
23. cf. *HG*, p. 38. The other distraints in the letter of 1537 were for £10 or less, except that against the countess of Crawford 'and her complices', who owed 200 merks: *Treasurer's Accounts*, vi. 346 (reading 'lairde' for 'lande').

behind these entries in the accounts of the Lord High Treasurer, they suggest that James Haldane was not enjoying the favour of James V.

That king, however, died unexpectedly on 14 December 1542, leaving the crown to his week-old daughter, Mary. The political community now wrestled with two overriding concerns: the future marriage of the infant queen and the succession to the crown in the event of her death, which, given the high incidence of infant mortality at the time, was by no means a remote possibility. By the end of 1543, the question of the queen's marriage divided those who favoured a dynastic alliance with England and those who wished to strengthen the Auld Alliance with France. Of the potential heirs presumptive, Matthew Stewart, earl of Lennox, was aligned with the earls of Glencairn, Angus, and Cassilis, all sworn to support the English king's plans for Scotland, which included both his securing custody of the royal infant and Scotland's rejection of papal authority. Lennox's rival, James Hamilton, earl of Arran, already recognized as governor and 'second person' of the realm, had found the embrace of Henry VIII too uncomfortable, and, after a 'godly fit' in which he presided over a parliament that ordered the dissemination of vernacular Bibles, he returned to orthodoxy and reaffirmed the alliance with France. The queen herself was with her mother in the safekeeping of James Haldane's brother-in-law, Lord Erskine, in Stirling Castle.[24]

During this period of acute political volatility, the Haldanes of Gleneagles did not present a seamlessly united front. Whether hedging their bets by a time-honoured strategy, or from ideological conviction, the laird and his heir trod different paths in 1544. In April, the rivalry between Arran and Lennox had escalated into armed conflict, when Arran led a large army to eject Lennox's garrison from Glasgow. The

No other sale of a pardon for 'certain crimes' in 1541 approached Haldane's 1,000 merks: one was for 500 merks, two for 300 merks, one for 100 merks, and six for lesser sums: ibid., viii. 13, 16–19.

24. The above is a bald summary of events best elucidated in G. Donaldson, *Scotland: James V–James VII* (2nd edn, Edinburgh, 1971), pp. 62–75; idem, *All the Queen's Men: Power and Politics in Mary Stewart's Scotland* (London, 1983), pp. 15–20; J. Wormald, *Mary, Queen of Scots* (2nd edn, London, 2001), pp. 43–60.

earl of Glencairn, a fervent Protestant and Anglophile, marched out to meet him on Glasgow Muir, with a force which included John Haldane, younger of Gleneagles, his brother Robert, and two other Haldanes (Patrick and John), 'coming with displayed banner' and 'pursuing his grace for his slaughter'. Their pursuit was fruitless, for Arran emerged victorious and Glasgow surrendered.[25] With his sons collaborating with the anti-French party, James Haldane kept close to the circle of his brother-in-law. In July 1545, after Henry VIII had turned from bribery to savagery with his 'rough wooing', the laird of Gleneagles, together with other 'substantious freindis' of Lord Erskine, was exempted from service against England in order to remain in Stirling and protect the queen and her French mother.[26] In January 1546, he saw his daughter Margaret married to Henry, son and heir of the queen's clerk of the rolls, James Foulis of Colinton.[27]

When Lennox fled to England after the fall of Glasgow, he ordered his captain at Dumbarton castle, George Stirling of Glorat, to surrender to the English; Stirling refused and held the castle virtually as a freelance for nearly a year, raiding the accessible countryside to provision his garrison. That countryside included lands within the barony of Haldane. In March 1546, James Haldane's intention to pursue Stirling through the courts for the resultant despoliation ('spulzie') of his and his tenants' goods was discouraged by the government, but compensation came in June 1546, when Haldane's property south-east of Loch Lomond was increased by the grant of Portnellan Muir, Ardoch, and Blairnavaid, lands which had fallen to the crown on Lennox's forfeiture after his conviction for treason.[28] A month later, the barons of the Lennox declared their readiness to use force to persuade George Stirling to allow government officials into Dumbarton, but James Haldane was

25. *Reg. Privy Seal*, iv, no. 2713; M. Merriman, *The Rough Wooings: Mary Queen of Scots, 1542–1551* (East Linton, 2000), pp. 141–2.
26. *The Register of the Privy Council of Scotland*, 1st ser. [hereafter *RPC*], i. 11.
27. *RMS*, iii, no. 3124; *HG*, pp. 41–2.
28. W. Fraser, *The Stirlings of Keir & their Family Papers* (Edinburgh, 1858), pp. 390–5; *RMS*, iii, no. 3264.

not among them.[29] It is possible that he was already incapacitated by whatever caused his death at the end of February 1547.[30]

Navigating Reformation politics: John (IV) and George Haldane, 1547–74

John Haldane did not immediately step into his full inheritance. For reasons which are unclear, part of the land granted to his father out of the forfeiture of the earl of Lennox was retained by the crown until 1549.[31] Moreover, when he took sasine of his baronies of Gleneagles and Haldane in May 1547,[32] two dowager ladies of Gleneagles were enjoying income from valuable parts of his estate: his mother, Margaret Erskine, held the manor of Dysart with its coal mines and salt-works, while his grandmother, Marjorie Lawson, still controlled Rusky and Lanrick.[33] Marjorie Lawson was now also lady of West Kerse, having married as her third husband Robert Menteith of West Kerse and Alva. The inventory in her testament, drawn up at Alva in June 1553 (and witnessed by representatives of her three marriages: a Haldane, a Stirling, and a Menteith), not only mentions property in the parish of Kilmadock (i.e. Rusky and Lanrick), but also in that of Glendevon, which must relate to Frandy, Glenhead, or Kaimknowe (or all three), the only Haldane ground in that parish. She was also in receipt of rent from Gleneagles mill and £20 annual rent from the Mains of Gleneagles.[34] Rusky and Lanrick returned to the laird's control after Marjorie's death in July 1553, and Dysart returned after Margaret Erskine's, five years later.[35]

29. Fraser, *Stirlings*, pp. 394–5.
30. GD198/127.
31. *Exchequer Rolls*, xviii. 483; Portnellan Muir and Ardoch were retained, but sasine of Blairnavaid was taken on 26 May 1547: GD198/231.
32. He took sasine of Gleneagles on 24 May and of Haldane the following day: GD198/128–9. Relief of 400 merks for both baronies had been paid on 2 April: *Exch. Rolls*, xviii. 411.
33. GD198/127; *Exch. Rolls*, xviii. 411.
34. NRS, CC6/5/2: test. 1553 Lawsone, Mariorie.
35. GD198/34; *Exch. Rolls*, xix, app. x.

John Haldane attempted to avoid payment of £40 relief on succession to Rusky and Lanrick, on the grounds that the exemption granted to the immediate heirs of those who fell at Flodden should apply to him in this instance, as it was the first opportunity for anyone to succeed, his recently deceased grandmother having been in possession since before the battle.[36] His case was rejected in 1555, but his attempt to save such a sum (the price of about a hundred ewe lambs) shows a concern for careful husbandry which may also have led him to make arrangements prior to his death in 1563 that enabled his executor to present an inventory of his moveable wealth, including rents, which amounted to no more than £134.[37]

In the years between these episodes of purely domestic concern, momentous events had changed Scotland: the advance of Protestantism, evident since the 1540s, surged after the burning of an aged apostate priest in St Andrews in April 1558; a riot in Perth a year later led to the enlistment of rival armies, one raised by the Protestant lords of the Congregation, the other loyal to the regent, Mary of Guise; government forces were driven out of Perth and Fife; the regent, who had been quite unconstitutionally deposed by the lords of the Congregation, died in June 1560, and the Reformation parliament of that summer abolished the pope's jurisdiction, banned the celebration of the Mass, and proscribed all but Protestant forms of worship.

How these events were viewed from Gleneagles is a matter for conjecture. The laird's wife, Elizabeth Lundie (alias Lundin, daughter of John Lundie of that ilk), came from a family in Fife whose head 'had lived in blindness' until his conversion to the reformed faith at the parliament of 1560.[38] It may be that Elizabeth had already abandoned her chief's earlier conservatism, for she brought up her children to win the approval of Protestant lairds of Lothian and the Merse. Her husband's escapade in 1544 on Glasgow Muir had been in the company of radical reformers, but whether or not he shared their religious fervour is unknowable. If

36. *HG*, p. 44; *Exch. Rolls*, xviii. 560.
37. CC8/8/3: test. 1575 Haldane, Johne. For his resignation of the baronies of Gleneagles and Haldane to his heir, see GD198/131–6; *RMS*, iv, no. 1489.
38. G. Donaldson, *All the Queen's Men*, p. 64.

he had, his subsequent behaviour suggests that his opinions moderated with age. There can be no question that he favoured some degree of reform; all his known connections were with men opposed to the orthodox establishment, but his name is not to be found on any religious bond pledging signatories to the cause of Protestantism. The connection most valued by the Haldanes was almost certainly that with Lord Erskine: Archibald Haldane, John's uncle, was constable of Edinburgh and Stirling castles, both of which lay in Erskine's custody;[39] Margaret Haldane, John's daughter, married, before 1561, David Erskine, the illegitimate son of the late master of Erskine; and John's sons, George and James, were to maintain the connection after their father's death.[40] The sixth Lord Erskine, John Haldane's cousin who had succeeded in 1555, was one of the five noblemen who threw down the Protestant gauntlet in December 1557, when they signed the First Bond, promising to 'establische the maist blissed worde of God and his congregatioune ... and forsaik and renunce the congregatioune of Sathan with all the superstitioune, abhominatioune, and idolatrie thereof'.[41] While patently a reformer, Erskine was no extremist and was to incur Knox's disapproval for his refusal to endorse the *First Book of Discipline*.[42] He subscribed to no more statements of reformist intent. John Haldane may have shared his cousin's moderate stance.

The Erskine affinity included the Cunninghams of Drumquhassle,[43] whose dealings with John Haldane are a reminder that too much emphasis may be placed on confessional and national affairs when seeking to understand relationships between individuals in this period

39. *HG*, pp. 35–6; for Erskine grants of land and rents to Archibald, see GD124/1/609; *Reg. Privy Seal*, viii, no. 2385.
40. *HG*, p. 50; below, pp. 53, 55.
41. *A Source Book of Scottish History*, ed. W.C. Dickinson et al. (3 vols, London, 1953–4), ii. 152. It used to be thought that the signatory was John Erskine of Dun, but handwriting evidence proves otherwise: D.F. Wright, 'Erskine, John, of Dun', *ODNB* (2004).
42. J. Wormald, *Court, Kirk, and Community: Scotland 1470–1625* (London, 1981), p. 118; *John Knox's History of the Reformation in Scotland*, ed. W.C. Dickinson (2 vols, London, 1949), i. 344 & n.
43. cf. NRS, GD124/1/587, 963, 1090; 124/10/40.

of religious upheaval and political turbulence. Men with shared doctrinal opinions, political views, and even lordly affinities, might still find themselves at loggerheads over local issues touching their landholding or honour. Such an issue seems to have lain behind the abduction of the laird of Gleneagles in 1553 or early 1554, when he was seized in his house ('place') of Lanrick by a party of Cunninghams, led by John Cunningham of Drumquhassle, bundled out of Menteith, and taken over twenty miles into the Lennox, where he was confined in the laird of Drumquhassle's house at Craigievern, a remote location on the eastern edge of Garadhban forest, north-east of Drymen, which may have been thought a more secure prison than Drumquhassle itself, bordered as it was by the Haldane properties of Spittal, Drumbeg, and the Catters.[44] There had been rivalry between the two families in the disposal of the Cremannan inheritance a century and a half earlier, but this discord was probably of more recent origin.[45] John Haldane had only taken possession of Lanrick in July 1553, after the death of his grandmother, Marjorie Lawson, and it is possible that his new broom disturbed interests which had become established during the years of her largely absentee landlordship. What precise advantage the Cunninghams expected to derive from Haldane's detention is, however, unknown, just as are the circumstances of his release. Our knowledge of this dramatic episode in John's career is restricted to the respite from prosecution 'for the tressonable taiking of Johne Haldane of Glennegyis', issued to his captors on 8 March 1554, four days before he himself received a respite for his escapade on Glasgow Muir ten years previously.[46] The coincidence in the timing of these respites, secured within a week of each other during the transference of the regency from Arran to Mary of Guise, points to the honest brokerage of Lord Erskine, using his influence with the queen mother to defuse an incipient feud between valued members of his affinity.[47]

44. *Reg. Privy Seal*, iv, no. 2508.
45. For the Cremannan inheritance, see above, p. 24.
46. *Reg. Privy Seal*, iv, no. 2713.
47. The acquisition of his own respite, evidently long withheld by Arran, may have reconciled John Haldane to that granted to his recent kidnappers.

John Haldane died in December 1563, shortly after granting to his spouse, Elizabeth Lundie, for her life, the lands of Rusky, Lanrick, and Auchrig in the barony of Haldane and resigning the rest of that barony, together with the barony of Gleneagles, to his eldest son, George.[48] George may not yet have been of full age, for the negotiations which resulted in the marriage in April 1565 of his sister Isobel to Patrick Hepburn, younger of Waughton and Luffness, were conducted without reference to him by his mother, assisted by the laird of Lundie and Lord Erskine.[49] George's lairdship coincided with the civil war which followed the enforced abdication of Queen Mary on 24 July 1567 and the coronation of her thirteen-month-old son, James VI, five days later. For the next six years, Scotland was torn by strife between the queen's party, which sought to restore Mary, and the king's party, which supported the government of four successive regents (the first two of whom were killed). The convention of estates, which, in June 1570, elected Matthew, earl of Lennox, as the second regent, was attended by the laird of Gleneagles.[50] He was also a member of the parliament held by the king's party, in August the following year, in the Canongate. This became known as 'the creeping parliament', because its members had to crawl on all fours to avoid gunfire directed at them from Edinburgh Castle, which was in the hands of the queen's supporters, who were simultaneously holding their own parliament in the Tolbooth, where they issued forfeitures against many of the king's party, including George Haldane.[51] Lennox's successor as regent in September 1571 was George's kinsman,

For the transfer of the regency and Erskine's closeness to Mary of Guise at this time, see P.E. Ritchie, *Mary of Guise in Scotland, 1548–1560* (East Linton, 2002), pp. 93–4.

48. GD198/131–6; *RMS*, iv, no. 1489; for his death, see CC8/8/3: test. 1575 Haldane, George.
49. NRS, GD70/19; George is unmentioned in the marriage contract. The match was very much a Lundie affair, since Patrick's mother was a Lundie.
50. *CSP Scotland*, iii. 267.
51. Donaldson, *All the Queen's Men*, pp. 121–2; *A Diurnal of Remarkable Occurrents*, ed. T. Thomson (Bannatyne Club, xliii, 1833), p. 244; *HG*, p. 55, confuses the complexion of the Tolbooth and Canongate parliaments.

the earl of Mar (as Lord Erskine had become in 1565). The king had been in his custody in Stirling Castle ever since his coronation in the church of the Holy Rude, and, when Mar died in October 1572, leaving a ten-year-old son as heir, George Haldane bound himself with other 'friends of the house of Erskine' to assist the boy's uncle, the master of Mar, in safeguarding the king and defending the castle for as long as he was within it.[52]

The laird of Gleneagles did not marry until it was clear that the war was approaching its end and that the king's party would win it. This became evident in the summer of 1572, and, by February 1573, most of Mary's leading supporters were prepared to accept the Pacification of Perth, which promised a return to the territorial *status quo ante bellum*.[53] On 15 February 1573 at Stirling, George Haldane signed a marriage contract with Janet (alias Jane, Jean, or Joan) Cunningham, a daughter of William, master of Glencairn (who was to succeed his father as sixth earl in December the following year). Her grandfather, Alexander earl of Glencairn, was a zealous Presbyterian, who had twice led troops in battle against Queen Mary. Moreover, he was the head of a name borne by many of Haldane's neighbours in the Lennox, while his own property in his barony of Kilmaronock marched both in the west and east with that of the laird of Gleneagles. George's choice of bride, therefore, not only advertised his credentials as a Protestant and a king's man, but also promised to repair damage done during his father's conflict with local Cunninghams a decade earlier.

The marriage contract stipulated that Janet was to receive the lands of Rusky and Lanrick after the death of George's mother, Elizabeth Lundie, who currently enjoyed them; while Elizabeth lived, Janet was to have the liferent of most of the Haldane lands in the Lennox.[54] The charter confirming the contract was sealed, and presumably the marriage celebrated, at Kilmaronock on 29 April 1573.[55] In August the next year,

52. GD124/10/40.
53. Donaldson, *All the Queen's Men*, p. 125; M. Lynch, *Scotland: A New History* (London, 1991), p. 221.
54. *RMS*, vi, p. 88 note; NRS, GD19/16 (Kirkpatrick of Closeburn Papers).
55. GD19/16.

George fell ill and drew up his will; a little over a month later, he was dead.[56]

Financial and political straits: Mr John (V) Haldane, 1574–91

George's successor, his younger brother Master John Haldane, was the first laird of Gleneagles to have a university degree. As younger sons probably anticipating careers in the law, he and his brother James had both matriculated in St Mary's College, St Andrews, in 1568 and graduated in 1571.[57] Contemporary with them at St Mary's was David Home, second son of the laird of Wedderburn in Berwickshire, and already recognized for his formidable intellect. As well as being a devoted religious reformer, he developed a political theory advocating government by altruistic aristocrats, whose pursuit of the common good was conducted without monarchical interference.[58] After James VI's accession to the throne of England, Home was to propose a complete union of both kingdoms and to moderate his republicanism, but, when the Haldane brothers first met him, he was an untrammelled radical. They found his company congenial, and the three became firm friends, with James accompanying Home to the Continent to pursue postgraduate studies together, and John seeking Home's elder sister as his bride.[59] John's first task was to approach the regent, the earl of Morton, for he had not quite achieved his majority when his elder brother died, and his marriage was consequently at the disposal of the crown. Accompanied

56. NRS, CC8/8/3: test. 1575 Haldane, George.
57. *The Early Records of the University of St Andrews, 1413–1579*, ed. J.M. Anderson (Scot. Hist. Soc., 3rd ser., viii, 1925–6), pp. 166, 275; *Acta Facultatis Artium Universitatis Sanctiandree 1413–1588*, ii, ed. A.I. Dunlop (Scot. Hist. Soc., 3rd ser., lv, 1964), pp. 436–8.
58. Ibid., p. 438; P.J. McGinnis & A.H. Williamson, 'Hume, David, of Godscroft', *ODNB* (2004).
59. D. Hume, *De Familia Humia Wedderburnensi Liber* (Abbotsford Club, 1839), pp. 71, 73. The Haldanes had entered Home circles in 1565, when John's eldest sister, Isobel, married Patrick Hepburn of Waughton; Isobel Home's aunt was a Waughton Hepburn: HMC, *MSS of Milne Home of Wedderburn Castle* (London, 1902), p. 6; above, p. 52.

by his uncles, Richard and Robert, and his brother-in-law, David Erskine, commendator of Dryburgh, the young laird found the earl in an unusually generous mood. Apparently without prompting from the family of the prospective bride, whose father was his first cousin, he had decided to show how he could be 'liberall upon occasion, and not unkinde or unmindefull of his friends'. He told Gleneagles that he had bestowed his wardship upon Isobel Home and that 'hee might take her and it together'; whereupon the Haldane party set off for Wedderburn. According to her brother, Isobel Home was 'of tall stature, grave expression, and sober behaviour', as befitted the daughter of a fiercely Calvinist mother. The interview proved satisfactory, and the marriage contract was agreed in December 1574.[60]

Isobel Home's settlement illustrates the paramount difficulty faced by her husband in the management of his inheritance: a shortage of land. Landowners did not readily use their ancestral patrimony to provide conjunct fees for their spouses, but John Haldane had no choice. Rusky and Lanrick were still in the possession of his mother, and the Lennox lands of the barony of Haldane were now in that of his sister-in-law. Isobel's immediate endowment was the liferent of the Mains of Gleneagles, the mill, Cairnquarter (Bardrill), and 'Carsburn', to be joined in 1580 by that of the Glen, Eastside (now East Mains), Glenhead, Hillkitty, Common Hill, 'Corrochie', Easter Kippen, and Dysart.[61] Had John Haldane's life ended as unexpectedly and his widow lived as long as his late brother's, the close of the sixteenth century could have seen the Haldanes of Gleneagles in irreversible decline. In the event, Isobel Home predeceased her husband, dying probably in the mid 1580s. No contract has survived for John's second marriage, which was to Barbara Johnstone, daughter of the laird of Elphinstone in East Lothian, but she is known to have been drawing rent from Cairnquarter in 1602.[62]

60. Hume, *De Familia Humia*, pp. 58, 68; David Hume of Godscroft, *The History of the House of Angus*, e. D. Reid (Scottish Text Soc., 5th ser., iv–v, 2005), i. 271; *HG*, pp. 58–9 (where Isobel, rather than John, is mistakenly depicted as the crown's ward); *Milne Home MSS*, p. 68; *RMS*, v, no. 1263.
61. *RMS*, v, no. 1263.
62. NRS, CC6/5/3: test. 1604 Patersone, James.

To a degree dependent on the lady's longevity, a wife's endowment was paid for by her tocher, but tochers received had to be reckoned against those being paid out. How much Isobel Home brought with her is unknown; a first instalment of £1,230 11s. 4d. was received by John Haldane in February 1575.[63] He should also have been in receipt of the balance of Janet Cunningham's tocher, for only part had been paid by the master of Glencairn when George Haldane died in 1574.[64] On the debit side, John had to provide for three unmarried sisters: Elizabeth (or Elspeth), Beatrix, and Jane (alias Jean, Joan, or Janet). George's will had stipulated that they were to be given the outstanding Cunningham debt, together with rents worth £710 owed him by his tenants. It is doubtful that this sum would have been enough for a single tocher. Details survive only for Jane's, which was 3,000 merks (£2,000).[65]

Jane was the youngest of John's sisters and had attracted the devotion of his friend, Mr David Home, who described her as possessed of beauty and innate charm, and, thanks to her mother's careful education, both virtue and piety.[66] Her attributes had not, however, escaped the attention of David's brother George, the laird of Wedderburn, and his more powerful suit prevailed. The marriage contract between John Haldane's sister and his brother-in-law was made in January 1578.[67] Bruised but unbowed, David Home maintained his intimacy with the Gleneagles family and used his good offices to secure as a husband for Elizabeth Haldane his neighbour in the Merse, Philip, heir to George Nesbit of that ilk, the contract being agreed in Elizabeth's mother's house at Lanrick in March 1582.[68] At an unknown date, Beatrix found a husband nearer home in Robert Colville of Cleish.[69]

The prominence given in the records of her children's marriages to Elizabeth Lundie, the senior surviving Lady Gleneagles, suggests that

63. *Milne Home MSS*, p. 47.
64. CC8/8/3: test. 1575 Haldane, George.
65. *Milne Home MSS*, p. 48.
66. *De Familia Humia*, pp. 70–1.
67. *Milne Home MSS*, p. 48.
68. *RMS*, v, no. 403.
69. *HG*, pp. 52, 333.

she played an active part in the affairs of her Perthshire family. She is known to have lent money to George Haldane to stock the Glen (now St Mungo's) with sheep and to furnish the Mains,[70] and it is unlikely that she withheld it from his straitened brother, who was displaying signs of desperation by the end of the 1570s. He attempted to collect rents and dues from tenants of that part of the barony of Haldane in the Lennox which, by the incontrovertible terms of her marriage contract, was enjoyed by his elder brother's widow. Janet Cunningham had remarried in 1577, returning to her own family's heartland in south-west Scotland to find her second husband, Thomas Kirkpatrick, younger of Closeburn, who proved a strenuous supporter of his wife's rights.[71] In 1580, faced with demands from rival landlords, the Lennox tenants sought legal clarification, and an unequivocal judgment was given against John Haldane.[72] The closest he came to possessing this part of his barony of Haldane was in 1586, when he paid Kirkpatrick and his wife 1,000 merks (£666 13s. 4d.) for a lease of Boturich castle and the Haldane lands attached to it.[73]

Financial worries were not the only source of anxiety for the laird of Gleneagles at the start of the 1580s. The rise to power of the teenage king's favourites, the half-French duke of Lennox and Captain James Stewart, an audacious adventurer who was promoted to the (not strictly vacant) earldom of Arran,[74] caused alarm to Anglophile Presbyterians like the Haldanes and their friends the Homes, who watched as James VI was encouraged to consider the Scottish Reformation the product of a seditious faction and to admire the monarchical absolutism of France. A plot to remove the king from the baleful influence of Lennox and Arran was executed in August 1582, when James was kidnapped at Ruthven House near Perth. The principal movers in the Ruthven Raid included John Erskine, the twenty-year-old earl of Mar, his cousin David

70. NRS, CC8/8/3: test. 1575 Haldane, George.
71. GD19/17–18; *RMS*, iv, no. 2702.
72. *HG*, p. 58; Register of Acts & Decreets, lxxix, 28 April 1580.
73. Register of Deeds, xxiv. 381; *HG*, p. 58.
74. *Complete Peerage*, i. 222.

Erskine, commendator of Dryburgh and Inchmahome, and the earl of Angus, whose secretary was David Home.[75] It may be wondered which had the greater influence on the Haldanes: the political theories of the laird's university friend and brother-in-law, which read like a blueprint for the manifestos issued by the Raiders, or the strength of the family's Erskine connection. The earl was a kinsman, while David Erskine was a brother-in-law; John's brother James was in the earl's retinue; another brother, David, served in the commendator's household, and Mr Richard Haldane, John's uncle, held tacks in the commendator's barony of Cardross; his great-uncle, Archibald Haldane, had for years been Mar's constable of Edinburgh Castle.[76] Richard was directly implicated in the king's detention, while John and his brother James became involved in its aftermath.

The plotters held power for as long as they held the king, but, after ten months, the king escaped and handed authority to Arran. Among those who found themselves 'putt out of the king's grace . . . and captives' in February 1584 was the laird of Gleneagles, in company with his brother-in-law, George Home of Wedderburn; another brother-in-law, Robert Colville of Cleish, was banished to Flanders or France; John's sister Margaret, David Erskine's wife, was in custody in Kildrummy (Aberdeenshire).[77] In April 1584, evidently released from confinement, both John Haldane and George Home were summoned to appear before the Privy Council and charged not to communicate with any of the Ruthven Raiders 'now abroad'; the political neutrality of another brother-in-law, Patrick Hepburn, younger of Waughton, apparently

75. D. Calderwood, *The History of the Kirk of Scotland*, ed. T. Thomson (8 vols, Edinburgh, 1843), iii. 637; McGinnis & Williamson, 'Hume, David of Godscroft', *ODNB*; for the Ruthven Raid, see Donaldson, *Scotland: James V–James VII*, pp. 178–83; idem, *All the Queen's Men*, pp. 140–7.

76. *Red Book of Menteith*, ed. Fraser, i. 544; ii. 365; *RMS*, v, nos. 636, 1012; *Reg. Privy Seal*, viii, nos. 1595, 2385; NAS, GD124/1/96–7, 609; for the Raiders' manifestos, see Calderwood, *History of the Kirk*, iii. 637–40, 683–7.

77. Ibid., iv. 25, 32, 72, 421; *The Hamilton Papers*, ed. J. Bain (Edinburgh, 1892), ii. 643.

made him acceptable to the régime as John's cautioner in £10,000 not to disobey this command.[78] The laird did, nevertheless, make contact with an enemy of Arran. In May 1585, in an attempt to alleviate the plight of his sister Margaret, who was 'in some distresse', being 'restrayned farre absent from hir frendis', he asked Queen Elizabeth's minister, Walsingham, to persuade Edward Wotton, the English emissary in Scotland, to intercede directly with the king on her behalf. Walsingham sent Haldane a letter of introduction to the envoy, suggesting that he try to have Margaret removed to the custody of her mother (at Lanrick) or her brother (at Gleneagles).[79] It may be that John Haldane had met Walsingham and established sufficient rapport with him, during the latter's brief mission to Scotland in the autumn of 1583, to feel emboldened to write to him, but it is as likely that contact was made through the agency of David Home, who was now in London, where he had joined a coterie of exiled Scottish ultra-Presbyterian divines, whose company the puritan Walsingham found congenial.[80]

The rebel lords had also fled to England towards the end of April 1584, after a failed attempt to hold Stirling. At the end of October 1585, they returned, raising an army as they moved north of the Tweed. Before dawn on 2 November, some 7,000 rebels entered Stirling, where their numbers were increased by 'manie gentlemen that were in the toun, as the lairds of Keir and Glennegeis'. John Haldane found himself in the company of his brother James, who was with the earl of Mar, and of their brother-in-law George Home of Wedderburn, who had joined the lords as soon as they had reached Kelso. Government forces numbered no more than 4,000. An agent reported to Walsingham that

---

78. *RPC*, iii. 648, 651.
79. *Hamilton Papers*, ii. 643.
80. C. Read, *Mr Secretary Walsingham and the Policy of Queen Elizabeth* (3 vols, Oxford, 1925), ii. 213–19; Calderwood, *History of the Kirk*, iii. 724–30. David Home was in London with Andrew Melville and others in October 1584: *Miscellany of the Wodrow Society*, ed. D. Laing (Edinburgh, 1844), pp. 451–2; cf. G. Donaldson, 'Scottish Presbyterian Exiles in England, 1584–88', *Records of the Scottish Church History Soc.*, xiv (1963), pp. 67–80.

'some conflict ther was, which lasted about two howris, and in the end
the lordis prevailed and have the upper hand, with the losse of xx^te men
on both sides; one gentleman slayne called Haddon belonging to the
Erle of Marre'. The gentleman called Haddon was James Haldane, who
had entered the burgh through its west port, the defence of which had
been entrusted to Colonel William Stewart, a man hated and feared as
'imployed by the king to apprehend anie subject, in anie corner of the
kingdome, that the court had anie querrell at'. He and Arran were the
two men whom the insurgents most wanted to capture. Arran had fled
across Stirling Bridge, throwing the key to its gate into the Forth as he
went, but the colonel made for the castle. James Haldane spotted him,
gave hot pursuit, and was in the act of seizing him, when Stewart's servant fired. James fell, dead or dying. David Home was so deeply affected
by his friend's death that, over forty years later, when describing the
Raid of Stirling in his history of the earls of Angus, he inserted a heart-
felt eulogy of Master James Haldane. 'He was a young Gentleman, much
lamented of all that knew him, being lately come out of France, where
(as also in Italy) he had lived divers years, with great approbation of all
his Country-men, being greatly beloved for his sweet courteous disposition. If it were lawfull here to bewaile a particular losse, I have just cause
to loose the reins of my private affection, and pay that tribute of sorrow
and teares which I owe to the memorie of so faithfull, upright, and trusty
a friend. For the present it shall suffise to say thus much, that before
him I found not any, and since have known but very few so hearty and
sincere friends, as he was to me from our childe-hood for many yeares.'[81]

The king dismissed Arran and readmitted the Ruthven Raiders to
his grace, but there was no return to the ultra-Protestantism of their
regime. Friends of David Home would have been dismayed to hear the
king defend the institution of episcopacy and denounce the intrusion
of Presbyterian ministers in matters of state. In March 1590, doubting
James VI's commitment to the persecution of Roman Catholics, the

81.   D. Hume, *History of House of Angus*, ed. Reid, ii. 354–5; Calderwood,
      History of the Kirk, iv. 382, 389–90, 448; *Calendar of Letters & Papers, re-
      lating to the Borders of England & Scotland*, ed. J. Bain (2 vols, Edinburgh,
      1894–6), i. 210.

kirk's General Assembly appointed commissioners to enforce its legislation against Jesuits; one such commissioner was the laird of Gleneagles,
deputed to act with Stirling of Keir and Murray of Tullibardine in
Menteith, the Lennox, and the diocese of Dunblane.[82] Mr John Haldane's
last appearance in surviving records is on 4 August 1590, when he was
Dunblane's commissioner on the General Assembly.[83] By 16 December
1590, his brother David had been appointed tutor of Gleneagles.[84] In the
interim, it would seem that John had become incapacitated by illness or
accident, for his death did not take place until April 1591.[85]

Domestic debt and foreign adventure: James (III) Haldane, 1591–1624

John's eldest son, James, underage at his father's death, was retoured
as heir on 3 December 1592 and took sasine of his inheritance on 24
October 1593.[86] His marriage would have to wait for a reduction in the
number of surviving dowager ladies of Gleneagles. His grandmother,
Elizabeth Lundie, Lady Gleneagles, remained at Lanrick and Rusky;
his stepmother, Barbara Johnstone, Lady Gleneagles, was in receipt of
income from lands at Gleneagles itself; while the Lennox lands of the
barony of Haldane were held, until Lanrick and Rusky became available, by James's aunt, Janet Cunningham, Lady Gleneagles, and now
also Lady Closeburn, as her husband, Thomas Kirkpatrick, had come

82. Calderwood, *History of the Kirk*, v. 43.
83. *HG*, p. 58.
84. *RPC*, iv. 803.
85. According to the retour for his son and heir, 3 October 1592, his baronies
    had been in non-entry for eighteen months, and an exchequer record of 18
    April 1593 notes that they had been in the king's hand for two years: NRS,
    GD198/142; *Exchequer Rolls*, xxii. 481. A Privy Council scribe's failure to
    call the laird defunct, when describing Mr Joseph Haldane as his brother,
    on 30 August 1591 appears to have been an error: *RPC*, iv. 674; cf. *HG*,
    p. 59.
86. NRS, GD198/142–4; David Haldane was still tutor on 26 August
    1592: *Calendar of the Laing Charters, A.D. 854–1857*, ed. J. Anderson
    (Edinburgh, 1899), no. 1248.

into his inheritance in Dumfriesshire. Revenue from the manor of Gleneagles remained encumbered for some time, for Barbara Johnstone was still alive in 1620, having in 1594 married her late husband's old friend and her sister-in-law's erstwhile admirer, David Home, now laird of Godscroft in the Merse.[87] Elizabeth Lundie's long life ended in the winter of 1598–99. On 9 April 1599, Thomas Kirkpatrick demanded possession of 'the lands and barony' of Rusky and Lanrick on behalf of his wife, and James Haldane handed over the keys of 'the manor place thereof', whereupon Kirkpatrick renounced all claim to the barony of Haldane in the Lennox.[88]

Relations between the two families, however, remained tense, for an old chicken came home to roost. Elizabeth Lundie had been the surviving executrix of George Haldane's will and testament, and her passing cleared the way for Janet Cunningham to set about righting a wrong which had clearly troubled her for twenty-five years. She produced her own record of her first husband's moveable wealth and persuaded the commissary court of Edinburgh to appoint her son, Thomas Kirkpatrick, younger of Closeburn, as executor of an adjusted inventory. Where there were no children to receive the 'bairns' part', a defunct's moveable wealth was divided in two, with the widow taking half. In 1574, George Haldane had passed over his wife and appointed as executors his mother and brother, who evidently considered that his widow was sufficiently compensated for her brief and childless marriage, and reduced her half-share by minimizing the value of his moveable assets. They presented an inventory which valued the contents of his houses at £10, the livestock at Gleneagles at £580, and rents owed from the tenants of the Lennox and Gleneagles at £710; all set against debts of £893. The inventory produced by Thomas Kirkpatrick in January 1599 estimated the value of the contents of Gleneagles and Boturich at George's death

---

87. *Milne Home MSS*, pp. 80, 88.
88. GD19/31. Although Rusky and Lanrick had been incorporated in the barony of Haldane in 1509, references to them as constituting a separate barony become the norm in the seventeenth century. Haldane gives no evidence for his statement that Elizabeth Lundie was alive in March 1605 (*HG*, p. 45), and I have found none.

as £159 (including twelve silver spoons worth £19); the value of the livestock was increased by £492, and of outstanding rents by £111: a total upward adjustment of £762.[89] Although the evidence is wanting, the presumption must be that Lady Closeburn presented James Haldane with a bill for £381, not a vast sum, but vastly irritating. There need be little wonder that, in 1602, James Haldane of Gleneagles was required to find surety in 2,000 merks not to harm Janet Cunningham or her husband, Thomas Kirkpatrick of Closeburn.[90]

The departure of the Closeburns from Haldane's lands in the Lennox in 1599 provided James with the wherewithal to endow a wife, and, on 26 January 1600, a marriage contract was made with Margaret Murray, daughter of his Perthshire neighbour, Sir John Murray, laird and future earl of Tullibardine; she would have the liferent of the barony of Haldane and bring with her a tocher of 9,000 merks (£6,000).[91] James would need to balance this sum against tochers he had to find for his four sisters: Margaret, who strengthened the family's link with the Homes of the Merse by marrying Sir John Home of Blackadder at an unknown date; Isobel, who by 1608 had married William Edmonstone, younger of Duntreath in Strath Blane, an estate so heavily encumbered that, shortly after succeeding to it, he became a pioneer in the plantation of Ulster; Jean, who took a tocher of 2,000 merks to James Colville, younger brother of the commendator of Culross; and Helen, who became in 1613 the second wife of a younger son of Sir David Lindsay of Edzell. In purely materialistic terms, by far the best of these matches was Margaret's, whose unspecified tocher was described by David Home, kinsman to both parties, as 'large enough'; if Jean's 2,000 merks exemplified the maximum that James could afford for the remaining sisters, the modesty of their alliances is explained.[92]

---

89. CC8/8/3, 32: test. 1575 Haldane, George; 1599 Halden, George.
90. *RPC*, vi. 735.
91. *HG*, p. 72 & note.
92. Ibid., pp. 64–6; *De Familia Humia*, p. 78; NRS, GD26/6/27 (Leslie Papers: contract for Jean Haldane, who is overlooked in *HG*); *RMS*, vi, no. 2180; vii, no. 2009.

James's financial difficulties were to become acute. His great-grand-father and namesake had sold the Haldane superiorities north of Loch Tay to Campbell of Lawers in 1526; in 1609 James disposed of the south-ern part of Agnes Menteith's Tayside inheritance, selling Ardeonaig to Lawers's descendant for 8,500 merks.[93] James's income would have been further increased by the return of Lanrick and Rusky after Janet Cunningham's death in about 1613,[94] and, in June 1616, he and his wife converted most of the tenancies on the Lennox lands of the barony of Haldane into feu farms, in return for 'certain great sums of money',[95] but the respite was temporary. In 1618, an order was made for the seizure of his houses and goods for non-payment of a principal debt of 16,162 merks and 2,000 merks in 'expenses'.[96] His wife had died in December 1617, and James decided to reduce his domestic expenditure, receiving the king's licence in 1618 to stay abroad for five years, during which his property would be protected, so long as he behaved like a dutiful subject.[97]

In September 1620, his sons, John and James, were given permission to follow him 'to whatsoever parts beyond sea they please for the doing of their lawful affairs'.[98] In the case of the brothers, these lawful affairs are known to have been military, with John probably, and James certainly, joining the many Scots already in the Netherlands, serving the prince of Orange in his war with the Habsburgs. James was to rise to the rank of lieutenant-colonel before being killed in action in 1629, having earned the admiration not only of his uncle, Sir Mungo Murray of Drumcairn, who declared that 'he hes not left the lyk behind him of ane Scottisman', but also of the prince of Orange and the elector palatine, who both went into mourning for him.[99] Nothing is known of his father's destination or

93. GD112/1/829 (Breadalbane Papers); *RMS*, vii, no. 742; above, pp. 26, 44.
94. Thomas Kirkpatrick contracted his second marriage in December 1614: *Kirkpatrick of Closeburn* (priv. printed, London, 1858), p. 41.
95. GD198/83.
96. *RPC*, xi. 287.
97. CC6/5/4: test. 1618 Murray, Margrat; *HG*, pp. 72–3 *RPC*, xi. 425.
98. *RPC*, xii. 362.
99. *HG*, pp. 73–4.

occupation in 1618, but the potential profit to be had in wars on foreign soil provided the most likely motive, and the Netherlands the most convenient location. This may not have been the first time that the laird had left Scotland: his uncle David had acted as tutor of Gleneagles in 1596–97; an otherwise unknown Andrew Haldane had served in 1599, and David had been back in harness in 1603, as he was to be after James's departure in 1618.[100] In 1603, the laird's absence is more likely to have been across the border than across the sea, for in March James VI had succeeded to the crown of England, and in April the Scottish king and his court moved south to London, followed by many in search of place or patronage. Their numbers were to be thinned, however, by the unfriend-liness of the English élite, and the expense of living where the official exchange rate was £1 sterling to £12 Scots.[101] Even when his nephew was at home, David Haldane took a leading part in family affairs, his consent being required for the sale of Ardeonaig and his participation needed in tackling problems emanating from the Highlands.[102]

With their lands in Strathearn, Menteith, and the Lennox lying at the frontier of Highland and Lowland Scotland, the Haldanes frequently found themselves called upon by the government to help police areas where central authority was ineffective. For the most part, clansmen were also tenants of their chiefs, who were able to maintain acceptable order in their regions, but, where this tenurial structure had been dis-located, a chief, while retaining the loyalty of his clansmen, lost his most effective sanction in disciplining their behaviour, and clans might splin-ter into gangs, a contemporary term for bands of raiders. This became the fate of the MacGregors, victims of the aggressive expansion of the Campbells of Glenorchy.[103] In 1564, the laird of Gleneagles had been among the barons of Menteith whose tenants were ordered to pursue the Clan Gregor 'until they be expelled forth of the said bounds'.[104] In 1585,

---

100. *RPC*, v. 365; vi. 823; xii. 176; CC8/8/40: test. 1605 Haldane, Johnne.
101. Cf. Brown, *Noble Society in Scotland*, p. 88.
102. *RMS*, vii, no. 742; *RPC*, viii. 669.
103. See *Campbell Letters 1559–1583*, ed. J.A. Dawson (Scot. History Soc., 5th ser., x, 1997), pp. 55–9.
104. *Red Book of Menteith*, ii. 401–2.

the laird had been summoned to provide information about Highland banditry in the Lennox, Menteith, Stirlingshire, and Strathearn.[105] Men without lords who would answer for them, known as 'broken men', were the focus of government attention. In 1587, landlords were made responsible, under heavy financial penalties, for the behaviour of their tenants, and John Haldane's name had been enrolled as that of a laird dwelling in the Highlands 'where broken men have dwelt and presently dwell'.[106] In 1590, David Haldane, as tutor of Gleneagles, and one 'on whose lands broken men dwell', had to find surety in £5,000 to keep 'good rule'.[107] Complaints were lodged against the Haldanes by tenants of Colquhoun of Luss in 1599.[107] When Colquhouns were slaughtered by the MacGregors in Glen Fruin in 1603, the government reacted by abolishing the name 'MacGregor'; in 1611, when anyone bearing the name might be killed with impunity, David Haldane received a commission to try those who harboured MacGregors within the earldom and stewartry of Menteith.[109]

It was James VI's intention not only to strengthen his authority in the Highlands, Islands, and Borders, but also to intensify the impact of government generally. Before his departure for the Continent in 1618, James Haldane had already served three times as a justice of the peace for Perthshire: in 1609, when the office was introduced to Scotland, in 1610, and in 1613. The king's terrified fascination with witchcraft produced an increased number of prosecutions, with James being commissioned to join the bishop of Dunblane in trying two women in May 1615.[110] If he had returned home by 13 December 1621, he may have been alarmed to hear that one Joan Anderson, on trial at Stirling, claimed that she had learnt her charms from 'ane man callit Litill Dik, servand to the auld laird of Gleneglis [presumably James's father], quhen he was charmen

---

105. *RPC*, iii. 718.
106. Records of Parliament of Scotland [hereafter RPS], 1587/7/70.
107. *RPC*, iv. 803.
108. *RPC*, vi. 823.
109. *RPC*, ix. 285.
110. *HG*, pp. 69–71.

ane hors in ane medow'.[111] James had certainly returned by February 1622, when he was appointed to commissions for licensing pearl fishing in the Forth and Teith, for negotiating the dispatch of raw wool to middlemen in England, and for the establishment of manufactures.[112] He accepted a further commission of the peace for Perthshire and the stewartries of Strathearn and Menteith in 1623, and his last appearance on administrative business was at a council of Highland landlords on 17 March 1624.[113] He died about two months later.[114]

Revolution and war: Sir John (VI) Haldane, 1624–50

John Haldane, James's eldest son, did not enter upon his inheritance until November 1625, eighteen months after his father's death, but he is known to have been in Scotland in the second half of 1624: in November he was in Edinburgh, and on 18 August he had contracted to marry.[115] His bride was Catherine, a sister of Sir John Wemyss of that ilk, who was to be ennobled as Lord Wemyss of Elcho in 1628, and was created earl of Wemyss during Charles I's visit to Scotland in 1633.[116] At Holyrood, on 12 July 1633, his final day before returning south, the king also knighted John Haldane of Gleneagles.[117] Catherine may not have lived to witness

---

111. *RPC*, viii. 345, 347.
112. *HG*, pp. 71–2.
113. *RPC*, xiii. 347, 461.
114. *HG*, p. 72; NRS, GD198/145. I have failed to find the evidence for General Haldane's statement that James had been knighted after his return from the Continent (*HG*, p. 71). No official source calls him a knight, and, had he been one, the title would certainly have been given him in the documents recording his son's succession, where he appears simply as 'James Haldene of Glennegas': GD145–7.
115. GD198/145; GD124/2/16; W. Fraser (ed.), *Memorials of the Family of Wemyss of Wemyss* (3 vols, Edinburgh, 1888), i. 205.
116. *Complete Peerage*, xii, part ii, p. 463.
117. *The Historical Works of Sir James Balfour* (4 vols, Edinburgh, 1824), iv. 366. Gen. Haldane misreads Balfour in saying that Haldane was dubbed at the unlikely hour of 4 a.m. (*HG*, p. 81): after listing a group of four

his promotion. She was certainly dead by December 1634, when John contracted to marry her sister-in-law, Margaret Fraser (whose brother Hugh, Lord Lovat, had married Catherine's eldest sister Isobel in 1614). Like John, Margaret was entering her second marriage, having first been the wife of Sir Robert Arbuthnott of that ilk (d. 16 March 1633), and she brought with her, as her jointure from that marriage, the lands of Arrats Mill near Brechin. For his part, Sir John Haldane (in 1638) gave Margaret the liferent of Lanrick and Rusky in Menteith, together with that of West Catter and Drumdash in the Lennox; the remainder of the barony of Haldane was made an appanage for their infant son, Mungo.[118]

John's association with Margaret Fraser added a new focus for Haldane marriages. Before May 1628, his sister Christian had found a local Perthshire match in a younger son of Murray of Ochtertyre;[119] in 1626, his sister Catherine married Robert Napier, younger of Kilmahew in western Lennox;[120] and in 1630, his sister Margaret married James Stirling of Auchyle, a neighbour of the Haldanes in Menteith.[121] The two remaining sisters, however, found their spouses in Kincardineshire and Aberdeenshire: Annabelle, by July 1638, had married James Wood of Balbegno in the Mearns, not far from Margaret Fraser's property at Arrats Mill, while Ann, in 1634, became the second wife of the master of Fraser, whose father, Lord Fraser, was based near Monymusk in Aberdeenshire.[122]

No evidence survives for the tochers provided by John Haldane for these ladies. He himself had received 10,000 merks with Catherine

---

lairds, including 'Gleneggies', the text reads 'These 4 in the morning being Friday'.

118. GD198/84–6; *RMS*, ix, no. 681; *Chronicles of the Frasers: the Wardlaw MS*, ed. W. Mackay (Scot. Hist. Soc., xlvii, 1905), p. 243.

119. *RMS*, viii, no. 1417.

120. *Genealogical Notices of the Napiers of Kilmahew* (priv. pr., Glasgow, 1849), pp. 9–10, 28–9; *HG*, pp. 76–7.

121. GD86/522; Fraser, *Stirlings of Keir*, p. 171; *Laing Charters*, no. 2051.

122. GD1/38; *RMS*, ix, no. 759. Lord Fraser was unconnected with Margaret's family, the Frasers of Lovat, until his grandson married her niece in 1658: GEC, *Complete Peerage*, v. 568.

Wemyss,[123] but his attempt to maximize the financial benefits brought by his second wife met with failure. Margaret Fraser's liferent of the lands of Arrat was granted by her first husband in lieu of the widow's right to a third of his property (her terce), but the marriage contract failed to specify whether this property was limited to Sir Robert Arbuthnott's patrimony or included his acquisitions ('conquests'), which were considerable. The loophole was a small one, and there was perhaps an element of desperation in Sir John Haldane's decision, in collaboration with his wife, to sue her eldest son for a terce of Arbuthnott's 'conquest lands'. On 22 March 1636 the lords of Session rejected Haldane's claim, having 'utterly blasted' his arguments, as the Arbuthnott family historian happily recorded.[124]

Sir John's financial problems obliged him to continue the drastic policy forced on his father and sell land. Since the mid sixteenth century, Balwill, Upper and Lower Ballaird, and Woodend in southern Menteith had formed a holding for a cadet line descended from a younger son of James (II) Haldane; in 1629, John Haldane resigned these lands, with Kepdowrie and Auchrig, to Archibald Campbell, Lord Lorne, who had them incorporated into a new barony of Balwill in 1630.[125] Further, in 1637 Sir John mortgaged Little Boturich to his tenant at Haldane's Mill for 2,000 merks, and two years later sold Kippen (near Dunning) and Craigbaikie to the land-hungry and cash-rich Sir Andrew Rollo of Duncrub.[126] The baronies of Gleneagles and Haldane were shrinking.

Sir John Haldane, however, was by no means the only laird to struggle against inflation and the costs of keeping up with increasingly expensive

---

123. The final instalment was paid in May 1627. Catherine's sister Isobel similarly took 10,000 merks to the master of Lovat in 1614, but their eldest sister had taken £10,000 to the earl of Tullibardine in 1599: *Mem. Wemyss*, i. 205, 211–12.

124. A. Arbuthnott, 'A continuation of the genealogie of the noble family of Arbuthnott', National Library of Scotland, Adv. Ms. 34.6.19, fos. 12–23; Acts & Decreets, v. 489; *Scots Peerage*, i. 302; *HG*, pp. 88–9.

125. GD86/522, 657; GD220/1/L/2/2/1–3, 9; GD220/1/L/2/4/1; *RMS*, viii, no. 1623.

126. GD198/98–9; *RMS*, ix, no. 886; cf. *Complete Peerage*, xi. 77, note (b).

changes in fashion, and, on the day of his investiture as a knight, he could reflect that the Haldane name still attracted members of the higher nobility. Through his first wife, he was brother-in-law to the earl of Wemyss; through his second, to Lord Lovat; and the earl of Tullibardine was his first cousin. More distant cousins were the Erskine earls of Mar and the Graham earls of Montrose. The Erskine connection remained significant, but relations between the Haldanes and the Grahams, close neighbours in Strathearn, had cooled. Both the laird's grandfather and the earl's had been antagonists at the time of the Ruthven Raid and its aftermath; the third earl of Montrose was a member of Arran's regime, which the Haldanes enthusiastically opposed, and had indeed been imprisoned at the insistence of the laird's colleagues, the banished lords whom he helped take Stirling in 1585.[127] Nevertheless, the fifth earl, who succeeded in 1626 at the age of fourteen, seemed eager to improve relations with his neighbour. There are records of him visiting Gleneagles in September 1628 and October 1629, each time distributing over £3 among the servants, while, in October 1628, 'Geneglis and his servands' joined fourteen others in a supper party given by Montrose at his house at Drumfad.[128]

Alas, the young earl and the slightly older laird were destined to find themselves on opposite sides of a yet more violent and bitter conflict than that which had divided their grandfathers. When at Holyrood in 1633, John Haldane would have noticed with disquiet how the king used the English Prayer Book and Anglican ceremonial. Eleven years later, the laird was in arms in defence of the Scottish Reformation, and the earl in defence of the king. In the interim, Charles I had unsettled the political classes of his northern kingdom by increasing taxation, threatening a revocation of royal grants stretching back further than the previous century, disappointing seekers of place and pensions by a heavy reliance on bishops in his administration, and presenting the image of an absolute monarch. Above all, he had caused widespread alarm, within and

127. *Complete Peerage*, ix. 148, note (b).
128. M. Napier (ed.), *Memorials of Montrose and his Times* (2 vols, Edinburgh, 1850), i. 147, 169, 196; E.J. Cowan, *Montrose: for Covenant and King* (London, 1977), pp. 12–13, 18.

without the élite, by his determination to unify, on his own terms, the churches of his kingdoms. Centred on episcopacy and royal supremacy, his plans manifestly had no place for presbyteries or General Assemblies. Dissent gathered steam throughout the 1630s, exploded in an Edinburgh riot in July 1637, when an attempt was made to use the Anglican liturgy in the High Kirk of St Giles, and was channelled in February 1638 into the National Covenant, whose subscribers – most of the nobility and untold numbers of lairds – swore to defend with their lives the Reformation of 1560, demanded the removal of bishops, and called for free parliaments. Royal authority in Scotland evaporated, a process epitomized by Gleneagles's unfortunate uncle, Archibald Haldane, constable of the undermanned and under-provisioned Edinburgh Castle, who was obliged in March 1639 to watch from the battlements as its outer gate was dynamited and its inner gates broken down; when General Leslie's covenanters poured in, Archibald wept tears of frustration; at a parley half an hour earlier, he had surprised the general by his unwillingness to surrender.[129]

The king's authority was replaced eventually by that of committees of covenanting noblemen, prominent among whom was the earl of Montrose. A state of defence was organized. Regiments were raised, with officers drawn from those who, like Gleneagles, had experience of Continental warfare. A revolution was taking place, but, as is the way with revolutions, its base narrowed and its objectives became more extreme. To Montrose it seemed that royal powers were being improperly usurped and that there was a danger of King Charles being replaced by King Campbell. The earl of Argyll was using the authority of the covenant to extend his dominance in the Highlands, while Campbell

---

129. J. Gordon, *History of Scots Affairs, 1637–1641* (3 vols, Spalding Club, 1841), ii. 209–10; *The Memoirs of Henry Guthry, late Bishop of Dunkeld* (2nd edn, Glasgow, 1747), p. 52; *The Letters and Journals of Robert Baillie, 1637–1662*, ed. D. Laing (3 vols, Bannatyne Club, 1841–2), i. 195; Balfour, *Historical Works*, ii. 320–1; *HG*, 62–4. The pacification of Berwick in June 1639 returned the castle to the king, who bought out the earl of Mar's hereditary custodianship, and so ended the Haldane connection with it. It finally surrendered to the covenanters in September 1640.

of Lawers, now earl of Loudoun and Lord Chancellor, was a zealot
obsessed by an ambition to presbyterianize England and Ireland. When
Charles I found himself at war with his English parliament, Loudoun
went to Oxford to tell his monarch that a hostile Scottish intervention
would only be averted by implementing his ecclesiastical plans. In the
event, the Scots negotiated a 'Solemn League and Covenant' with the
English parliament, agreeing to raise an army of 21,000 troops, for the
maintenance of which their allies were to pay £30,000 sterling a month,
and in return for which the churches of England and Ireland were to be
reformed on the model of the Scottish kirk. In January 1644, a covenanting army crossed the border; the next month, Montrose accepted the
king's commission as lieutenant-general of his forces in Scotland. Civil
war had broken out.[130]

Sir John Haldane had already participated in Perthshire's contribution to the covenanting war effort, serving in August 1643 as a collector of taxes to raise 1,220,000 merks Scots, and as a commissioner for
recruitment, with the expectation that he would command men within
the sheriffdom.[131] By February 1644, his brother Mungo had joined
Tullibardine's Perthshire regiment, with the rank of captain.[132] During
1644 and much of 1645, Sir John's services were in demand on parliamentary business as a commissioner for Perthshire barons and, during
November and December 1644, in liaising between the Committee

130. For general accounts of the events of which the above is the baldest
     outline, see R. Mitchinson, *Lordship to Patronage: Scotland 1603–1745*
     (London, 1983), pp. 22–56; Donaldson, *Scotland: James V–James VII*,
     pp. 295–333; Lynch, *Scotland: A New History*, pp. 248–76.
131. RPS, 1643/6/66, 91; *HG*, p. 82, where an assumption is made that Sir
     John was identical with the Major Halden who is found in the Loudon-
     Glasgow Regiment. Major Halden, however, is never referred to as a
     knight or a laird, and, as the Perthshire committee had selected Sir John as
     a potential colonel, the identification must be wrong; a more likely candi-
     date is the John Halden who appears as one of Lord Loudoun's servants
     in 1640: *Memoirs of Henry Guthrie*, p. 70; cf. *Papers relating to the Army of
     the Solemn League and Covenant, 1643–1647*, ed. C.S. Terry (2 vols, Scot.
     Hist. Soc., 2nd ser., xvi–xvii, 1917), i, pp. 55, 57 77.
132. Ibid., pp. xlii, 75, 77–8.

with the Army, first at Newcastle and then in Edinburgh, and the Scots commissioners in London, who were trying to extract some of the maintenance for their troops promised by the English parliament.[133]

Covenanters were already deeply shocked and dismayed by a series of spectacular defeats inflicted upon them within Scotland by Montrose, whose forces, largely Irish and Highland enemies of the Campbells, had ravaged Argyll and the eastern Highlands. The earl of Argyll reluctantly relinquished command of the covenanting army in Scotland to a professional soldier, William Baillie, but continued failure and outspoken criticism from his own officers led to his resignation early in August 1645. On 15 August, however, before his replacement could arrive, his demoralized troops faced Montrose at Kilsyth, north-east of Glasgow. Argyll asked Baillie for advice; Baillie called for the opinion of other noblemen, including Lord Loudoun, whose regiment included a Major Haldane. When Montrose attacked, the covenanters were already in disarray, trying to alter their position, but unclear what their new one should be. The main body of Loudoun's men advanced when Baillie thought they had been told to hold their position, and Major Haldane used his own initiative to lead a party of musketeers towards a house in a glen controlled by Montrose; ordered by Baillie to retreat, he took no notice.[134] The covenanting army was destroyed, its surviving officers and men scattering in all directions. Although Baillie thought the episode worthy of record, it is highly improbable that Haldane's disregard of an order contributed appreciably to the outcome. The chain of command had been fatally weakened before the battle began, and the lack of confidence in Baillie's judgement displayed by the noblemen in his army was evidently shared by Major Haldane.[135]

Loudoun's regiment was broken up after, or, perhaps more accurately, by the battle of Kilsyth, and within a week Major Haldane had joined

133. RPS, 1644/6/2; 1645/1/2, 16; 1645/7/82; 1645/7/8/11; 1645/7/24/2, 9; *Correspondence of the Scots Commissioners in London, 1644–1645,* ed. H.W. Meikle (Roxburghe Club, 1917), p. 50; *HG,* p. 82.
134. *Letters & Journals of Robert Baillie,* ii. 421–2; Cowan, *Montrose,* p. 219.
135. D. Stevenson, *Revolution and Counter-Revolution in Scotland, 1644–1651* (London, Royal Historical Society, 1977), pp. 33–5.

Captain Mungo Haldane in Tullibardine's Perthshire regiment.[136] He arrived just in time to witness the war come to Gleneagles. Montrose's persistent problem after a victory was to hold his army together. While his agenda was to secure Scotland for the king, and deprive the English parliament of the Scots army by drawing it north of the border, the Irish and Highlanders had different priorities, chief of which were the pursuit of private feuds, the accumulation of booty, and the protection of their homes once they had returned to them with their loot. A party of Atholl men, MacGregors, and 'other broken Hieland men', retracing the route by which Montrose had led them to Kilsyth,[137] had found thin pickings in the parishes of Muckhart and Dollar (which had suffered on the outward march, when MacLeans settled old scores by wasting the countryside around Castle Campbell), and turned north to explore Glendevon. On Thursday 28 August, they found Frandy, where the MacGregors drove off 280 wethers. Atholl men moved into the wood of Gleneagles itself, seizing a horse (worth £100) belonging to the laird and a nag (worth £18) belonging to his forester, whose cottage they entered, stealing blankets, sheets, clothing, and 'ane pair of shone aff his feitt'. Word spread among returning victors from Kilsyth that the detour was worthwhile, and a week later, on 6 September, Robert Fleming of Moness (in Aberfeldy) appeared with more Atholl men. On this occasion, Andrew Christie, the tenant of Frandy, lost 560 wethers, 90 ewes, 14 cattle, and 5 horses; his house was stripped of furniture, bedding, clothing (including 'ane night bonnett'), unmade plaids, spades, kitchen ware, cheeses, butter, 'the thrid pairt of the Bible', 'ane psalme buik', and £12 out of his purse; altogether, he incurred losses in these two raids assessed at £4,300 Scots. The raiders also pillaged two houses at the southern end of Gleneagles: James Christie at Corrachie lost blankets, linen, clothing, shoes, and cheese, all valued at £40, while Donald Stalker at Bought Hill had his sword taken from him as he watched Moness's men appropriate

136. *Papers relating to the Army*, i, pp. xxxvi, 77.
137. Montrose had moved from Bridge of Earn down Glenfarg to Kinross, west to Muckhart and Dollar, and on to Alloa, before crossing the Forth above Stirling: Cowan, *Montrose*, pp. 215–16; *Memoirs of Henry Guthrie*, p. 191.

his wife's black serge gown, his own long-tailed scarlet coat with silk buttons, a pair of breeches, linen, and a brass pan (all worth £42 10s.). Moness did not venture further than the Glen of Gleneagles (now St Mungo's), where his men snatched some lengths of plaid, and no more dwellings were ransacked, although three other tenants lost sheep that were grazing within reach of the raiders, and the laird's cook, Patrick Dennistone, lost his three-year-old horse, worth £20.[138]

Meanwhile, Montrose's ally, Alasdair MacDonald, left the royalist camp at Bothwell with his Highlanders and about 500 of the 2,000 Irishmen he had brought with him, and set out for the west Highlands, where Argyll was reported to be mistreating his kinsmen.[139] Haldane lands in the Lennox lay in his path. In early September, £2,380 worth of damage was done 'when McDonald was returning to the Hielands after the battell at Kylsythe', as twenty-five cottages were pillaged and livestock rustled at Catter, Drumdash, Auchencarroch, Dumbain, Haldane's Mill, Ledrishbeg, Boturich, Knockour, Blairnyle, Blairlusk, and Shanacles. The land was not wasted, for it would appear that MacDonald was in a hurry, but for at least one of Sir John's tenants the damage caused was bad enough: three cows, a horse, twelve wethers, linen in various stages of preparation, and £40 in cash, all assessed at £155 10s. 8d., comprised the sum of the losses suffered by John McHutcheon in Knockour on the south-eastern bank of Loch Lomond; it amounted, he said, to 'almost all he had'.[140]

News of Kilsyth brought General Leslie back from England with part of his covenanting army. Seven days after the laird of Moness had visited Gleneagles, Montrose's much reduced and hopelessly outnumbered force was shattered by Leslie at Philiphaugh near Selkirk. Montrose fled north, heading for Atholl. En route, he paused at Kilmahog in Menteith to garrison neighbouring Callander with MacGregors and Irishmen. Haldane territory was again vulnerable to raids, with tenants in Lanrick and Rusky this time being the sufferers. The presence at Callander of

---

138. NRS, PA16/4/50, mm. 1–4.
139. Cowan, *Montrose*, p. 232; Stevenson, *Revolution & Counter-Revolution*, p. 36.
140. NRS, PA16/4/49, mm. 12–15.

'Irishes' gave especial cause for fear, as they had earned a reputation for being 'too cruell: it seemed to them there was no distinction betuixt a man and a beast, for they killed men ordinarly with no more feilling of compassion, and with the same carelesse neglect that they kill ane henn or capone for ther supper'.[141] For the first time there is record of fatalities during raids on Sir John's tenants: at Chapel (west of Lanrick House) Andrew Stewart's brother-in-law was killed as 'the enemie' looted whisky, ale, cheese, butter, £30 in cash, plaids, bedding, and two horses; and at Borland (east of Ruskie) 'Irishes and others' came by night, slew John Young in front of his wife, took his gun, sword, dirk and belt, his purse containing 25 merks, stripped his corpse of his clothing and 'his plaid that was about him', removed bedding, clothes, and shoes, secured a couple of horses and four wethers, drank 'ane haill brewing of aill', and then smashed all the widow's brewing vessels, 'to hir great losse'; to her greater loss they also found £100 in cash, which her husband had 'provydit to pay his master the laird of Glenegles'.[142] In Broich (south-east of Lanrick) the raiders found a cordwainer (Mungo Morisone); as well as finished shoes, they stole all his leather, ransacked his dwelling, taking £30 out of his chest, 'ane pynte of aquavita with the bottell', and £8's worth of malt; before leaving with two cows, an ox, two sheep, and a workhorse, they destroyed his shoemaking equipment. Other tenants of the barony of Lanrick did not receive such thorough attention: probably the most prosperous, John Haldane in Sauchans, must have been able to defend his property, for all that he lost were three cows; similarly, the laird's house at Lanrick itself was untouched, and his only personal loss was limited to a pair of workhorses which John Stewart at 'the Greneheid' had in his custody 'as hynd'. The total value put upon the damage incurred by Lanrick's tenants was £865 Scots. Rusky Tower was safe on the island in its little loch, and the raiders' attention was focused to the south-east, where their interest was mostly in livestock (especially cows) and clothing. Outside this area, only Ballabeg (south-west of Loch Rusky), received a visit, probably by the MacGregors on their way

141. P. Gordon of Ruthven, *A Short Abridgement of Britane's Distemper, 1639–1649* (Spalding Club, 1844), p. 161.
142. PA16/4/50, mm. 8, 10.

further south, and out of Haldane ground, to Cardross, where they had learnt that the tenant of Wester Borland had lodged 346 merks (£235 13s. 4d.) 'for saftie'. Including this sum, the value of the losses of Rusky's tenants in September 1645 totalled £917 Scots.[143]

In October 1645, Montrose was back in the Lennox, occupying Buchanan Castle, and accompanied by 1,500 horse and foot. His hope was to retake Glasgow. In the meanwhile, Haldane's extensive property at Catter on the opposite bank of Endrick Water proved a convenient source of provisions: eighteen tenants were pillaged, including three cottar women, each of whom lost 'all that sche had in hir house', the total worth being £52. Worst hit was Thomas Stevie in Finnich Tennant, whose livestock worth 440 merks was driven off, and whose house was ransacked and 500 merks stolen, as he lay 'deadlie woundit in his bodie'. At the end of November, Montrose abandoned his design on Glasgow and retired towards Strathspey. On their way north, a stray party of McNabs, moving through Menteith, stole meal from a Haldane tenant in Auchinsalt, and cows and sheep worth £120 from John Haldane in Sauchans.[144]

As Montrose withdrew, so did a winter set in which was worse than any could remember. In February 1646, over 1,000 starving Campbells appeared in Menteith, driven from their lands in Argyll by Alasdair MacDonald, and looking for royalists to pillage. Montrose ordered Patrick Graham, younger of Inchbrakie, and John Drummond, younger of Balloch, to assemble a force from Atholl to confront them.[145] As they marched south, the Atholl men targeted Gleneagles. Sir John Haldane was convinced that his 'constant affection to the caus in hand' made his lands and tenants the particular prey of 'the rebellis and enemies of

143. Ibid., mm. 7–10; PA16/4/49, m. 11.
144. Ibid., mm. 11, 14–16; PA16/4/50, mm. 7–8; Cowan, *Montrose*, pp. 240–1; Stevenson, *Revolution & Counter-Revolution*, p. 45; G. Wishart, *The Memoirs of James Marquis of Montrose, 1639–1650*, ed. A.D. Murdoch & H.F.M. Simpson (1893), p. 160 & n.
145. *Memorials of Montrose and his Times*, ed. M. Napier (2 vols, Maitland Club, 1848–50), ii. 625; Cowan, *Montrose*, p. 244; Stevenson, *Revolution &c.*, p. 48.

this kirk and kingdome'.[146] The earlier raids may have been opportunis-
tic; this was different, and it was thorough. 'The Athol men and other
adherents of the enemie came under the command and conduct of
Young Balloch and Inchbrakie' on 11 February, and at least over ninety
stayed overnight. Thirty-two were billeted on Donald Stalker in Bought
Hill, whom they stripped of coat, breeches, and shoes, and 'tournd him
naked' into the night; sixty were quartered upon Alexander Monteith in
Carsburn, who was forced to provide meal, bread, cheese, chickens, and
a barrel of ale. Walter Christie in the Glen (St Mungo's) had his cottage
door broken up for firewood and burnt, and his neighbour, Alexander
McGhie, similarly watched his chests and beds go up in flames. The
forester reported that 'they malitiouslie destroyit the young groath of
the Wood and especiallie the young firre trees', as well as timber already
'cuttit to burne and other uses'. They took what grain and straw they
needed, and destroyed the rest. At Frandy, Andrew Christie endured his
third raid; apart from two horses, each worth £50, and £80 in cash, his
losses on this occasion were limited to cloth and clothing; their value
nevertheless amounted to £414, for his store of plaid, worsted, and other
wool fabric was extensive; the stolen apparel included 'ane gowne and
ane bellicott [petticoat] of my wyffes, pryce quherof ten pounds; mair
tua stand [two outfits] of well maid clothes of my own and my sones and
ane bonnett, pryce quherof valued tuell [twelve] pounds'. There seem to
have been few items of clothing that that the Atholl men did not want.
Not only men had their shoes removed: Walter Thomson's mother at
Kaimknowe had 'ane pair of new schone takin aff hir feit', while, in the
Mains, the new coat worn by John Buchanan's wife was taken off her
back; Alexander McGhie's losses included 'his bairnes clothes, cotts
[coats] and sarkes [shirts]'; at East Side (now East Mains) the bairns of
John Cairns also lost their shirts. The cordwainer, Jerome Johnstone,
dwelling in the Mains, had the implements of his trade seized, as well as
a pair of boots, but appears to have been able to hide his stock of leather.
Perhaps he deposited it in the castle, which presumably remained a safe
haven, as it is unmentioned in all accounts of depredations in 1645 and

146. *HG*, p. 83; RPS, 1645/11/244.

1646. Plunder was taken from 31 tenants dwelling in Gleneagles and its neighbouring farms on 11 and 12 February 1646; household goods, grain and straw, horses and sheep formed the bulk of the loot. Apart from fifteen horses, the livestock figures were low – 127 sheep and only one ox – which gives an indication of the extent of the customary slaughter of beasts before the onset of winter. The previous September, when Moness raided only eight tenants, 762 sheep and 18 cattle were driven off. The cost of February's raid was put at £1,578 Scots.[147]

Balloch and Inchbrakie led their men into Menteith, where they routed the Campbells at Callander. Once again, Haldane property lay in their path. Eight tenants in the barony of Lanrick suffered £470 worth of damage, but the Atholl men did not touch reserves of grain or straw. The wanton destruction for which Gleneagles had been picked out was not in evidence here, nor when they raided five tenants in the barony of Rusky, where their most lucrative visit was to Barbara Graham at 'Guyoke'. Her losses in September had been restricted to some cattle kept in the byre at Earn, worth £90, but now the Atholl men found eight serviceable horses worth 400 merks, an abundance of cloth and clothing, including an outfit of new clothes 'with ane hieland coatte', extensive kitchen ware and numerous cooking implements, three stone of cheese and one of butter, and 'ane great Bybill and ane littil Bybill and tua prayer buiks, estimate to sixteen pounds'. The lady's losses contributed £607 to Rusky's total of £1,009 Scots.[148]

The cost of the raids on the barony of Gleneagles in August and September 1645 and in February 1646 amounted to £6,832 11s. Scots, of which Andrew Christie in Frandy, 'who was altogether haryed', bore the brunt with losses totalling £4,642 15s. 8d. Totals for the depredation in the baronies of Lanrick and Rusky in September and November 1645 and February 1646 were £1,546 8s. 8d. and £2,090 10s. 4d. respectively, and for that in 'the easter and wester baronies of Haddon' in September and October 1645 they were £4,485 10s. 4d. The grand total was £14,955 0s. 4d. Scots (equivalent to £1,246 5s. sterling).[149] Sir John had also

147. PA16/4/50, mm. 2–10.
148. PA16/4/49, m. 11.
149. PA16/4/50, mm. 6, 9; 16/4/49, mm. 12, 16.

suffered damage amounting to £1,884 16s. 2d. Scots, which had been incurred at his wife's property at Arrat in Angus, initially as early as 1639, when Argyll's covenanters had commandeered provisions during their inconclusive campaign against royalists in the north-east, and latterly, in April 1646, when havoc was caused in Angus as it was criss-crossed by 'Irisches', MacGregors, and Camerons, with the covenanting army in pursuit.[150] Sir John petitioned for the exemption of his lands from the monthly maintenance imposed for the support of the army in Scotland, since his entire Perthshire property had been utterly wasted, 'and nothing left to my tennantis except the houssis … quherby my tennantis ar rendered so unable that they have not sowin the ground this yeire'.[151]

The question of the maintenance of the Scottish army in England was only one of the sources of friction which developed between the two national régimes. The English army had become home to a militant religious individualism, advocating the independence of separate congregations, as much opposed to Presbyterian intolerance as to episcopal authority. Frustrated by Parliament's inability to defy its army and establish an English kirk, covenanting leaders sought an agreement with the king, who had placed himself in their hands in May 1646. In January 1647, the Scottish leaders despaired of their negotiations with Charles I, and sold him to the English for half the maintenance money due to them, whereupon the covenanting army returned north of the Border. The ambition to extend Scottish influence over the southern church, however, remained, and contact with the king was restarted. In an agreement known as 'the Engagement' he promised to introduce Presbyterian church government in England for a trial period, and the Scots sent an army south to support royalists in August 1648. Cromwell cut it to pieces in Lancashire, entered Scotland, and helped to establish a government which excluded from public office all who had been sympathetic to the Engagement or who were classified as royalists. Returning south, he then orchestrated the quasi-judicial killing of the king. In a display more of outraged national pride than of royalism, the Scottish parliament proclaimed the late king's son, Charles II, king of Great Britain, secured

150. PA16/4/46; cf. Cowan, *Montrose*, p. 66.
151. *HG*, pp. 83–4; Supplementary Parliamentary Papers 1646, nos. 166–7.

a commitment from him to impose their Presbyterianism upon England and Ireland, and prepared for war with England.

Such was the context in which Sir John Haldane lived the last four years of his life. In November 1646, he represented the stewartry of Menteith and the Bruce lordships in Fife of Culross and Tulliallan on a committee of war.[152] In January 1647, he was appointed lieutenant-colonel of a Perthshire regiment to be raised by Walter Scott, and in March served on the Perthshire committee for war. He was on the same committee just over a year later, on 18 April 1648, after the Engagers put Scotland on a war footing.[153] In February 1649, after the proclamation of Charles II, the anti-Engagers repeated the procedure, and the laird of Gleneagles was listed as a colonel of horse or foot for Perthshire.[154] In March, when there were rumblings of a royalist revival in Atholl, he joined Sir Charles Erskine of Alva and Sir James Rollo of Duncrub in alerting Parliament to the hazards faced by landowners in the Ochils 'threw thair lying neir the hieland upon the west end thairoff, whairthrow many broken men takis occasione to spoyll and tak away the haill[whole] bestiall [livestock]'; permission was sought to keep 'sum considerable number of men' to guard against such depredations. Parliament restricted the number to no more than twenty.[155] It clearly expected that able-bodied men would soon be needed elsewhere. Sir John's services were required in May on a commission to discover abuses by the collectors of tax in Perthshire in 1643; as he had been one of them, he may have had inside information.[156]

On 24 June, Charles II landed at Garmouth in Spey Bay to claim his kingdoms. On 6 July, 'considering the preparations made by sectaries in England to invade this kingdom', the laird of Gleneagles was appointed colonel of one of the two Perthshire regiments of foot.[157] On 22 July, Cromwell crossed the Tweed. Purged of all who had not

152. RPS, 1646/11/32; *HG*, p. 84, with Tullibardine in error for Tulliallan.
153. RPS, 1648/3/79.
154. Ibid., 1649/1/133.
155. Ibid., A1649/1/56; 1649/1/247.
156. Ibid., 1649/5/22; cf. 1643/6/66.
157. Ibid., A1650/5/116.

opposed the Engagement, the Scottish government was anxious to display to God that its cause was His rather than the king's, and, in the first week of August about eighty officers were dismissed on suspicion of being 'malignants'.[158] Sir John Haldane's political reputation was sufficiently unblemished for him to survive the purge. God's approval seemed to have been won, as Cromwell's 16,000 men were reduced by sickness to about 11,000, but, when this force met 20,000 Scots at Dunbar on 3 September, its professionalism and experience, coupled with Cromwell's military genius, overwhelmed the army of the Solemn League and Covenant, whose superior numbers were largely made up of raw recruits and inexperienced junior officers. Eventually, the Scots cavalry broke; some foot regiments surrendered; others fought to the death. About 10,000 prisoners were taken, and 4,000 Scots lay dead. Somewhere among them lay Sir John Haldane, together with his lieutenant-colonel, Robert Melville, and his major, John Cockburne.[159] His regiment had not surrendered.

158. Stevenson, *Revolution & Counter-Revolution*, pp. 174.
159. Ibid., pp. 177–9; Balfour, *Historical Works*, iv. 98.

IV

Private Debt and Public Affairs

Survival: John (VII) and Mungo (I) Haldane, 1650–85

The Haldanes of Gleneagles were described in about 1680 as a family which 'had fallen into great decay'.[1] The financial problems with which its lairds had grappled for over half a century reached alarming proportions under the strain of war, both civil and national. In 1649, such were the straits in which Sir John found himself that, for 11,000 merks, he mortgaged the whole barony of Haldane to his brother-in-law, Robert Napier of Kilmahew (the annual rental of the Gleneagles barony at that time being £2,413).[2] It is highly unlikely that he had received any recompense for the harrying of his lands and tenantry, let alone for the costs incurred in raising his regiment, before the catastrophe at Dunbar threw responsibility for the family's solvency upon his eldest son and namesake. John Haldane and his stepmother, Margaret Fraser, petitioned the king in parliament at Perth that none of the lands belonging to the laird of Gleneagles should have soldiers quartered upon them or be subject to 'public dewes', in view of 'their sad lamentable condition through ... the loss and spoylling of their guidis and means by the former

1. Arbuthnott, 'Continuation of genealogie of Arbuthnott', fos. 12–23; for the date see *Scots Peerage*, i. 273.
2. NRS, GD198/88–9; W. Gloag (ed.), *Rentall of the County of Perth, 4th August 1649* (Perth, 1835), pp. 80, 84, 96.

rebelliounes'.[3] The fact that their petition was granted on 18 December 1650 was, however, of little moment, for that same month Cromwell entered Edinburgh; he took Perth and Stirling eight months later, crushed the Scottish army at Worcester on 3 September 1651, and, the following month, announced the union of England and Scotland. Aristocratic and lairdly debtors, of whom Haldane was but one among very many, were to find the new regime particularly uncongenial. A system of efficient and impartial central courts replaced the maze of judicatories which had previously favoured local interests and delayed the pursuit of legal action. In 1652, the diarist John Nicoll noticed how 'our nobles of Scotland, gentrie, barrones ... wer forcit to attend the Englische judges at thair courtes in Scotland as commoun men'. In January 1653, a decree eased the path for the heirs of creditors to reclaim either capital or collateral due from the heirs of debtors.[4] It was not a propitious time to inherit an encumbered estate.

On 3 March 1653, John Haldane was retoured as his father's heir in the baronies of Gleneagles and Haldane, within which his stepmother enjoyed the liferent of Lanrick and Rusky, as well as two holdings in the Lennox, while the income from the remaining lands in the barony of Haldane had been conveyed to his stepbrother, Mungo.[5] John took sasine on 8 November 1653, and, within five months, his lands were being apprized for payment of debts. Between April 1654 and November 1659, lands and superiorities in the baronies of Gleneagles and Haldane had been sold to meet debts totalling a minimum of £38,198 13s. 4d. Scots.[6] Grants of Haldane property issued in the name of the Lord Protector spoke of John Haldane's ownership in the past tense.[7]

3.   RPS, A1650/11/11; *HG*, p. 92.
4.   J. Nicoll, *A Diary of Public Transactions* (Bannatyne Club, 1836), pp. 103–5; Mitchinson, *Lordship to Patronage*, pp. 64–7, 93–4; Donaldson, *Scotland: James V–James VII*, pp. 347–50; Lynch, *Scotland: A New History*, pp. 286, 291.
5.   Above, p. 68; GD198/148–151.
6.   *RMS*, x, nos. 271, 276, 290, 661, 674; GD198/88–93, 152.
7.   *RMS*, x, nos. 276, 290; a deed dated 9 June 1656, granting Gleneagles to Agnes Murray, relict of Duncan Campbell, who was owed 2,855 merks Scots, is preserved at Gleneagles.

According to the descendants of his half-brother Patrick, such was the disorder of his affairs 'that, despairing ever to extricate himself from the confusion they appeared to be in, John went abroad and engaged himself in foreign service'. The service he entered was that of Charles X of Sweden, who had invaded Poland in 1655, and whose army he joined. He may have accompanied his first cousin, Lord Lovat's son James Fraser, who left Scotland in 1656 with the regiment raised for the Swedish king by Lord Cranstoun.[8] It was among the Scottish community in Poland that John died, unmarried, soon after the restoration of Charles II in 1660; he was certainly dead in June 1662, when Mungo, the elder son of his father's second marriage, was designated 'of Gleneges'.[9]

John Haldane's heir was not at Gleneagles when news of his half-brother's death reached Scotland. Mungo Haldane was living with his wife, Anna Grant, on his mother's estate near Brechin. The fact that, in 1674, their eldest son John was entered not into a St Andrews college but into King's College, Aberdeen, may give an indication of the temporary reorientation of Haldane attention. Anna was a daughter of John Grant of Lurg and niece of the laird of Grant; she had borne her husband three children before dying, perhaps in childbed, in June 1662, when Mungo recorded that they had no 'insicht nor plenishing [furniture nor furnishing], being in the house with his mother, the lady Glenegas'. Margaret Fraser had leased to her son and daughter-in-law half her ground at Arrats Mill and Isackston (in Dun, between Brechin and Montrose)

8. *HG*, p. 93; D. Graeme, *Answers for Anne Haldane* [&c] ... *all Daughters of the deceased John Haldane of Lenrick ... to the Petition of Mr Patrick Haldane, Advocate* (10 July 1766), p. 1; *Chronicles of the Frasers*, p. 417; G.E.C., *Complete Peerage*, iii. 495–6; A.F. Stuart (ed.), *Papers relating to the Scots in Poland 1576–1793* (Scot. Hist. Soc., lix, 1915), p. xxii. John was still in Scotland on 5 March 1656, when he borrowed 2,000 merks from James Holbourne of Menstrie: *RMS*, x, no. 517.
9. *HG*, p. 93; W. Drummond, *The Genealogy of the Most Noble and Ancient House of Drummond, 1681* (Glasgow, 1889), p. 175; NRS, CC3/3/6, test. 1665 Grant, Anna. It is possible that the portrait at Gleneagles, formerly thought to be of Sir John (VI) Haldane, is of his son, John VII.

for an annual rent of barley and meal worth £450 Scots.[10] As an infant, in 1638, Mungo had been granted much of the barony of Haldane in the Lennox, but control of this appanage had been submerged in the cascade of debt-collection which threatened to engulf the Haldanes in the 1650s. The barony had been conveyed in December 1655 by John Haldane to John Napier of Kilmahew, whose father had received a mortgage of it in 1649.[11] The lands of the barony of Gleneagles itself had been apprized for sale by various creditors between 1654 and 1659, and were referred to in 1668 as having formerly belonged to Sir Harry Stirling of Ardoch.[12] In 1657, it would appear that Stirling had bought up debts, the interest on which was being uplifted within the barony of Gleneagles,[13] and in 1664–65 he was in receipt of ferm duty paid by at least one tenant (at Common Hill and Glenhead) who referred to him as the 'maister'.[14] Neither Napier nor Stirling, however, was a hostile predator. John Napier's mother was John Haldane's sister, Catherine Haldane, while Harry Stirling (who became a baronet in 1666) was his brother-in-law, having married Isobel Haldane.[15] Among John Haldane's other creditors was Sir James Halkett of Pitfirrane, whose loan of 7,000 merks had been made available through the agency of the covenanting colonel, Robert Halkett, who had married John's aunt, Jean Haldane.[16] Patrick Smyth of Braco, who, in 1658, took over some of the Haldane debt owed to John Drummond of Balloch, maintained sufficiently cordial relations with

10. *Fasti Aberdonenses* (Spalding Club, 1854), p. 493; CC3/3/6, 1665 Grant, Anna.
11. NRS, GD198/88–93; above, p. 83.
12. *RMS*, x, nos. 271, 276, 290, 661, 674; xi, no. 1140; GD198/35.
13. NRS, RH9/4/32; cf. *RMS*, x, no. 674.
14. NRS, CC6/5/13, test. 1664 Thomsone, John; 1665 Thomsone, John. In August 1662, Harry Stirling of Ardoch was accused of forging a testament in the name of 'John Hadden of Glenegies' and 'using the same to get payment of sumes', but the accuser failed to proceed, and the episode remains unexplained: *Proc. of the Judiciary Court from 1661 to 1678*, i, ed. W.G. Scott-Moncrieff (Scot. Rec. Soc., xlviii, 1905), 48.
15. *HG*, pp. 76–7; Fraser, *Stirlings of Keir*, p. 119.
16. *HG*, p. 89; Drummond, *House of Drummond*, p. 175; NRS, GD198/152.

the Haldanes to marry Mungo's daughter Janet in 1682.[17] Such creditors were evidently conducting a holding operation, filling the breach until the Haldanes of Gleneagles had recovered some degree of solvency. In June 1666, John Napier, while accepting a mortgage of the capital messuage of Boturich, conveyed the lands and barony of Haldane to Mungo Haldane, and, a year and a half later, Sir Harry Stirling resigned the lands of the barony of Gleneagles to allow Mungo to receive sasine in them on 7 February 1668.[18] When Sir Harry died in February 1669, he had received 23,125 merks (£15,416 13s. 4d. Scots) of the principal sum of 25,000 merks owed him by the laird of Gleneagles.[19] There was light at the end of the tunnel.

A major contribution to this recovery was made by Mungo's younger brother, Patrick. His source of funds is unknown. According to family tradition, he was the favourite child of his mother, Margaret Fraser, who may have been in a position to help him financially; it was recalled by a Fraser kinsman who visited her in her widowhood 'in her hospitable house at Arrats Mill' that she 'lived most comfortably, a happy, fortunate woman'.[20] Patrick was intimate with the Stirlings of Ardoch, being nominated in 1669 as a curator during the minority of Sir William, and serving as factor of that estate during the 1670s and early 1680s,[21] but such employment was an indicator of his standing in local society rather than a source of capital. As early as December 1655, he had been able to lend £1,000 Scots to his half-brother John Haldane, and, by 1672, he had acquired £22,000 worth of debt held against the family estate. Margaret Fraser's death, not long after sitting for her portrait in 1666, released the

17. *HG*, p. 99; J. Burke, *A Genealogical and Heraldic History of the Commoners of Great Britain & Ireland* (London, 1833), p. 229; for connections between Smyth and various Drummonds, see *House of Drummond*, pp. 54, 126, 189.

18. NRS, GD198/35, 94–9; *RMS*, xi, no. 1140.

19. NRS, CC6/5/15, test. 1670 Stirling, Hary. Sir Harry died with £42,472 Scots out on loan; his own debts totalled £13,214.

20. *HG*, p. 280; *Chronicles of the Frasers*, p. 243.

21. Dunblane Register of Deeds, 3.172; 4 (1/2/1681). In 1674, Robert Stirling, tutor of Ardoch, was Patrick's cautioner in executing the will of his late wife, Helen Dow: CC6/5/17, test. Dow, Helen.

lands of Lanrick, in which she had enjoyed a life interest; on 12 August 1668, their rents and dues were transferred to Patrick. As the annual income from Lanrick was reckoned to be about £1,000, and no land was sold at that time at so high a rate as twenty years' purchase, the debts in Patrick's possession exceeded its value, but, in a demonstration of brotherly love, he waived any residual rights he might have over the baronies of Gleneagles and Haldane. In consequence, in 1673 Mungo was able to seek from the king a fresh charter setting out his title to his patrimony, including the superiority of Lanrick and Rusky, and, in 1675, in accordance with a contract existing between the two brothers, 'all and haill the lands of Lanerk [Lanrick]' were conveyed to Patrick.[22]

The transference to a cadet line of the inheritance which Agnes Menteith had brought to them in 1459 was the most significant cost paid by the Haldanes of Gleneagles in emerging from decades of financial crises. Nevertheless, it must have been gratifying to Mungo to have that emergence recognized in May 1674, when he was included in a committee of six Perthshire lairds charged with superintending 'the better management' of the estates of the earl of Atholl; he was also to be one of three receivers of rents earmarked for repayment of principal sums owed by the earl; in 1676, he shared the supervision of plans for rebuilding Dunkeld House.[23] Further indicators of the restored standing of the Haldanes of Gleneagles were the marriages Mungo was able to arrange for his children: in 1677, his son and heir, John, married Mary Drummond, who brought a tocher of 10,000 merks from her father, Lord Maderty; in 1681, he gave his elder daughter, Margaret, with a tocher of 9,000 merks, in marriage to the rich baronet, Sir Patrick Murray of Ochtertyre; and, the following year, her half-sister, Janet, with

22. 'Unto the Right Honourable the Lords of Council and Session, the Petition of Mr Patrick Haldane, Advocate, June 19 1766', pp. 1–3; D. Dalrymple, *Decisions of the Lords of Council and Session from 1766 to 1791*, i, ed. M.P. Brown (Edinburgh, 1826), 168–70; Reg. Privy Seal, 1660–1782, iv. 536; *HG*, p. 280. Margaret Fraser's dated portrait is at Gleneagles.
23. John, seventh duke of Atholl, *Chronicles of the Families of Atholl and Tullibardine* (5 vols, Edinburgh, 1908), ii. 164–5, 172–3.

10,000 merks, became the spouse of the prosperous landed merchant, Patrick Smyth of Braco and Methven.[24]

After a hiatus of more than a generation, in 1678 the laird of Gleneagles returned to public affairs with his appointment, in company with his brother Patrick of Lanrick and his son's father-in-law Lord Maderty, as a commissioner of supply for Perthshire and Stirlingshire.[25] Their primary task was to settle the value of estates for assessment to the land-tax and then to supervise its collection, but commissioners were also required to cooperate with justices of the peace in the maintenance of roads, bridges, and ferries, and their accumulation of extra responsibilities soon made them 'the most important officers in Scottish local government'.[26] Mungo Haldane also sat as one of the two members for Perthshire in the 1681 parliament summoned by the king's brother and commissioner in Scotland, James duke of York and Albany.[27] The main business which James had for this parliament was to enact 'The Test', which it did with the minimum of debate. The Act required all members of parliament and their electors, and all office holders in church or state, to swear to adhere to the Protestant religion as defined in 1567, but to renounce the Covenant, defend the king's supremacy, and attempt no alteration in church or state. This oath, which would surely have troubled his covenanting father, was evidently acceptable to Mungo, for, in 1682, 1683, and 1684, he took the Test when accepting the king's commission to maintain peace in the Highlands, and when he took his seat in the parliament of 1685.[28] His commitment to the Restoration regime had been demonstrated in 1678, when he served as a lieutenant in the king's Life Guards under the command of the duke of Montrose; he may therefore have been present the next year at Bothwell Brig, where the Life Guards formed part of the government force which scattered rebellious

24. *HG*, pp. 98–9, 126; *Complete Baronetage* (5 vols, Exeter, 1900–06), iv. 291–2; Drummond, *Genealogy of Drummond*, p. 190.
25. *RPS*, 1678/6/22.
26. Donaldson, *Scotland, James V–James VII*, p. 399.
27. *RPS*, 1681/7/2.
28. *RPCSc.*, vii. 509; viii. 137, 536; ix. 193, 197, 200; x. 211.

covenanters of the south-west.[29] In 1683, Mungo held a captaincy in the troop of horse commanded by the earl of Perth, the most enthusiastic persecutor of radical dissidents.[30]

At root the discontent was ecclesiastical. The return of the king had brought the return of bishops and lay patrons. The Restoration settlement was surprisingly moderate, closer to the regime of James VI than to that of his son, but it had no place for the General Assembly; the National Covenant was declared unlawful, and parochial ministers instituted since the abolition of lay patronage in 1649 were required, on pain of depriva-tion, to obtain the restored patron's presentation and the bishop's colla-tion. Over a third of the ministry refused to cooperate and was deprived. To the government's alarm, the reaction of many congregations was to gather for worship in conventicles – illicit meetings, often large and in the open air. Few members of the landed class were to be found among these dissidents, but, while the bloodthirsty fanaticism and doctrinaire incom-petence of the covenanting regimes of the late 1640s had eroded their loyalty to the covenant, for many an attachment to Presbyterianism had acquired the strength of family tradition. Mungo Haldane seems to have been one such moderate. A story, passed down to the nineteenth-century descendants of one of his servants named Gould, who was a conventicle man, told how the laird helped him evade arrest.[31] Gould may not have been the only conventicler in his service: in April 1682, Mungo was told by the marquess of Atholl, hereditary sheriff of Perthshire, to execute the law against conventiclers, and, seven months later, he accepted a bond by one John Pattone for payment of the appropriate fine; it is possible that this man was identical with the John Paton, 'gardener in Gleneagles', who died in 1727, and that Mungo was prepared to employ conventiclers who kept their dissent within acceptable bounds.[32]

29. M. Linklater & C. Hesketh, *John Graham of Claverhouse, Bonnie Dundee: For King and Conscience* (London, 1989), p. 51; *HG*, pp. 333–4; *Chronicles of Atholl & Tullibardine*, i, App., p. xl.

30. Marchioness of Tullibardine, *A Military History of Perthshire 1660–1902* (Perth, 1908), p. 105; J. Miller, *James II* (3rd edn, New Haven, 2000), p. 213.

31. *HG*, p. 96.

32. Dunblane Commissariat Deeds, 24 April & 17 November 1682; CC6/5/23, test. 1731 Paton, John.

On 23 April 1685, Mungo was in Edinburgh for the opening of the first parliament of the reign of James VII (and II), but, on 8 May, fellow members were told of his death, and a warrant was issued for a new election to his Perthshire seat.[33]

Darien, the Union, and Jacobites: Union Jack, John (VIII) Haldane, 1685–1721

Mungo's death came three months after that of King Charles II. The succession to the crowns of Scotland and England of his Roman Catholic brother James was the signal for rebellion by the earl of Argyll, who had been in exile since refusing to take the Test in 1681. Mungo's 25-year-old son and successor, John Haldane, not only showed himself willing to take the Test when he stepped into his father's shoes as a commissioner of supply for Perthshire on 13 May, but also, within a couple of weeks, was marching against the rebels with the Perthshire Horse, participating in a combined naval and military action which pursued Argyll from the Kyles of Bute, along the eastern shore of Loch Fyne, south to Glendaruel, and eventually across the Clyde to capture near Paisley.[34] The new laird of Gleneagles evidently found no difficulty in serving the new king.

Before the end of 1685, John Haldane lost his wife, Mary Drummond, who, in seven years of marriage, had borne five sons, of whom three survived to adulthood. Her father, the third Lord Maderty, was a firm royalist, but ill health had caused his retirement from public life in 1684, leaving him to concentrate on the library he had founded at Innerpeffray, of which he persuaded his son-in-law to become a trustee, a function which has been performed ever since by the lairds of Gleneagles.[35] In October 1687, John decided to leave Scotland on business, appointing his brother David as factor during his absence in England and elsewhere.[36]

33. RPS, M1685/4/7, 11; for his inventory, see CC/5/19, test. 1686, Haldane, Mungo.
34. *HG*, pp. 334–5; *Chron. Atholl & Tullibardine*, i. 238–42.
35. *HG*, p. 126; *Complete Peerage*, viii. 348, n. (g).
36. *HG*, p. 101; Dunblane Commissariat Deeds, 28 Dec. 1687.

Nothing is known of John's activities until after King James's promotion of Roman Catholicism had led to the loss of his southern kingdom to his Protestant daughter Mary and her husband and cousin, the Dutch stadholder, William of Orange, who jointly acceded to the throne of England in February 1689, James having fled into exile the previous December. On 14 March 1689, the laird of Gleneagles took his seat as a representative for Perthshire in the convention of estates which met in Edinburgh to determine Scotland's reaction to these events.[37] Numbers of convinced Williamites and Jacobites were probably matched by those whose minds were yet to be decided, until letters from William and James were read out on 16 March. William's was vague and conciliatory; James's uncompromising and aggressive, threatening condign punishment of all who defied his authority. The unity of the Jacobites, never strong, was shattered: some followed Viscount Dundee in leaving the convention and taking to arms; others, like Haldane's kinsman, the marquess of Atholl, remained to pick their way cautiously through the proceedings of a convention now dominated by Williamites. On 23 March, Haldane followed Atholl in signing the letter in which the convention congratulated William 'on being rewarded by God with success in delivering us, and in preserving to us the Protestant religion.'[38] King James's presence in Ireland aroused fears of an invasion from that quarter, and forces were marshalled south of the Tay, with John Haldane appointed initially a captain of the Stirlingshire militia and then, on 30 March, captain of a troop of horse in western Perthshire. On 27 April, he also became a commissioner of supply to raise money in Dunbartonshire and Perthshire to fund this military readiness.[39]

John had evidently accepted the validity both of the convention's declaration on 4 April that the Scottish throne was vacant, and of its offer to William and Mary a week later. However, when William summoned the convention to reassemble on 5 June as his first Scottish parliament,

37.   RPS, 1689/3/2.
38.   RPS, 1689/3/58. John Haldane was the marquess's second cousin once removed.
39.   RPS, 1689/3/82, 189; M1689/3/8.

John Haldane absented himself.[40] The marquess of Atholl, from whom John may earlier have been taking his cue, became ill with indecision and took himself off to Bath.[41] The parliament was adjourned until 17 June, giving absentees time for reflection, and John did indeed travel to Edinburgh on the sixteenth with the intention of attending. His doubts, however, returned after an altercation with an enthusiastic Williamite, the earl of Eglinton, whose troopers had committed 'unheard of incivilitys' in Perthshire. John recited a list of complaints about gentlemen's horses being commandeered, weapons requisitioned, and provisions taken without payment. Eglinton responded with aspersions upon the loyalty of Perthshire people and a threat to advise the king, to whose privy council he had just been admitted, to billet more troops upon them.[42] No longer in a mood to take his seat, John joined a number of other commissioners and noblemen in ignoring a deadline of 3 July and incurred a fine of £100 Scots.[43]

On 30 June 1689, the laird explained his position to Lord Murray, the marquess of Atholl's heir: 'I hav not as yet been in the house by reson that evrie member who went in uer obliged to taike the oth of alegance, and I do acknowledge that I am so litel fond of oaths as not to be desirous to taik anie mor nor what I hav already ingadged in'.[44] The oath required of members of parliament ran: 'I do sincerely promise and swear that I will be faithfull and bear true allegiance to their majesties King William and Queen Mary, so help me God'.[45] In accepting his commissions in March, John must have taken the military oath, swearing 'that I shall demean my selfe faithfully to the estates now presently mett',[46] but this in no way contravened his oath, made when he took the Test in 1685, to bear faith

40. RPS, 1689/6/2.
41. *Chron. Atholl & Tullibardine*, i. 277, 282, 285.
42. *HG*, p. 163; HMC, 12th Report, App. viii: *MSS of the duke of Athole and of the earl of Home* (1891), p. 38.
43. RPS, 1689/6/18, 30; A1689/6/9.
44. HMC, *MSS Athole & Home*, p. 38.
45. RPS, 1689/3/108.
46. RPS, 1689/3/35; cf. Colin, earl of Balcarres, *Memoirs touching the Revolution in Scotland 1688–1690* (Bannatyne Club, 1841), p. 22.

and true allegiance to James VII, his heirs and lawful successors. He had yet to be convinced that William and Mary came into the latter category. Lord Murray, who was credited with preventing his father from adopting an openly Jacobite position, shared the laird's dilemma, later explaining that his 'backwardness in acting either in one side or the other' was owing to his uncertainty about where his duty lay. Viscount Dundee helped remove that uncertainty, when he attracted large numbers of Atholl vassals to his Jacobite standard and seized Blair Castle in July 1689. Lord Murray collected as many of his friends, followers, and vassals as he could to oppose Dundee, but his force melted away, and he waited at Moulin (near Pitlochry), taking no part when the government's army confronted the Jacobites at Killiecrankie on 27 July. It seems that John Haldane was one of Lord Murray's friends who did not abandon him, but undertook a watching brief on his behalf. Two days after the battle, it was presumed by a correspondent of Murray's that the laird of Gleneagles would already have given him a full account of the government's defeat.[47] Further evidence of John Haldane's closeness to Lord Murray is his association in January 1690 with Murray, Murray's brother-in-law Lord Lovat, and kinsman Murray of Strowan, as a cautioner for Murray's Jacobite brother Lord Dunmore in keeping the peace.[48]

It is possible that Lord Murray was responsible for persuading John that his conscience might allow him to swear allegiance to William and Mary because they *were* king and queen, not because they *should* be. On 22 April 1690, when parliament had resumed its session, he took the oath of allegiance; in June he once again accepted a commission of supply

47.   J.R. Young, 'Murray, John, first duke of Atholl', *ODNB* (2004–14); *Chron. Atholl & Tullibardine*, i. 303–4; G. Lockhart, *The Lockhart Papers, containing Memoirs and Commentaries upon the Affairs of Scotland 1702–1715* (2 vols, Lndon, 1817), i. 72; Linklater & Hesketh, *Bonnie Dundee*, pp. 198–203, 222. General Haldane suggests (*HG*, p. 104) that the laird fought on the Williamite side at Killiecrankie, but he held no commission in any of the forces under General Mackay's command, and, had he participated in, and survived, a fight in which over a third of the combatants perished (including Dundee), it is odd that Murray's correspondent did not mention it.

48.   *Chron. Atholl & Tullibardine*, i. 328.

for Perthshire.[49] The bar was raised, however, after the appointment in 1692 of a zealous Presbyterian, James Johnston, as joint secretary of state for Scotland, with special responsibility for managing parliament, heralding a greater emphasis on the principles of the revolution of 1688 and a purge of members whose position was considered equivocal. In 1693, all members were required to sign the Assurance, declaring 'that their majesties King William and Queen Mary are the only lawfull undoubted soveraigns of this realm as well *de jure*, that is, of right king and queen, as *de facto*, that is, in possession and exercise of the government', and engaging 'with heart and hand, life and goods' to defend their title against 'the late King James and his adherents'.[50] This Assurance John Haldane could not make and consequently was not only fined £600 Scots, but also unseated.[51]

After six years of widowhood, John had remarried in February 1691. For his wife he had looked to the southern slopes of the Ochils and been accepted by Helen Erskine, only daughter of Sir Charles Erskine, first baronet of Alva, a laird of unimpeachable Presbyterian stock, like the Haldanes of Gleneagles, to whom Helen was distantly related, John Haldane being her fifth cousin.[52] It was perhaps through this revived connection that John entered a business partnership with the Erskines' neighbour, Sir John Shaw of Sauchie, whose estate lay on the southern side of the River Devon, between Alva and Alloa. Planning a considerable investment in fishing for herring and white fish off Greenland and Archangel, the two men had come across a new method of making salt for curing the catch, and, despite opposition from the saltmasters, in October 1696 they obtained a parliamentary Act facilitating their purchase of plots of ground suitable for salt-working on the northern

49. RPS, 1690/4/2, 8, 44.
50. *Source Book of Scottish History*, ed. Dickinson et al., iii. 218; J.R. Young, 'Johnston, James', *ODNB* (2004–14).
51. RPS, 1693/4/28.
52. Both traced descent from Robert, fourth Lord Erskine (d.1513). Helen Erskine, Lady Gleneagles, died at Haddington on 4 July 1739: *London Evening Post*, 10–12 July 1739, issue 1819.

shore of the Forth between Alloa and Culross.[53] Shaw's interest in trade, further manifested by his attempt to build a harbour at his western estate at Greenock, matched Haldane's, which was becoming absorbed in the newly established Company of Scotland trading to Africa and the Indies.

The Act by which the Scottish parliament set up this company, on 25 June 1695, was the product of years of Scots' resentment at their exclusion by the Navigation Acts from the English colonial trade and their general desire to share in England's prosperity, a desire sharpened by their loss of traditional markets owing to King William's war with France. They were encouraged by London merchants seeking to bypass the monopoly of the English African and East India Companies by competing lawfully under another flag: that of Scotland. The company was given the monopoly of trade between Scotland, Asia, Africa, and the Americas, with exemptions from customs duties, the right to found colonies, and to call upon public funds in compensation for any damage suffered. The London promoters fixed the capital at £600,000 sterling, half to be raised north of the border. Given the attractiveness of the terms of the company's charter, the London subscription book opened and closed within a fortnight in November 1695, all £300,000 being pledged. Meanwhile, the stock of the East India Company had been falling dramatically, and few should have been surprised when it mobilized its political strength in the English parliament. The outcome was ominous for its fledgling rival: the king declared that his commissioner for Scotland had misinterpreted his instructions in giving the royal assent to the Scottish Act, and the House of Commons threatened to impeach the company's English participants. In January 1696, the commitments subscribed in the London book were withdrawn, the company's London headquarters were closed, and the enterprise was left to the Scots.[54]

53. RPS 1696/9/156, 178; *Darien Papers, 1695–1701* (Bannatyne Club, 1849), p. 32.

54. See generally D. Hamilton, 'The Company of Scotland and its investors', *ODNB* (2004–14); D. Watt, *The Price of Scotland: Darien, Union and the Wealth of Nations* (London, 2007); G. Clark, *The Later Stuarts, 1660–1714* (2nd edn, Oxford, 1955), pp. 281–5; W. Ferguson, *Scotland, 1689 to the Present* (Edinburgh, 1968), pp. 26–34.

The Edinburgh subscription book was opened on 26 February 1696, the amount to be raised set at £400,000 sterling. Two days later, the name of John Haldane of Gleneagles was put down for £600, well in excess of his annual rent-roll; by 25 March, he had found more funds, or more confidence, and increased his commitment to £1,000 (equal to the sum promised five days later by the marquess of Montrose, and double that subscribed by the marquess of Atholl). His Erskine brothers-in-law, Sir John and Robert, had accompanied him on 28 February, when each promised £300, while his partner, Sir John Shaw, pledged £1,000 on 20 March.[55] John was also the channel through which a total of £3,100 was pledged by kinsmen and neighbours, who asked him to subscribe on their behalf.[56] By August 1696, over 1,300 people from a broad cross-section of Scottish society and politics had underwritten the sum required in a heady atmosphere of enthusiastic patriotism, engendered by anger at the behaviour of the English parliament and eager anticipation of profits to come.

John Haldane was among the thirty-one directors elected to the board of the company in May 1696; before the end of the month, he had become chairman of the board's 'committee of improvements', and a member of the joint committee composed of this and the two other standing committees. In the autumn, he was appointed with three other directors to go overseas 'upon special affairs'. He could barely contain his excitement: 'there has nothing fallen out of a long time that makes a greater noise in the world than this does,' he wrote, 'and the eyes of

55. *Darien Papers*, pp. 375, 380, 383, 387–8; for rent-rolls, cf. Ferguson, *Scotland, 1689 to the Present*, pp. 73–4; H.G. Graham, *The Social Life of Scotland in the Eighteenth Century* (2 vols, London, 1899), i. 4.

56. His brother David (£200); brother-in-law, Sir Patrick Murray of Ochtertyre (£1,000); cousin, and wife's brother-in-law, Sir William Stirling of Ardoch (£400); cousin once removed, George Stirling of Herbertshire (£250); neighbours, William Oliphant of Gask (£500), and his uncle James Graham of Orchill (£300); and £300 from three lesser fry: *Darien Papers*, pp. 379, 382–3, 388, 404, 407–8; for the relationship between Gleneagles and Herbertshire, and Oliphant and Graham, see Fraser, *Stirlings of Keir*, pp. 171, 175–6; L.G. Graeme, *Or and Sable* (Edinburgh, 1903), pp. 435–6.

every body is upon us'. He travelled via London, where his tasks were to engage such 'proper seamen' as would be fit for the company's service and to examine the books of the company's London agents. Exhibiting an acumen in accountancy which re-emerged among his descendants in the nineteenth and twentieth centuries, he uncovered embezzlement on a worrying scale, perpetrated by a man whom he found to be 'the greatest vilan and most notorious lyer in nature', whose activities had presented him with a problem, than which he 'never had a ticklisher point to manadge'; he then set off for Holland and Hamburg, where he and his companions were to raise capital, buy ships, and negotiate with the senate of Hamburg for a free port in the Hanse towns.[57] Here they reckoned without the already established English Merchant Venturers, and Sir Paul Rycaut, the English resident, informed the Hamburg senators that his master, King William, disowned the commissioners of the Scottish Company and would view with hostility those who abetted them. Events had hardly taken an unpredictable course, but Rycaut's sabotage caused bitter resentment and a sense of betrayal. His 'memorial' to Hamburg's senate was translated and widely circulated in Scotland, where it enhanced the king's reputation for untrustworthiness, under which he had laboured since the Glencoe massacre in 1692.[58]

One of Haldane's companions on the Continental mission was William Paterson, a major contributor to the foundation of the company, with a background in London banking and Caribbean plantation. The

57. D. Watt, *The Price of Scotland: Darien, Union and the Wealth of Nations* (Edinburgh, 2007), pp. 91, 111, 114. The Hanse towns were Hamburg, Lübeck, and Bremen. Haldane also visited Glückstadt on the Elbe estuary and Tonningen on the Eider: *Papers relating to the Ships and Voyages of the Company of Scotland . . . 1696–1707*, ed. G.P. Insh (Scot. Hist. Soc., 3rd ser., vi, 1924), p. 25.

58. *Darien Papers*, pp. 14, 18, 25–7; W. Fraser, *The Annandale Family Book of the Johnstones, Earls and Marquesses of Annandale* (2 vols, Edinburgh, 1894), ii. 129; D.W. Hayton, 'Haldane, John (1660–1721) of Gleneagles', *The History of Parliament: the House of Commons 1690–1715*, ed. D. Hayton et al. (2002); Hamilton, 'The company of Scotland'. For the directors' 'international roadshow', see Watt, *The Price of Scotland*, pp. 91–103.

failure to make progress with the Hanseatic League shifted the company's attention towards a scheme which Paterson had conceived in the 1680s and had already presented to his fellow directors. His plan was to establish a colony, New Caledonia, at Darien on the Caribbean shore of the Isthmus of Panama, which he described as 'the door of the seas and the key to the universe'. It was also considered by the king of Spain to be subject to his sovereignty. If William III had been unhelpful to the Company of Scotland when its activities disturbed the House of Commons, he was downrightly antagonistic when they threatened to compromise his relations with Spain, an ally in his war with France.

The first settlers made landfall in November 1698. They soon found that their provisions were inadequate, and, close to starvation, they were rapidly succumbing to disease. A sloop was sent to obtain supplies from Jamaica. It returned, not with food, but with the news that King William had ordered his governors of English colonies in North America and the West Indies to ban assistance of any kind to the Scots; fearing that the Company had collapsed and no more settlers would arrive, and confronted by an advancing Spanish force, they abandoned their settlement. Unaware of the unfolding disaster in the isthmus, the laird of Gleneagles was to be found in an Edinburgh coffee-house on 5 April 1699, cheerfully exhibiting a chip of gold, which had come from a source in Panama.[59] In the summer of 1699, he revisited London, searching for some way of circumventing the English parliament's obstructionism. A brief spell under arrest at the suit of a Company creditor was not encouraging, but his efforts were appreciated by one seasoned observer of public affairs, who wrote on 5 June that Gleneagles 'has left noe stone unturned, and, tho' he shows great temper [restraint], he has all the fire and zeal that is requisite to be both indefatigable and incorruptible'.[60] Neither fire nor zeal, however, was enough to save a second expedition, which sailed from the Clyde in the autumn. Its progress was marred by internal discord, and ended by a Spanish land assault and naval blockade. On 31 March 1700, New Caledonia capitulated.

59. Ibid., p. 17.
60. *Annandale Family Book*, ii. 184; Hayton, 'Haldane, John'.

As a member of the committee for equipping ships, the laird of Gleneagles must bear some responsibility for the first expedition's shortage of provisions, and, despite his reputation as a man of 'honour and worth', his inexperience in the world of finance and commerce, shared by many other directors, contributed to the catastrophe that awaited the inadequately researched or resourced enterprise of Darien. He himself was inclined to blame 'the divisions and animosities' among the settlers. Most Scots had no doubt that the failure was owing to what the company's directors described as 'the unkind behaviour of our neighbour nation'.[61]

Before news reached Scotland that New Caledonia had ceased to exist, the directors marshalled influential support to petition the king to recall the Scottish parliament, so that it might confirm the legality of the settlement on the isthmus, debate the problems it faced, and suggest remedies. John Haldane collaborated in drafting the address and was included in a deputation of four, led by the marquess of Tweeddale, who waited on his majesty at Kensington Palace, at four o'clock on 25 March 1700, to present it. They kissed hands in the bedchamber; the king heard the petition and told them that, as he had summoned parliament to sit on 15 May, they could have been spared the trouble of coming to see him. One of the emissaries, Sir John Home of Blackadder, could not refrain from expressing the hope that his majesty would look upon the address, not only as petitioning for a parliament, but as witnessing the concerns of the nation for the Indian and African company; to which the king replied that these concerns would be known to parliament; meanwhile, he had to go to Hampton Court and would permit the deputation to attend him to his coach.[62]

Having striven for parliament's recall, Gleneagles predictably sought to re-enter it, and a refusal of the member for Dunbartonshire to sign the Association presented his opportunity. Since the discovery of a Jacobite plot to assassinate William III in 1696, members were required to sign

61. *Darien Papers*, pp. xix n., 281; *Journal of the Hon. John Erskine of Carnock, 1683–1687*, ed. W. Macleod (Scot. Hist. Soc., xiv, 1893), p. 245; Watt, *The Price of Scotland*, p. 92.
62. *Darien Papers*, pp. 283–4; *Annandale Family Book*, ii. 203–4.

an 'association', professing that he was the rightful king, in addition to swearing allegiance, taking the Test, and making the Assurance. All these requirements an older and less scrupulous John Haldane now felt able to meet. He took his seat for Dunbartonshire on 29 October 1700, not having been returned until after the adjournment of the stormy session in May, which had produced resolutions to confirm the legality of New Caledonia and promise it help. When parliament reassembled in October, it was known that the colony had been beyond help since 31 March, but the Company of Scotland remained, and its directors and investors required confirmation of the lawfulness of the Darien operation, lest their right to compensation, enshrined in its charter, be prejudiced. As far as the king was concerned, any matter touching on Spanish sovereignty was to be avoided, so, when John Haldane voted to embody the Company's title to New Caledonia in an Act, rather than present another address, he unequivocally aligned himself against the Court party. Indeed, he had already done so by moving a resolution to condemn Rycaut's actions in Hamburg as 'an encroachment on the sovereignty and independency' of Scotland.[63]

The sullen resentment which pervaded the northern kingdom was not lifted when Queen Anne failed to summon the Scottish parliament within twenty days of her accession after William III's death on 8 March 1702, as required by law; she waited for ninety days, during which interval war was renewed against France, a measure many Scots considered contrary to their interests. John Haldane and seventy-two other members followed the duke of Hamilton, the leader of the opposition or 'Country' party, in seceding from parliament when it did meet on 9 June. They thus effectively ensured that this tenth session of a parliament originally elected in 1689 was its last. New elections were held, and, on 6 May 1703, Gleneagles took his seat as a member for Perthshire in a house where the Country party enjoyed a 'fluctuating majority'.[64]

63. RPS, 1696/9/16; 1700/5/17; 1700/10/2, 6, 179; D. Hume of Crossrig, *A Diary of the Proceedings in the Parliament and Privy Council of Scotland, 1700–1707* (Bannatyne Club, 1828), p. 46.
64. Ferguson, *Scotland: 1689 to the Present*, pp. 37–8

This parliament was dominated by the long-standing desire of Scots for freedom of trade with England and her colonies, and the increasingly urgent matter of the succession to the throne, problems closely allied to the overarching need to define and defend Scottish sovereignty in relation to its larger, richer, and more powerful southern neighbour. The last of Queen Anne's large but unhealthy progeny had died in 1700. As far as London was concerned, the succession had been settled the following year, when the English parliament recognized the right of James I and VI's granddaughter Sophia, electress of Hanover, and her issue, and passed over the claims of the issue of James's other grandchild, James II and VII. The Scottish parliament had yet to pronounce upon the matter, and John Haldane and his colleagues had no desire to hurry that pronouncement, valuing the leverage its delay offered them in securing concessions on other issues. No one thought that Gleneagles had become a Jacobite: 'tho' opposed to the court,' an observer noted of him and others, 'they were never esteem'd staunch friends to the royal [Jacobite] interest'.[65] One issue at the forefront of his mind and the minds of many members of this parliament, as investors in the Company of Scotland, was recognition of their claim upon public funds. Indeed, it was upon this point that somewhat half-hearted negotiations for a constitutional and commercial union had foundered early in 1703.[66] In July 1704, John Haldane supported the duke of Hamilton's motion to postpone nominating the queen's successor 'until we have had a previous treaty with England in relation to our commerce and other concerns with that nation'.[67]

James VI and I had foreseen the need for a closer relationship between his 'twa antient and famous kingdomes' than one limited to a union of the crowns, while the activities of the Company of Scotland had taught William III that 'difficulties may too often arise with respect to the different interests of trade between the two kingdomes unless some way be found to unite them more neatly and completely', and, in 1700, he had hoped that his ministers might engineer 'some happy expedient for

65. *Lockhart Papers*, i. 92.
66. Ferguson, *Scotland, 1689 to the Present*, p. 38.
67. Ibid., p. 43; Hayton, 'Haldane, John', *Hist. Parliament*.

making England and Scotland one people'.[68] Legislation presented by the Country party in Scotland's parliament during 1703 and 1704 made it clear that the alternative to union was commercial and political chaos: the Act anent Peace and War provided for an independent foreign policy, while the Act of Security threatened the dissolution of the union of the crowns after Anne's death. The queen withheld consent to the latter; the Scots withheld supply; the queen relented; the English parliament retaliated in 1705 with the Alien Act, by which natives of Scotland were to be treated as aliens, and trade between the two countries prohibited, until the Scottish parliament should pass an Act settling the crown upon the successor to the crown of England. Having made clear what the consequences of separation would be, the Alien Act offered the alternative: commissioners would be appointed to negotiate constitutional union as soon as the appointment of similar commissioners was authorized in Scotland. In September 1705, the Scottish parliament asked the queen to make the necessary nominations, and in November the hostile clauses of the Alien Act were repealed.[69]

By now, commercial realism had tempered John Haldane's reaction to the Darien catastrophe. In the parliamentary session of 1704, it was noticed that the marquess of Montrose, Haldane of Gleneagles, Erskine of Alva, and others, 'all formerly of the Cavalier or Country parties, did now desert them, and ... did promote the measures of England'.[70] Haldane's association with Montrose (his first wife's cousin twice removed) was more than a meeting of minds. The 22-year-old marquess had embarked on his political career bolstered by a considerable aggrandizement of his importance as a landowner: the lands of Graham of Braco and of the earldom of Menteith, together with the newly acquired Buchanan Castle estate, had come to him as a child, and he had recently stretched his resources to buy the Lennox and Darnley estates of the duke of Richmond, making himself by far the most influential of Gleneagles's neighbours in Strathearn, Stirlingshire, and Dunbartonshire. The

68. *Source Book of Scot. Hist.*, iii. 456–7, 469.
69. Ibid., pp. 470–80.
70. *Lockhart Papers*, i. 98–9; C.A. Whatley, *The Scots and the Union* (Edinburgh, 2006), p. 303.

Haldanes are henceforward to be found in Montrose's affinity rather than that of Atholl. When the secretary of state for Scotland was asked to consider John Haldane for preferment in December 1704, he thought 'all should be delayed till Montrose was employed'; he had no doubt who John's patron now was, and, unlike the duke of Atholl, the young marquess strongly favoured both a Hanoverian succession and union with England.[71] So far as preferment was concerned, John had let it be known, when courted by ministers in October, that he would never 'change my thoughts or inclinations to my country for any advantages a slippery and uncertain Court could give me'.[72]

In essence, by the Treaty of Union the Scots sacrificed their parliament in return for equality of commercial rights. They were also able to retain their own legal system and ecclesiastical establishment, and, because their resources were so much smaller than England's, their share of the national debt was balanced by the transference from the English to the Scottish exchequer of an 'Equivalent', part of which was to return the capital of the Company of Scotland together with interest at 5 per cent, whereupon the company would 'dissolve and cease'. In acknowledgement of his past work on committees for trade and for auditing public accounts, as well as on the board of the Scottish Company itself, parliament appointed John Haldane to the committee for calculating the Equivalent; he also sat on a subcommittee for adjusting public debts and standardizing the coinage, and, at the end of the exercise, received thanks as one who had been 'at much pains, acted very diligently, and made several reports to the house'.[73] The sum agreed upon was £395,085 10s., of which £232,884 5s. 0⅔d. was set aside on behalf of the Company. At last, on 16 January 1707, the Treaty of Union was ratified by the Scottish parliament by 110 votes to 67; on 25 March, the session was adjourned;

71. R.M. Sunter, 'Graham, James, first duke of Montrose', *ODNB* (2004–14); *Correspondence of George Baillie of Jerviswood, 1702–1708* (Bannatyne Club, 1842), pp. 28–9 & cf. pp. 25, 27; for Atholl, see *Lockhart Papers*, i. 73.

72. Hayton, 'Haldane, John'.

73. RPS, 1700/10/25; 1703/5/144; M1704/7/21; C1706/10/1; Sir J. Clerk of Penicuik, *History of the Union of Scotland and England*, trans. & ed. D. Duncan (Scot. Hist. Soc., 5th ser., vi, 1993), p. 100.

on 28 April, Scotland's parliament was dissolved by Proclamation, and, on 1 May 1707, the Union came into existence.[74] Tension remained high until the Equivalent arrived; it had yet to appear on 15 July, when John told the earl of Mar that government supporters 'have bin nou struggling these 2 days to keep violent resolutions from being taken'; at last, English gentlemen arrived, and the specie and exchequer bills were trundled into Edinburgh Castle on 5 August; John told Mar that 'the common people belive it to be nothing but pouder and shott'.[75] By the end of the month, shareholders in the Company of Scotland began to recover their money, and the Company was wound up.

John Haldane had followed Montrose in voting for every article of the Treaty of Union.[76] Montrose's reward was a Scottish dukedom and selection as one of the sixteen representative peers of Scotland in the House of Lords; Haldane's was selection as one of the thirty Scottish barons from the last Scottish parliament, to sit in the House of Commons when the parliament of Great Britain met on 23 October 1707.[77] He immediately made his mark, being nominated in November to the committee on the Address, moving in December that the militia and commission of the peace should be placed on the same footing in Scotland as in England, and being appointed to draft the bill to rescind the Scottish Acts of Security and anent Peace and War; he supported the abolition of the Scottish Privy Council, and, in February 1708, joined committees to draft bills relating to the salmon fishery and linen industry. The respect which he had so swiftly achieved in the House was demonstrated on 8 January 1708, when he was asked to join two English Whig lawyers on a committee to prepare amendments to the Regency Act.[78]

74. Ferguson, *Scotland: 1689 to the Present*, pp. 52–3; M. Fry, *The Union: England, Scotland, and the Treaty of 1707* (Edinburgh, 2006), pp. 282–290.
75. NRS, GD124/15/642/1, 2 (Erskine Papers). £100,000 sterling came in specie, the rest in exchequer bills: *Memoirs of the Life of Sir John Clerk of Penicuik (1676–1755)*, ed. J.M. Gray (Scot. Hist. Soc., xiii, 1892), p. 69.
76. RPS, 1706/10/42, 65, 76, &c.
77. RPS, 1706/10/307.
78. Hayton, 'Haldane, John'; HMC, *Report on the MSS of the earl of Mar and Kellie* (1904), i. 424.

In accordance with the terms of the Triennial Act, the English parliament which the Scottish representatives had joined was dissolved in the
spring of 1708, and elections were called throughout the fledgling United
Kingdom. John Haldane stood for Perthshire, with the support of the
duke of Montrose, who told a cousin that everyone who knew the laird of
Gleneagles recognized 'his integratie and honestie', and that, since 'he is
already bothe weall knouen and much estimead by the best in Ingland', it
would be a great advantage to the shire to have such a representative.[79] The
election took place in a feverish atmosphere induced by a French attempt
to take advantage of the widespread unpopularity of the union by landing
the Pretender 'James VIII' at the head of 5,000 men on the southern shore
of the Firth of Forth. Bad navigation, rough weather, and the presence
of a British squadron combined to foil the enterprise, but a number of
suspected and confirmed Jacobites were held in custody, among them the
duke of Atholl and his candidate for the Perthshire seat, the earl of Bute's
brother, Dougald Stuart. Atholl probably viewed Haldane's alignment
with Montrose, and promotion of the Hanoverian and unionist cause,
as a betrayal of their past friendship, and, even though, on 19 April, he
had been placed under close house arrest at Blair, forbidden to converse
with anyone outside the hearing of the captain of the guard, he was able
to orchestrate a campaign against Gleneagles.[80] Correspondents wrote
to the secretary of state for Scotland, expressing their concern to 'hold
out Glenegles'; on 20 May, Haldane was reported to be 'canvassing for
himself', and the outcome to be 'dubious'; on 2 June, the duke of Atholl
was optimistic that, 'if I have my liberty soon', his assistance to Dougald
Stuart would prove decisive. On 8 June, both he and Stuart were bailed;
on the fourteenth, the elections were 'near over', and Gleneagles had
indeed been 'held out'.[81] His erstwhile parliamentary colleagues 'reckoned
more upon the disappointment of Gleneigies then tenne others'.[82]

79. *HG*, p. 111.
80. For Atholl's confinement: *MSS Mar & Kellie*, i. 440; NAS,
    GD112/39/216/16 (Breadalbane Muniments).
81. *MSS Mar & Kellie*, i. 438, 443, 445; GD112/39/216/16.
82. NRS, GD112/39/217/31. For the conduct of the election and John's
    challenge to its outcome, see D.W. Hayton, 'Perthshire', *Hist. Parl.:
    Constituencies 1690–1715*; GD112/32/217/24.

In 1710, John stood both for the county and for the burghs district of Perthshire, but suffered a double defeat. Montrose's backing for his candidature for the seat of Stirlingshire in 1714 was insufficient to counter the Erskine and Livingstone influence deployed in favour of the Jacobite Sir Hugh Paterson.[83] John thereupon decided to accept a non-political office of profit under the crown, which effectively meant abandoning his parliamentary career. In December 1714, he accepted appointment as a commissioner of police, with an annual salary of £400, the other commissioners being a marquess, five earls, one earl's brother, and the cousin of another. This newly instituted commission used the word 'police' in the sense of the Greek *polis*, which was indeed its eighteenth-century pronunciation; it was intended to supervise the working of central government in Scotland by reporting on papists and non-jurors, proposing ways of taming the Highlands, maintaining high-ways, dredging rivers, relieving the poor, and directing crown patronage in the Kirk. The declared intention was commendable, but the thought behind it more to do with propaganda than administration, and, by about 1730, the commission was simply a collection of sinecures.[84] In July 1715, John collected another 'job', as a commissioner for levying the customs of tonnage and poundage in Scotland, followed in December 1716 by one as commissioner for Scottish customs, subsidies, and other duties, which carried an additional annual salary of £400, and, before his death, he had been granted a pension of a further £400.[85]

83. Ibid.; Hayton, 'Haldane, John'; GD220/5/332, 357, 367 (Montrose Muniments); GD124/1/1141 (Erskine Papers). For John's petition against the burghs result, see *Journals of the House of Commons* (1803), xvi. 419.
84. GD86/852 (Sir William Fraser Charters); P.W.J. Riley, *English Ministers and Scotland* (London, 1964), pp. 185–6; E. Burt, *Letters from a Gentleman in the North of Scotland* (London, 1815), i. 134. Haldane (*HG*, p. 110), followed by Hayton (*ODNB*), mistakenly places Haldane's appointment in 1707, which pre-dates the establishment of the commission. He is also mistaken in giving John a parliamentary seat in 1715, confusing him with his son Patrick: *HG*, pp. 114, 123.
85. *HG*, p.123; Hayton, 'Haldane, John'.

John's receipt of official favour demonstrates that he was untarnished by the Jacobite activities of close kinsmen during the rising of 1715. Queen Anne had died on 1 August 1714, when the elector of Hanover was proclaimed as George I. A flurry of Jacobite activity, more dare-devil than dangerous, included such examples of defiance as Rob Roy MacGregor's drinking the Pretender's health at Crieff market cross in October and departing unscathed, despite the presence of soldiers in the town; in February next year, Gleneagles learnt that MacGregor had repeated the performance and had 'bin up and down in severall houses of this countrie'.[86] Even so, in April he felt able to report to Montrose that the country was quiet after the disappointment of Jacobite hopes in the elections to George I's first parliament.[87] It was the calm before the storm. On 6 September 1715, the earl of Mar raised the standard of King James VIII and III at Braemar.

Gleneagles's personal relationship with Mar had been a good one. The Erskines, whose chief Mar was, had a long-standing connection with the Haldanes, revived by John's marriage to the earl's kinswoman, Helen Erskine.[88] Politics, however, took Mar towards the Tories and Gleneagles towards the Whigs. As early as 1708, they had sparred in attempts to influence an election in Clackmannanshire, and Mar wrote to Haldane, hoping 'that political differences should not break private friendships'.[89] This they irrevocably did in October 1715, when Highlanders from Mar's Jacobite army based at Auchterarder were detached from an abortive advance on Stirling to raid Gleneagles, removing even household furni-ture in addition to livestock, grain, and fodder – the more usual objects of military plunder. In the first week of November, Mar quartered about 1,000 men on the Gleneagles estate, which was denuded of horses, sheep, and cattle, while barns and granaries were emptied, the dwellings of tenants and shepherds looted, and even the laird's closet burgled. Two years were to elapse before tenants were in a position to resume

86. *HG*, p. 114; HMC, *Third Report*, Appendix, p. 378; NRS, GD220/5/506.
87. GD220/5/506.
88. John Haldane was Mar's fifth cousin once removed, and Helen his second cousin twice removed.
89. NRS, GD124/15/886.

payment of rent. A letter of complaint to Mar from Lady Gleneagles's sister-in-law, the wife of the Jacobite Sir John Erskine, produced an order to the commander at Auchterarder to control his men.[90] A week later, the Jacobite army moved towards Dunblane to meet government forces at Sheriffmuir on 13 November. The battle resulted in stalemate, and the Jacobites remained in the neighbourhood. Orders were given that forty men accustomed to threshing be sent to thresh what corn was still standing at Dalreoch, part of a property in Abruthven, including Easter and Wester Balgour and a ferry over the Earn, which John Haldane had bought from the Atholl estate for £25,825 Scots in 1696, and kept in hand as a demesne farm; another forty, dispatched on a similar task to Gleneagles itself, went under the supervision of officers to avoid a repetition of the outrages of the previous week.[91]

Such outrages, however, were to be magnified and multiplied in the new year. When Mar decided to retreat northwards before the approaching government army on 17 January 1716, he sought to delay its advance by denying it supplies and shelter. Accordingly, commands were issued for the destruction of Auchterarder, Blackford, Muthill, Dunning, and Crieff. Before dawn on 25 January, amid 'the most terrible blowings and falls of snow that ever man saw', Auchterarder was ransacked and put to the flames, 142 houses being destroyed, and the population left to freeze. Included in the devastation was the estate of John Haldane's brother David at Aberuthven (feued to him by Montrose in 1706). David had emptied his house and retired with his family to Stirling at the outset of the rebellion. The Highlanders told his staff that, if the roof was removed, they would be satisfied, but, when the servants were upon the roof, their ladders were taken away and the building torched. Attention was then given to the dwellings, cattle, and grain of David's tenants.[92] Later that

90. *HG*, pp. 114–16; A.G. Reid, *The Annals of Auchterarder and Memorials of Strathearn* (Crieff, 1899), pp. 89–90.

91. Ibid., pp. 97, 141; *HG*, p. 288 (by a slip, giving the price as sterling).

92. 'Accounts of the burning of the villages of Auchterarder, Muthill, Crieff, Blackford, Dalreoch, and Dunning, about the beginning of the year 1716', *Miscellany of the Maitland Club iii* (Edinburgh, 1843), pp. 450–7;

morning, a detachment of 200 or 300 clansmen (out of a total of some 600) set off to Blackford. 'When they came to that part of the road which is about half a mile to the northward of Gleneagles, some of the clans, who had quartered there about the time of the battle of Dumblain [Sheriffmuir], proposed to go to it, but the storm blew so strong, and the snow was so deep, that the rest did not aggree to it, so they went on their way to Blackfoord.'[93] After further merciless destruction and savagery at Blackford, the clansmen rested on the Sabbath before moving on to Muthill and Crieff, which were burnt on the twenty-eighth.[94] Dunning also suffered on the twenty-eighth, and the operation was completed the next day, when Dalreoch was revisited. Horses and cattle had been taken long before, and John Haldane's servants had already been ordered by the Jacobite garrison at Duncrub to thresh corn ready for transport to the army at Perth; at 3 a.m. on the twenty-ninth, men arrived to collect the meal and burn the buildings. A false alarm that government troops were approaching led to the Highlanders' precipitate departure, allowing one tenant to save his house by giving the rebel officer a guinea (in 1716, worth 30s.), and the boatman at Haldane's ferry on the Earn likewise paid to preserve his cottage.[95] A commission of inquiry, established in 1722 to assess the damages incurred during these five days of terror, offered £383 13s. 4d. sterling to David Haldane and £611 8s. to the laird of Gleneagles, sums which were to be raised out of the sale of forfeited estates and which remained unpaid until 1781.[96]

The Jacobite rising ended when its leaders sailed for France on 4 February 1716, leaving their followers to face the government's retribution. Within John Haldane's family, his Jacobite cousin, John Haldane of Lanrick, seems to have kept a low profile and managed to shift for himself, but two nephews and one brother-in-law required his help.

Reid, *Auchterarder & Strathearn*, pp. 98–124. For David's infeftment by Montrose, see NRS, GD220/1/H/3/1/1 (Montrose muniments).
93. 'Accounts of the burning', p. 460.
94. Ibid., pp. 468–74.
95. Ibid., pp. 463–8.
96. Reid, *Auchterarder & Strathearn*, pp. 159–70; NRS, E605/61/3, 6; CC6/5/28, test. 1777, Haldane, David.

PLATE 1. (Above left)
Margaret Fraser, lady
of Gleneagles, 1666;
'a happy fortunate
woman'.

PLATE 2. (Above right)
James Haldane of
Airthrey (1728–68);
a painting by Sir
Joshua Reynolds.

PLATE 3. (Left)
Capt. Robert Haldane,
R.N. (*c.* 1723-61); a
painting by Sir Joshua
Reynolds: 'the devil
take me how time has
slipt away'.

PLATE 4. Lt Col. James Haldane (1692–1742), diplomat and soldier.

PLATE 5. The Entailer: Robert Haldane (laird 1760–68); a painting by Sir Joshua Reynolds

PLATE 6. (Left) Patrick Haldane (laird 1755–60), 'the curse of Scotland'; a painting possibly by George Knapton.

PLATE 7. (Below left) Brigadier-General George Haldane (1721–59) as he wished to be seen: a painting by Sir Joshua Reynolds, 1755.

PLATE 8. (Below right) Brigadier-General George Haldane as others saw him: a caricature by George Townshend, Marquess Townshend, in the National Portrait Gallery, London.

PLATE 9. Admiral Adam Duncan, Viscount Duncan (laird 1799–1804), 'a seaman every inch of him'; a painting by Sir Henry Raeburn, 1798, in Trinity House, Leith.

PLATE 10. The third earl of Camperdown (laird 1867–1918); a caricature from *Vanity Fair* by 'Spy' (Leslie Ward), 1895.

PLATE 11. Robert Haldane (1764–1842), propagator of the gospel; engraving of a sketch by Dr César Malan at Geneva, c. 1817.

PLATE 12. James A. Haldane (1768–1851), 'Boanerges of the evangelical movement'; caricature by John Kay, 1801.

PLATE 13. Alexander Haldane (1800–82), the loyal father; a painting by William Gush, 1878.

PLATE 14. Sir Nicholas Chinnery (1804–1868), the lonely father; a painting by Thomas Harper, 1836.

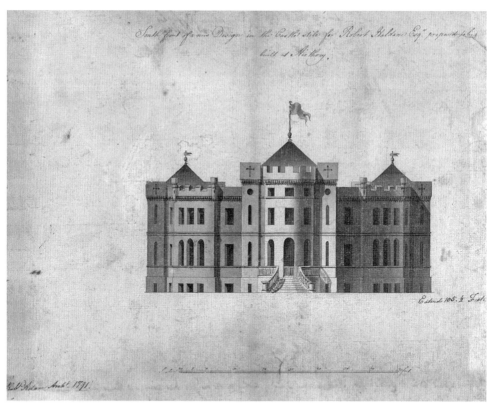

PLATE 15. Airthrey Castle; Robert Adam's sketch of the south front, 1791.

PLATE 16. Auchengray (built 1809) today.

PLATE 17. (Above left) Anna Chinnery-Haldane (1844–1907), the heiress.

PLATE 18. (Above right) Alexander Chinnery-Haldane (1842–1906), bishop of Argyll and the Isles.

PLATE 19. (Left) Travelling on diocesan business.

PLATE 20. Alltshellach.

PLATE 21. Dunbeg.

Among prisoners held in Edinburgh Castle were the sons of his sister Margaret and his half-sister Janet. Since prosecutions in Scotland were likely to be thwarted by hostile juries, it was proposed to transfer certain prisoners for exemplary trial in Carlisle. Armed with letters of contrition, John went to London in January 1716 to intercede with Lord Townshend, secretary of state for the north, on behalf of Margaret's son William Murray, younger of Ochtertyre, and Janet's son David Smyth, younger of Methven.[97] He was successful in having David's name removed from the list of those to be taken to Carlisle, and later, in thanking the minister, assured him that 'that gentleman is extreamly sorie that he should ever have joined in the late horid rebelion', and was resolved ever after to be King George's dutiful and loyal subject.[98]

Although assuredly equally sorry, William Murray was treated less sympathetically. He was still in Edinburgh Castle on 7 August, when his wife received news that his uncle's latest appeal had been denied. On 1 September, the laird wrote to the secretary of state, pleading for the too easygoing nephew whom he had 'knouen from his infancie', blaming his transgression on his youth (he was thirty-three years old), and giving assurances of his future loyal conduct. On the fifth, however, the younger of Ochtertyre was marched to Carlisle.[99] After applying to friends in London, from whom he still had hopes of finding favour, John decided, on 22 October, to write to the king's private secretary. He began by deploring the use of habeas corpus, newly introduced into Scotland, to force the military to release suspected rebels, and was equally critical of the stratagems by which forfeited rebels were managing to retain enjoyment of their estates. Having established his anti-Jacobite credentials, he proceeded to show why his nephew deserved clemency: 'he is young, good natured and easie to an extream degree, lives in a countrie

---

97. *HG*, p. 336. After his dismissal during 1715, the duke of Montrose's duties as secretary of state for Scotland were shared by two other ministers, Lord Townshend and Lord Stanhope. Matters concerning rebels were handled by Townshend, who is almost certain to have been the recipient of Haldane's letters, where he is addressed simply as 'my lord'.

98. *HG*, p. 118.

99. *HG*, pp. 117–19.

that is much disafected, and where most of the nobility and gentrie went into the rebelion. By them he was seduced, joyned with them, and was taken in actual rebelion not manie houres after he had joyned.' The letter concludes with the information that the Murrays of Ochtertyre were 'a family of considerable interest in this countrie', and John's personal assurance that, 'if his majestie extends his mercie and clemencie to this young gentleman, they will always use it in his majestie's service'.[100] Other voices were probably telling the king, not untruthfully, that Ochtertyre was a nest of Jacobites, and William remained in Carlisle.

Despairing of the efficacy of the written word, in mid November John sent his eldest son Mungo to London to 'throu himself' at the feet of Lord Townshend, while drawing on his own experience to warn William's father that lack of news from Mungo would 'not arise from remissness or neglect butt from that constant and assiduous attendance which must be given when one pretends [attempts] to doe service either to themselves or friends att a court'.[101] Meanwhile, a younger son James, in the early stages of a planned diplomatic career, was working on his cousin's behalf at Hanover, where King George was in residence. Murray's trial took place at the end of December, with him pleading guilty in the expectation of an early pardon. A Jacobite agent in London reported to Paris that 'young Murray of Achtertyre is saved by the Haldanes', but his relief was premature.[102] On 15 February 1717, Murray feared that 'I still run the hazard of being condemned'. On that very day, however, good news was on its way from Hanover. 'It's with the utmost pleasure,' wrote James Haldane to his cousin, 'I give you joy of the favour his majesty has gratiously been pleased to show you. He has resolved to pardon you, and in order to it his orders goes to England by this post to put a stop to your tryall, and, if the case will allow of it before your pardon is expeded, to set you at liberty on account of your health, which I hope is not so bad as I represented it. . . . I gave a memorial to the king in my father's name, representing your case in the most favourable maner.

100. *HG*, pp. 335–7.
101. TNA, State Papers, Scotland, 54, bundle 12, no. 250; transcript in Gen. Haldane's 'Notes collected for the history of the Haldanes' (2 vols, typescript, at Gleneagles; hereafter 'Notes'), ii. 648; *HG*, p. 120.
102. HMC, *Calendar of the Stuart Papers*, iii. 377–8.

I assured him of your hearty and early repentance, and that my father would not ask so great a favour for you if he was not persuaded you would endeavour to deserve it by your future good behaviour, and by renouncing these principles that had drawn you into so great a misfortune.'[103] In England William Murray was considered healthy enough to wait until June 1717 for his release, but the fact that he obtained it showed that John Haldane had been the right man to orchestrate the campaign on his behalf. William's Jacobitism, however, proved unquenchable, and, had the Spanish-backed attempt at a rising in 1719 not been snuffed out so swiftly, his involvement would have been revealed and have proved a severe embarrassment to his uncle.[104]

John's skill as a mediator was further tested by his wife's brother, Sir John Erskine of Alva. Jacobites had thought him 'well affected' at the beginning of the century, but Haldane introduced him to the circle of the duke of Montrose, and that influence, combined with the desire to retrieve his investment in the Company of Scotland, resulted in his voting for the Union. Disillusionment with the rewards that came in its wake, however, returned him to the affinity of the earl of Mar, the head of his family name. Although he played no military role in the rising of 1715, he joined the Pretender's court, and, in 1716, found himself on the Continent facing a life in exile. In the aftermath of the rising, a servant revealed to government officials that Erskine had been working a clandestine silver mine on his estate at Alva, the entry to which remained a secret. The information was sent to the Scottish mint, of which John Haldane was a commissioner, and John realized its potential to secure his brother-in-law's rehabilitation. In July 1716, 'Gleneagles has brought things so about as to obtain a pardon to Sir John for life and fortune and a share of the mine, providing they'll discover all about it'. When approached, however, Lady Erskine denied all knowledge of the existence, let alone the whereabouts, of the mine, 'at which all his friends are very angry, especially Gleneagles, who thought he had brought him well off'.[105]

103. *HG*, p. 122.
104. *HG*, p. 104; T.L.K. Oliphant, *The Jacobite Lairds of Gask* (Grampian Club, London, 1870), p. 64.
105. 'Erskine Papers', *Miscellany* (Scot. Hist. Soc., ii, 1904), p. 414.

At the end of August 1716, Erskine's nephew, Sir Henry Stirling of Ardoch, was sent to bring him back to Britain with the confirmation from Lord Townshend that 'full discovery of the place of the bonnywally [ore]' would be followed by a pardon. Erskine required a good deal of reassurance about the percentage of the ore that he would be allowed to retain, as well as about his liberty, before he arrived in Scotland in the middle of October. Gleneagles was told that the pardon was conditional upon Erskine's revealing the entry to the mine in person, and his presence when experts examined it. (Sir Isaac Newton was asked to go down, but declined and was replaced by a certain Dr Justus Bradshagen.) Erskine was concerned that, if not enough was found, there would be no pardon, and, if too much, his knowledge of the Ochil mines would no longer be needed, and his pardon be revoked. Haldane's delicate task was to mediate between his suspicious and volatile brother-in-law and an increasingly impatient Lord Townshend, and there is a suggestion that the laird was close to the end of his tether on 19 November, when he protested to the secretary of state that 'in this afair, and everie other where your lordship is pleased to lay your commands upon me, I shall indevor to behave my self as becomes an honest man and one who has always indevored to preserve the character that is due to a gentleman.'[106] Eventually, the mine was examined, a sample sent to Sir Isaac Newton, who reported that 'the ore is exceeding rich', and Erskine's pardon was confirmed.[107]

John Haldane's application to responsibilities laid upon him made him a perfect trustee. In 1704, Innerpeffray Library came under the potentially predatory attention of the Auchterarder presbytery, whose members were anxious to promote the General Assembly's policy of providing Highland Protestant clergy with libraries stocked with suitable books to counter the influence of the Roman Catholic faith among the Gaelic population. They asked the minister at Blackford to approach one of Innerpeffray's two trustees – his parishioner, the

---

106. *HG*, p. 125; TNA, State Papers, Scotland, 54, bundle 12, no. 250.
107. HMC, *Eighth Report* (1881), pp. 84–6; *Stuart Papers*, ii. 376, 395–6, 422, 496, 499; iii. 76, 90; D.W. Hayton, 'Erskine (Areskine), Sir John', *Hist. Parl.: House of Commons 1690–1715*; *HG*, p. 125.

laird of Gleneagles – to seek permission for them 'to augment and inspect' the library. Alert to the danger such interference might pose to the independence of his trust, the laird made clear his reluctance to comply, but sent the minister on his way with a diplomatic pleasantry: he would be happy to cooperate should the presbytery wish to erect its own library, and, should any minister meet difficulty in borrowing a book from Innerpeffray, he would like to know.[108] John would appear to have been similarly assiduous in the exercise of his duties as a heritor of the parish of Blackford, attending a session of the elders in 1698 to charge them with the preparation of lists of the needy poor, after he and his fellow heritors had resolved to organize their relief.[109] The minister at Blackford, it may be noted, was occasionally called upon to officiate in Gleneagles Chapel, for it was there that he baptized John's youngest son Robert in 1705, when inclement weather persuaded the laird that his wife and child ought not make the journey to the parish church.[110]

Robert was sent to sea, and on his way to riches, in the service of the East India Company, with whom his father had presumably established a more amicable relationship than that which prevailed during his directorship of the Company of Scotland.[111] For his son John (born in Edinburgh in 1693), the laird found a profitable placement as collector of customs at Prestonpans.[112] Not long before his death in 1721, he arranged the marriage of his elder daughter Margaret to Charles Cockburn of Sandybeg, a lawyer-son of his colleague in the boardroom of the Scottish Company, the Lord Justice-Clerk, Adam Cockburn of Ormiston.[113] John's original intention for James (b.1692), the eldest

108. *HG*, p. 126; cf. R. Chambers, *Domestic Annals of Scotland* (3 vols, Edinburgh, 1859–61), iii. 250–3.
109. *HG*, p. 125, citing NRS, CH2/500/1 (Blackford Kirk Session minutes), 20 November 1698, transcribed in Haldane, 'Notes', i. 269.
110. *HG*, p. 126, citing CH2/500/1, 18 March 1705, transcribed in 'Notes', i. 270. Gravestones on the south side of the chapel record burials in 1686, 1697, and 1701. For the growing fashion for private baptisms, see Graham, *Social Life*, i. 245.
111. *HG*, p. 293.
112. *HG*, p. 183.
113. *HG*, pp. 123–4, 297; Watt, *Price of Scotland*, p. 51.

surviving child of his second marriage, was a career in the law, and, in September 1714, he approached the duke of Montrose's right-hand man to solicit the post of bailie of the regality of the Lennox for the young advocate, who 'not haveing reccommendation or interest enough to bring him quickly into business ... thought this might contribute something to it'.[114] The Haldanes, however, while being the duke's valued clients, were not Grahams, and such a position was reserved for bearers of the name. Ten months later, John bought James a commission in the Life Guards, a select regiment in which a cornetcy cost £3,200. Before his father's death, James had not only progressed to major, but also set out on a diplomatic career which took him as resident to various German principalities between 1716 and 1720.[115]

John's plan for Patrick (b.1683), the younger of his two surviving sons by his first wife Mary Drummond (d.1685), had also been that he should represent the family at the bar, and, to give him the income needed before his practice was established, he sought sinecures for him in the academic world. The idea may have been suggested by Mary's brother-in-law, the earl of Hyndford, with whom John had retained contact as his fellow trustee at Innerpeffray, and who happened to be chancellor of Glasgow University. An attempt with his support in 1704 to secure a Glasgow regency failed, but St Andrews proved more amenable, electing Patrick to the chair of Greek at St Salvator's in 1705. This post, however, was poorly remunerated, and in 1707, when John was able to request rewards for his parliamentary contribution to the Union, he included the creation of a chair of ecclesiastical history at the New College, which was to carry a salary of £105, and was earmarked for Patrick.[116] By 1716, Patrick possessed a seat in parliament (for Perthshire Burghs) and membership of highly paid commissions, as well as his legal practice,

---

114. NRS, GD220/5/811, 5 Sept. 1714, cited by R.M. Sunter, *Patronage and Politics in Scotland 1707–1832* (Edinburgh, 1986), p. 62.

115. For James's career, see below, pp. 189–95.

116. R.R. Sedgwick, 'Haldane, Patrick (c.1683–1769), of Bearcrofts', *Hist. Parl.: House of Commons 1715–1754*, ed. R. Sedgwick (1970); R.L. Emerson, *Academic Patronage in the Scottish Enlightenment* (Edinburgh, 2008), pp. 382, 410–11.

and John must have been content that there was little more he needed to do on his behalf, beyond granting him the rents from five holdings in the baronies of Haldane and Gleneagles as a wedding present in 1720.[117]

For his heir Mungo (b.1682), John sought to lay the foundations of a career in public life. As soon as he reached his majority, his status was enhanced by investment with the title to the family estate: he became 'fiar of Gleneagles', while his father retained a life interest in its revenue. In 1702, he became a commissioner of supply for Perthshire; in 1708, he was considered as a possible parliamentary candidate for Dunbartonshire, and the rents of certain Haldane lands in the Lennox were transferred to him to satisfy the necessary property qualification.[118] In 1715, he secured election to parliament as the member for Stirlingshire,[119] not only thereby avenging the early termination of his father's parliamentary career, but also perhaps giving John confidence that his stewardship of the Gleneagles inheritance was drawing to a successful conclusion.

John's health began to fail in the autumn of 1720. In September, accompanied by his wife and daughters, he went south to take the waters at Bath, where he met the king's private secretary, whose aid he had requested on a nephew's behalf five years earlier. One of his last acts on his return was to endow his younger daughter Helen with a bond for 10,000 merks Scots, to be paid as her tocher in the event of her marriage.[120] Ten days later, on 26 June 1721 in his sixty-first year, he died in Edinburgh, and was buried in St Giles' Cathedral in the chapel of his patron, the duke of Montrose.[121]

117. NRS, GD198/168–170; for Patrick's career, see below, pp. 124–47.
118. *HG*, p. 129; RPS 1702/6/44; D.W. Hayton, 'Dumbartonshire', in *Hist. Parl.: Constituences 1690–1715*; NRS, GD198/163–4. His father retained Haldane's Mill, which he used as a residence when in the neighbourhood, Boturich Castle being ruinous: *HG*, pp. 106–7; W. Macfarlane, *Geographical Collections*, ed. A. Mitchell (3 vols, Scot. Hist. Soc., li, 1906–08), i. 353.
119. J.M. Simpson, 'Haldane, Mungo (1682–1755), of Gleneagles', in *Hist. Parl.: House of Commons 1715–54*.
120. NRS, CC6/5/23, test. 1731 Haldan, John.
121. *HG*, pp. 123–4.

Mungo (II) Haldane, 1721–55

Within three months of his succession, Mungo faced financial embarrassment. His father had secured a loan of £200 under the guarantee of Mungo Graham of Gorthy, a friend and sometime colleague, and the duke of Montrose's 'general man-of-business, uniting the functions of factor, personal secretary, political lieutenant, and election manager'.[122] Learning of John's death, the creditor duly presented the bond to Gorthy, who in turn advised Mungo that a demand for payment had been received. 'It is,' replied Mungo, 'you may be sure, noe small trouble to me to finde my affairs in such a state; that a demand of so small a summ, as that is, should be hard upon me if it be insisted on peremtorily to so short a day, especially when it may also give you trouble for your kind and good office in joining with my father in the bond. All that I can say is that I shall doe all that in me lys in the short time I have to gett the effects and moveables my father left turned to ready money to answer that demand as soon as possible.'[123] We may be sure that Mungo made every effort to retain Gorthy's goodwill, but we know that he was unable to make prompt payment of his half-sister Helen's tocher of 10,000 merks Scots (£555 sterling), when she married Alexander Duncan of Lundy in 1724; it was still unpaid in 1731.[124]

The time Mungo had to spend in Scotland in 1721 was short because of his responsibilities in the House of Commons, in which he had sat as member for Stirlingshire since 1715, voting with the Whig ministry in every recorded division of George I's first parliament and being listed as a docile client of the duke of Montrose.[125] When new elections were called in 1722, however, it suited the duke to put up his chamberlain, John

122. D.W. Hayton, 'Graham, Mungo (1650–1754), of Gorthy', *Hist. Parl.: House of Commons 1690–1715*. Graham's mother was a Murray of Ochtertyre, sister-in-law of John's sister Margaret; he had been John's colleague on the Equivalent commission, and as MP for Perthshire before the Union, and as a representative Scottish MP at Westminster after it.

123. NRS, GD220/5/994 (Montrose Muniments).

124. CC6/5/23, test. 1731 Haldan, John.

125. J.M. Simpson, 'Haldane, Mungo (1660–1755), of Gleneagles', *Hist. Parl.: House of Commons 1715–54*.

Graham of Killearn, for the Stirlingshire seat and persuade Mungo to stand for Dunbartonshire, which the duke of Argyll's influence made a less secure proposition. Mungo's reluctance to comply was overcome by 22 February 1722, when the duke was 'glad to hear that Mungo Haldane has come to a better understanding of his interest, [and] a point where he will stand'. 'Sure I am,' the duke told Gorthy, 'he had no other game to play.' Mungo was elected by twenty votes to twelve, but on the petition of his Campbell opponent, in January 1725, twelve of his supporters were declared unqualified to have voted, and he was unseated.[126] A by-election for Perthshire in 1726 returned him to parliament, but the Atholl interest defeated him the following year, in the general election caused by George I's death.[127] While travelling on the Continent in the summer of 1723, Mungo had visited Rouen, where he had sought out Lord George Murray, one of the duke of Atholl's exiled Jacobite sons, to offer what service lay in his power, and had brought back a letter for the duke, but his willingness to serve as a postman for his grace had evidently won him no favours.[128] By 1730, he had decided to turn his back on a parliamentary career; his father had heralded a similar decision by accepting appointment as a commissioner of police, which, with its salary of £400 p.a., was an office of profit under the crown; on John's death, this place had been kept in the family by its transference to his brother David Haldane of Aberuthven, who had no parliamentary ambitions; the loan was now called in, and David resigned so that his nephew Mungo could succeed to the sinecure at the end of 1730.[129]

Prior to departing on his Continental tour in 1723, Mungo arranged for his Scottish affairs to be managed during his absence by his stepmother, his brother Patrick, his uncle David Haldane, and his cousin David Smyth of Methven, with two making a quorum so long as Patrick was of the number.[130] Helen Erskine, Lady Gleneagles (or Mrs Helen

126. GD220/5/838, no. 22; Simpson, 'Haldane, Mungo'.
127. Ibid.; Ramsay, *Scotland & Scotsmen*, i. 119, n. 2.
128. *Chron. Atholl & Tullibardine*, ii. 356.
129. *HG*, pp. 130, 289; above, p. 107.
130. Register of Deeds, Durie Office, 31 July 1725, transcribed in 'Notes', ii. 581.

Haldane, as she was sometimes called, as English usage spread north-wards), remained at Gleneagles in possession of her widow's terce; the 300 sheep on the hills, and seven young horses in the paddocks ('parks') near the house, which were rustled by Highlanders in April 1723, belonged to her and her tenants.[131] That Patrick's presence was essential was to be expected, since he was the younger of Gleneagles, and so remained throughout the lairdship of his bachelor brother, but it is clear that Mungo positively valued his advice. When negotiating exchanges of ground with the Montrose estate in 1738 and 1739, he was content for Patrick to correspond independently with Graham of Gorthie, and on one occasion was anxious that nothing should be finalized before he could arrange a meeting between the two.[132]

The exchange in question helped satisfy both Mungo's expressed desire for 'elbow room' near his house and the duke's wish to control the immediate neighbourhood of Buchanan, which had become his seat after the destruction of Kincardine Castle by Covenanters in 1646. For £1,260 Scots, Mungo sold his superiority over five tenancies in the Lennox bordering the policies of Buchanan Castle, and, for £2,838 Scots, the duke sold pendicles of Kincardine lying to the north of Gleneagles at Lochside, Peterhead, Loch, Cairn, Loaningfoot, and Loaninghead; the transaction was begun in 1736, and completed in 1741.[133] In 1745, wishing to 'square his enclosures', Mungo paid James Moray of Abercairny £755 Scots for the lease of Muiralehouse, to the west of Peterhead, and, in 1751, 'in order to make him convenient and clear up their marches', Abercairny also sold Mungo some ground to the south of Gleneagles at Bruich Hill, on the western border of Frandy, the price being £1,908 6s. 8d. Scots.[134]

131. *HG*, p. 130; *Chron. Atholl & Tullibardine*, ii. 352, 355; Helen is called 'Mrs Helen Haldane, Lady Gleneagles' in Mungo's registration of factory in 1725: Durie Register, *loc. cit.* She died at Haddington in 1739: above, n. 52.

132. NRS, GD220/1/1432, 1456, 1458 (Montrose Muniments).

133. GD220/1/K/4/5/1; GD220/1/K/5/1/2; GD220/5/902, no. 10; GD198/226; the reference to 'elbow room' was made by a later Abercairny: GD24/1/60, July 1782 (Papers of Stirling Home Drummond Moray of Abercairny).

134. GD198/227–9; GD24/1/60, July 1782.

In seeking to extend and enclose his pastures, Mungo was responding to opportunities offered by the free access to English markets opened by the Union. A particular source of profit was the trade in black cattle, which Mungo and his brother hoped to exploit by turning the Mains of Gleneagles into a stock farm. The plan probably originated with Patrick; since 1720, he had owned Bearcrofts near Falkirk, whose importance as a cattle market had grown in response to English demand.[135] By 1742, Patrick had come into contact with an Edinburgh barber and wigmaker, Neill McKinnon, a native of Mull, who had decided on a radical change of career. In September 1743, Patrick granted him a lease for nineteen years of his farm at Carbrook in Plean, at £880 p.a. rising to £1,000 Scots; in 1742 and 1743, he subscribed loans to McKinnon for £56 sterling; on 9 April 1744, Mungo granted McKinnon a lease for nineteen years of the West Mains of Gleneagles, with enclosures, glen, and hill ground, for an annual rent of £1,566 16s. 8d., rising to £1,606 16s. 8d. Scots in the third year; between 1743 and 1745, Mungo combined with Patrick to advance to McKinnon loans totalling some £500 sterling (£6,000 Scots) 'for his use in purchasing black cattle for stocking the farms set in tack to him'. The drover himself lived primarily at Carbrook, with West Mains occupied by his servant, William Hepburn. The investment sadly proved disappointing: Neill McKinnon died in May 1746, two months after his servant. An Edinburgh lawyer bought the debts owed to Mungo and Patrick, and in 1752 was still pursuing McKinnon's son and heir Donald, who had left Edinburgh to set up as a journeyman barber and wigmaker in London.[136]

Although the duke of Montrose had not felt able to sell all the ground attached to Kincardine that Mungo wanted, the negotiations had been amicable. Political differences and social rivalry, however, all too easily acerbated relations with James Moray of Abercairny. Abercairny was a Jacobite, Gleneagles a Whig; Abercairny was rich, Gleneagles was not; each was 'of antient pedigree as any in Strathearn', although the only

---

135. A.R.B. Haldane, *The Drove Roads of Scotland* (London, 1952), p. 152.
136. NRS, CC6/5/25, Dunblane CC, 1746 Hepburn, William; ibid., 1746 McKinnon, Neill; CC8/8/114, Edinburgh CC, 1753 McKinnon, Neill.

documentary evidence in the Haldane charter-chest that pre-dated Moray's had been faked.[137] Feeling that somehow he had been outwitted during the purchase of Muiralehouse, Mungo visited Moray, and the ensuing confrontation inspired eight stanzas of doggerel, written obviously to be read by people who knew the protagonists, and therefore to be trusted as giving a recognizable impression of their characteristics.[138] A convivial atmosphere darkened when 'Glen … grew cankir'd and grew surlie'; Moray said he would punch the nose of 'any little Whig'; Haldane scoffed that the other should think himself 'a grandee' and reminded him that, although over sixty, he could still handle 'sword or pike'. In short, the poem confirms an image of irascibility that attaches to Mungo in a reminiscence told, in the first half of the nineteenth century, by a centenarian tenant who related how, towards the end of his life, Mungo had forbidden Sunday trading in Blackford churchyard, and, when defied, had confronted the assembled packmen with his sword drawn, chased them down the hill on which the church then stood, and returned to deposit their scattered wares into the adjacent loch.[139] Earlier evidence of Mungo's temper was noticed in 1708, when he was reported as 'being very quarrelsome' during a meeting of the Perthshire electoral court, whose composition was being challenged by his father.[140] Mungo's irascibility would not have been smoothed by the apparent onset of rheumatism, which caused him, in spring 1739, to complain that 'the continuance of this bad weather does continue still so to affect me in my health that I am really good for nothing, and it is with difficulty enough that I am now able to write'.[141]

137. Above, pp. 14–15.
138. NRS, GD51/10/27 (Melville Castle Papers).
139. A. Haldane, *Memoirs of the Lives of Robert Haldane of Airthrey and of his Brother James Alexander Haldane* (4th edn, London, 1855), pp. 6–7. For two or three 'small lochs' near Blackford church in the 1790s (later drained), see *Statistical Account 1791–1799*, iii. 206.
140. GD112/32/217/24 (Breadalbane Muniments).
141. GD, 220/5/1456 (Montrose Muniments).

A bachelor, Mungo Haldane died at Gleneagles on 1 June 1755, in his seventy-third year.[142] The benevolence, that might have been enjoyed by the son he never had, had been bestowed upon his brother's son, George, who was born in about 1721. It was to Gleneagles that George came to recuperate from wounds received in battle on the Continent in 1745. To him Mungo gave most of the £400 he received annually as a commissioner of police, and, in 1748, made him the fiar of part of his estate, transferring to him Frandy in Glendevon, Camoquhill in Balfron, Knockhill and Craigbaickie in Dunning, Letter in Menteith (west of Loch Rusky), Middle Catter in the Lennox, Belhie in Aberuthven, and the recently acquired pendicles of Kincardine, while granting the life rent to his father Patrick.[143] It is conceivable that the decorated gate

142. *The Scots Magazine* (1755). An entry in the minutes of the Blackford Kirk sessions for 27 April 1700 records the summons of Mungo Halden to appear at the next meeting to respond to Christian Haldane's claim that he was the father of the child she was carrying. Duly summoned by the beadle, he appeared on 5 May, acknowledged paternity, and promised to submit to the discipline of the church, 'but pleaded that he might be forborn for some time, which the session, considering the circumstances, thought meet to do, and provided he once compeared in public to be rebuked'. Accordingly, on 17 May, he 'was upon the stool of repentance, and publickly rebuked for his scandal of fornication with Christian Haldane', and paid £6 Scots as a penalty for both of them: NRS, CH2/500/1 (Blackford Kirk Session Minutes), 7 & 27 April 1700; 5 & 19 May 1700; 16 January 1704; transcribed in Haldane, 'Notes', i. 268–9. If the subject of the kirk's rebuke was indeed the younger of Gleneagles, as has been assumed (*HG*, p. 134), his compliance is remarkable, but the name 'Mungo' was not unusual, and there were more Haldanes in Blackford parish than the laird's family: they are found at the time at Glen (St Mungo's), at the Mains, and outside the estate at Peterhead and Panholes, and 'Mungo' was current in the family at the Mains in 1727: Blackford Kirk Minutes, 14 May 1727, transcribed in 'Notes', i. 286. The younger, moreover, is most unlikely to have been consistently absent from Gleneagles between May 1700 and January 1704, since he was appointed a commissioner of supply for Perthshire in 1702: RPS 1702/6/44. In sum, it would be rash to assume that he was the father of Christian Haldane's child.

143. *HG*, p. 163; NRS, GD198/175–9.

piers, which bear the date 1749 and Mungo's initials, possibly together with George's, were commissioned to celebrate the latter's elevation to this partnership.[144]

'The curse of Scotland': Patrick Haldane, 1755–60

Known also as Peter (the usual Anglicization of the Gaelic 'Padraig'), Patrick Haldane was seventy-two years old when he succeeded his elder brother. After graduating at St Andrews in 1701, he had applied himself to the study of law, initially in Edinburgh, an application eventually financed by his tenure of two chairs at St Andrews: from 1705 to 1707 that of Greek, and from 1707 to 1718 that of ecclesiastical history, the latter being a complete sinecure.[145] Between 1711 and 1714, he had joined the large Scottish contingent studying civil law at the Dutch university of Leiden (both Dutch and Scots property law sharing a classical Roman basis, whose leading contemporary exponents were jurists in the United Provinces).[146] He returned home to be admitted advocate in January 1715, and, shortly thereafter, to be appointed a commissioner of the Equivalent. Two months later, he was in London, sitting in the House of Commons as member for Perth Burghs. He voted with the Whig government in all recorded divisions, and when, in April 1716, it sought to prolong its existence by extending the maximum duration of the present parliament, and of all future parliaments (until 1911), from three to seven years, Patrick made his mark with 'an excellent allegorical speech comparing our times to those of Solon and Pisistratus in the Greek and those of Sulla in the Roman history'.[147] This demonstration

144. *HG*, pp. 132, 149, 161; the letter 'G' used to be discernible above Mungo's initial on one of the pillars: Haldane, 'Notes', i. 288.

145. See above, p. 116.

146. Cf. J. Cairns, 'Importing our lawyers from Holland' in G. Simpson (ed.), *Scotland and the Low Countries, 1124–1994* (East Linton, 1996), pp. 36–53.

147. R.R. Sedgwick, 'Haldane, Patrick (1683–1769), of Bearcrofts', *Hist. Parl.: House of Commons 1715–54*; B. Williams & C.H. Stuart, *The Whig Supremacy, 1714–1760* (2nd edn, Oxford, 1962), p.164; Cambridge Univ. Lib., Cholmondeley (Houghton) MSS, A. Corbière to H. Walpole, 27 April 1716, cited by Sedgwick, 'Haldane, Patrick (1683–1769), of Bearcrofts'.

that Patrick's tenure of the chair of Greek at St Andrews had not been a total charade elicited from John Snell, the Tory member for Gloucester, the observation that 'he did not wonder that a gentleman, who had given up the liberties of his own country in order to sit here, was now ready to give up those of England too'.[148] Scottish members were outraged, and Mr Snell was obliged to apologize to the House. It was to be the last time that Patrick would enjoy the unqualified support of his countrymen.

In the summer of 1716, while finding time to win a lively election for the provostship of St Andrews, he exchanged his membership of the commission of the Equivalent for that of a new commission, established in the aftermath of the late rebellion, to value and dispose of the estates forfeited by convicted Jacobites. Whereas his previous post had carried an annual salary of £500, his new remuneration was to be £1,000 a year, but he was to pay dearly for the difference. Since neither of the other two Scots on the commission, the impoverished Henry Cunningham of Boquhan and Robert Munro of Foulis, was a lawyer, it was Patrick to whom his colleagues turned when seeking to negotiate the maze of the Scots legal system,[149] and his were the shoulders that had to bear most of the resentment felt in Scotland for the activities of the commission.

Patrick was offended by the compliance of the Court of Session in allowing forfeited estates to pass under the control of spurious creditors, often of the culprits' kin, who appointed factors similarly affiliated, who in turn acted for the benefit of the forfeited persons.[150] 'It is very observable,' he complained, 'that only in Scotland all the obstructions that could be thought on have been thrown in the commissioners' way to render their commission ineffectual.... And a prejudice is taken

---

148. Cambridge U.L., *loc. cit.*, cited by S. Matthews, 'Snell, John (1682–1726), of Lower Guiting', *Hist. Parl.: House of Commons 1715–54*; *The Correspondence of the Rev. Robert Wodrow*, ed. T.M. M'Crie (3 vols, Edinburgh, 1842–3), ii. 165, where the speaker is wrongly called 'Mr Haldane of Gleneagles', thus misleading Gen. Haldane into attributing Patrick's speech to his father: *HG*, p. 123.

149. HMC, *Cal. Stuart Papers*, ii. 231, 260.

150. P. Haldane, *The Case of the Forfeited Estates in Scotland* (2nd edn, London, 1718), pp. 4–8, 14–16, 24–6.

against them by some people who don't like this commission, because it tends to suppress a Jacobite interest.'[151] Patrick's conviction that Scottish Jacobitism was more dangerous than English led him, in February 1718, to oppose a petition from the wives and widows of attainted Scots, asking that their jointures be granted after their decease to their children, whereas he had supported a similar petition from ladies south of the border.[152] In Patrick's view, the king's clemency 'hath tended to render the rebels more confident of their own strength, and consequently more obstinate enemies to the government; insomuch that that degree of tenderness ... is really become unsafe'; should the king 'think any of the forfeiting persons deserving of his favour', care should be taken 'that what is bestow'd on them be given only for their subsistence, or during pleasure, which may be afterwards encreas'd, according as they shall be found by their future behaviour to deserve it; and that in such a manner as to put it out of their power to have so great an influence in the country as formerly, lest some of them ... should be tempted ... to rebel again.'[153] Although, in June 1717, Patrick helped frame the necessary parliamentary bills to allow the countess of Southesk her jointure and restore to Lady Nairne the estate she had brought to her husband,[154] his reputation for severity was largely deserved and earned him a host of enemies, not only among Jacobites but also among their loyalist friends and relations, and politicians who thought that future peace was more likely to be assured by reconciliation. A not unsympathetic commentator was to observe that 'there are few instances of more general odium against any man, he being execrated by Whigs and Tories, Episcopalians and Presbyterians'.[155] His brother Mungo once reminded him how he had advocated a less uncompromising zeal in the execution of his duties: 'Peter, Peter, often have I told you your behaviour to the unfortunate families would stick to you like Burgundy pitch-plaster.'[156]

151. Ibid., p. 34.
152. *Cal. Stuart Papers*, vi. 106.
153. Haldane, *Forfeited Estates*, pp. 38–9.
154. *Journals of the House of Commons* (1803), xviii. 579, 587.
155. J. Ramsay of Ochtertyre (1736–1814), *Scotland and Scotsmen in the Eighteenth Century*, ed. A. Allardyce (2 vols, Edinburgh, 1888), ii. 480.
156. Ibid., ii. 483.

John Ramsay of Ochtertyre considered that Patrick 'thought he should recommend himself to the administration by the exhuberance of his zeal', and that, 'perhaps contrary to his inclination, he took a more active part in seizing estates and rejecting claims than a good-natured man would have wished'.[157] That may have been the case, but it is also possible that Patrick acted as he did because he thought it was right to do so. After all, he was not alone in condemning the way the Court of Session had allowed attainted rebels to save their estates by the manipulation of fictitious debt. His father's attitude was much the same,[158] and both may have been influenced by the lord justice-clerk, Adam Cockburn of Ormiston. John Haldane had sat with Ormiston in the last Scottish parliament, worked closely with him in the boardroom of the Scottish Company, and in 1721 was to marry his daughter Margaret to the lawyer's younger son. Since 1700, Ormiston's elder son had been married to a daughter of the earl of Hyndford, whose wife was Patrick's aunt, and who had offered his patronage in 1704 to try to secure Patrick a regency at Glasgow University.[159] Adam Cockburn's legal career had prospered greatly after the revolution of 1689. He was considered 'a bigot to a fault, and hardly in common charity with any man out of the verge of Presbytery, but otherwise a very fine gentleman in his person and manners; just in his dealings, [and] hath good sense'. His reputation as a member of the commission appointed in 1695 to enquire into the Glencoe massacre, and his zeal in detecting disaffection with the revolutionary settlement, earned him such opprobrium that, when cardplayers referred to the nine of diamonds, a card mysteriously known as 'the curse of Scotland', they called it 'the justice-clerk'. As this unpopularity had not slowed its subject's promotion to the bench of the Court of Session, Patrick may not have minded when 'Peter Haldane', in its turn, came to be synonymous with 'the curse of Scotland'.[160] Indeed, it may

---

157. Ibid., ii. 480.
158. *HG*, p. 336.
159. Above, pp. 115, 116.
160. J. Macky, *Memoirs of the Secret Services* (London, 1733), pp. 224–5; G. Brunton & D. Haig, *An Historical Account of the Senators of the College of Justice* (Edinburgh, 1832), pp. 478–80; D.J. Patrick, 'Cockburn, Adam, of Ormiston, Lord Ormiston', *ODNB* (2004–14).

be that Patrick sought to model his own career on that of his father's old colleague.

Patrick's ambition to become a lord of Session was almost comically manifested when he heard of the death of Lord Minto in May 1718; he immediately left London for Edinburgh, 'thinking to be preferred to his lordship's gown, which missing [he] is now on his return'.[161] A condition for elevation to the bench of Scotland's supreme civil court was five years' practice as an advocate, and Patrick had only been called in 1715.[162] It is to be hoped that he was enlightened in his remarkable ignorance before he could embarrass himself in Edinburgh. When the next vacancy occurred, on the death of Sir John Lauder of Fountainhall in September 1721, five years and eight months had elapsed since Patrick had been admitted to the faculty of advocates.

In 1721, both the faculty and the Court of Session mirrored the acrimonious rivalry in contemporary Scottish politics between the Argathelians and the Squadrone. The former took their name from the latinized version of Argyll, whose duke was their leader, and sought to accommodate Jacobites rather than alienate them. The Squadrone, who looked for leadership to the secretary of state, the duke of Roxburghe, while occasionally jealous of Scottish rights, saw a close integration with England as the surest way to secure the Protestant succession in Scotland. Patrick's father, like his patron Montrose, had been associated with the Squadrone from its inception in the prelude to union, and Patrick followed in his footsteps. Its principal agent in the legal world was the lord advocate, and dean of the faculty, Robert Dundas of Arniston. In opposition to him, and in close association with the duke of Argyll, was the lord advocate-depute, Duncan Forbes, brother of the laird of Culloden.

Into this cockpit strode Patrick Haldane, when Roxburghe and Montrose persuaded the king to nominate him for the vacant seat in the Court of Session. A horrified Duncan Forbes told his brother on 19 December 1721 that 'we are frightened out of our witts here that Peter

161. HMC, *Fifth Report on MSS in Various Collections* (1909), p. 263.
162. Minto's successor was Sir Walter Pringle of Newhall, an advocate of thirty-one years' standing: Brunton & Haig, *Senators*, p. 496.

Haldane will be made lord of Session in place of Fountainhall'; he fore-saw a decisive shift in favour of the Squadrone in the balance between the political factions on the bench, with the duke of Argyll needing to 'look to his own interest, ... which will be mortally wounded, if not killed quite dead, by such a judge'.[163] The agile and able Forbes set about masterminding a campaign to stop Haldane, whose own champion, the hard-drinking Robert Dundas, soon found himself marginalized in the faculty of advocates of which he was dean. In the Court of Session itself, Patrick's membership of the commission for forfeited estates weighed against him, not because of excessive zeal in the persecution of Jacobites, but because the commissioners were seen by many lords of Session, especially by the lord president, Sir Hew Dalrymple, as rivals, challenging their own position as 'trustees of the property of Scotland' by forming a 'new judicatory with a parliamentary power, from whence there's no appeal'.[164]

The first line of attack by Patrick's opponents was to question his qualification for promotion. Although five years had passed since his admission as advocate, the faculty complained that his attendance at the Westminster parliament had left only thirty months for actual practice at the Scottish bar. The lords of Session duly found that he could not be admitted, whereupon Lord Advocate Dundas appealed to the House of Lords, in itself a controversial move, since nothing in the Treaty of Union gave the Lords appellate jurisdiction over the Scottish court. The lords of Session regretfully informed the king of the ineligibility of his nominee, and Patrick's supporters confidently awaited the royal reaction. The duke of Montrose reported that 'the king looks upon his prerogative as struck at, and, as all his ministers take it in this view, they have all the just resentment that one could wish against such as have blowen the coall upon this occasion'.[165] George I duly insisted on his prerogative; the Court played for time; on 12 February 1723, the judgment arrived from the House of Lords granting the lord advocate's

---

163. *Culloden Papers* (London, 1815), p. 75; Argyll's immediate interest concerned a disputed provost's election in Inverness.
164. Ibid., p. 147; *Cal. Stuart Papers*, vi. 106.
165. NRS, GD220/5/838, no. 8: Montrose to Gorthie, 15–16 January 1722.

appeal and ordering that Patrick be put 'upon his trial' (the examination of his legal knowledge which was the preliminary to his accession to the bench).

His critics now excavated legislation from 1579 and 1592 which provided 'that, when any vacancy happens in the Court of Session, the king shall present and nominate a man that fears God, of good literature, practice, judgment, and understanding of the laws, of good fame, having sufficient living of his own, &c, who shall be first sufficiently try'd by the ordinary lords of Session; and, in case the person presented by the king's majesty be not found so qualify'd by them, . . . it shall be lawful for the said lords to refuse the person presented to them'.[166] The lord president 'was sorry to find himself obliged to say that Mr Haldane's fame and character were bad'.[167] Numerous witnesses were collected, many of them Jacobites and most depending on hearsay, to support allegations that Patrick was a secret supporter of the Pretender, whose health he had frequently knelt to drink, that he had sung bawdy songs to the tunes of psalms, that he had been guilty of bribery and false imprisonment of voters during his election as member of parliament for Perth Burghs in 1715 and as provost of St Andrews in 1716. These allegations Patrick flatly denied in every particular and produced witnesses of his own to challenge them, but was unwise to argue that, even had he used 'trifles' as bribes, 'there are too few men of good name, or fame, remaining in Britain if such transactions as these be thought sufficient to defame'.[168]

It may be thought unlikely that Patrick's antagonists should have chosen to attack his character had there been no grounds for so doing, but the neatness with which allegations of sedition, blasphemy, and bribery fitted the statutory conditions for unfitness renders them suspicious, and it is worth noting that, in February 1723, when the *Edinburgh Evening Courant* reported of Patrick's trial: 'We do not hear of any great discoveries yet made to his prejudice', the Edinburgh magistrates seized

166. Anon., *The Case of Mr Patrick Haldane, Advocate: with Some Remarks upon his Defence* ([Edinburgh], 1723), pp. 3–4.
167. *HG*, p. 140.
168. *The Case of Patrick Haldane*, pp. 33–4.

all copies of the issue.[169] At a distance of three centuries it is impossible to untangle the truth from evidence which left contemporaries divided. In any case, his adversaries were simply playing for time. Developments in London, not Edinburgh, would decide the composition of the Court of Session, and Duncan Forbes, who was orchestrating the campaign against Patrick in the southern capital, had grounds for feeling that time was on his side. The death, in 1722, of the earl of Sunderland had removed the most powerful obstacle to the rise of Sir Robert Walpole. Walpole had no reason to favour Patrick Haldane, who had taunted him with inconsistency in 1716, in a display of sarcasm which the great man is unlikely to have forgotten.[170] Of greater significance, however, was the fact that Roxburghe and the Squadrone had allied themselves with Walpole's rivals: first with Sunderland, and then with his protégé Lord Carteret. When Carteret was disgraced in April 1724, Walpole, now supreme, turned to Argyll as his partner in the management of Scotland.

Put to the vote, Patrick's candidacy for the bench was approved by a majority of two, but that majority included the votes of two extraordinary lords of Session, whose right to vote was challenged by the ordinary lords, who had divided seven to six against him. The challenge was referred to London, where the king dismissed it, but Walpole stressed the destabilizing potential of Patrick's unpopularity in Scotland. The king, who took Patrick's reverse as a personal affront, offered him the consolation prize of membership of the commission of excise in England, which carried a salary of £800 a year, £300 more than that of a lord of Session; on 30 May 1724, under pressure 'to make peace with my opposers', Patrick accepted. Four days later, Fountainhall's seat in the Court of Session was granted to Andrew Fletcher of Milton, an intimate of Argyll's brother, the earl of Islay.[171] The following

---

169. Chambers, *Domestic Annals of Scotland*, iii. 439; J. Finlay, 'Advocacy, patronage, and character at the eighteenth century Scots bar', *The Legal History Review*, lxxiv (2006), 104.

170. R. Wodrow, *Analecta* (4 vols, Maitland Club, 1842–3), iii. 144; cf. 155; *HG*, pp. 145–6.

171. *HG*, pp. 146, 154; W. Sliford, *The Court-Register & Statesman's Remembrancer* (London, 1733), pp. 173–4; for a detailed account of the various stages of Patrick's trial, and how the Court of Session divided,

year, Patrick's champion, Robert Dundas, fell victim to Walpole's axe, after opposing the extension of the malt tax to Scotland, and was replaced as lord advocate by Argyll's client, and Patrick's principal adversary, Duncan Forbes.[172] It did not take long for Patrick to read the runes: in 1726, when another vacancy appeared on the Session's bench, 'Mr Peter Haddin has changed hands, and is gone into the duke of Argyle'.[173] His candidature, however, never got off the ground.

Nevertheless, Patrick's approach to the Argathelians was taken seriously by the duke's brother, Lord Islay, whose influence moderated Sir Robert Walpole's antipathy. Unfortunately, the removal of one obstacle to advancement was balanced by the acquisition of another. Patrick had somehow managed to offend the prince of Wales, who succeeded his father as king in June 1727. Of the nine commissioners of excise, Patrick was alone in failing to have his appointment renewed by George II. Early in 1728, Islay persuaded Walpole to suggest that a vacancy in the separate commission for customs and excise be filled by Haldane, but the new king's response was discouraging: he ordered the minister 'to tell Peter that he, nor no such rascall, ever shou'd have any imployment from him'. According to the correspondent who reported this news to Duncan Forbes, 'on this ... Peter has walked for Scotland, with an intent to sacrifyse the remainder of his days for the good of the country in a private way'.[174]

Patrick had married in 1720. His bride was Margaret Forrester, a sister of the fifth Lord Forrester, and granddaughter of a sometime lord of

see R. Scott, 'The politics and administration of Scotland, 1725–1748' (Edinburgh Univ., Ph.D. thesis, 1981), pp. 219–59.

172. R. Scott, 'Dundas, Robert, Lord Arniston', and J.S. Shaw, 'Forbes, Duncan', *ODNB* (2004–14); Ferguson, *Scotland: 1689 to the Present*, p. 142.

173. Wodrow, *Analecta*, iii. 290; the vacancy was caused by the death of Sir Francis Grant of Cullen on 26 March, and filled by Sir Gilbert Elliot of Minto on 4 June 1726: Brunton & Haig, *Senators*, pp. 489, 500.

174. Sliford, *Court-Register*, p. 174; *Culloden Papers*, p. 136 (the undated letter is placed in 1728 by its mention of the appointment of Gwynn Vaughan, who was listed as commissioner on 19 July 1728, and by Patrick's own statement in a letter of 1750 that he had resided in Scotland for the last 22 years: Sliford, *Court-Register*, p. 168; *HG*, p. 154).

Session and dean of the faculty of advocates; her brother moved in circles firmly supportive of Patrick, appointing as guardians for his children in his will of 1723 not only Patrick but also the dukes of Montrose and Roxburghe, and Robert Dundas the lord advocate.[175] By their marriage contract of 5 August 1720 Patrick received a tocher of 10,000 merks Scots, but bound himself to find £20,000 sterling for the purchase of lands for himself and the heirs male of the marriage, and to provide Margaret with an annuity of £200, secured on the said lands, should she survive him, as well as a dower house or £30 a year in lieu. That month, Patrick bought the barony of Bearcrofts in Falkirk parish, some seven miles south-east of the Forrester estate of Torwoodhead (now lost in Grangemouth), and Wester Saltcoats in nearby Polmont.[176] Command of such funds was the product of his assiduous attendance at Westminster: in the heady spring of 1720, the South Sea Company selected members of parliament whose goodwill was judged to be worth having and credited them with stock which they might 'sell' back to the company at a future date, taking any increase in the market price as 'profit'. Patrick was among the recipients of these barely concealed bribes, being credited with £2,000 on 23 March; on 30 May, he was listed as borrowing from the company £11,500 against £3,800 stock (which never seems to have been transferred as security); his allocation had been made when £100 stock was selling at £285; in June it was selling at £745; in July at £1,000. Then, the bubble burst. We can only conjecture that Patrick sold in time, for there is no paper trail, but a hostile pamphlet in 1723 attributed the improvement in Mr Haldane's fortune to 'the transactions of the year 1720'.[177]

Patrick's marriage contract was sealed in the house of his bride's brother-in-law, William Stirling of Herbertshire, who had married Lilias

175. *Complete Peerage*, v. 558; her maternal grandfather was Sir Andrew Birnie of Saline, who was culled from the bench of Session at the accession of William and Mary: Brunton & Haig, *Senators*, pp. 407–8; for the will of George, fifth Lord Forrester, see TNA, PROB 11/618/164.
176. NRS, GD86/858 (Sir William Fraser Charters); *HG*, pp. 337–8.
177. *Commons Journals*, xix. 569, 575; *Case of Patrick Haldane*, p. 23; W.A. Speck & M. Kilburn, 'Promoters of the South Sea Bubble', Themes, *ODNB* (2004–14).

Forrester in 1718. In the years to come, Patrick was occasionally to be found staying at Herbertshire, in Dunipace on the river Carron, no more than eight miles west of Bearcrofts. The two brothers-in-law combined in a business venture in 1735, and, in 1740, were partners in the purchase of a wood in Dunipace from the widow of the fifth Lord Forrester, while they shared the tack of her dower estate of Torwoodhead, including the farm at Carbrook, which (as we have seen) Patrick leased to Neill McKinnon.[178] The lairds of Bearcrofts and Herbertshire had married into a family of absentee landlords, and cooperated to exploit the legitimate opportunities willingly offered by their in-laws.[179]

Such exploitation was necessary for Patrick, since his annual income had been reduced by £1,000 in 1725, when the commission of inquiry into the forfeited estates was wound up, and by a further £800 in 1727, when George I's death terminated his commission of excise in England. Confronted by the new king's hostility, in 1728 he returned to Scotland to resume his practice at the bar. His unpopularity with a large section of the landed class was a damaging handicap, but he did have a lucrative practice as an election lawyer.[180] He managed to edge into the authorities' favour, in 1735 being appointed an assessor to whom the Edinburgh magistrates would turn for advice, being made a lord advocate-depute in

178. NRS, GD38/1/869 (Dalgaise Muniments); GD86/886, 909; GD220/5/1458 (Montrose Muniments); Fraser, *Stirlings of Keir*, p. 176; above, p. 121.

179. Their brother-in-law, the fifth Lord Forrester, was a colonel in the Horse Guards, who, when not on active service, seems to have spent more time on his wife's estates in Oxfordshire and Middlesex than on his own in Scotland, before dying in France in 1727, leaving a three-year-old heir (whose guardians included both Patrick and William Stirling); his widow became a lady of the bedchamber to the princess royal, who married the prince of Orange in 1734, and she died in Holland in 1743; his son, the sixth lord, served in the Royal Navy, was given his own command in 1744, showed initial promise, but was cashiered for habitual drunkenness two years later, and died in Middlesex in 1748 at the age of twenty-four; the seventh lord, a cousin, died in Wiltshire in 1763: *Complete Peerage*, v. 558–9; anon., *Lives of Illustrious Seamen* (London, 1803), p. 146.

180. Ramsay, *Scotland & Scotsmen*, pp. 482–3.

1737, and solicitor to the board of excise in Scotland in 1741. In 1740, he thought it worthwhile to buy a house in the fashionable James's Court off the Lawnmarket.[181]

It was not perhaps Patrick's finest hour, when, on 16 September 1745, he refused to advise the lord provost, who wanted to know from his assessor if it would be treason to read a letter from the Young Pretender, then at the city gates at the head of an army of some 3,000 men, while Edinburgh's volunteer force had dwindled, that morning, from 400 to 42. Patrick said 'it was a matter of too high a nature for him, and therefore he would give no advice upon it', whereupon he walked out, leaving the beleaguered provost to exclaim: 'Good God, I am deserted by my arms, and by my assessors!'.[182] In fairness to Patrick, it must be noted that he was the only assessor who had not fled the city, and the provost's subsidiary questions, asking 'if read, whether [the letter] should be answered, and what answer should be given' were more political than legal, patently seeking to share a responsibility that, unluckily, was his alone. The following day, the rebels entered the city, and Patrick left it. He is next heard of on 17 January 1746, as an eyewitness to the battle of Falkirk, when the Jacobite army passed through the Forrester lands of Torwoodhead, whose tower house may have been his temporary base, on its way to defeat government forces on the hilly ground to the south.[183]

Patrick's account of the battle was sent to his brother Mungo at Gleneagles, which had been in the path of the rebels on their way south in 1745, but seems to have suffered no more than the pillage of stored meal.[184] After Falkirk, the direction of the government's suppression of the rebellion was entrusted to the duke of Cumberland, under whom Patrick's son George (his exact contemporary, both having been born in

181. *HG*, p. 147, 153, 338.
182. *The Trial of Archibald Stewart, Esq; Late Lord Provost of Edinburgh* (Edinburgh, 1747), pp. 58, 113, 166–7, 175–6; J. Gilhooley, 'The Edinburgh Local Defence Volunteers of 1745', *Edinburgh History Magazine*, i (1989), 4–7.
183. *HG*, pp. 149–52.
184. NRS, GD220/5/1632 (Montrose Muniments).

1721) had served in June 1745 at Fontenoy, where he had been wounded and also gained the duke's 'high favour'. After recuperating at Gleneagles, he won further plaudits during the pursuit of the rebels to their ultimate defeat at Culloden on 16 April 1746.[185] A month before Culloden, Patrick had been appointed joint-solicitor-general for Scotland, evidence that, whatever accusations of Jacobitism had been cast at him in the early 1720s, they were not shared by a government under pressure in 1746. Later that year, at the suggestion of the duke of Cumberland (doubless primed by George), he was also made sheriff-depute of Perthshire. In that capacity he examined captured rebels and interrogated witnesses.[186] He must have felt some awkwardness when, in 1747, he was required to serve as advocate-depute in the prosecution of Edinburgh's late provost for dereliction of duty in surrendering the capital,[187] but he could at least reflect that his circumspection had not excluded him from preferment.

Patrick's propensity to antagonize those whom it would have been better to cultivate, however, had not deserted him, and he seems to have passed it on to his son. For some time before the general election of 1747, he had been establishing an interest for George in the constituency of Stirling Burghs, courting the hammermen and tailors, threatening a hostile postmaster with dismissal, and even going to the remarkable length for a lawyer of waiving his fee for work done for Stirling itself, in recognition of which he was given the freedom of the burgh on the eve of the election.[188] For years, the predominant influence in this particularly venal constituency had been that of the dukes of Argyll, usually closely allied to the Whig administration in London. In 1741, however, the mercurial second duke had fallen out with Walpole, and an opposition member was returned for Stirling Burghs. Two years later, that duke was succeeded by his brother, who had never wavered in his loyalty to the government, but whose uncertainty of his ability to influence the election of 1747 was such that he refused to appear in Scotland until it

185. *HG*, pp. 160–1; Ramsay, *Scotland & Scotsmen*, ii. 484 n.
186. *Chron. Atholl & Tullibardine*, iii. 211; *HG*, p. 153; Perth & Kinross Council Archives, B59/30/72, nos. 1, 6–7, 10.
187. *Trial of Archibald Stewart*, p. 23.
188. *HG*, p.153; Sunter, *Patronage and Politics in Scotland 1707–1832*, pp. 39, 48.

was over.[189] Patrick must have sensed an opportunity to further his son's career and at the same time win the gratitude of the government, which, in 1747, was controlled by Henry Pelham and his brother, the duke of Newcastle, and George stood as a candidate in the Whig interest.

In the event, however, the third duke decided to put up an alternative government candidate, and, as both Pelhams looked to him for the management of Scotland, his nominee had their support. Patrick told Henry Pelham that he had not learnt of Argyll's recommendation until too late, adding that the chances of the duke's candidate were anyway 'hopeless', since he had never visited or corresponded with any of the burghs. Pelham remonstrated, but Patrick would not consider George's withdrawal. His son, back in Flanders, where he fought at Roucoux and Lauffeld, obtained election leave from the duke of Cumberland and appeared in London, where he had an audience of the prince of Wales at Leicester House, but failed to call upon Pelham before continuing his journey north. He won the election, but his father felt it necessary to apologize to Pelham, both for his victory and for his negligent behaviour in London, assuring him of the new member's loyalty to Argyll and himself, and promising that he would be 'as zealous to support his majesty's servants as any member of the House'. The assurance is unlikely to have impressed Pelham: zealous supporters of George II's ministers did not pay court to his estranged son at Leicester House, which was a magnet for disappointed place-seekers and a medley of opposition figures.[190] The name of George Haldane, in fact, was included in a list drawn up by the prince of Wales in 1750 of 'particular friends' whose presence in parliament was to be ensured at the general election which would be triggered by his father's death.[191] It was not the king, however, but the prince who died, in March 1751.

189. A. Murdoch, 'Campbell, Archibald, third duke of Argyll (1682–1761)', *ODNB*.

190. E. Haden-Guest, 'Haldane, George (1722–59)', *Hist. Parl.: House of Commons 1715–54*; E. Cruickshanks, 'Stirling Burghs', *Hist. Parl.: Constituences 1715–54*.

191. Haden-Guest, 'Haldane, George (1722–59)'; cf. Williams & Stuart, *Whig Supremacy*, p. 339.

George's confidence that Pelham's brother, the duke of Newcastle, would overlook his association with the opposition, and be the agent of his preferment, appears to have been unshakeable, despite evidence to the contrary. When he solicited the duke's influence, late in 1747, to obtain leave to purchase a company in the Guards, he was passed over in favour of 'a person in every shape extremely deserving, tho' a much younger officer than myself'; when, in 1750, two years after the peace of Aix-la-Chapelle, he pointed out to the duke that circumstances were hardly propitious for him to see much return on the £3,000 he had so far spent on his commissions, and asked for a military governorship in Ireland, or, failing that, the governorship of Pendennis castle, he was refused. In the general election of 1754, the Haldanes spent a great deal of money preparing to oppose ministerial candidates in three constituencies: George's uncle Robert stood (unsuccessfully) against the duke of Argyll's client in Stirlingshire, while George contested both Stirling and Perth Burghs. He retained Stirling Burghs in a spiteful campaign, losing in one constituent burgh (Inverkeithing, largely owing to the bad impression left by his assault on the provost, to whom he had given a black eye in 1752), but winning another, Queensferry, by such persuasive expenditure that the magistrates announced, before the vote, that 'as the members of this town council are already resolved upon Colonel George Haldane as the gentleman they propose should represent them in the next Parliament, they make this public intimation that such as are concerned in knowing it may save trouble and expense to themselves, as the council is determined to admit of no further solicitations or potherings on that head'. Perth Burghs he contested 'for no other reason', thought Argyll, 'than to distress Administration'. George hoped, in negotiating his withdrawal from Perth Burghs, to earn Newcastle's gratitude, but what he and Robert actually achieved, at extortionate expense, was the inexorable hostility of the duke of Argyll, whom Newcastle was loath to offend. Hence, George was again refused in June 1755, when he asked Newcastle for the place on the commission of police which had been vacated by the death of his uncle Mungo and which had been held by a Haldane since the commission's inception; two months later, his request to be included in the household of the young prince of Wales, or else to be given a post attached to the Scottish exchequer, was ignored;

in September of the same year, hearing that new regiments of foot were about to be raised, he begged the duke to use his 'great situation' (he had succeeded his brother as first lord of the treasury in 1754) to secure him preferment and so 'prevent injustice being done to those who have the honour to be reckon'd among the number of your friends', but it became clear that injustice was, nevertheless, to be done; despite his support for subsidy treaties with Russia and Hesse-Cassel, the year ended with his failure to be made commissary to the Russian troops, or a member of the board of ordnance. His desperation expressed itself in the barely polite hope that 'your grace will ... have some consideration for your friends as well as for many that are not so'. His grace would have consideration for those who could offer something in return, other than upsetting the duke of Argyll, but when George asked him 'if I have done anything that could possibly offend your grace', the duke blandly assured him of his 'kind intentions'.[192]

The Commons journals show George to have been an assiduous workhorse during his 10½ years in the House: serving on the committee of privileges, reporting on the state of highways in Scotland, preparing bills to improve harbours south as well as north of the border, identifying and making recommendations about laws which had expired or were nearing expiry.[193] It was remembered that, 'though no orator, [he] was well heard in the House'.[194] He was reported to have been 'one of the warmest' of the pro-government speakers at the opening of the 1751 session, but other performances reflected his links with the opposition. In March 1751, he 'talked high for inquiries' into the administration of General Philip Anstruther, who was accused of corruption as lieutenant-governor of Minorca.[195] Here he may also have been grinding an axe of

192. E. Haden-Guest, 'Haldane, George (1722–59)', *Hist. Parl.: House of Commons 1754–1790*, ed. L Namier & J. Brooke (1964); for George's letters, see *HG*, pp. 161–9; for his campaign in Stirling Burghs in 1754, see Sunter, *Patronage and Politics*, pp. 31–5; *London Evening Post*, 26–9 January 1754, issue 4090.

193. *Commons Journals*, xxvi. 5, 416–17, 511–2, 860, &c; xxvii. 463, 596, &c.

194. Ramsay, *Scotland & Scotsmen*, ii. 484 n.

195. H. Walpole, *Memoirs of the Reign of King George the Second*, ed. Lord Holland (London, 1846), i. 57.

his father's. Thirty-three years previously, before George had been born, Patrick had entered a crowded coffee-house, seen the then Colonel Anstruther, tapped him on the shoulder 'in a familiar, friendly way', and the following exchange had taken place.

> *Haldane*: 'Dear Phill, how comes it that you and I, who were once so great comrads, are now lyke to wear out of acquaintance?'

> *Anstruther*: 'Faith, Hadden, the reason is very plain: when we were first acquaint, I took you for ane honest man, but now that you are knowen to be a rascall, and the greatest villan of mankind, it needs not be thought strange that I look down on you, but rather a wonder that any man of honour or honesty converses with you.'

> *Haldane*: 'That is, colonel, language not to be borne.'

> *Anstruther*: 'By God, it is true tho.'

> *Haldane*: 'I will take another time to resent such treatment.'

Whereupon, Anstruther gave the address of his lodging and said that he would await Haldane's commands. None came, and Haldane was seen to have been outfaced.[196] It would, of course, have been rash for the lawyer to have challenged the professional soldier, but the humiliation must have rankled, and George's loyalty to his father was such that the opportunity to avenge him would have weighed more heavily than any advantage to be expected by toeing the government line.

In speaking against the treaty buying Saxony's alliance with a subsidy of £32,000 in 1752, George was attaching his wagon to the rising star of William Pitt and assuredly displeasing Newcastle, whose scheme the subsidy was.[197] In following Henry Fox by opposing the Marriage Act of 1753, George may have been prompted by Fox's friend, the duke of Cumberland; his motive is unlikely to have been personal conviction,

196. *More Culloden Papers*, ed. D. Warrand (2 vols, Inverness, 1925), ii. 186–7.
197. Haden-Guest, 'Haldane, George', *Hist. Parl.: House of Commons 1715–54*; cf. Williams & Stuart, *Whig Supremacy*, p. 344 & n.

since the provisions of the Act did not extend to Scotland, and the bill had been drawn up and championed by Lord Chancellor Hardwicke, whose influence did, as George was fully aware. In 1750, his father had written to Hardwicke, seeking nomination for a vacancy which had opened on the bench of Session. It was an inept letter, expecting an energetic, reforming chancellor to promote its writer because 'I am now somewhat advanced in years, and not so well able as I have been to undergo the fatigues of the barr'; nor could Patrick resist complaining of his exclusion from the bench, thirty years earlier, 'for no other reason that I have ever yet heard sudgested' but that of diligence as a commissioner for the forfeited estates. George was similarly unable to avoid the reference when asking the same chancellor, shortly before the general election of 1754, to recommend Patrick for a place in the court of the exchequer.[198] Both solicitations proved fruitless, and it may be wondered if either father or son was aware of the close friendship and mutual respect which had existed between Hardwicke and Duncan Forbes, the prime mover against Patrick's elevation to the bench in the 1720s.[199]

While trying to exploit his apparent personal rapport with Newcastle, and, at the same time, maintain his connections in opposition circles, George was in danger of falling between two or more stools, but, during the political merry-go-round of 1757, his luck changed. After barely five months of office, Pitt was dismissed in April 1757 and set about orchestrating a manifestation of public support, in which George had an opportunity to offer his service: he used his influence to obtain for Pitt the freedom of the guild merchants of Stirling. It is questionable how much Pitt, in fact, owed to such demonstrations, but he did not forget those who delivered them. On 29 June, a coalition was formed, with Newcastle as first lord of the treasury and Pitt as secretary of state. By 14 August, rumour had spread that, in return for services rendered to the new secretary, George Haldane was to be governor of Jamaica. On

198. Haden-Guest, 'Haldane, George', *HG*, pp. 153–5.
199. Williams & Stuart, *Whig Supremacy*, p. 274.

27 January 1758, his appointment was gazetted, together with his promotion to colonel.[200]

Meanwhile, his father's powers were fading. Although John Ramsay saw Patrick take 'a very active part' at a Michaelmas head court at Stirling in 1753, when he 'was perfectly master of the business', he also witnessed appearances in crown causes between 1752 and 1755, which 'conveyed no high idea of his abilities, his pleadings bespeaking neither eloquence nor vigour of mind'.[201] The lord president, Robert Dundas, told Hardwicke in 1753 that Patrick was 'quite daised, as we express it', and no longer pulling his weight as a solicitor-general and lord advocate-depute.[202] Five years earlier, at a meeting on shire business at Moncrieff, the 'naturally distant and reserved' joint-deputy king's remembrancer, David Moncrieff of Moredun (in Gilmerton), was accosted by an inebriated Patrick, who, by his prey's account (related to the duke of Atholl), 'said many abusive things about all the gentlemen, me in particular, not even sparing his grace the duke of Argyle; but, as he was mortally drunk, I told him we should discuss that point at Edinburgh; so I left him, and came to town. As soon as he arrived, I asked him if he remembered what he had said at Moncrieffe; ... [he said] that he did not, for he was mortally drunk. I said I was glad of it, and should take no further notice of it. But, the infamous fellow continued in all companies to say that the lord privy seal, the deputy remembrancer, the comptroller at Alloa, and collector of Kircaldie ought to be complained of to the king for leading a disaffected party in Perthshire.... On Saturday last, I took him aside in the Parliament House, and told him that I was confounded to find he had expressed himself in the above manner, as we were as well affected

200. *The Yale Edition of Horace Walpole's Correspondence*, ed. W.S. Lewis (48 vols, New Haven, 1937–83), xxxvii. 497 & n. 9; P. Langford, 'William Pitt and public opinion', *Eng. Hist. Rev.*, lxxxviii (1973), 61; idem, *A Polite and Commercial People: England 1727–1783* (Oxford, 1989), p. 226; *HG*, pp. 168–9

201. Ramsay, *Scotland & Scotsmen*, ii. 483 & n. 2.

202. Sedgwick, 'Haldane, Patrick', *Hist. Parl.*; P.C. Yorke, *The Life and Correspondence of Philip Yorke, Earl of Hardwicke* (3 vols, Cambridge, 1913), i. 621–2.

to the government as he was, and most of us had given more proof of our loyalty than he had done.... He later that day came up and said I had been finding fault with him for what he had said, but (said he) "I do say that the lord privy seal (and so on) do join with a disaffected partie", so I answered: "If you do say so, you tell a damn'd, malicious, calumnious lie," folded my fist, and told him: "You old dog, nothing but the place we are in protects you from being used as you deserve". He roared out to get me gone, so that the whole Parliament House were alarmed.'[203] The sad picture is presented of a bitter, disappointed man, aware that his early promise had been unfulfilled, 'tired of knocking at preferment's door', and occasionally seeking solace in a bottle.[204]

In April 1755, Patrick resigned his office of solicitor-general and was granted an annual pension of £400 'by his majesty's bounty'.[205] A little over a month later, on 1 June, his brother Mungo died, and he became laird of Gleneagles. He had been a widower since 1747 at the latest,[206] perhaps for many years before that, and his domestic life was presumably shared by his daughter Margaret. In 1758, however, she set out to join her brother in Jamaica and assume the role of governor's lady, for George was a bachelor, although he had a mistress who had borne him two sons.[207] Upon a lucrative gubernatorial term depended the financial health of his house. Unfortunately, expectation of future profits led George to amass new debts on top of those incurred through the family's prodigality during the general election of 1754. The notion of squaring his expenditure to his income was foreign to George, of whom it

203. *Chron. Atholl & Tullibardine*, iii. 385; G. Seton, *The House of Moncrieff* (Edinburgh, 1890), p. 64.
204. Matthew Arnold, *The Scholar-Gipsy*, line 35. For reference to Patrick's early promise, see Ramsay, *Scotland & Scotsmen*, ii. 479.
205. *HG*, p. 155; CC8/8/123, test. 1776, Haldane, Patrick.
206. *HG*, p. 159.
207. John, who entered the service of the East India Co., and died in the wreck of his ship the *Nancy* off the Scilly Isles in 1784; Henry, born in London in 1756, served in the Royal Engineers in the American war of independence, then in India, followed by many years of poor health and poverty in England and Dunkirk, supporting a wife and seventeen children, before dying in 1825: *HG*, pp. 177–82.

was said that 'his luxury exceeded all bounds'.[208] However, it may at least be surmised that deep gambling played no part in his extravagance: a record survives from 1752 of 'George Haldane at Bearcrofts' challenging Walter Little of Liberton to a curling match 'for the sum of £24 Scots [£2 sterling], to be eaten and drunk whenever they please', which envisaged a lavish dinner, but was not the wager of a heavy gambler.[209]

To live in Jamaica, however, *was* a gamble. George's uncle, Lieutenant-Colonel James Haldane, had succumbed to fever on the island in September 1742, after a residence of barely a year, while Henry Cunningham, one of Patrick's fellow Scots on the commission for forfeited estates, had arrived as governor on 18 December 1735 and died two months later.[210] George was some twenty-four years younger than Cunningham had been, but he knew that his age was no defence against the diseases that awaited visitors to Jamaica: his cousin Adam Cockburn had died there in 1747 in his twenty-second year.[211] Anticipating his appointment, in 1757 he transferred to his father the lands which had been settled on him by his uncle Mungo, in consideration of which Patrick provided funds to help satisfy his son's creditors and equip him for his new situation.[212]

On 9 May 1758, George resigned his seat in parliament and, the same day, was given the brevet rank of brigadier-general, with instructions to participate in an expedition against French possessions in the Caribbean prior to taking up his post. As his ambitions were primarily military, he must have relished his involvement in the capture of Guadeloupe, before he made landfall in Jamaica in April 1759.[213] The Creole planters,

208. Ramsay, *Scotland & Scotsmen*, ii. 484 n. 1.
209. NRS, GD122/3/17 (Liberton Papers).
210. *HG*, pp. 193–4; E. Cruickshanks, 'Cunningham, Henry (c. 1677–1736) of Boquhan', *Hist. Parl.: House of Commons 1715–54*.
211. *HG*, p. 297.
212. GD198/180–3; *HG*, p. 169.
213. *HG*, pp. 170–2. George's furniture, stores, and coach had arrived in Jamaica some four months in advance: *London Evening Post*, 6–9 January 1759, issue 4864.

who were 'much displeased' with having a Scot for their ruler,[214] were soon given a measure of his style: the cost of his four-day welcoming entertainment, which was to be met from the island's revenue, was £716 18s. The first Act passed by the house of assembly during George's rule doubled his salary of £2,500 and provided £12,000 for the purchase of a fully stocked estate for his use.[215] No one, however, questioned the energy and ability which he devoted to his duties, and he rapidly established a reputation for 'wise, prudent, and impartial administration'.[216] He set about inspecting the island's fortifications, extending the provision of common gaols, improving transport, and reviewing the standards of the clergy.[217] On 20 July, he wrote to London on the subject of Jamaica's defences, but apologized that sickness had prevented him from drawing up 'an exact state of the fortifications'. The sickness was probably yellow fever, and, six days later, he was dead.[218]

The personal tragedy for Patrick was also a financial catastrophe. When he heard that the principal proprietors of the colony were proposing to make a handsome present to George's sister, he hoped 'that this present will go towards relieving the family estate of its great debts incurred in providing for the late governor'.[219] It was the vain hope of a desperate man. With no other realistic solution to his financial plight, and now without a son to inherit his patrimony, Patrick decided to sell Gleneagles. His decision was eased, and may have been prompted, by the presence of a potential buyer within the family. His half-brother Robert had made a fortune in the naval service of the East India Company, and his hunger for land had not been assuaged by his purchase, first of Plean, and recently of Airthrey, both near Stirling. On 26 January 1760, the legal

---

214. Brit. Lib., Add. MS 30,001, fos. 4–7: Mary Ricketts to Eliz. Jervis, 23 June 1757. I am grateful to Mr Simon Ricketts for this reference.
215. *HG*, p. 173.
216. *HG*, pp. 175–6.
217. G. Metcalf, *Royal Government and Political Conflict in Jamaica 1729–1783* (London, 1965), pp. 145–9; *HG*, pp. 173–5.
218. *HG*, p. 175.
219. NRS, GD224/1005/1 (Montague-Douglas-Scott Papers: Townshend Corr.).

process was begun whereby the baronies of Gleneagles and Haldane were transferred from Patrick to Robert; it was completed on 4 April.[220]

By the rule of male primogeniture, which had governed the descent of Gleneagles since the fourteenth century, Patrick's heir would have been Captain James Haldane, the son of his eldest half-brother, the late Colonel James Haldane. It was perhaps on his behalf that Patrick sought to reclaim Lanrick for the senior Haldane line, after the death on 28 December 1764 of John Haldane, the last male representative of the Lanrick family. An inveterate Jacobite, John, together with his elder son Alexander, had participated in the rebellion of 1745–46, and, before fleeing to France, endeavoured to protect his property from forfeiture by transferring its title to his second son Patrick, while reserving the liferent to himself. This was precisely the sort of strategem that the commissioner for forfeited estates had been determined to thwart after the rebellion of 1715. John duly returned from France when he judged it safe to do so; in 1757, his son Patrick transferred Lanrick to his six sisters, reserving his father's and his own life interest; in 1761, Patrick died, followed by his elder brother Alexander two years later, and by their father at the end of 1764. At this juncture, Patrick Haldane late of Gleneagles retained Henry Dundas, the son of his old ally Robert Dundas of Arniston, and now setting out on his brilliant legal and political career, to argue that, on the failure of Lanrick's male line, the estate ought to revert to the heirs of Mungo (I) of Gleneagles. On 17 December 1765, however, Lord Auchinleck found that the disposition made in 1757 in favour of the six sisters had been within the legal power of their brother; Patrick appealed the following year, but in vain.[221] The sisters sold Lanrick to Sir John Murray Macgregor for about £14,000.[222]

On 14 April 1765, Patrick's daughter Margaret married Charles Barclay-Maitland, brother of the earl of Lauderdale, and laird of Tillicoultry, a property on the southern side of the Ochils which had

220. GD198/185–8.
221. D. Dalrymple, *Decisions of the Lords of Council & Session, 1766–91*, i. 170–1; H. Dundas, *Unto the Rt. Hon. The Lords of Council & Session, the Petition of Mr Patrick Haldane, Advocate* (Edinburgh, 1766), pp. 2–6, 9–14, 18–30.
222. *HG*, p. 286.

come to him with his first wife. Margaret died childless within three years of marriage,[223] whereupon Patrick went to live with Mr William Bennet, minister of Duddingston, and an old friend who had been entrusted with his son George's education. The occasions already found to remark upon Patrick's propensity to make enemies should be balanced by evidence of his ability to maintain long friendships; apart from that with Mr Bennet, his friendship with Lady Jane Douglas lasted from 1720 until her death in 1753, while Patrick Spark served him as his first clerk for forty years and was nominated with Mr Bennet as an executor of his will.[224]

On 9 August 1768, 'considering that I am now in the eighty-fifth year of my age, and, altho' I be in health of body and soundness of mind, yet the period of life being extremely uncertain at the said age', Patrick drew up his last will and testament. On 10 January 1769, he died. He had spent his final years at Duddingston 'with comfort, in the company of a sensible, worthy man, forgetting and forgotten by the political world'.[225] He asked to be buried, not at Gleneagles, where his successor Robert Haldane had been buried twelve months earlier, but at Duddingston in the family vault of his neighbour Sir Alexander Dick of Prestonfield. There, in the cemetery, a marble obelisk was erected by his grandson, George's illegitimate son John, in memory of 'one of the best parents and worthiest of men'.[226] As John is unlikely to have been out of his teens when his grandfather died, this encomium must reflect the sentiments of his father and reminds us that, for all the animosity he was capable of arousing, Patrick retained the loyalty and respect of those who knew him best.

223. *HG*, p. 159.
224. W. Fraser, *The Douglas Book* (4 vols, Edinburgh, 1885), ii. 482, 490; *HG*, p. 156; CC8/8/123, test. 1776, Haldane, Patrick.
225. Ramsay, *Scotland & Scotsmen*, ii. 484–5.
226. *HG*, pp. 157, 178. The fifteen-foot-high monument is described in *The Public Advertiser*, 1 November 1788; it was sculpted by the Falkirk mason, Walter Gowans, at a cost of £200, bequeathed for the purpose by John Haldane, who died in 1784 in a shipwreck depicted in bas relief on the obelisk.

East India captain and Entailer: Robert Haldane, 1760–68

The youngest of Union Jack's children by his second marriage, Robert Haldane had been baptized in the family chapel at Gleneagles on 18 March 1705, when two days old. Fifty-five years later, he returned as laird, having outlived his four elder full brothers, and commanding greater financial resources than either of their surviving sons. Robert (born *c*.1723), the son of John Haldane (1693–1726), was beginning to receive significant prize money as a captain in the Royal Navy, thanks to the outbreak of the Seven Years' War in 1756, but he had a happy-go-lucky disposition which made him an unlikely saviour of his family's ancestral estate. In 1754, for example, when about thirty years of age, he had sent a begging letter to his great-uncle, Patrick Campbell of Monzie, in which he cheerfully signalled the use to which a loan might be put: 'Ever since I have been in town, the devil take me if I know how the time has slipt away; what with love, what with company, claret, and other diversions, I'm almost fallen in to the same scrape as Mr John Carstairs, that went out to ask his own name.'[227] Robert's gallantry and seamanship in action off the south-east coast of India in 1760 fully atoned for having run his ship aground in Plymouth Sound in 1748, but his health was poor, and he died in August 1761. Meanwhile, James (b.1728), the son of Colonel James Haldane (*c*.1692–1742), had by 1760 benefited from the financial privileges of a captain for only one voyage in the maritime service of the Honourable East India Company.[228]

His uncle Robert had entered the same service at an early age. A combination of fine seamanship and signal business acumen brought him success. He received his first command when appointed captain of the 498-ton *Haselingfield* at the end of 1742, and his prospects were sufficiently bright for him to have been accepted in marriage on 28 September of that year by Elizabeth Holmes, widow of a captain in the Royal Navy, and sister of Sir John Oglander, Bt, of Nunwell in the

227. The Campbell of Monzie Papers, Univ. of Guelph Lib., Archival Collctions: www.electronicscotland.net/canada/library11.htm.
228. For the careers of Capt. Robert, RN, and Capt. James, HEIC, see *HG*, pp. 184–7, 197, and below, p. 196.

Isle of Wight and Parnham in Dorset. She was possessed of land and securities worth £4,400 'and upwards', which her possibly nervous brother insisted be converted into a trust fund.[229] The marriage took place in London (Robert's residence being given as in Mortimer Street), and, two months later, Robert set sail for Whampoa, the chief port of Canton. A typhoon in the South China Sea completely dismasted his ship on 12 and 13 September 1743; by cannibalizing the long boat to improvise a foremast, Robert managed to reach the Chinese mainland, where he procured fourteen tow-boats to bring him into Whampoa on 8 November. The ship's owners showed their appreciation of his achievement by presenting him with a silver-gilt salver weighing nearly 200 ounces, and he showed his pride by commissioning a series of punchbowls commemorating the event. Between 1746 and 1755, Robert commanded the 499-ton *Prince Edward* on three voyages to India, Java, and China, each taking about two years.[230] The captain of an Eastindiaman received a salary of £10 a month, plus a negotiable percentage of a voyage's profit, but his main source of income derived from the privilege of carrying, as 'private trade', a sixteenth of the tonnage of his vessel. Shrewdly exploited, this liberty could make a captain's fortune.

Captain Robert Haldane proved to be shrewd. By 1751, he had bought the barony of Plean, south-east of Stirling.[231] In spring 1753, using Plean as security, he managed to borrow £2,300 of his wife's trust money, probably to finance his own trading activities; he was certainly anxious that his lawyer, the fashionable and expensive Alexander Hume Campbell, 'settle' the transaction the evening before he was due to set sail for Bombay and the Malabar Coast, the voyage perhaps being that

229. Isle of Wight R.O., OG/I/11 (Articles made on the marriage of Mr Robert Haldane mariner with Mrs Elizabeth Holmes widow); *HG*, p. 293.

230. *HG*, pp. 293–4; Brit. Lib., IOR/L/MAR/B573 (*Prince Edward* paybook & ledger, transcribed in Haldane, 'Notes', i. 229–32); J. Sutton, *Lords of the East: The East India Company and its Ships (1600–1874)* (2nd edn, London, 1981), pp. 162–8.

231. For the date, see Haldane, 'Notes', ii. 373, citing the seating allotment in the new church of St Ninian's, in Stirling Record Off.

on which he was rumoured to have made £70,000.[232] In 1759, he bought the barony of Airthrey, centred about 6½ miles north of Plean.[233] The following year, as we have seen, he made the substantial purchase from his half-brother Patrick of the baronies of Gleneagles and Haldane, to which lands in Trinity Gask were to be added in 1766.[234]

Robert's ambition was to use his wealth, not only to establish himself as a landowner, but also to launch a parliamentary career. In 1753, on the eve of setting sail for India, he entered his name as a candidate for Stirlingshire in the forthcoming general election in opposition to a client of the duke of Argyll. In February, he was reported to be on the point of resigning command of his ship to his nephew James, but business considerations led to a change of mind, and he sailed in April. The absentee candidate was defeated, but on his return, in July 1755, he prepared a petition to unseat his opponent. His nephew George Haldane, successfully re-elected for Stirling Burghs, tried to persuade the duke of Newcastle to use his influence with Argyll to bring Robert into Parliament as soon as a Scottish burghs seat fell vacant, in return for which favour Robert would drop his petition. Newcastle, however, seems to have shared the opinion of his late brother, Henry Pelham, who had found 'none of this country [i.e. Scotland] who call themselves Whigs so obnoxious as this India captain'; no deal was done, and the petition was abandoned. Nevertheless, when George Haldane accepted the governorship of Jamaica in 1758, he was succeeded in Stirling Burghs by his uncle Robert, and 'nobody was prepared to offer their service in opposition to him.'[235]

232. Isle of Wight R.O., OG/I/11 (Oglander muniments); *HG*, p. 297; for Hume Campbell, see E. Haden-Guest, 'Hume Campbell, Hon. Alexander (1708–60)', *Hist. Parl., 1715–54.*
233. *HG*, p. 296.
234. NRS, GD198/185–8, 230; above, pp. 145–6.
235. E. Haden-Guest, 'Haldane, Robert (1705–67) of Plean and Airthrey', *Hist. Parl., House of Commons 1754–90*, citing Brit. Lib., Add. 32860, fos. 78, 262, 486 (transcribed in Haldane, 'Notes', ii. 498–9); E. Cruickshanks, 'Stirling Burghs', *Hist. Parl., House of Commons 1715–54.* Robert's considered transfer of command of the *Prince Edward* is recorded in the *London Evening Post*, 20–22 February 1753, issue 3450.

When the next general election fell due, in 1761, Robert had increased his territorial presence within Stirlingshire, and extended it to Perthshire and Dunbartonshire. Moreover, before owning an acre in Scotland, he had acquired an interest south of the border through the connections of his wife, Elizabeth Oglander, whose brother owned some 8,000 acres in the Isle of Wight, Somerset, and west Dorset. Robert adopted a scatter-gun approach in his campaign to secure re-election in 1761: he contested not only Stirling Burghs but also Perth Burghs, Perthshire, Dunbartonshire, and Bridport in west Dorset.

The constituency of Stirling Burghs, comprising Stirling itself, Dunfermline, Inverkeithing, Queensferry, and Culross, was notorious for the expense required to nurse it. Various interests exerted pressure on burgh voters, competing to control the individual councils, each of which chose a delegate to vote at the returning burgh – a procedure in which provosts might play a decisive role. Reasonably confident of the strength of his position in Culross and Dunfermline, Robert sought to secure Inverkeithing by becoming its provost himself in 1760 and seeking re-election in that office in 1761 against Admiral Holborn, who was also his parliamentary opponent. Robert's campaign was managed by his nephew, George Cockburn, and, like Holburn's, involved a mixture of bribery and violence. Holburn, for example, took upon himself the payment of one voter's debt of £140, while the shoemakers' corporation was wooed by the Haldane camp with a commitment to buy £300 worth of footwear. Where bribery was deemed insufficient, the candidates resorted to physical coercion, with Holburn using the press-gang to intimidate voters, and Haldane mobilizing tenants and staff from Gleneagles to ride into the burgh armed with sticks and oak saplings. Both parties used the threat of kidnap during the period of actual voting.[236]

236. W. Stephens, *The History of Inverkeithing and Rosyth* (Aberdeen, 1921), p. 224; *HG*, pp. 295–6; E. Haden-Guest, 'Stirling Burghs', ibid., 1754–90; Sunter, *Patronage and Politics in Scotland*, pp. 165–7; *Petition of Robert Haldane, Esqre, Provost of the Burgh of Innerkeithing, to the Lords of Council & Session* (6 March 1761; at Gleneagles).

The admiral won the municipal vote (although it was declared so irregular that it was annulled), whereupon Robert transferred his supporters in the parliamentary election to another candidate, and contested Perthshire. He had already withdrawn from Perth Burghs, and, on the day before the election, he withdrew from Perthshire too. Here he had hoped to take advantage of the division which had opened in the Atholl camp, as the duke proposed to replace the sitting member, his half-brother Lord John Murray, with his son-in-law John Murray of Strowan. The night before the election, however, Lord John instructed his supporters to vote for Strowan, 'upon which Mr Haldane's friends went away, and did not vote'.[237] Robert was more optimistic about his chances of being returned for Bridport, where he would have been encouraged to stand by his brother-in-law, Sir John Oglander. Sir John's future son-in-law, the Tory Sir Gerard Napier, was certain to be returned for one of the borough's two seats, since the Whigs had already decided that 'it would be imprudent to oppose him' as 'he is just come into vast circumstances'. Robert's opponent, however, was a member of Lord Coventry's family, which had represented the borough for several generations, and he repelled the Scottish newcomer.[238] Meanwhile, it became apparent that, two days before his return as member for Dunbartonshire, John Campbell of Mamore had succeeded to the dukedom of Argyll, whereupon Robert Haldane promptly announced his candidature for the vacant seat. On 23 April, he asked the secretary of state for the north, Lord Bute, for support, claiming that 'our family interest is not inconsiderable'. Inconsiderable or not, as far as any duke of Argyll was concerned it was undesirable, and the new duke arranged for a nephew's succession as member for Dunbartonshire, explaining to Bute that, 'as Mr Haldane has been in the country with a view of offering his service, I thought no time was to be lost, by taking some measures to secure it for the interest of our families'.[239] Robert now concentrated on a petition to reverse the

---

237. E. Haden-Guest, 'Perthshire', *Hist. Parl., H. of Commons 1754–90*.
238. M.M. Drummond, 'Sir Gerard Napier (1739–65) of Crichell More', *Hist. Parl., H. of Commons 1754–90*. A debt of £197 'anent Mr R. Haldane's election for Bridport' remained unpaid at his death: NRS, CS96/3914, p. 9.
239. E. Haden-Guest, 'Dunbartonshire', *Hist. Parl., H. of Commons 1754–90*.

Bridport result, but, on 2 March 1762, it was rejected, and, having 'gone all round the compass', as Horace Walpole quizzed, his search for a seat had been in vain.[240]

The lure of a parliamentary seat, however, remained strong, and Robert continued to nurse both Bridport and Stirling Burghs in preparation for the general election due in 1768. In the Scottish constituency, he enjoyed the assistance of a plutocrat whose influence was to have a decisive bearing on the history of Gleneagles. Sir Lawrence Dundas, whose baronetcy was acquired in 1762, had grown rich as commissary to the army in Scotland, a position obtained through the favour of the duke of Cumberland, whose troops he had supplied during the suppression of the 1745 rebellion. He became friendly with another member of Cumberland's circle, George Haldane, whom he helped win Stirling Burghs in 1747. It was perhaps George who introduced Dundas to his uncle Robert, who received his support in his failed campaign in Stirlingshire in 1754. Much of Dundas's fortune, which had become colossal during the Seven Years' War, when he received contracts on a vast scale, was invested in East India Company stock and ships, so that an acquaintance between him and Captain Robert Haldane would have been mutually satisfactory. They also shared an antipathy to the duke of Argyll. Whatever its basis, a rapport undoubtedly existed between the two men: when Robert sat for his portrait by Reynolds, he ordered two pictures, one of which passed to his Haldane successors, the other to the descendants of Lawrence Dundas. Just as his pockets were deeper, so was Dundas's ambition higher than Robert's. He aimed at the creation of his own parliamentary interest, and, by 1767, when his property portfolio included large estates in Stirlingshire, Fife, Orkney, Shetland, Yorkshire, and Hertfordshire, with great houses in St Andrew Square, Edinburgh, and Arlington Street, London, he controlled eight or nine members of parliament. As part of his plan to enlarge that group, in 1761 he tried to advance Robert's bid to overturn the Bridport result by securing the support of Lord Shelburne (to whom he had made a substantial loan),

240. Eadem, 'Haldane, Robert', *Hist. Parl., H. of Commons 1754–90*.

and he also lavished expenditure in promotion of Haldane's interest in Stirling Burghs in anticipation of the 1768 election.[241]

In May 1766, the ties that bound Haldane and Dundas became tighter, with the marriage of Robert's nephew, George Cockburn, son of his sister Margaret, to Sir Lawrence's niece, Bethia Dundas. She brought a tocher of £3,000, while Robert, after borrowing £2,500 of that tocher, settled £5,000 on the bridegroom, payable on the first Whitsun or Martinmas after his death, and secured upon the lands of Gleneagles.[242] Precisely one month after this alliance had been sealed, Robert entailed the baronies of Gleneagles and Haldane upon George Cockburn and the heirs male of his body. Should Cockburn's male line fail, the entail would open, in turn, to the sons of Robert's sister Helen; that is, to Colonel Alexander Duncan, younger of Lundie, and his male heirs, and, in the event of their failure, to his younger brother, Captain Adam Duncan, RN, and his male heirs. Only if they failed would the succession to Gleneagles devolve to the male line of Captain James Haldane, the son of Robert's deceased elder brother Colonel James Haldane.[243] Since

241. Eadem, 'Dundas, Sir Lawrence, 1st Bart. (c.1710–81)'; 'Haldane, Robert', *Hist. Parl., H. of Commons 1754–90*. A mezzotint of Robert Haldane by C. Clint was taken from the portrait in the possession of Dundas's son in 1805. Reynolds's bill to Robert (£52 10s.) was paid by George Cockburn in April 1768: NRS, CS96/3914.

242. NRS, GD65/216–17 (Dundas of Fingask); W.M. Morrison, *The Decisions of the Court of Session*, xviii (Edinburgh, 1804), App., part i, no. 10 (pp. 21–5). Also in May, Lawrence bought Bethia's brother Thomas a commission in the Dragoon Guards; it is likely that he also underwrote Bethia's tocher, as her father, Lawrence's elder brother, was financially dependent upon him: Mrs Dundas of Carronhall, *Dundas of Fingask: Some Memorials of the Family* (Edinburgh, 1891), pp. 57–9, 61. For the loan of most of the tocher to Robert see Lord Haldane's petition to the Court of Session, 19 Dec., 1812, p. 2 (at Gleneagles).

243. Two copies of the Deed of Tailzie, one contemporary, the other mid nineteenth century, are preserved at Gleneagles; abbreviations are found in *Memoranda relating to the Family of Haldane of Gleneagles* (priv. printed, London, 1880), pp. 18–19; Haldane, 'Notes', i. 349–50 (transcription from 'Register of Deeds' [Mackenzie], cciv, part 1, 18 August 1768). The sons of

Robert's stated motive behind the 'deed of tailzie' was 'for the support and continuation of my name and family', some explanation must be sought for his relegation to the last reversionary interest of the only nephew who would not have to change his name in order to meet that condition, and, indeed, who would be the senior male representative of the family once Patrick Haldane, late of Gleneagles, had died.

Robert's relationship with George Cockburn was a good one (Cockburn had been his election agent in Inverkeithing in 1761, and he had granted him the liferent of certain lands in the baronies of Gleneagles and Haldane as soon as he had bought the lairdship),[244] but there was no ill will between Robert and James, nor had there been between Robert and James's father. In April 1742, having accompanied the colonel to Portsmouth prior to his return to his regiment in Jamaica, Robert promised to take care of his fourteen-year-old son and signed a joint bond assuring the boy's mother of an annuity of £100. The colonel's will, drawn up in Jamaica three months later, made Robert executor in trust for his son, 'knowing well the good use he will make of the trust'.[245] It was almost certainly through Robert's good offices that James was brought into the East India Company after reaching a lieutenant's rank in the Royal Navy; he was serving as his uncle's fourth mate on board the *Prince Edward* in February 1753, when Robert was reported to be about to resign command to him, presumably in order to concentrate on a political career; Robert in fact deferred his resignation until the next voyage, when, in 1757, he did indeed hand the *Prince Edward* over to his nephew.[246] When he drew up his own will in January 1766, James bequeathed £500 to his uncle Robert 'as a small testimony of my gratitude for the favour and protection he has always shown me'.[247] According to James's grandson Alexander Haldane (1800–82), it was 'well known

Robert's other older brother, John (d.1726), had both died unmarried – Robert in 1761 and David in 1753: *HG*, p. 187.

244. NRS, GD198/237–8, 244–6.
245. TNA, PROB 11/743/333 (transcribed in Haldane, 'Notes', i. 5–9).
246. Brit. Lib., IOR/L/MAR/753C (transcribed in 'Notes', i. 231–2); *London Evening Post*, 20–22 February 1753, issue 3950.
247. TNA, PROB 11/941/139; *HG*, p. 199.

that Robert Haldane introduced Captain James at the county balls in Perthshire and Stirlingshire as his heir not only to Airthrey but also to Gleneagles'.[248]

Two explanations for the Entailer's change of mind circulated within the Haldane family. One, that Captain James was averse to a residence on the northern side of the Ochils,[249] is hardly compelling, requiring an heir to decline an inheritance embracing thousands of ancestral acres spread over three shires, because the principal messuage faced the wrong way. An alternative theory, entertained by Alexander Haldane, was that Robert's mind was altered by Sir Lawrence Dundas, who was thought to have argued that, since Robert had 'with his own money purchased the family property from Patrick, his elder brother by his father's first marriage, to leave it back again to the son of another brother by the first marriage, past the children of his full sister' was 'not fair'.[250] The flaw in this theory is that James's father was not the youngest son of John Haldane's first marriage, but the eldest son of his second, and thus Robert's full brother. This is stated in the genealogy written in mid eighteenth-century script, and pasted onto the stretcher of Aikman's portrait of Union Jack, giving his year of birth as 1692, seven years after the death of John's first wife, and a date confirmed by a legal deposition of 1730 stating his age as 'about 38'. The identity of Colonel James's full siblings appears to be confirmed by his will, drawn up during the lifetime of both Mungo the laird and Patrick the younger of Gleneagles (sons of the first marriage), but mentioning neither, making Robert executor and trustee, and requiring him, not the laird, to supervise the testator's burial at Gleneagles, 'the vault of my ancestors'.[251] If Dundas had used the reasoning attributed to him, Robert would surely have indicated his error.[252]

248. *HG*, p. 198.
249. Haldane, *Memoirs of Robert & James Alexander Haldane*, p. 8.
250. *HG*, p. 198.
251. TNA, PROB 11/743/333; C24/1469 ('Notes', i. 5–9; ii. 381).
252. Nevertheless, it was an error which remained current among James's descendants, until someone looked on the back of Union Jack's portrait in the 1920s: Haldane, 'Notes', ii. 536a-537; *HG*, p. 188.

It is hard to resist the conclusion that what changed Robert's mind was the marriage of his nephew George Cockburn to Bethia Dundas, and that the man who helped change it was indeed Bethia's uncle, as Alexander Haldane believed, but the wrong words were put into his mouth. Not only was Robert in Dundas's debt for the generosity of his political favours, and doubtless eager to secure them for the future, but he was also deeply in his debt financially: between December 1763 and the month of Cockburn's marriage in 1766, he had borrowed from 'the nabob of the north' no less than £10,000 (at 5 per cent interest), followed by £500 in November 1767, all of which remained outstanding at his death.[253] Explicit evidence is lacking, but it is not unlikely that Sir Lawrence was taking over a loan of £10,000 which had been made to Robert in 1756 by Charles Townshend. With his property portfolio at that time limited to Plean, Robert had offered as security the estate of his brother-in-law Alexander Duncan of Lundie, and consideration of this major financial favour may have played a part in Robert's decision to give his Duncan nephews the second and third interests in the entail.[254] It seems certain that the reversal of James Haldane's position in the line of succession to Gleneagles had more to do with his uncle's indebtedness than his own supposed lack of interest.

At the end of his life, Robert was in debt but not insolvent. He had been obliged to dispose of Plean, and his will, drawn up on the same day as the entail (9 June 1766), provided for the sale both of the Airthrey estate to pay £14,000 worth of debt and of recently acquired ground in Trinity Gask to meet any remaining obligations. His total liability, when he died eighteen months later, appears to have been £33,625, which included £7,500 owed to his heir, George Cockburn. Moneys owed to him amounted to no more than £1,627 10s., but the sale of the unentailed estates of Gask and Airthrey, plus his personal estate of at least £4,000, should have met all his creditors' demands.[255]

---

253. NRS, CS96/3914 ('State of affairs of the deceased Robert Haldane, Esquire of Gleneagles, 1796').

254. NRS, GD224/85 (Papers of Montague-Douglas-Scott).

255. CC6/5/29, test. 1784, Haldane, Robert; Lord Duncan's petition to the Lords of Council & Session, 19 December 1812, pp. 2–3; 'Memorial for Lord Viscount Duncan, January 1801' (at Gleneagles), pp. 6–7.

Robert and his wife divided their time, during his last years, between Gleneagles ('our summer quarters') and Airthrey. Between 1759 and 1767, having 'conceived to himself the fashionable modern fancy of beautifying his place in an elegant manner', he spent an estimated £2,000 in laying out the park at Airthrey and constructing a wide new public road outside it, to replace the narrow lanes which intersected his ground and passed close to the door of his house, and which he obtained authority to close. Here, at 'his little paradise', in a house filled with evidence of nearly a lifetime's connection with India and the Far East, he signed both his will and the entail in 1766, and here he died, in his sixty-second year, in the early hours of New Year's Day, 1768, leaving instructions for his burial at Gleneagles.[256] His widow, Elizabeth Oglander, was left an annuity of £400 and a life interest in the house of Airthrey, which would be cancelled should she choose to reside elsewhere. Robert may have expected her to return to her own family south of the border, but she evidently liked Airthrey, for it was there that she died, in straitened circumstances, in 1779.[257] Creditors forced a public roup (auction) of her horses, cattle, household furniture, jewellery, and books. As a poignant reminder of past prosperity, 'an old post chaise' was sold to pay the bill of an Edinburgh coachmaker, whose rent for its 'stance' in his yard was outstanding. Among the jewels were mourning rings of Elizabeth's father, Sir William Oglander, and aunt, Ann Strode, but apparently nothing with a Haldane connection. It is, of course, not possible to judge how

256. H. Dundas, *Unto the Rt. Hon. The Lords of Council & Session, the Petition of Mungo Haldane, Esq: General-accomptant of the Excise-office, London; Lieutenant-colonel Alexander Duncan, Younger of Lundie; and Captain Adam Duncan of his Majesty's Navy, Disponees of the Lands and Estate of Airthery, in Trust for Behoof of Robert Haldane, Eldest Son of the deceased Captain James Haldane* (Edinburgh, 1770), pp. 2–3, 5, 7, 10, 31. Robert's reference to Gleneagles as 'our summer quarters' is in a letter of 17 June 1766 among the Oglander papers at Nunwell, seen by Sir Aylmer Haldane in 1937. Robert's date of death is variously given as 31 December 1767 or 1 January 1768.

257. Mackenzie, Register of Deeds, cciv, part 1, 18 August 1768; transcribed in Haldane, 'Notes', i. 350.

much the books reflected her interests as distinct from her husband's. Forty-one volumes were listed in the inventory, of which thirty were theological (including fourteen volumes of sermons) and four historical. An account of a sensational trial for incest and murder (*Katharine Nairn's Trial*, Edinburgh, 1765), containing witnesses' testimony of the most intimate kind, suggests that its reader was not easily shocked, while it is to be hoped that only someone with a sense of humour would possess Jane Collier's *Essay on the Art of Tormenting* (London, 1753) – advice on how to nag, 'with some general instructions for plaguing all your acquaintance'. We may but speculate who bought for whom *The Government of the Tongue*, written by the author of *The Whole Duty of Man*.[258]

258. CC6/5/28, test. 1780, Oglander, Elizabeth.

V

Gleneagles Without Haldanes

Folly and fraud: George (Cockburn) Haldane, 1768–1799

George Cockburn, or rather George Haldane, as he was known after his succession in accordance with the terms of the entail, was the elder surviving son of Charles Cockburn of Sandybeg. A small property on the Scottish Tyne, Sandybeg had been carved out of the barony of Ormiston as an appanage for Charles, the younger son of Adam Cockburn of Ormiston, the lord justice-clerk and lord of session who had been a business colleague of George's other grandfather, Union Jack Haldane. Ormiston had been held by George's paternal ancestors since 1368 and, under the regime of Adam and his elder son John, became the object of bold experiments in agricultural improvement. John not only extended his father's policy of granting long leases at low rents, but also initiated manufacturing enterprises, and rebuilt both his house and the adjacent village. The capital outlay, however, coupled with the inevitable delay before his improvements bore financial fruit, had proved unsustainable; between 1747 and 1749, encumbered with a debt of £10,000, the barony of Ormiston was sold to John's creditor, the earl of Hopetoun. The head of the family after John's death in 1758, his English-based son and George's cousin, Captain George Cockburn, RN, married the sister and eventual heir of the all but landless sixth Lord Forrester, who had drunk himself to death in 1748 at the age of twenty-four, after being cashiered from the navy for habitual intoxication. Since that marriage produced no male heir, Gleneagles's new laird may have considered himself unlucky not to have arrived as the younger of Ormiston. As it was, he came as the scion of a poverty-stricken family, his tiny patrimony of Sandybeg being the sole remnant in Cockburn hands of its ancient barony, and that he soon sold.[1]

The collapse in the fortunes of the Cockburns of Ormiston, which took place when George was in his late teens, may have contributed to the feelings of insecurity suggested by the pretensions he displayed when laird of Gleneagles. At some time in the 1770s, he attempted to revive, in his own person, the Haldane claim to the earldom of Lennox, but progressed no further in this futile and foolish enterprise than persuading Sir Lawrence Dundas to urge his client Alexander Wedderburn of Westerhall, solicitor-general and future Lord Chancellor, to give it moral support. Perthshire neighbours, who dubbed him 'monarch of the glen', doubted that he expected his claim to be taken seriously, but considered that his vanity was served by the public reminder that the baron of Gleneagles had once possessed a legitimate claim to an ancient earldom.[2] The exercise, however, earned him widespread and long-lasting ridicule; in 1782, when he joined the county committee to support the establishment of a militia in Scotland, the *Public Advertiser* slid into heavy sarcasm: 'The members of the Perth committee are all men of ability and attached to the interest and happiness of their native country. Some of them I know to be so, particularly Mr Haldane of Gleneagles, who some years ago was claimant to the title of earl of Lennox. When men of such character and worth take the lead in matters of so much

1.   T.H. Cockburn-Hood, *The House of Cockburn of that Ilk* (Edinburgh, 1888), p. 156; R. & H.A. Cockburn, *The Records of the Cockburn Family* (London, 1913), pp. 132–6; J. Colville (ed.), *Letters of John Cockburn of Ormiston to his Gardener, 1727–1744* (Scot. Hist. Soc., xlv, 1904), pp. xvii, xliii; R.H. Campbell, 'John Cockburn of Ormiston', *ODNB*; R.S. Lea, 'Cockburn, John, (c.1679–1758) of Ormiston', *Hist. Parl., 1715–54*; D. Wilkinson, 'Cockburn, John, (c.1679–1758) of Ormiston', *Hist. Parl., 1690–1715*; above, pp. 115, 127, 134 & n. 179.
2.   *Memoranda relating to the Family of Haldane of Gleneagles* (priv. pr., 1880), pp. 34–7; cf. J. Brook, 'Wedderburn, Alexander (1733–1805)', *Hist. Parl., 1754–90*; E. Haden-Guest, 'Dundas, Sir Laurence', *Hist. Parl., 1754–90*.

importance, a happy issue may be looked for.'[3] Towards the end of his
life, George made an equally absurd enquiry about the possibility that
he was heir to the Forrester title, despite the lack of a drop of Forrester
blood in his veins.[4] Moreover, his Haldane kinsmen were scandalized by
his assumption of supporters to the Haldane coat of arms, which were
the prerogative of the head of the family.[5] Scottish custom, however,
allowed supporters to the holders of ancient baronies, and, while not the
Haldane chief, George was unquestionably the Gleneagles baron.

An advocate like his father and grandfather, George cannot always
have been an object of scorn. He had evidently impressed both
Lawrence Dundas and Robert Haldane, both men of wide experience. His efficiency and ruthlessness as Robert's election manager in
Inverkeithing in 1761 had been successful, and, between 1768 and 1794,
he worked enthusiastically and effectively on behalf of his father-in-law
in his constituency of Stirlingshire. Although 'not much attached to any
party', he was thought to be 'very desirous of getting into parliament
himself', but never actually contested a seat, although, with the backing
of Sir Lawrence Dundas, he came close to so doing in Dunbartonshire
in 1768, and, in 1789, allowed his name to be mentioned as a possible
candidate for Perthshire.[6]

By his own account, George Haldane's custodianship of the
Gleneagles estate was notable for 'a course of improvements in building,
planting, and inclosing', while an independent observer praised his introduction of sixteen of 'the finest rams' (Spanish, Cheviot, Southdown,
and Ryland), which promised to double the value of the wool-clip in the
glen. He was also the only proprietor in the parish of Blackford to sow
wheat, albeit only for the use of his own household. In 1779, he found
it 'absolutely necessary' to build a new set of offices, and the next year

3. *Public Advertiser*, 29 Nov., 1782, issue 15,135.
4. *HG*, p. 298.
5. Ibid.
6. Sunter, *Patronage & Politics in Scotland*, pp. 90–1; above, p. 151; E. Haden-
    Guest, 'Dunbartonshire', *Hist. Parl., 1754–90*; C.E. Adams (ed.), *View
    of the Political State of Scotland in the Last Century (1788)* (Edinburgh,
    1887), pp. 91, 261, 327; NRS, GD112/39/339, 341.

to make 'an addition to the mansion house'.[7] He also laid out capital on all the farms in the glen and improved the wright's shop, while the date 1776, incised on the lintel of Bargate Cottage, bears surviving evidence of his building-work in the policies of Gleneagles. No evidence survives of George's relations with his tenants, but, as has already been remarked, his neighbours had little respect for him, and two found him downright objectionable. He wanted to tidy Gleneagles's western border with the laird of Abercairny by exchanging some thirty acres, to which his neighbour was perfectly well disposed 'so long as it was consistent with his entail'. However, George's attempt in 1781 to force matters by buying up pieces of contiguous ground and then petitioning the sheriff to enforce an exchange in accordance with the Act to Encourage Improvement, left Abercairny 'in high rage'. Relations did not improve in 1790, when George cut a canal through his neighbour's land at Drumlochie, claiming rights to water which was being used to supply Abercairny's local manufactory.[8] In 1780, George's aggressive assertion of fishing rights on the Earn at Gask elicited the lofty disdain of Oliphant of Gask, who affected respect for his neighbour's 'genteel way of thinking', and sent his underfactor to discuss the matter, 'for, you know, I'm nobody'.[9]

Within the Haldane and Duncan families (the substitute heirs of entail), George's management of his estate earned bitter censure. One solitary achievement could be credited to him. Soon after his succession, he lighted upon the debenture for nearly £4,260 issued by the government in 1722 to claimants for compensation for damage done in Auchterarder and Blackford and their environs by Jacobite rebels in 1716. In 1770, as the most significant claimant both socially and financially, George led his neighbours and tenants in an attempt to prise the money, plus interest, out of the exchequer. The petition for interest was refused, but, by November 1777, George had received the principal sum, which

7. J. Robertson, *General View of the Agriculture in the Southern Districts of the County of Perth* (London, 1794), p. 71; NRS, CS96/3914, p.16; *Statistical Account of Scotland, 1791–99*, iii. 207.
8. NRS, GD24/1/60.
9. T.L.K. Oliphant, *The Jacobite Lairds of Gask* (Grampian Club, 1870), pp. 389–90.

he retained for four years before releasing shares to other claimants, having deducted £499 for his own estate's 'burning losses', £200 for expenses incurred in three journeys to London between 1770 and 1778, and £1,035 for legal costs.[10]

George's management of his predecessor's debt, however, verged upon fraudulent malpractice. The Entailer had provided that trustees, of whom George was one, should pay debts to a limit of £14,000 out of the sale of the estate of Airthrey, whose residue was to be conveyed to Captain James Haldane; anything above £14,000 was to be met from the estate at Trinity Gask, but the entailed baronies of Gleneagles and Haldane were in no way to be alienated or subject to further encumbrances than those they already bore. In 1812, the second Lord Duncan expressed his opinion that the funds left by the Entailer for the discharge of his debts were 'most ample', but had been misapplied by George Haldane for his own benefit.[11] Firstly, there was the matter of Robert's personal estate (reckoned in 1801 to have been worth no less than £4,000), which included the contents of Gleneagles. Although Robert Haldane's will had given George the authority to dispose of his moveable possessions at Gleneagles, such power should not have been exercised until the inventory had been confirmed. Some livestock was auctioned in May 1768 (raising £58), but no evidence survives for the disposal of the remaining stock (valued at £150), nor for the contents of the house (valued at £533 4s.). Sixteen years passed before George thought proper to confirm his uncle's testament, by which time, as a 'memorial' drawn up for the first Lord Duncan politely suggested, 'it may well be supposed many articles intromitted with and disposed of by him must have wholly

10.   Reid, *Annals of Auchterarder*, pp. 161–70; CS96/3914, p. 17.
11.   The following account is based on 'Memorial for Lord Viscount Duncan, January 1801', 'The Petition of Robert Viscount Duncan to the Lords of Council and Session, 19 Dec. 1812' (both at Gleneagles), and NRS, CS96/3914 (a 'State of Affairs' drawn up in 1792 by accountants on George's behalf); see also *HG*, pp. 297–8; E.D. Sandford, *A Treatise on the History and Law of Entails in Scotland* (2nd edn, Edinburgh, 1844), pp. 414–17; W.M. Morison, *The Decisions of the Court of Session*, xviii (Edinburgh, 1804), App., part i, no. 10 (pp. 21–3).

escaped his remembrance'. All the plate, wines, and bed and table linen had slipped out of sight. So had most of Robert's books, for the value of £50 which George put upon them (while claiming that a bookseller had priced them at no more than £22) was probably less than a third of the true worth of Robert's library. That the house was rendered deficient as a gentleman's residence may be surmised from the fact that George did not move into it until 1776, up to which time it had been occupied by a solitary maidservant.[12]

Airthrey had been sold immediately, bought, as the Entailer had clearly intended, by Captain James Haldane, but for more than the stipulated £14,000. After Robert's death, George had met James in London, and, by representing 'the miserable and involved state in which their uncle had left their affairs', induced him to pay £17,000 for the estate, plus £500 for the furniture in the house, and a further £1,000 for a farm acquired by Robert after 1766; payment reached George between March 1768 and August 1771, when the last instalment was made on behalf of James's infant son and heir. Despite this relief, four years after his succession, George had cleared no more than £2,000 worth of the most pressing obligations, many arising from contracts for building-work in progress at the time of Robert's death.

George's failure to alleviate significantly the estate's burden of liability derived not from incompetence but from dishonesty. When, in 1792, he unsuccessfully petitioned the Court of Session to authorize the sale of part of the entailed estate, he sought essentially to show that the funds assigned for the discharge of debt were inadequate. First, he exaggerated the size of that debt, claiming that it amounted to £33,625, a figure reached by including £7,500 due to himself (£5,000 being his marriage settlement payable on his uncle's death, and the rest part of the tocher he had received, and which had been lent to Robert). George borrowed extensively on the security of this £7,500, and it was not until 1802, three years after his death, that the Court of Session declared that the sum was a charge, not upon the entailed estate, but upon Robert Haldane's personal estate; since George had inherited that estate, he had himself

---

12. NRS, CC6/5/29, test. 1784, Haldane, Robert; CS96/3914, pp. 15–16.

inherited the charge. In borrowing against the expectation of that settlement he was, in effect, borrowing against the expectation of a settlement of which he was already the beneficiary.[13] In addition, George not only claimed 'management expenses' of £2,900, as if he had been acting as the factor of the heirs of entail, but also charged against them the £525 he paid in annuities to his own mother. He also considered that he had a legal claim to reimbursement for the improvements he had made at Gleneagles, Aberuthven, and, prior to 1785, at Trinity Gask, in building, planting, and enclosing, whereby he claimed to have considerably increased the rental, but 'at a great advance on his part', which, in 1792, he put at £4,873. In reality, he felled more timber than he planted and, by accepting large premiums ('grassums') for low leases, left the estate under-rented. By exaggerating the debt, he exaggerated the interest payable, while simultaneously understating the estate's rental income. He thus claimed that annual interest of £1,838 had to be met from a rental of £1,100. The figures he used, however, were not comprehensive, and omitted Gask, the true rental being closer to £2,200.

George's most serious deception won him absolute control of the Gask estate for 63 per cent of its value. This he achieved by staging a mock auction in 1785, in which a reserve of £10,000 was based on a fictitious rental of £460. There was only one bid, of £10,500, and the bidder proved to be George's writing clerk, a Mr Fago. No conveyance, however, was made to Mr Fago, and six years later George offered to add £4,000 to the pretended price paid by Fago, and transfer £14,500 to the heirs of entail, provided that they allowed him to sell the estate for his own benefit. They agreed, and he successfully interpreted their agreement as freeing him from any obligation to use his proceeds to help extinguish the Entailer's debts. In the event, the second auction, using a true rental of £715, raised £22,750, enabling George to remove Gask from the heirs of entail and pocket £8,250 at their expense.

George had complained that, upon Robert Haldane's death on New Year's Day 1768, 'his affairs were found to be in a very embarrassed state'. The embarrassment of his own was prodigious, and his bankruptcy

13.　Morison, *Decisions*, xviii, App., part i, p. 22; Sandford, *Treatise*, pp. 416–17.

patent, when he himself died in Edinburgh on 2 March 1799, at the age of sixty-nine. By a warrant of the Dunblane commissariat, a public auction of the late laird's effects was held at Gleneagles, and lasted for four days at the beginning of May 1799. Excluding heirship goods (such as ancestral portraits and plate), it raised £1,186 9s. 0½d., about half of which came from domestic items, the most valuable being a 'large silver server' (£52 16s.) and an 'epergne with 4 branches' (£40 9s. 4d.). George's coach was sold separately for £55. Altogether there were 826 lots, some reflecting the career of the Entailer, such as sea chests, India chests, India boots, India bed covers, an 'old trunk with Chinese lumber', and wine from the Cape. There also remained twenty-eight bottles of port and thirteen of white wine, which had been laid down by Union Jack, while relics of a still more distant past survived in 'a parcel of arrows and an old helmet'. Positively new-fangled, on the other hand, was the 'cuckow clock' in the servants' hall.[14]

George was buried, not at Gleneagles like his first wife, Bethia Dundas, but in Greyfriars' churchyard in Edinburgh. Bethia had died in May 1770, having borne one daughter. George's second marriage took place on 16 December 1779, in Blackford church, to Margaret Drummond, daughter of the late Jacobite, the fifth Viscount Strathallan, who had been attainted and whose peerage had been forfeited in 1746. They had three daughters, of whom the longest-lived died aged twenty-one, and three sons, only one of whom, George Augustus, survived his father. Like his siblings, however, George Augustus's health was frail, and he died, unmarried, in his eighteenth year on 26 October 1799. His seven-month lairdship is notable only for his mother's felling of timber standing to the south of Gleneagles, a house denuded of furniture and furnishings by the roup of the previous May, and presumably reduced to a skeleton staff.[15]

14. CC6/5/30, test. 1800, Haldane, George. A deadline of 12 June 1801 was to be set for creditors 'to produce their interests' in the process of multiple poinding: *Caledonian Mercury*, 23 May 1801, issue 12,433.
15. *HG*, pp. 300, 338.

National Hero: Adam Duncan, Viscount Duncan of Camperdown, 1799–1804

On the death of George Augustus, the Cockburn line in the entail was extinguished, and the succession to Gleneagles opened to the descendants of Helen Haldane and Alexander Duncan of Lundie. Compared with the Haldanes of Gleneagles, or indeed the Cockburns of Ormiston, the Duncans were *arrivistes*, their presence at Lundie Castle dating only from the 1660s, when Alexander Duncan, a prosperous Dundee merchant, bought the barony from the Campbells. In about 1745, some twenty years after their marriage, Helen and Alexander transferred their residence closer to Dundee, to Gourdie House, which was renamed Lundie House.[16] Their eldest son and successor, Colonel Alexander, had died childless in 1796, leaving Lundie and the inheritance of entail to his brother Adam. Adam had gone to sea in 1746 as a fifteen-year-old midshipman on board the sloop HMS *Tryal*, under the command of his cousin Robert Haldane (son of Union Jack's son John, collector of customs at Prestonpans). He remained with Robert when the latter transferred to the frigate *Shoreham* in November 1747 and, early the next year, saw action against French privateers off the Breton coast.[17] Left to find another posting when his cousin resigned his command in September 1748, Mr Midshipman Duncan found it aboard the *Centurion* under Captain the Hon. Augustus Keppel, whom he served initially as midshipman, then successively as third, second, and first lieutenant thoughout the Seven Years' War. At this stage of his career, crowds of admirers used to follow the young lieutenant through the streets of Chatham; standing six feet four inches tall, and of 'gigantic' build, he was said to be 'the biggest and finest man in the navy'.[18] Of greater significance was the admiration he earned from Keppel for the qualities he displayed as an officer in voyages to North America, West Africa, and

16. A.J. Warden, *Angus or Forfarshire: The Land and People* (4 vols, Dundee, 1884), iv. 200, 269; *Dundee Courier & Argus*, 10 Sept., 1897, issue 13,792.
17. *HG*, pp. 184–5; Earl of Camperdown, *Admiral Duncan* (London, 1898), pp. 4–5; for Robert Haldane, see above, p. 148.
18. Camperdown, *Duncan*, pp. 14–15.

the West Indies, and, in February 1761, four months before his thirtieth birthday, he was promoted captain. The need to recover his health after service in the Caribbean in 1762, followed by the outbreak of peace in 1763, led to some sixteen years of unemployment, from which he was rescued by Admiral Keppel, in 1778, with appointment to a command in the Channel fleet. Further employment was consequent upon Keppel's arrival at the admiralty in 1782 as first lord, and between 1783 and 1786 Adam commanded Portsmouth's naval defences. However, although promoted rear-admiral of the blue in 1787, and of the white in 1790, and then vice-admiral of the blue in 1793, he was not employed again until 1795, when the French Revolutionary War was in its second year.[19]

Adam was given command of the North Sea fleet, a motley assemblage of converted Indiamen, superannuated fighting-ships, and captured prizes, tasked generally with patrolling an expanse of sea between the Pentland Firth and the English Channel, and specifically, after the Netherlands had become a French client state in May 1795, with blockading the Dutch fleet in its base on the Texel. Despite the inadequate force at his disposal, Duncan maintained the blockade for two years, even during the mutiny which spread from the Channel fleet to his own in May 1797. He dealt with rumblings aboard his flagship *Venerable* by sheer force of personality: physically restrained by his officers from running a mutineer through with his sword, he summoned the ringleaders, assured them that promises of increased pay would be honoured, emphasized the enormity of the crime of mutiny, and finally pardoned the offenders. He was able to report to the admiralty that 'Good order was again established, and I have the satisfaction to say they have behaved very properly ever since'. When a rising broke out on the *Adamant*, the admiral went on board and addressed the ship's company: 'My lads, I am not in the smallest degree apprehensive

19. For Adam's service under Keppel, and for his career generally, see P.K. Crimmin, 'Duncan, Adam, Viscount Duncan (1731–1804)', *ODNB*; also D. Stockdale, 'Admiral Duncan, naval officer, Scots gentleman, and British hero' in J. Murray (ed.), *Glorious Victory: Admiral Duncan and the Battle of Camperdown, 1797* (Dundee, 1997), pp. 25–39.

of any violent measures you may have in contemplation, and, though I assure you I would rather acquire your love than incur your fear, I will with my own hand put to death the first man who shall display the slightest sign of rebellious conduct.' He then asked if anyone present presumed to dispute his authority, and, when one intrepid seaman said, 'I do,' he seized him by the shirt, thrust him over the side, dangled him by one arm, and invited his mates to contemplate the outcome of his presumption. In reply to his report on 15 May, Lord Spencer, the first lord, expressed 'the sincere satisfaction I felt at reading the very dexterous manner in which you contrived to get rid of the rising disturbance on board the *Adamant*.'[20] Nevertheless, Duncan was unable to prevent the rest of his force from joining the mutinous ships at the Nore, and, whereas the mutinies on *Venerable* and *Adamant* had tested his courage and natural authority, an equal test of his ingenuity was presented by the need to maintain a blockade of the entire Dutch fleet with only two ships of the line. In the event, he disguised each vessel differently each day and kept up such a display of signalling that the Dutch were persuaded that the rest of the North Sea fleet was just beyond their horizon. This pretence was maintained until he received reinforcements from the Channel fleet, and, finally, from returning mutineers.

The Dutch and English fleets were, therefore, numerically equal when the sixteen Dutch men of war left the Texel on 6 October 1797. Duncan received the news while revictualling at Yarmouth. He immediately set sail and met the enemy on 11 October, five miles off the coastal village of Camperdown (Camperduin in Bergen, North Holland), south of the isle of Texel. To prevent Dutch ships, with their shallower draught, from reaching shoal water, Duncan attacked without waiting to form a regular line of battle, ordering each captain to engage a selected opponent. The Dutch fought with determination and bravery, and casualties were heavy on both sides. Engaging the Dutch admiral's flagship, the *Venerable* was surrounded by enemy ships, with only Duncan and the pilot left alive on the quarterdeck, while de Winter, the Dutch admiral, was almost the only man left standing on his vessel when he offered to

20. Camperdown, *Duncan*, pp. 98–111.

surrender his sword. 'I would much rather take a brave man's hand than his sword,' responded Duncan, before inviting de Winter to his cabin for a game of whist.[21]

Adam Duncan's victory was total: he had lost no ships and taken eleven; commanding a ramshackle fleet, with crews emerging from a state of mutiny, he had removed the threat from the Dutch fleet, and with it the danger of an invasion of Ireland; he had restored the prestige of the British navy and the morale of the British people. The battle was to be recognized as 'one of the most complete victories in the age of fighting sail', but some contemporaries criticized Duncan for his departure from standard tactical practice, considering that, by trusting to the initiative of his captains and the courage of their men, and throwing them into a mêlée, he had been lucky rather than skilful. His answer was that he had had no time 'for tactique or manoeuvre', and, indeed, his Dutch opponent told him that 'your not waiting to form line ruined me'. Years later, Lord St Vincent, who remembered Duncan as 'a gallant officer [with] no idea of tactics', recalled that he attacked at Camperdown 'without attention to form or order, trusting that the brave example he set would achieve his object, which,' he was obliged, almost reluctantly, to add, 'it did completely'.[22]

Britain responded to news of Camperdown with rapturous delight. Adam Duncan himself was showered with the freedom of cities and towns throughout the kingdom; when travelling to a presentation at the Guildhall in London, admirers unhitched the horses from his carriage, and themselves dragged it up Ludgate Hill. Medals were struck in his honour, portraits commissioned, and valuable gifts of plate conferred. The government granted him an annual pension of £2,000, while the prize court eventually awarded him and his men £150,000, of which his share as admiral was £18,750. By a unique dispensation, he was enabled to buy shares on the London Stock Exchange at seven-eighths

21. N. Mostert, *The Line upon a Wind: An Intimate History of the Last and Greatest War fought at Sea: 1793–1813* (London, 2007), p. 232.

22. M.A. Palmer, *Command at Sea: Naval Command and Control since the Sixteenth Century* (London, 2005), pp. 180, 184, 186; J.S. Tucker, *Memoirs of Admiral the Earl of St Vincent* (2 vols, London, 1844), ii. 282.

of the market price.[23] On 30 October, he was created Baron Duncan of Lundie and Viscount Duncan of Camperdown, a rank in the peerage which some thought an inadequate recognition of his services. In June of that year, Admiral Jervis, while receiving an equivalent pension, had been given an earldom after destroying the Spanish fleet off Cape St Vincent. When Adam's aunt, Lady Mary Duncan, told Henry Dundas, the secretary for war and Scotland's political manager, that 'the whole nation thinks the least you can do is to give him an English earldom', she expressed a view held within the royal family by vice-admiral the duke of Clarence, and one that he did not forget: among the coronation peerages granted by William IV on 12 September 1831 was the earldom of Camperdown, bestowed upon Adam's son and heir Robert, whose brother and sisters, as the sailor king's special tribute to the memory of their father, were given the rank of earl's children.[24]

Recurrent bouts of ill health obliged Lord Duncan, in April 1800, to retire to Lundie, the 6,800-acre Forfarshire estate which he had inherited in 1796 on the death of his elder brother. He had also, on the death of George Augustus Haldane in October 1799, inherited the entailed baronies of Gleneagles and Haldane. He was not, in fact, served heir to Gleneagles until January 1801, an occasion he celebrated with 'an elegant entertainment' at Hunter's in Perth.[25] At the beginning of August, he indicated the principal use to which he and his descendants were to put the newly acquired estate, when he announced his desire to preserve game at Gleneagles, Frandy, and Aberuthven, and requested 'that no gentleman will shoot or hunt there this season without his written authority'.[26] Of even graver concern was his inheritance's encumbrance with nearly £21,000 of debt. He swiftly set about disentangling the personal debts

23. C. Lloyd, *St Vincent and Camperdown* (London, 1963), p. 159; for the nation's gratitude, see D. Swinfen, '"The Nation Joyful": Admiral Duncan and Camperdown' in Murray (ed.), *Glorious Victory*, pp. 41–6.
24. Lady Mary suggested 'Earl of Lundie, Viscount Texel, and Baron Duncan': Camperdown, *Duncan*, pp. 261–3; G.E.C., *Complete Peerage*, ii. 518, n. (a); *HG*, p. 303.
25. *Aberdeen Journal*, 2 Feb.,1801, issue 2769.
26. *Caledonian Mercury*, 8 August 1801, issue 12,466.

of his penultimate predecessor from the obligations which lay upon the entailed estate, and, in 1802, succeeded in obtaining an acquittance of £7,500 from the Court of Session.[27] How he would have dealt with the remaining debt will never be known. He twice offered his services to the admiralty after the renewal of war in 1803, and, on the second occasion, was returning from London to his Edinburgh house in George Square, when, on 4 August 1804, he reached the border at Cornhill-on-Tweed. While in the capital, he had consulted his doctor about the abdominal pains which had been plaguing him, and been told that he had 'only to attend to [his] digestion'. At Cornhill's inn, after obediently 'eating a moderate dinner and taking his pint of wine as usual, he went to bed in good spirits', but awoke in great pain, and did not live to see the dawn.[28]

Adam's widow, Henrietta Dundas, survived him until 1832. They had married in June 1777, he aged forty-six, she twenty-eight. Her father was Robert Dundas of Arniston, lord president of the Court of Session, whose younger brother, Henry, was already making his mark in national politics, in which he was to play a major role, joining his niece's husband in the Lords in 1802 as Viscount Melville. Adam and Henrietta's happy marriage produced nine children, two of whom died young: William, aged nine, in 1789, and Alexander, aged twenty-two, in 1803.[29]

Just as the Haldane ancestors of Adam's mother had passed down a tradition of staunch Presbyterianism, so had the Duncan ancestors of his father. Adam embraced it fully. When he addressed his crew a week after he had calmed their mutiny on the *Venerable*, he devoted much of his speech to the offence caused him by their addiction to profane oaths, and such was the unaffected conviction with which he displayed his piety that he was heard with respect and achieved the desired moderation in behaviour.[30] Sailors, in fact, seem to have felt an instant affinity to their warm-hearted, fair-minded, courageous, giant of a commander. One of his men, hearing that he was about to be ennobled, wrote: 'They can't make too much of him. He is heart of oak; he is a seaman every

27. *HG*, p. 302; above, p. 165.
28. Camperdown, *Duncan*, pp. 354–5.
29. *HG*, p. 303.
30. Camperdown, *Duncan*, pp. 1, 106.

inch of him, and, as to a bit of broadside, it only makes the old cock young again.'[31] At much the same time, Adam himself wrote to Robert Dundas: 'Honours seem to flow on me. I hope my head will keep right.'[32] His modesty, like his spirit, was indomitable.

Robert Dundas Duncan-Haldane, Viscount Duncan and earl of Camperdown, 1804–59

Robert, who added to 'Duncan' the Haldane name of his paternal grand-mother, was nineteen years old when he succeeded to his father's estates and titles, his elder brother Alexander, a lieutenant in the Grenadier Guards, having died in Malta the previous year. In January 1805, the second Viscount Duncan married his sister-in-law Janet, daughter of the Berwickshire baronet, Sir Hew Hamilton-Dalrymple.[33] He was soon introduced to the financial embarrassment contingent upon the lairdship of Gleneagles. In 1805, the kirk session of Blackford sought to recover from him a debt initially incurred by the Haldanes in 1733, when Mungo (II) had borrowed £100 Scots from the parish poor fund. Resort to this convenient source of cash became habitual, and, by 1762, the debt had reached £2,598 Scots or £216 10s. sterling. Robert Haldane gave the kirk treasurer his bill for this sum, but it remained unpaid, and with accruing interest had reached £280 in 1769, when George (Cockburn) Haldane substituted his bill for the Entailer's. Needless to say, there was no delivery of cash. Lord Duncan was reluctant to honour any bill issued by his insolvent predecessor, and the Court of Session agreed that the debt was personal to George, and did not lie upon the entailed estate.[34]

The debts which *were* incumbent upon that estate, however, had to be addressed. Discussion between Lord Duncan and Robert and James Haldane, his second cousins who represented the reversionary interest in the entail, resulted, in February 1813, in a petition to the Court of

31. Lloyd, *St Vincent & Camperdown*, p. 158.
32. Stockdale, 'Admiral Duncan' in Murray (ed.), *Glorious Victory*, p. 38.
33. Robert's sister had married Janet's brother in 1800: *HG*, pp. 303–4.
34. D. Hume, *Decisions of the Court of Session, 1781–1822* (Edinburgh, 1839), no. 192 (pp. 245–7).

Session, presented by Duncan for himself and his infant children, and by the Haldane brothers, requesting leave to sell parts of the estates of Gleneagles, Haldane, and Aberuthven, in order to discharge the debts of Robert Haldane the Entailer, 'thus freeing the remainder from debts for which they may be evicted'. An Act of Parliament empowering the court to allow the sale was duly passed.[35] The lands selected for disposal comprised all those brought to the Haldanes by Agnes Menteith in 1490 as her quarter-share of the earldom of Lennox, plus all those acquired in 1493 in compensation for John Haldane's surrender of superiority in the earldom. This withdrawal from the area south-east of Loch Lomond in effect brought the territorial existence of the barony of Haldane to an end. The lands of Aberuthven were untouched, and all that was sold out of the barony of Gleneagles in the public roup in 1815 was the small and isolated property of Knockhill south of Dunblane. The auction realized £11,944, with prices based on twenty-five years' income at the current rental; an additional £360 came from the sale of superiorities, and a few lands were sold privately to the duke of Montrose and others in January 1816.[36] The process of completing the liquidation of the Entailer's debts at last began.

Leaving Gleneagles to slumber as a hunting lodge, and making no attempt to put the estate in order, Lord Duncan set about building himself a grand neoclassical residence to the east of Lundie House, the 'plain old building' remarkable only for the colossal red lion rampant which was attached to a wall in its office block. This had adorned the prow of the Dutch admiral's flagship at the battle of Camperdown, been transported from Sheerness to Dundee, and arrived at the victor's house in November 1799. Lundie House itself was demolished and its magnificent replacement, Camperdown House, completed in 1828.[37] Sitting

35. *The Statutes of the United Kingdom, &c.*, xxiii, p. xv, no. 69; cf. *Caledonian Mercury*, 25 Feb.1813, issue 14,227.
36. NRS, CS228/D/9/28; CS32/12/84.
37. Fourth Earl of Camperdown to Brodrick Chinnery-Haldane, 18 July 1918 (at Gleneagles); Warden, *Angus or Forfarshire*, iv. 200–1; *Dundee Courier*, 14 March 1849, issue 1,697; Swinfen, 'The Nation Joyful' in Murray (ed.), *Glorious Victory*, p. 46 & pl. 25.

in the Lords throughout his adult life, initially as the second Viscount Duncan, and from 1831 as the first earl of Camperdown, and, like his father, a Whig, Robert was associated with the moderate reformers who looked to Lord Lansdowne for a lead. He favoured the Reform Bill in 1830, and in 1858 gave his support to the reform of Scottish universities, and, although 'no enemy to the established church', voted against church imposts in Scotland.[38]

Gleneagles saw its laird during the shooting season, and probably seldom outside it. A desire to protect his game from interference combined with a financial interest in the tolls paid by road traffic between Glendevon and Muthill to persuade the earl in 1845 to prevent the Scottish South Midland Railway from surveying the glen with a view to driving a branch line through it, connecting Crieff and Dunfermline. Meanwhile, the Scottish Central Railway was in the process of bringing its line between Dundee and Glasgow close to the northern entrance to Gleneagles, but the convenience of this development, both for the earl travelling between London and his Scottish properties, and for his tenants transporting their produce, was obvious. In 1856, a railway station, called Crieff Junction, opened a little over a mile from his house, and soon the annual August departure of earls of Camperdown from Euston to Gleneagles became a regular announcement in newspaper society columns. In 1912, the station's name was to be changed to 'Gleneagles', and the seed planted for a dispute which was to exercise the restored Haldane lairds for much of the twentieth century.[39]

The first earl of Camperdown died at his London house on 22 December 1859, in his seventy-fourth year, and was succeeded by his second but eldest surviving son, Adam.

38. M. Escott, 'Forfarshire (Angus)', *Hist. Parliament, 1820–32.*
39. *Dundee Courier*, 16 July 1844, 14 Oct., 1845, 20 Jan., 1846; issues 1,454, 1,519, 1,533. The scheme for a branch line through Gleneagles was revived by the Scottish Central Railway in 1861, but abandoned the following year as too expensive: *Dundee Courier & Daily Argus*, 24 June, 16 Nov. 1861, 10 Jan., 22 March 1862; issues 2,480, 2,507, 2,626, 2,687.

Adam Duncan-Haldane, second earl of Camperdown, 1859–67

Born in 1812, and educated at Eton and Trinity College, Cambridge, Adam's elevation to the peerage ended a career on the Liberal benches of the House of Commons which had begun in 1837, when he was elected member for Southampton. In 1841, he exchanged his seat for that of Bath, where his father had a house, and which he represented for the next eleven years. In 1852, he failed to secure election for Bury (Lancashire), but a by-election brought him in for his home county of Forfar. Between 1855 and 1858, he served under Palmerston as a lord of the treasury, but his great achievement had taken place in 1851, when the window tax was abolished largely as a result of his untiring advocacy since 1845, when he first drew attention to 'the poor who were suffering from impure air and want of light in their dwellings', as a consequence of architects building 'houses hardly fit for people to live in, because they desired to put in as few windows as possible in order to avoid the tax'. He also campaigned, but in vain, in favour of a secret ballot for parliamentary elections.[40]

In September 1864, the second earl fell seriously ill while resident at Gleneagles; when strong enough, he travelled south, but never fully recovered his health, and died in his fifty-fourth year, on 30 January 1867, at his father-in-law's Warwickshire seat of Weston Park near Long Compton. In 1839 he had married Juliana, the eldest of the three daughters and coheiresses of Sir George Philips, Bt, a Whig reformer, whose father's vast cotton wealth had provided the funds for the erection, in 1828, of the enormous neo-Jacobean Weston Park, which formed part of Juliana's inheritance. She and Lord Camperdown had two sons, Robert, the heir, and George, an engineer who went to America. They also had a daughter, Julia, who, in 1858, married the fourth Lord Abercromby; from Camperdown, where the wedding took place, the couple proceeded to Gleneagles for a few days, en route for Weston, London, and Rome.[41]

---

40. *Hansard*, lxxvii, c. 826; cx, c. 68; cxviii, c. 293; *Morning Post*, 1 Feb., 1867, issue 29,662; G.E.C., *Complete Peerage*, ii. 518.
41. P. Reid, *Burke's & Savills Guide to Country Houses, ii: Herefordshire, Shropshire, Warwickshire, Worcestershire* (London, 1980), p. 185; *Dundee Courier*, 13 Oct. 1858, issue 2197.

Before leaving Scotland, they probably visited Airthrey, inherited by Abercromby's father from an uncle who had bought it in 1798 from Robert Haldane. While the landed profile of their Duncan cousins waxed, that of the Haldanes had distinctly waned.

Robert Philips Haldane-Duncan, third earl of Camperdown, 1867–1918

Born on 28 May 1841, Robert was educated at Eton and Balliol College, Oxford, where he took a first-class degree in classics. His inherited Liberal credentials secured his entry to Gladstone's first administration in December 1868 as a lord-in-waiting, followed in 1870 by appointment as civil lord of the admiralty, which he remained until the government's defeat at the polls in 1874. Gladstone's return to power in 1880 was not accompanied by Lord Camperdown's return to office, and it seems unlikely that he sought it. When Gladstone's third administration foundered on the issue of Irish home rule in 1886, he withheld his support, and became a Unionist.

His sense of public duty found its expression on committees of local government in Forfarshire and Warwickshire, where, in the tactful words of his *Times* obituary, 'he was greatly trusted and popular, although certain ardent spirits were sometimes inclined, when rapid action was desired, to regard his customary insistence upon the due formalities of business and discussion as a hindrance to the aims they had in view'. The obituarist, in fact, suggests that there may have been a Wodehousian dimension to the third earl: 'direct, fearless, and honourable, incapable of unworthy compromise, and abhorring every form of self-advertisement or personal display'; breeding cattle on the home farm at Lundie, not in any way on a commercial basis, but 'always greatly pleased when he won a prize'.[42] His time was divided between London, where he regularly attended the House of Lords; Weston, where he hunted; Camperdown, where he farmed; and Gleneagles, where he shot. A bachelor, his devoted companion in all his residences was his

42. *The Times*, 7 June 1918, issue 41,810.

sister, Lady Abercromby, whose death in 1915 exacerbated the anxieties of wartime and aged him rapidly.[43] He died shortly after his seventh-seventh birthday, on 5 June 1918, at Weston Park, which had passed to him from his mother twenty years earlier.

Earl Robert had moved decisively into the Conservative camp since his departure from the Liberals in 1886, and their return to power, first under Campbell-Bannerman in 1905 and then under Asquith in 1908. He vehemently objected to the Scottish Landholders Bill, opposition to which was orchestrated in the Lords by the parliamentary lawyer, Sir John Seymour Lloyd, who became a close friend. The introduction by Lloyd George of a budget in 1909 which raised death duties, and introduced super-tax and duties on increased land values, provoked a reaction which led, in 1911, to the limitation of the power of the Lords to resist the Commons, which in turn produced an obsessive siege mentality among the patrician landowning class. Even when he wrote a letter of condolence to Brodrick Chinnery-Haldane on the death of his aunt Alexina in December 1911, Lord Camperdown devoted most space to an expression of alarm that 'an entirely new spirit has developed in the country; and in the government especially. It is difficult to understand how men of education and honesty can support, and much less can one comprehend how they can take part in, the present government.'[44] Brodrick should have had little doubt that his lordship was thinking particularly of his cousin, Richard Haldane, who sat with Lloyd George in Asquith's cabinet. The third earl's friendship with Sir John Seymour Lloyd and his loathing of Richard Haldane were to have unexpected consequences for the future owner of Gleneagles.

The heir to the earldom was Robert's 73-year-old brother. In 1888, after a successful career in engineering, George Haldane-Duncan had gone to Boston in the United States to marry Laura Adams Blanchard, whose first husband had died three years previously, and whose father was the Massachusetts flax magnate and philanthropist, John Dove. It was in Boston that George decided to establish his residence. His

43. Ibid.
44. Lord Camperdown to B. Chinnery-Haldane, 28 Dec. 1911 (at Gleneagles); for Seymour Lloyd, see *The Times*, 27 July 1939.

childless marriage ended with his wife's death in 1910, after which he devoted his energy and resources to charitable work, largely for the benefit of the unemployed in Boston.

With the Duncan titles on the brink of extinction, and a double imposition of Lloyd George's death and land-value duties in rapid sequence appearing to be a real threat, the decision was taken to leapfrog the fourth earl in the succession both to Camperdown and to Gleneagles, Weston being left by Earl Robert to his local agent, Henry Warriner.[45] Camperdown, with the Lundie estate, passed by entail to the earls' only first cousin in the male line, Georgiana, countess of Buckinghamshire. At Gleneagles, the entail opened to the senior male representative of the line of the Entailer's elder brother James, and, in the person of Brodrick Chinnery-Haldane, the Haldanes came home.

Gleneagles in the nineteenth century

During their absence, Gleneagles had emerged from relative isolation. Road communication through the glen towards Muckhart and thence into Fife was greatly improved during the 1830s, while transport facilities were revolutionized in 1856 by the arrival of a railway connection with Dundee, Glasgow, and Crieff.[46] At the same time, reclamation during the 1850s brought nearly a hundred acres of moorland into cultivation, and in 1863 a new nursery for trees was formed to help compensate for the amount of forest land that had been converted into good arable soil.[47] In October 1860, the *Glasgow Herald* reported that rents on the 7,000-acre Gleneagles estate had risen by between 20 per cent and 30 per cent; in 1861, they went up by between 10 per cent and 15 per cent.[48] These rises

45. Warwickshire County Rec. Off., CR1635; Weston Park was demolished in 1933. For the fourth earl's obituary, see *The Times*, 7 December 1933.
46. *Statistical Account of Scotland 1834–45*, x. 300–1; above, p. 176.
47. *Morning Post*, 7 Nov. 1860, issue 27,111; *Dundee Courier & Daily Argus*, 6 Jan. 1863, issue 2,935.
48. *Glasgow Herald*, 29 Oct. 1860, iss. 6,489; *Dundee Courier &c.*, 14 June 1861, iss. 2,446.

are reflected in the gross annual values given to the estate of £2,330 in 1812, £2,457 in 1859, £3,004 in 1867, and £3,479 in 1873.[49]

The nineteenth century saw a decline in the population of the glen. Including the Haldane ground in Glendevon, a total of 185 in 1841 fell to 95 in 1901, the steepest drop (29 per cent) occurring between 1851 and 1861.[50] The number of dwellings in the glen was consequently reduced: both those at West Gate had gone by 1861, that at East Gate by 1871, by which year the bothy at North Mains had also vanished; of the four 'shops' listed in 1871, two survived in 1891, and none in 1901; one of the two dwellings at Jock's Brae in 1871 had gone ten years later, and the survivor by 1901, by which time Cauldhame had also lost one of its two cottages; the number of crofts at Muiralehouse fell from three to two between 1841 and 1851, and from two to one between 1861 and 1871. These statistics reflected a general exodus from the countryside to the towns as people sought work in the new factories. The four handloom weavers found in 1841 were survivors of a once much larger body of labourers who disappeared as mechanization replaced them; the three cotton weavers had gone by 1851, and the sole linen weaver by 1861. Moreover, the farms which employed most of the estate's inhabitants were amalgamating. Frandy's hill acres were transferred to St Mungo's in 1843, and its farmhouse, occupied in 1841 by a grazier with his wife and children, a female servant, and two agricultural labourers, was home, ten years later, to a single shepherd and his family. It continued to house shepherds for the rest of the century, the occupant in 1901, Joseph McLaren, being notable, with his wife and Cameron mother-in-law, as the only Gaelic-speaking residents on the estate.

The arable lands of East Mains were similarly reallocated in 1850, and the two-roomed farmhouse with its one-roomed bothy was made

---

49. Rental of Gleneagles & Aberuthven, 1812 (Camperdown MSS at Gleneagles); wills of Robert & Adam Duncan Haldane, earls of Camperdown, 1860, 1867 (NRS, SC45/31/15, 20); *Scotland: Owners of Lands & Heritages, 1872–73* (HMSO, 1874), p. 161. It must be remembered that these figures include those for Aberuthven, whose value was about one-third of that of Gleneagles.

50. These figures and most of what follows are taken from the census returns for 1841–1901.

available for the families of a ploughman, a farm hand, and a journey-man blacksmith. The occasion for this development was a violent tragedy in Auchterarder, when the farmer of East Mains, William Jack, a fifty-year-old with a history of mental illness, called on his brother, became enraged over an old family dispute, and stabbed him to death. He was immediately arrested and sent to Perth.[51] His land was taken over by the gamekeeper, John Anderson, who lived in the big house (the Mains) and already leased the home farm. In 1851, he had 351 acres and employed seven workers, but, following his bankruptcy seven years later, these acres were kept in hand and the farm's hill pasture transferred to John Cairns, who was in no danger of insolvency.[52]

Based at St Mungo's, and leasing between 5,000 and 6,000 acres of grazing, the Cairns family occupied the pinnacle of the glen's resident society throughout the nineteenth century. In 1798, William Cairns 'in Mungo's Wells of Gleneagles' had even bought up part of the debt of his laird, George Cockburn Haldane. The Cairns's house began the century with ten rooms and ended it with sixteen, while, having managed with two domestic servants in the forties and fifties, their household in 1881 included a housekeeper, a governess, a nursemaid, and a housemaid. Guests dining with Robert Cairns in the 1830s were served and ate their soup, and ladled their gravy, with silver spoons. At his death in 1843, as well as his tack of St Mungo's, Robert had land in Buttergask (west of Blackford), and interest in two textile mills in Tillicoultry, while his moveable funds totalled £4,330. His son William (died 1851) acquired commercial property in Auchterarder and Muthill, and a hill farm at Lategreen (south of Dunning), while his grandson, John Monteath Cairns, added stock-farms at Dalchruin in Glen Artney (near Comrie) and at Mount in the Campsie Fells (near Balfron), enlarged his presence in the neighbourhood of Gleneagles by taking leases on the hill farm of Backhills (bordering Frandy) and the arable farm of Banheath (south

---

51. *Caledonian Mercury*, 9 May 1850, issue 19,987.
52. Ibid., 20 Nov. 1858, issue 21,577; wills of first and second earls of Camperdown (1860 & 1867: SC45/31/15, 20). For the sale of furniture and stock at the Mains and North Mains in October 1858, see Camperdown MSS, no. 42 (at Gleneagles).

of Blackford), and expanded his interests in and around Auchterarder by acquiring five small farms to the west and south of the town, and the Crown Hotel within it. Also in the town centre he built a substantial house called Glencairn, which he left to his widow, and which is now a residential care home. When John Monteath Cairns died in April 1899, his total moveable wealth was £21,305, which, like his land, was divided among his four sons and five daughters. Behind the dry record of his household in the census returns for 1881 and 1891 lies a domestic history which must have absorbed the interest of the glen: in 1881, the list of those living under the roof of John Cairns and his wife Jessie included Janet Herdman, the seventeen-year-old daughter of their housekeeper; before the year ended, Jessie Cairns had died, and, in 1891, Janet's mother was still housekeeper, but Janet was now the 61-year-old Mr Cairns's recently wed second wife.[53]

Below the grandees at St Mungo's, the next level of Gleneagles society was occupied by the tenants of two hill farms, Glenhead and Kaimknowe (both lying in the parish of Glendevon), and those of two arable farms, West and North Mains. Each of the hill farms grazed 700 acres, and each was based on a house which doubled in size as the century progressed – Glenhead from four to eight rooms, Kaimknowe from five to eleven. Both tenancies remained in the same families throughout the period. A Forbes had been at Glenhead since 1798 at the latest, and, like Cairns in St Mungo's, albeit on a more modest scale, had interests beyond the bounds of the estate. John Forbes, in 1822, also farmed nearby at Whiterigg (east of Glendevon), which he left to his eldest son, bequeathing his tack of Glenhead to a younger; this junior line flourished, with its representative Duncan, in 1862, leaving stock worth £2,390 on his farms of Glenhead, Wester Downhill (south of Glendevon), and Thornton (in Fossoway, south-east of Glendevon).[54] Not quite as prosperous, but as long established, also having arrived at Kaimknowe before 1798, the

53. Wills of Robert, William, & John Cairns (1844, 1852, & 1899: SC49/31/38; SC44/44/9, 44). The translation of a bond for £500 to Wm Cairns in 1798 is among the Camperdown MSS at Gleneagles.

54. Wills of John & Duncan Forbes (1817 & 1862: CC6/5/33; SC49/31/74); NRS, E/326/10/11/119 (farm horse tax roll 1797–98).

Kirks temporarily expanded and diversified their operation within the estate when, in the 1860s, James Kirk took an extra 800 acres of grazing together with 350 acres of arable, and moved his base to North Mains. The arable experiment had been abandoned by 1881, when James Kirk was back at Kaimknowe with a much enlarged farmhouse but limited again to pasturing his livestock on 700 acres. His son and heir embarked on a different course of diversification by becoming an auctioneer in Auchterarder.[55]

North and West Mains were the only significant arable farms on the estate in tenant hands, after John Anderson's failure at East Mains and the home farm itself. Each had between 120 and 150 acres, and each was based, during the first half of the century, on a six-roomed house. Two rooms were added to West Mains by 1881, while North Mains was rebuilt during the 1880s, renamed 'the Kinnaker' (or 'Kinacher', or 'Kinniker'), and on completion briefly occupied by one of John Cairns's sons. At West Mains, the Robertsons failed to prosper. In 1841, the farmer's youngest son William was listed as a labourer; ten years later he had been appointed an assistant gamekeeper, but, late on Christmas Eve 1856, his dead body was found on the railway track near Loaninghead, where he had been drinking; apparently, he had wandered along the line for some hundred yards before being struck by the mail train. Two years later, his eldest brother John, who had succeeded to West Mains, was declared bankrupt.[56]

William Robertson had been living with his wife and young family in one of the cottages or 'shops' which were scattered around the northern part of the glen. With one or two rooms with a window, they were home to artisans and those farm workers who did not live within a farmer's household, or in his bothy. Bothies were usually occupied by two or three young bachelors; so were some cottages, but usually the latter housed labourers with families; St Mungo's two-roomed cottage in 1881 was home to a ploughman, his wife, and eight children aged between seven months and twelve years; in the 1840s, on the drove road west

55. Wills of John & James Kirk (1900 & 1901: SC49/31/180, 186); NRS, E/326/10/11/119.
56. *Caledonian Mercury*, 11 Aug. 1858, iss. 21,490.

of St Mungo's, two similarly sized labourers' families occupied a pair of double-roomed dwellings at Jock's Brae. Apart from general farm-hands, ploughmen, and shepherds, occupants of cottages in the glen included blacksmiths at Peterhead, shoemakers at Cauldhame, numerous carpenters, a forester at Lochside, a toll collector on the glen road (until replaced by shepherds in the 1870s), and, from the middle of the century, railway workers at Cauldhame; in 1871, there lived a laundress in one of the 'shops', and a seamstress in another.

An inhabitant of another 'shop' in 1841 was listed in the census as Benjamin Taylor, aged twenty, teacher. He occupied a building erected in 1824, and described in 1861 as containing one room with a window. This was the space, thirty feet by sixteen, which served as the school-room; writing desks ran the length of the north and east walls, with a fireplace at the western end, and an entrance in the southern wall. Since the floor was below road level, flooding was frequent, and since the ceiling was low, complaints that the ventilation was 'insufficient' were regular. Unless there was an additional windowless room, this was also where the teacher lived. It being consequently impossible to recruit married men for the job, teachers were inexperienced and transitory: a twenty-year-old in 1841, another in 1851, a nineteen-year-old in 1861, and a twenty-two-year-old in 1871. The last lodged with a farm-worker and his wife in Bargate Cottage rather than dwell in the 'damp and draughty' schoolhouse. New desks and a few new seats appeared in 1871, and, in response to an inspector's call for immediate action, 'proper and separate offices for boys and girls' were supplied at the back of the building. The lack of a teacher's house was at last remedied in 1878, when a new, adjoining, four-roomed cottage was provided for Thomas Tindall, a graduate of Aberdeen University, who moved in with his wife, two-year-old son, and wife's parents.

The school was overseen by three managers: the farmers of St Mungo's, and North and West Mains. Weekly rates of subscription were 2½d. for infants and 3d. or 3½d., according to parents' means, for boys and girls. Before the Scottish Education Act of 1872 made education compulsory for five- to thirteen-year-olds, children aged ten were working as 'agricultural servants' at St Mungo's, Glenhead, and Muiralehouse in 1841, aged eleven at Kaimknowe in 1851, aged twelve at Glenhead and

Muiralehouse in 1851, and at Peterhead in 1871. There were thirty-six pupils on the school's books in 1872, but the average attendance over the year was twenty-seven. Regular reasons for absence were 'the older boys being sent to work during harvest', 'older pupils lifting potatoes', 'larger boys in fields preparing turnips', 'assisting at shearing the sheep', 'senior pupils kept at home, this being seed-sowing week', and occasionally attendance was adversely affected by markets in Auchterarder and Doune. When childhood diseases struck, as did scarlet fever in 1871, 1875, and 1910, chickenpox in 1879, measles in 1880, and diphtheria in 1887 and 1889, the school might be closed for a week or more. Occasions for half-day holidays came in 1871 with the queen's fiftieth birthday, in 1873 with a local ploughing match, and in 1874 with the Caledonian curling match; a New Year's Day holiday was introduced in 1879 to replace that on Handsel Monday, a week later when gifts (handsels) were customarily exchanged in this part of Perthshire.

The curriculum in 1870 comprised Bible study, dictation, reading (often history), writing, 'figures', and 'lessons on the human heart, eye, and blood circulation'. The purchase, in 1874, of four large wall maps of Scotland, England, Europe, and Asia permitted the introduction of geography, while a class in Latin was started in 1875, and, three years later, one in botany. Botany was dropped in 1883, but French was added to Latin as a 'special subject'. Inspectors in 1871 found all pupils in arithmetic able to say the multiplication tables; in 1875, the school was judged to be 'taught with considerable vigour' and to be 'on the whole in very fair order'. A more probing investigation of Mr Tindall's efforts in 1878 found that 'the reading is generally good, and the handwriting satisfactory, but there is much room for improvement in arithmetic of all classes'. The following year 'results are not at all satisfactory', with spelling and arithmetic 'very bad' and grammar, geography, and history 'very inefficiently taught'. Decided improvement was detected in 1880, when 'singing has been introduced with good effect and the drainage is somewhat better'.

Despite the effective singing, however, water still came into the sewing room, and, in fact, all was not at all well within this department. Sewing had been introduced in 1871, with girls taking instruction from Mrs Stevenson, a 61-year-old joiner's widow who lived alone in one of the neighbouring 'shops'. Classes took place for an hour after the boys had been dismissed at four o'clock. The sewing mistress's position was a sensitive one, for mothers, asked to provide their daughters with the material needed for lessons, were inclined to dispatch their offspring with garments in need of repair or alteration, and to complain if the returned items failed to meet their expectation. It took a year to find a replacement for Mrs Stevenson after her retirement in 1875, and, in 1881, the community was riven by a plot to depose the reigning mistress, Mrs King at Loaninghead (not available for teaching during the harvest), and replace her with Mrs Tindall, the master's wife. Despite Mrs King's resort to what Mr Tindall described as 'disgraceful language' in November 1881, she withstood the attempted coup, the defeated Tindalls left Gleneagles, and, in February 1882, a new master, John Scott, ten years older with a wife and five sons, arrived from the Trossachs Public School.

After twelve months, inspectors reported that Mr Scott had 'greatly improved the school', but the building and fittings were considered, in 1893, to be 'far from conforming to modern ideas of suitability', and so, shortly before the Scotts left, the ceiling was raised and the walls replastered. The twentieth century began optimistically. In 1908, inspectors acknowledged that 'in a somewhat remote rural district such as this, oral composition is attended with peculiar difficulties, and a special effort to overcome them would have its reward in improved sentence formation', but they concluded that 'much success attends the work of this little school'.[57]

The school's log book records a number of warnings to the pupils not to trespass on any of the grass 'parks' to the north of the big house. That house, as we have seen, was used as a shooting-lodge, with the visits of the proprietors limited to late summer and early autumn, unless prolonged by illness like that of the second earl of Camperdown in 1864. The permanent residents throughout the nineteenth century were gamekeepers and housekeepers. Between 1841 and 1891 both were supplied by the Anderson family. In 1841, accommodation within the house was shared by John and Mary Anderson with their young family,

57. School records, from which this account is drawn, are in Perth & Kinross District Archive, CC1/5/7/167–8, and NRS, ED18/2250. The school closed in 1921.

and William and Isabella Tutin, in their sixties with their two spinster daughters; John was both gamekeeper and farmer of the Mains, and William a retired gamekeeper on the Lundie estate, brought down to Gleneagles by Lord Camperdown to give the younger man the benefit of his experience. Anderson continued as keeper after his bankruptcy in 1858, by which time Mary had died and he had remarried. After his own death in 1866, his widow Margaret, twenty-four years his junior, remained as housekeeper into the 1890s, with between twenty-one and twenty-four rooms assigned to her charge, while successive gamekeepers, all from the Lundie estate, occupied two or three rooms.

Anything entering Gleneagles air space was in danger of being brought down. In 1841 'a magnificent white swan with a black beak and seven foot wingspan' was shot by one of the keepers and sent to Edinburgh museum for stuffing. 'Great slaughter of game' was reported in the glen in both 1860 and 1861, with one gun bagging 17½ brace of grouse; other game were partridge and, rarely, woodcock. The keepers were much exercised by the need to control an abundance of foxes, apparently seldom seen in the glen in the first half of the century. A hunt was organized in August 1860, when 'a party of gentlemen with hounds engaged in the chase', but a less formal method of control was resorted to in July 1878, when eighteen beaters, ten guns, and dogs constituted 'a fox hunt at Gleneagles'.[58]

58. *Morning Post*, 13 March 1841, iss. 21,890; *Glasgow Herald*, 16 & 25 Aug., 6 Oct. 1860, iss. 6,425, 6,435, 6,470; *Caledonian Mercury*, 24 Aug. 1861, iss. 22,435; *Dundee Courier & Daily Argus*, 22 July 1878.

VI

Haldanes Without Gleneagles

Prologue: James Haldane and his son, James Haldane of Airthrey, 1692–1768

The senior Haldane line was to be absent from Gleneagles for 150 years. The progenitor of the absentees was James, born in 1692, eldest son of Union Jack Haldane and his second wife, Helen Erskine. Without realistic expectation of a landed inheritance, since two sons of his father's first marriage survived, James needed a profession to provide his income and was prepared to hop from one to another in search of success. His first choice, the law, did not produce rapid enough results, and he seems to have abandoned it after the duke of Montrose failed to employ him in a legal capacity in 1714.[1] The next year, his father made the substantial investment of £3,200 to secure him a cornetcy in the Fourth (Scots) Life Guards, and, in November 1715, he was with the government forces that surrounded a Jacobite army at Preston in Lancashire, a county to which he was to return.[2] He progressed to captain in 1717 and major in 1721, ranks purchased by paying the difference between the value of his old commission and that of his new one.[3]

1. Above, pp. 115–6.
2. *HG*, p. 188.
3. J. Childs, *The British Army of William III, 1689–1702* (Manchester, 1987), p. 57.

The years between the conclusion of a treaty with France in 1716 and the outbreak of war with Spain in 1739 were years of peace, which for a professional soldier meant half-pay and inaction. James occupied himself in the summer of 1716 in St Andrews, helping his half-brother Patrick secure election as provost and earning the obloquy of his opponents by threatening them with imprisonment and trial in Carlisle as Jacobites, unless they changed their voting intentions.[4] At the same time, James was sounding out the possibility of an additional and conceivably alternative career as a diplomat. In August 1716, he was selected as George I's resident at the court of Peter the Great in Russia.[5]

His suitability for this appointment was unquestionable. No one at this time was a more reliable channel of access to the tsar than his personal physician, Dr Robert Erskine, and James was his nephew. The government would have hoped that the kinship might be useful in retaining Tsar Peter's cooperation with Hanover and Denmark against Swedish aggression in northern Europe, and James's father, who was currently orchestrating an effort to obtain a pardon for his Jacobite brother-in-law Sir John Erskine, would have hoped that his son might energize Dr Erskine to seek the tsar's intercession on behalf of Sir John, who was the doctor's brother.[6] The tsar, however, was unpredictable. James's commission was signed by George I on 15 September 1716, and the Russians expressed approval, but, before the end of the month, Russian troops had been quartered in Mecklenburg, which infuriated George, who hoped to bring it under Hanoverian control. Rumours that Peter was contemplating support for a new Jacobite attempt in Britain further delayed James's mission, and eventually the plan was dropped.[7] In November 1717, James was sent instead as resident to the court of the

---

4. *Memoranda re Haldane of Gleneagles*, p. 31; Anon., *The Case of Mr Patrick Haldan Advocate with Some Remarks upon His Defence* (1723), pp. 11–13.
5. Ibid., pp. 27–30; *HG*, p. 189.
6. Union Jack's cousin, Sir Henry Stirling of Ardoch, was already in Europe on a similar mission.
7. R. Wills, *The Jacobites of Russia, 1715–1750* (East Linton, 2002), pp. 42–61; L. Hughes, *Russia in the Age of Peter the Great* (New Haven & London, 1998), p. 313; Williams & Stuart, *Whig Supremacy*, p. 167; *HG*, pp. 189–90.

landgrave of Hesse-Cassel, whose capital was little more than seventy miles south of Hanover, so that James was able to use access to George I to plead the case for his Jacobite cousin, William Murray.[8] In 1719, he was transferred to the court of the elector palatine at Heidelberg, with the delicate task of telling the Roman Catholic elector to behave better towards his Protestant subjects. The predictable outcome was the recall of the elector's resident from London and James's departure from Heidelberg 'without taking leave'. His diplomatic career, in effect, came to an end.[9]

Back at home in 1722, James stood unsuccessfully for election in the Whig interest to the Tory-controlled Lancastrian borough of Clitheroe. He was to fail again, ten years later, when he contested Preston, another Tory borough in Lancashire. These contests were expensive, involving the purchase of 'burgages', urban property whose tenants voted according to the owners' instruction. Burgages, however, could be sold when no longer needed, and, in any event, James does not seem to have been short of money in 1722. Like his half-brother Patrick, to whom he was close at this time, he may have emerged with profit from the feverish speculation which gripped the stock market in 1720. He cooperated in financial dealings with Patrick's brother-in-law, Lord Forrester, who had become his colonel in the Fourth Troop Life Guards in 1719, and was able to buy not only burgages in Clitheroe but also agricultural property in Lancashire.[10] Moreover, by 1724 he had advanced loans amounting to at least £6,000 to Sir Lawrence Anderton, Bt, of Lostock (near Bolton).

It is not certainly known what originally drew James to Lancashire. Opportunities may have been opened to him after the Jacobite defeat at Preston, to which he contributed, and which involved many local families. The Andertons were one such family, but contact with Lawrence may not have been made until James was in Germany. Sir Lawrence

8. Above, pp. 112–3; James's letter of credentials, signed by George I, is at Gleneagles.
9. *HG*, pp. 190–1.
10. TNA, C24 (Town Depositions)/1469; C11 (Chancery Proc.)/1479/19 (both transcribed in 'Notes', ii. 381); above, p. 133; E. Cruickshanks, 'Clitheroe' and 'Preston', *Hist. Parliament 1715–54*.

had inherited a profound commitment to the Roman Catholic faith, which among the Lancashire gentry was not unusual, but his situation was unique: Sir Lawrence was a monk. When his predecessor died in 1710 at the Jesuit college of St Omer's, he was to be found among the English Benedictines at Dieulouard in Lorraine. His younger brother Francis thereupon argued that Lawrence, being a monk, was 'dead in law', and, as Lawrence himself put it, 'did artfully get into possession of my whole estate and keep me out of the same'. As a zealous Jacobite, Francis joined the rising of 1715, was captured at Preston, convicted of high treason, and forfeited the family estates to the crown, whereupon their disposal became a matter for the commission of which Patrick Haldane was a leading member. Lawrence may now have decided that he could not idly watch the dispossession of his family. By this time, he had moved to the English monastery of Lamspringe in the bishopric of Hildesheim, within twenty miles of Hanover and little more than seventy from Cassel, at either of which contact could have been made with James Haldane. The Jacobite grapevine, which unquestionably reached Lamspringe, was wholly cognizant of James's efforts on behalf of William Murray, while there was no secret about the relevance to the Andertons of the influence of James's half-brother Patrick. Rumour that both Haldanes had been hedging their bets in 1714 by mixing in Jacobite circles in Paris, whether true or false, may have further emboldened the monk-baronet to approach James.[11] In an alternative scenario, it may have been James who made the first approach, suggesting that it was time for Sir Lawrence to rescue his patrimony, and that he, as Patrick Haldane's half-brother, was, for an adequate reward, in a prime position to help.

However the first contact was made, when Sir Lawrence put off his cowl and returned to England to ask the government to relinquish the title deeds to his lands in Lancashire, Yorkshire, and Westmoreland, his heavy legal costs were met by James Haldane. In July 1723, he assigned to James the rents of his Lancastrian estates, estimated at £12,000 (a

11.   *Memoranda*, p. 31; Anon., *The Case of Mr Patrick Haldan Advocate with Some Remarks upon His Defence* (1723), p. 9.

sum which would have included a generous allocation for interest on the principal loans) 'in satisfaction of the trouble, charges, and expenses he had been at, or should be put to, in helping Sir Lawrence Anderton'; James also bought a part of the Lostock estate which bordered his own recently acquired ground in the county, issuing a bond for £500, and paying the balance of the purchase price in cash. When it became clear to him that Anderton's agent would never willingly release to him a penny of the assigned rents, James applied to the baronet for some security against their payment. Sir Lawrence was now living at Chalfont House in Buckinghamshire, in company with one Ludovic Fenwick, who assured James that securities had been drawn up, but failed to divulge their whereabouts, and, when Sir Lawrence died in October 1724, no record of them could be found. Even his instruction to return James's £500 bond was denied by Fenwick, and neither his will nor any of its codicils contains a mention of obligation to James Haldane. It may be that Sir Lawrence Anderton was not as otherworldly as he seemed, or, more likely, that his affairs were controlled by unscrupulous knaves. In either case, James's fingers were badly burnt, and his attempt to rescue something of his Lancastrian investment involved him in a legal quagmire, with Sir Lawrence's prior status as a monk being used to question his right to dispose of any Anderton property. When James died, eighteen years later, his suit against Sir Lawrence's executors for '£6,000 or thereabouts' was still unresolved.[12]

James's death took place in September 1742 off the east coast of Jamaica. He had set out for the West Indies, in April, to join Guise's regiment as lieutenant-colonel, having resigned from the Life Guards in October 1741. War had broken out with Spain two years earlier, and

12. This account of James's dealings with Anderton is based on the Chancery Proceedings, TNA, C11/64/32; 80/18; 2584/5 (transcribed in 'Notes', ii. 386–90); both men's wills, PROB 11/743/333 (transc., 'Notes', i. 5–9), & 11/596/403; T. Leach (ed.), *Modern Reports, or Select Cases adjudged in the Courts of King's Bench, Chancery, Common Pleas, & Exchequer* (London, 1795), case 25; *Complete Baronetage* (5 vols, Exeter, 1900–6), iv. 92; W. Farrer & J. Brownbill (eds), *Victoria County Hist., Lancashire*, iii. 200–8, 295–9.

reinforcements were being dispatched to replenish the losses suffered during a disastrous combined naval and military expedition against Cartagena (now in Colombia).[13] James and his younger brother Robert met in London on 19 April to settle financial matters between them and together travelled to Portsmouth. Once in Jamaica, James established himself at Snowhill, north of Kingston, but within three months his health collapsed, and, on 11 July, in his fiftieth year, he drew up his last will. He rallied sufficiently to attempt a return voyage to England, but, on 17 September, three days out of Port Royal, he died.[14]

The will is written informally, probably just as James dictated it.[15] He remembered his nineteen-year-old nephew Robert Haldane, a lieutenant in the Royal Navy, whose propensity for good living was perhaps recognized in the bequest of all his wines and other goods stored in a warehouse in Kingston,[16] as well as drinking glasses, cutlery, table linen, and much of his wardrobe: eighteen of the best Holland shirts, eight white and yellow waistcoats, his scarlet and blue frockcoats laced with gold and silver, together with his watch, sword, and cane. A blue greatcoat, two scarlet coats, some breeches and worsted stockings were left to one George Hog, who resided with him and whom he was helping to obtain a military commission. 'My dear little friend Lieut. Cumins, for whom I intended much better things,' was left a tent, field bed and bedding, a tweezer-case, and 'my apothecary's shop which I require he shall keep in memory of me'. To his servant, William Rantree, James left 15 moidores (about £20) 'to carry him to England'. Other cash dispositions totalled 250 moidores (about £340), which included the costs of embalming and repatriating his body for burial at Gleneagles, 'the vault of my ancestors'.

13. H.W. Richmond, *The Navy in the War of 1739–48* (3 vols, Cambridge, 1920), i. 123–4; R. Cannon, *Historical Record of the Sixth or Royal First Warwickshire Regiment* (London, 1839), pp. 58, 61; HG, pp. 193–4; J. Spain, 'Guise, John (1682/3–1765)', ODNB.

14. HG, p. 194.

15. TNA, PROB 11/743/333; Haldane, 'Notes', i. 5–9.

16. For Robert, see above, p. 148.

The principal part of the will relates to James's only child, his fourteen-year-old son and namesake, and to his wife Margaret. At an unknown date in or before 1727, Miss Margaret Pye had eloped with James from the young ladies' boarding school where she was a pupil. The couple married at once, and their son was born during 1728. Before setting sail from Portsmouth in April 1742, James made arrangements for his brother Robert to hold securities for £1,450 on the boy's behalf and also to guarantee the payment of an annuity of £100 to Margaret. These arrangements were confirmed by the will drawn up in Jamaica, which gave Robert custody of all James's effects in England, including arrears of pay, to be held for the use of his son; it also authorized Robert to pursue his claim against Sir Lawrence Anderton's estate and pay to Margaret £500, if so much were to be recovered. Finally, James willed that his journals, papers, and books were to be sealed up and sent to Robert, whom he appointed 'my executor in trust for my said son James Haldane [and] his mother, knowing well the good use he will make of the trust I repose in him'. The three pages containing the last will and testament arrived safely, but the other documents, which may have included evidence of James's marriage, have now vanished.[17]

17.   For the elopement and marriage, see the petition to Lyon King of Arms of James's great-grandson, Alexander Haldane: 'Notes', i. 13–16. The year of young James's birth is derived from his epitaph in Lundie churchyard: A. Jervise, *Epitaphs & Inscriptions from Burial Grounds & Old Buildings in the North-East of Scotland* (2 vols, Edinburgh, 1875–79), ii. 65. The lack of documentary evidence for the marriage suited George Cockburn Haldane when he proposed to claim the earldom of Lennox, since an assumption that James had no legitimate descendants was essential to his case. The fact that Margaret Pye is always referred to in the colonel's will as the mother of his son, and never as his wife, has no significance, given the informality of the document. Had his son not been regarded as legitimate in 1766, when Robert drew up the entail, he and his issue would not have been included among the substitute heirs; nor would he have been considered for marriage to his Duncan cousin in 1762: see 'Notes', i. 1–4, 14–19, derived from information given by Alexander Haldane to his son, who entered it in a prefatory note to his diary for 1878 (at Gleneagles).

The future Entailer had every intention of justifying his late brother's trust. Having followed his elder cousin Robert into the Royal Navy, young James was serving as a lieutenant when his uncle brought him into the East India Company, where he was to prosper. In February 1753, about to set out in the *Prince Edward* for India and Java, Robert was on the point of resigning his command to his nephew, when his plans suddenly changed, and James had to be content as his fourth mate for the 28-month voyage.[18] A year and a half after their return, however, the *Prince Edward* was indeed handed over to James, who commanded it on two voyages to India between 1757 and 1762. He then acquired a part-share in the considerably larger vessel, the *Duke of Albany*, in which he made two further voyages between 1763 and 1767, at the conclusion of which he was expected to join the board of the East India Company.[19]

After Brigadier-General George Haldane's death in Jamaica in 1759, James had become the senior male Haldane below his uncle Patrick, and, although the ancestral estates were bought by his uncle Robert in 1760, James continued to be treated as the younger of Gleneagles. The thought occurred to Patrick that his patrimony might after all be preserved for his direct descendants, if James were to marry his surviving child Margaret.[20] In December 1762, however, in the interval between his last voyage on the *Prince Edward* and his first on the *Duke of Albany*, James chose to marry, at Lundie House, his cousin Katherine Duncan. On 28 February 1764, Katherine gave birth to a son, who was named after his father's uncle and patron, Robert. On the eve of setting sail in January 1766, James drew up a will including a bequest of £500 to his uncle 'as a small testimony of my gratitude for the favour and protection he has always shown me'.[21]

18. *London Evening Post*, 20–22 Feb. 1753, issue 3,950.
19. Brit. Lib., IOR/L/MAR/553 A, B; 573 C, D, E (transc. In 'Notes', pp. 231–2); A. Haldane, *The Lives of Robert Haldane of Airthrey & his Brother James Alexander Haldane* (4th edn, Edinburgh, 1855), p. 10.
20. 'Notes', pp. 22–3, citing information from James's grandson, Alexander Haldane.
21. PROB 11/941/139.

It was probably not until he made landfall in England in September 1767 that James learnt the terms of the entail executed by Uncle Robert. He had sailed for India thinking himself the heir to Gleneagles and Airthrey, for that was what Robert had led him to believe and almost certainly had intended; he returned to find Gleneagles destined for George Cockburn and Airthrey, by the terms of his uncle's will, to be sold; out of the proceeds of that sale, £14,000 was assigned to creditors, and the residue bequeathed to James. Since eighteen months were to elapse to allow for James's return from his voyage, before the sale could take place, it is evident that the Entailer's hope was that James should buy Airthrey for £14,000. Robert died on New Year's Eve 1767, and James, persuaded by Cockburn's alarmist and, as it proved, dishonest account of the state of their late uncle's affairs, agreed to buy Airthrey for £17,000 rather than £14,000, and pay an extra £1,500 for the contents of the house and an additional farm. James disbursed the first instalment in March, but enjoyed his purchase for barely three months, falling victim to a sudden and fatal illness while accompanying his pregnant wife on a visit to her family at Lundie House. He died on 30 June 1768 and was buried at Lundie. His second son, who received his name and that of his father-in-law, was born a fortnight later.[22]

Leaders of Scottish evangelism: Robert Haldane, sometime of Airthrey, later of Auchengray, and his brother, James Alexander Haldane, 1764–1851

The fusion of Haldane and Duncan genes had proved eminently successful in the person of the hero of Camperdown. The alliance of James Haldane and his cousin Katherine Duncan produced two equally remarkable offspring.

The widowed Katherine gave up her London residence near Cavendish Square and brought the four-year-old Robert, his three-year-old sister Helen, and newly born brother James Alexander to live near

22. Above, pp. 155–7; *HG*, p. 197–200; Memorial of Lord Duncan, p. 7 (at Gleneagles).

her parents in Dundee. Death was to be a frequent visitor during the boys' childhood. In 1771, their grandfather Alexander Duncan of Lundie died, and his widow, Helen Haldane, joined their household; in 1774, their mother Katherine succumbed to a fatal respiratory disease, and the orphans' upbringing was taken over by their grandmother, while their official guardianship passed to their uncles, Alexander and Adam Duncan; their sister, always frail, died two years later, followed, in 1777, by their grandmother. Robert was now thirteen, and James nine. The household was devoutly Presbyterian, inspiring Robert with a childhood ambition to become a minister, the domestic staff being given an opportunity to judge his suitability from the regular Sunday sermons he delivered in the servants' hall. A resident tutor had charge of the brothers' education, but they had also been sent to the grammar school in Dundee 'that they might mingle with other boys, and profit by the stimulus of competition.'[23] The lack of a father's presence was to a degree compensated by that of their uncle Adam Duncan, then a captain in the Royal Navy, who came to live with them, and manage their affairs, during a period of naval unemployment. In June 1777, however, a month after their grandmother's death, Uncle Adam married, and new arrangements were required. The decision was taken to enrol the boys in the High School of Edinburgh; the house in Dundee being given up, Robert and James were boarded in Charles Street with the rector of their new school. In due course, both went up to the university in Edinburgh, but Robert left in 1780 to travel to Portsmouth and join the ship's company of the *Monarch*, commanded by his uncle Adam, who had been recalled to service and doubtless had not discouraged his nephew's adventurous spirit.[24]

The peace of 1783 brought to an end Robert's short but eventful naval career, in which he had participated in the relief of Gibraltar and seen action under the command of the future Earl St Vincent. At the age of

23. Haldane, *Lives*, pp. 14–15, 19; for biographical sketches of Robert and James see D. Lovegrove, 'Haldane, Robert (1764–1842)' & 'Haldane, James Alexander (1768–1851)', *ODNB* (2004).
24. Haldane, *Lives*, pp. 14–19.

twenty, after quitting the service, he returned to Edinburgh to resume his academic studies, and, in 1785, celebrated coming of age while on the customary grand tour. Shortly after returning home, in April 1786, he married Katherine Cochrane Oswald, three years his junior, a daughter of George Oswald of Scotstoun (east of Clydebank), a successful Glasgow tobacco merchant and banker, and the son of a Presbyterian minister. In the autumn, they settled at Robert's estate of Airthrey, where their only child, Margaret, was born in April 1787. The improvement and beautification of Airthrey was to occupy him for the next ten years.[25]

His younger brother, meanwhile, had trodden a similarly conventional path. After university, in 1785, at the age of seventeen he declined an offer from Mr Coutts, an old friend of his father, to join his bank and entered the Honourable East India Company, as his guardians had always intended, for the Haldanes owned the chief interest in the *Melville Castle*, one of the Company's chartered ships, whose command was earmarked for James once he passed his twenty-fifth birthday. The interim was to be spent acquiring the necessary skill in seamanship. His initiation was as a midshipman aboard the *Duke of Montrose*, bound for Bombay and Macao, and returning to Deptford in June 1787, after a voyage of twenty-eight months. His second voyage, as the fifth officer on the *Phoenix*, took him to Calcutta, where he spent six months enjoying the indulgent hospitality of a resident kinsman, who introduced him to 'one constant round of excitement and fashionable dissipation'.[26] Serving as third officer on his next voyage, aboard the *Hillsborough*, he was provoked by a captain of dragoons who had earned notoriety as a successful duellist. Angered by James's refusal to participate in a cruel practical joke, the dragoon emptied a wine glass in his face, in response to which James hurled a heavy tumbler at the other's head. Satisfaction was demanded, the challenge accepted, and the ensuing duel took place on St Helena. James's pistol exploded in his face, and his opponent's also misfired. It was generally agreed that honour had been satisfied,

25. Ibid., pp. 25–36.
26. Ibid., pp. 42–3, 47.

and James safely returned to England, rejoining his old ship, the *Duke of Montrose*, for a fifteen-month voyage as second officer.[27]

By the time the *Montrose* regained Deptford, on 19 June 1793, James was an experienced seaman and an accomplished navigator. He was within a month of his twenty-fifth birthday, and, after passing the required examination, was appointed captain of the *Melville Castle* for its voyage to Madras and Calcutta, due to sail in January 1794. In so far as any maritime enterprise could be certain, James's prosperity seemed assured, and he felt that his future was one that he could ask a young lady to share. On 18 September 1793, he married Mary Joass, only child of Major Joass, the resident deputy-governor of Stirling Castle. The pair had first met during one of James's visits to nearby Airthrey. Mary was a modest heiress (albeit in funds rather than in land, as her father had sold his Banffshire estate of Colleonard), but any objection to her marrying a younger son was overcome by the determination of the young couple and the high opinion held of James by Mary's uncles, the generals Sir Ralph and Sir Robert Abercromby.[28]

James and his bride took up residence in Sackville Street off Piccadilly, while the East India fleet was assembled. The *Melville Castle* arrived in Portsmouth on 31 December 1793, but prevailing contrary winds delayed the fleet's departure throughout the winter and early spring of 1794. The delay exhausted supplies for the crews, and in March the men of the *Melville Castle* received an advance of pay to alleviate their discomfort. A similar gesture, however, was refused by the captain of the *Dutton*, whose crew promptly mutinied. The captain disembarked, his officers were besieged on the quarterdeck, boats carrying armed men from other vessels approached the ship, shots were fired over the mutineers' heads, and alarm spread that the powder magazine was about to fall into their hands. At this point, Captain James Haldane appeared alongside, boarded, forced his way, sword in hand, onto the quarterdeck, which he cleared by calmly asking the men what they hoped to achieve when so overwhelmingly outnumbered within the fleet. Two drunken mutineers

27. Ibid., pp. 49–50, 52–3, 58.
28. Ibid., pp. 59–60.

persevered in their attempt to force the door of the magazine, but James levelled his pistol, threatened to fire unless they desisted, called for the ship's irons, and such was his natural authority that they were instantly produced and placed on the men. The mutiny over, Captain Haldane returned to the *Melville Castle*.[29] When the fleet at last weighed anchor, in May 1794, however, the *Melville Castle* sailed without him.

Living aboard his ship in Portsmouth harbour for four months gave James ample opportunity for reflection. Friends suspected that the unaccustomed gravity of this sociable man of action was not unconnected with dismay at the thought of parting from his young wife, who, by February 1794, was carrying his first child. Such may indeed have been the case, but it did not monopolize his thinking. Awareness of the responsibilities of marriage, coupled with those of commanding a large ship's company of officers, men, soldiers, and passengers, led James to explore his own character and question the nature of true contentment. For advice, he turned to Dr David Bogue, a Scottish Presbyterian minister who, in 1777, had established an independent Congregational chapel at Gosport, which, between 1779 and 1787, had been the headquarters of Adam Duncan. When visiting the future admiral in 1783, his nephews had attended Dr Bogue's ministry, and the foundation of lasting friendships was laid. A voracious reader, when James set out on his first voyage, he had taken with him a large trunk full of books selected by the minister, who combined classical and modern literature and history with a few carefully chosen religious works.[30] The latter, however, had been read 'as a task', just as his daily prayers had become perfunctory. During the return voyage of the *Montrose* in 1793, undertaken in convoy with a large number of Indiamen, even his natural abstemiousness had been eroded, as he joined in the convivial exchange of hospitality within a fleet whose maxim was that no ship should send a party away sober.[31] By his own account, up to this time James's religious life had been conventional and superficial. He had been content to observe

29.   Ibid., pp. 62–4.
30.   Ibid., pp. 20, 29, 44.
31.   Ibid., pp. 46, 51.

a Presbyterian Sabbath when he was within the bounds of Presbytery and to neglect it elsewhere; his wife was shocked at his disregard of the Lord's day during their London residence in the first months of their marriage.[32] Challenged to a duel, as we have seen, he had failed to turn away, a failure to which he referred some ten years later in a public room at Buxton, when he told a young blood who had immediately reopened a window which he had closed at his wife's request, that 'there was a time, sir, when I should have resented this impertinence, but I have since learned to overlook insults, as well as to forgive injuries.'[33]

James turned the months of enforced physical idleness at Portsmouth into a period of intense intellectual exercise. Prompted by Dr Bogue, he became 'more regular in prayer and attending public worship', and read studies on the sacraments. His conclusion changed his life, as he explained to an old shipmate in a letter of 1801: 'I never was acquainted with solid, rational happiness till my attention was turned to religion. My former merriment was really like the crackling of thorns under a pot. I was governed by passion, and under such a guide no wonder I missed my road.... My present peace of mind does not arise from any vision or supposed new revelation I have received. I had a book by me which from prejudice of education, and not from any rational conviction, I called the Word of God, ... and treated it with the greatest neglect, living in direct contradiction to all its precepts, and seldom taking the trouble to look into it.... I went on thus till, having much time on my hands when the Melville Castle lay at the Mother Bank, I began to think I would pay a little more attention to this book. The more I read the more worthy it appeared of God; and after examining the evidences with which Christianity is supported, I became fully persuaded of its truth.'[34] Life at sea had distanced him from this truth, and he would turn his back on that life.

Negotiations began for the sale of James's interest in the *Melville Castle*; an offer was made of £9,000 for his command, plus a large additional sum for his captain's share in the property of the ship and stores.

32. Ibid., pp. 21, 60.
33. Ibid., p. 54.
34. Ibid., pp. 65–6.

Both his own and his wife's uncles thought his decision mistaken. He received encouragement only from his brother Robert. Negotiations for the sale were protracted to within two days of the fleet's departure. Then, with the deal done, James went to Scotland to rejoin his wife Mary, who had been caring for her ailing father in Stirling Castle. There, on 6 October, their daughter Elizabeth was born. On 1 November, Major Joass died, and the young family left the castle to take up residence in George Square, Edinburgh.[35] James's son Alexander understood that, so far as his father had any fixed plan, it was 'to become a landed proprietor, retire to the country, and lead a quiet, useful, unambitious life'. He thought of buying the estate of Garnkirk, north-east of Glasgow, but Mary disliked the locality, and his bid to acquire the Chesterhill estate, near Dalkeith, was unsuccessful.[36] His future was indeed to be useful, but it was to be neither unambitious nor quiet.

James's search for a country seat may have been inspired by his elder brother's achievement at Airthrey. Aged only twenty-two when he settled there in 1786, Robert conceived a grand plan for both the old house and its surroundings. His late uncle and namesake had enclosed the park, but its formality was now sadly unfashionable, and Robert employed the Whites of Durham, a father and son team who had studied under Capability Brown, to rectify matters. The new scheme included an artificial loch covering nineteen acres, several plantations, enlarged gardens, summer houses commanding the most picturesque views, and a hermitage, which, alas, remained uninhabited. Such was his success in transplanting mature trees that his advice was sought for the Botanical Gardens of Edinburgh.[37] The whole was surrounded by a stone wall, four miles in extent. On completion, his attention turned to the house, and he commissioned a design for its replacement from Robert Adam, who offered the choice of a classical villa or a castellated, D-shaped mansion. The latter won Robert's approval, but, to supervise the building works, he engaged one of Adam's past associates, who undercut the architect's

35.   Ibid., pp. 67–8.
36.   Ibid., p. 115.
37.   Ibid., p. 37 n.

estimate by 5 per cent. Completed in 1791, Airthrey Castle cost Robert £37 6s. 2d. for its design and £3,755 13s. for its construction.[38]

James visited Airthrey soon after returning to Scotland in the summer of 1794 and found that his brother had been swept along on the tide of radical idealism that had flooded political debate in Britain since the fall of the Bastille in Paris in 1789. Robert later said that he had felt the world to be on the brink of 'the universal abolition of slavery, of war, and of many other miseries that mankind were exposed to, which appeared to me wholly to result from the false principles upon which the ancient governments have been constructed. I rejoiced in the experiment that was making in France.' Although Paris in the summer of 1794 was in the grip of the Terror, and France had been at war with Great Britain for over a year, he ascribed 'all or most of the enormities of the French solely to the state of degradation to which I thought their minds had been reduced during the ancient despotic government'.[39]

On 1 July, accompanied by his brother, Robert attended a meeting of the freeholders of Stirlingshire to consider a national call to arm volunteers in the interest of public order. Asked to speak by the chairman, Robert opposed the measure on the grounds that it would enable the government to send more regular forces out of the kingdom to fight a war of which he disapproved, and so, by an unintended consequence, weaken its internal security while putting arms in the hands of many who were accused of disaffection. He contrasted patriots who loved peace and wished to remove just grievances, with those who 'hugged their prejudices' and held to maxims of government belonging to the seventeenth rather than the late eighteenth century.[40] It was a bold

38. I. Anderson, 'The history of Airthrey Castle and estate' (2003), sites.scran. ac.uk/ada/documents/castle_style/airthrey/airthrey_history.htm; J Fleming, 'Seton Castle's debt to ancient Rome: Robert Adam's castle style II', *Country Life* (30 May 1968), p. 1,447; Haldane, *Lives*, pp. 36–9. The Scottish baronial turrets, etc., to be seen today, were added later in the nineteenth century.

39. R. Haldane, *Address to the Public concerning Political Opinions, and Plans lately adopted to promote Religion in Scotland* (Edinburgh, 1800), pp. 4–5; *Lives*, pp. 79–80.

40. *Address*, pp. 7–9; *Lives*, pp. 81–2.

speech to have made before the duke of Montrose and other principal landholders of the shire in a feverish atmosphere of radical agitation and authoritarian reaction, and gave the orator the quite unjustified reputation of being a firebrand, which dogged him for some years to come.

An immediate consequence was Robert's near ostracism by neighbouring country gentlemen.[41] The society in which he now exchanged ideas and analysed current affairs became predominantly clerical. The ministers, Dr Campbell of Kippen, Mr Somerville of Stirling, Mr Shireff of St Ninian's, and Dr Innes, chaplain at Stirling Castle, were regular visitors to Airthrey and, during discussions which went on late into the night, led Robert's search for a better world away from political theory to the Word of God. The Bible became his constant study, and past certainties began to totter. 'My views of government,' he wrote, 'became very different. Instead of laying to its charge all the moral evils by which mankind is afflicted, I was taught to refer them primarily to a very different source.' He perceived 'the melancholy fact that human nature was deeply and radically depraved'.[42] The excesses of the French revolutionaries were not, after all, to be laid at the door of the *ancien régime*. The scriptures were unequivocal that governments should be obeyed. When asked to subscribe money for the defence of agitators on trial in England for sedition, he replied that his political sentiments had been quite misunderstood. 'Had I ever known of anything dangerous to government, even if I had lived in Turkey, where they have one of the worst governments, I should have accounted it my duty immediately to reveal it.'[43] The savage tragedy being played out in France was the consequence, not of Bourbon despotism, but of man's original sin. Henceforward, Robert's philosophy was to be firmly based on a verse in St Paul's Epistle to the Romans: 'Wherefore as by one man sin entered into the world, and death by sin, and so death passed upon all men, for that all have sinned.'[44] When, in 1817, a student in Geneva questioned his teaching of

41. *Address*, pp. 9–10; *Lives*, pp. 82, 86.
42. *Address*, pp. 96–7.
43. Ibid., pp. 21–2; *Lives*, p. 102.
44. Romans 5:12.

original sin, Robert simply pointed to this verse, and the young man had to concede that he saw the doctrine in the Bible. 'But do you see it in your heart?' asked Robert.[45] From this essential starting-point, the route to a righteous life and ultimate salvation was signposted by the Word of God, and Robert decided that to propagate that Word was to be his life's work.

Towards the end of 1795, the London Missionary Society was founded by several evangelicals, prominent among whom was David Bogue, who hailed its interdenominational principle as 'the funeral of bigotry' and whose academy at Gosport was to become a seminary for missionaries.[46] Among the first donations received by the society were two, each of £50, from Robert and James Haldane. Robert's enthusiasm for missionary work then blossomed into a grand scheme: he would sell Airthrey (the product of an earlier grand scheme) and finance a mission to Bengal. After discussing his plan with his wife and two ecclesiastics, he went south to persuade Dr Bogue to join them; they all would spend the remainder of their lives, based in Benares, spreading the gospel among the Hindus, and Robert would place £25,000 in a trust which would continue to fund the work in the event of his death. Possibly mindful of the fate of a far more worldly expedition (to Darien) which had involved his ancestor Union Jack Haldane, Robert set about securing the good-will of the East India Company, whose leave to settle in Bengal was a prerequisite. It was not forthcoming. Although he may have succeeded in dispelling suspicions of subversive intent based on memories of his speech to the Stirlingshire freeholders, the court of directors was convinced that a mission to the seat of the holiest shrine in Hindustan would cause nothing but disquiet and disorder, and be thoroughly bad for business. Their official refusal to cooperate was delivered in January 1797. A lengthy, carefully argued appeal was similarly rejected a few months later, and, although some urged him to persevere regardless, Robert was too sensible to engage in such a risk. An alternative focus

---

45. T. Stunt, *From Awakening to Secession: Radical Evangelicals in Switzerland and Britain* (Edinburgh, 2000), p. 34; *Lives*, p. 404.
46. M. Laird, 'Bogue, David (1750–1825)', *ODNB*.

for his energy and philanthropy had, moreover, been suggested by the activities of his brother.[47]

James Haldane had considered joining the Benares mission, but his wife's health and their increasing family made it unlikely that he would have been able to do so.[48] He had, in any case, begun a missionary career of his own in Scotland. James had attended the General Assembly of the Church of Scotland in 1796, when the motion 'That it is the duty of Christians to carry the Gospel to the heathen world' was defeated by the Moderates, who made much of the needs of Scotland's own people. Their sincerity may have been questionable, but their facts were not. James became involved in a movement to establish Sabbath schools in Edinburgh and its neighbourhood. When his friend, the Grassmarket ironmonger John Campbell, set up such a school in the colliery town of Loanhead, James attended its opening, but 'such was his reluctance to make himself conspicuous' that he could not be persuaded to address the assembled parents and children. He did agree, however, to accompany Mr Campbell on a week's tour of the Clyde valley, distributing thousands of tracts on the road from the one-horsed chaise in which they travelled and holding meetings in Glasgow, Paisley, and Greenock, describing how readily and how cheaply such schools might be established. He himself decided to extend the movement into the north of Scotland, accompanied by a minister who would preach in the towns and villages. Before he set out, however, his instinct for self-effacement was overcome when he agreed to step into an absent preacher's shoes at the mining village of Gilmerton, south of Edinburgh. The power, energy, and earnestness with which he delivered his first sermon, on 6 May 1797, were remembered over forty years later, when a miller, who had been in the congregation, stopped him in Edinburgh's High Street with thanks for preaching the

47. Haldane, *Lives*, pp. 89–114; D. Mackichan, *The Missionary Ideal in the Scottish Churches* (London, 1927), pp. 105–6; D.W. Lovegrove, 'Unity and separation: contrasting elements in the thought and practice of Robert and James Alexander Haldane' in K. Robbins (ed.), *Protestant Evangelicalism: Britain, Ireland, Germany and America c.1750 – c.1950* (Oxford, 1990), pp. 164–5.
48. *Lives*, p. 94.

gospel to him at Gilmerton all those years ago. The little boy, who had been encouraged by his uncle Adam Duncan to declaim heroic verses from atop a side table in their house in Dundee, had found his vocation.[49]

Hailed as the Boanerges of the evangelical movement,[50] James set out from Edinburgh with two friends in July 1797 on a preaching tour, whose focus was to be the north of Scotland and the Orkney Islands. Travelling in a light open carriage, stocked with specially printed tracts and pamphlets, they began their labours as soon as they reached North Queensferry, where they preached to about fifty people in a school-room. As they moved north, congregations were addressed in hospitals, marketplaces, churchyards, streets, and greens, on riverbanks, and by the seashore. Numbers grew: 500 at Inverness, 600 at Elgin, while gatherings at Kirkwall, where a fair had attracted many from outlying islands, were estimated by James to have reached 1,200, 3,000, 4,000, 'even to upwards of 6,000 persons'. At Thurso, James's congregation grew from 300 on the first day to 800 the next morning and 1,500 that evening, from 1,700 in the morning of the third day to 3,000 in the evening, and thereafter seldom fewer than 3,000.[51] At Brechin, for the first time, the preachers availed themselves of the services of the town-drummer to announce their presence, elsewhere bellringers were used, and in the Orkneys the people alerted their neighbours by lighting beacons on hilltops. At Kirriemuir in Forfar, James initially listened to the local minister's sermon, then addressed the departing congregation from the market cross; nearly 1,000 stopped, and were told plainly that what they had heard inside the kirk 'was not the Gospel', and were urged 'to search the scriptures for themselves'; as for their minister, prayers were offered to God 'that He might give him repentance to the acknowledgment of the truth.'[52] This became a regular mode of proceeding and predictably provoked official hostility as well as exciting keen local interest.

49. Ibid., pp. 15, 123–41.
50. Ibid., p. 140; Mark 3:17.
51. *Lives*, pp. 154–64, drawn from J.A. Haldane, *Journal of a Tour through the Northern Counties of Scotland and the Orkney Isles, in Autumn 1797* (Edinburgh, 1798).
52. *Lives*, p. 147.

Part of James's audience was undoubtedly attracted by the novelty of seeing an East India captain of good family turning out in all weathers as an itinerant street preacher. He was described by someone who heard him in Banff as arriving on horseback, wearing a blue, braided greatcoat, with his hair powdered and tied behind, as was then usual for gentlemen. He dismounted, handed his horse to an attendant and proceeded to speak distinctly and simply, but with such power that fifty years later that member of the Banff congregation vividly remembered his repetition of the words, 'Except ye repent, ye shall all perish': 'I never closed an eye nor even retired to rest that night'.[53] James's preaching, delivered by a voice that combined strength and range, was above all exciting. One listener later compared its effect to an electric shock;[54] few who heard it remained indifferent to the concerns of eternity. The stamina of the voice's owner was also remarkable. After addressing thousands, often more than once a day, in the open air, sometimes travelling many miles in the course of a few days, repeatedly crossing turbulent seas when in Caithness and Orkney (all of whose twenty-nine islands he visited), James at last arrived at the schoolhouse in Auchterarder to deliver the closing sermon of his tour on 7 November 1797, but it was not until he drove on to Airthrey that he found he had lost his voice.[55]

The achievement of this first tour was to awaken religious life in parts of the country neglected by the established church. Before the end of 1797, to continue the work, James and his brother Robert decided to establish 'The Society for Propagating the Gospel at Home', whose first general meeting took place in Edinburgh on 11 January 1798. Its sole intention was contained in its title; it was non-denominational; it conferred no ordination on its preachers and schoolmasters; there were to be no public collections or private donations of money from those among whom they preached or taught; the entire enterprise was to be funded by Robert.[56]

53. Ibid., p. 153; R. Hill, *Journal of a Tour through the North of England and Parts of Scotland* (London, 1799), p. 11.
54. *Lives*, p. 174.
55. Ibid.
56. Ibid., p. 178.

Robert's decision to sell Airthrey had not been altered by the realization that his plan for a mission to Bengal would have to be abandoned. On 9 January 1798, *The Times* newspaper advertised the sale of most of the Airthrey estate: about 2,440 acres producing a rental of £2,052, the house, 160 acres of parkland, gardens, and orchards, a lake covering 19 acres, and a let coppermine. Robert retained certain lands let on long leases, and thus easily managed, which brought in about a third of the value of the whole property, and he still owned Lochton and Keithock in Forfarshire, properties purchased for him out of a trust fund during his minority by his guardian, Colonel Alexander Duncan.[57] Katherine, his wife, displayed her approval of the reduction in the family's establishment by relinquishing her carriage, an expense which she would never again allow.[58] Airthrey was bought privately for about £87,000 by General Sir Robert Abercromby, an uncle of James's wife Mary, and, on 16 June 1798, Robert Haldane bade farewell to his estate and domestic staff. The sale of a property which was largely his own creation was the most unequivocal demonstration of his commitment to evangelicalism. An admirer later recalled that 'the world looked on and smiled, and pitied the infatuation, and even friends could scarce excuse the folly', but Robert rejoiced that he had surrendered 'a place and a situation, which continually presented objects calculated to excite and to gratify the lust of the eye and the pride of life'. 'Instead of being engaged in such poor matters,' he wrote, 'my time is more at my command, and I find my power of usefully applying property very considerably increased.'[59]

The immediate focus of his philanthropy was the Society for the Propagation of the Gospel at Home. Already committed to defraying the expenses of the society's preachers and schoolmasters, he now set about establishing seminaries to supply graduates to perform those tasks, educating pious young men 'who fear God, who honour the king,

---

57.　Ibid., pp. 134, 194; *Times*, 9 Jan., 1798, issue 4,088.
58.　*Lives*, p. 274.
59.　Ibid., pp. 195, 592; R. Haldane, *Address*, p. 60; the price of Airthrey is given by Robert's grandson in a prefatory note to his diary for 1878 (at Gleneagles).

and who do not meddle with matters of government'.[60] About eighty
students were selected for education at his expense for up to three years
under tutors in Edinburgh, Glasgow, and Dundee.[61] In England, two
generations earlier, George Whitefield had founded preaching centres,
or tabernacles, in his campaign to inject enthusiasm into religion;
now, encouraged by English friends, Robert decided to transport this
model to Scotland. First, a lease was taken on the Circus, an erstwhile
Edinburgh theatre, where, on 3 February 1799, in a ceremony lasting five
hours, his brother James was ordained 'to be pastor of a church on the
Congregational plan'. Next, Robert bought an adjacent site in Greenside,
at the head of Leith Walk, and built for his brother a tabernacle larger
than any of Edinburgh's churches; when opened in July 1801, it could seat
3,200, with standing room for a further 800. Subsequently he financed
the establishment of similar large places of worship in Glasgow, Dundee,
Perth, Elgin, Thurso, and Wick.[62]

It was estimated that, between the years 1798 and 1810, Robert gave
away nearly £70,000 in furtherance of the propagation of the gospel
in Scotland.[63] His liberality, however, was controlled by economic
prudence, and any who hoped to benefit from his fortune 'as a wreck
cast upon the shore, to which all ought to be allowed to help themselves', were disappointed.[64] In 1798, for example, he became interested
in a scheme to bring about thirty children of African chiefs from Sierra
Leone to Britain for education, before returning them home five years
later to take their part in the public affairs of their country. The governor and the Sierra Leone Company accepted Robert's offer to bear
the cost of the children's travel, maintenance, and education for that
period, estimated at between £6,000 and £7,000, on the understanding
that he would control the project, and that it would be conducted in
Scotland. He accordingly took the lease of a house on the western edge

60. *Address*, p. 83.
61. *Lives*, p. 274.
62. Ibid., pp. 219, 274, 278–9.
63. Ibid., p. 342.
64. Ibid., p. 302.

of Holyrood Park and furnished it to await the children's arrival. They never reached Edinburgh. The Sierra Leone Company waited until they had landed in England before telling Robert that his services would be limited to financing the enterprise and that the children's education would be based in Clapham, under the company's control. Robert made it categorically clear that, without the sole management of the project, he would not bear its sole expense. The governor insisted that the education of Sierra Leone's future chiefs should be predominantly secular and eventually found alternative funding, but he had discovered that Robert Haldane's benevolence was ruled by a keen determination to control how his money was being spent.[65]

The colonial authorities' suspicions about the effects of an evangelical education were as strong as those of the establishment of the Church of Scotland about the effects of itinerant lay preaching. The size of congregations attracted by the Haldanes and their associates, and the class from which those congregations were predominantly drawn, prompted an alarmed General Assembly to place 'vagrant teachers and Sunday-schools, irreligion and anarchy' within the same category, prohibit the use of kirk premises by unlicensed preachers, and threaten legal proceedings against unauthorized teachers of Sunday schools.[66] Such fulminations, however, served only as spurs to the Haldanes in the furtherance of their mission.

James had spent the summer of 1798 on a second preaching tour, which took him to Peebles, Biggar, Hamilton, and Greenock, before moving south into Ayrshire and Galloway.[67] When he accepted the pastoral care of the Circus church, he stipulated that he should be allowed to continue his summer programme of evangelizing 'in the highways and hedges', and in 1799 he revisited the north of Scotland and Orkney, and extended his mission to Shetland; the following summer, he toured Arran and Kintyre; in 1801, now accompanied by his wife and five children, he based his activities at Dumfries, where he settled

---

65.   Ibid., pp. 191–2, 202, 230–3.
66.   Ibid., pp. 236–7; Lovegrove, 'Unity and separation', p. 166.
67.   *Lives*, pp. 184–5.

for four months before leaving his family, to spend September in Ulster, where he found that his 'unsophisticated, Bible-searching, non-clerical way of faith' had a strong appeal for the Scottish settlers.[68]

Like his brother, and indeed anyone else who had sat at the feet of Dr Bogue in Gosport, James believed that the scriptures had been dictated by the Holy Spirit and combed them for guidance. In his effort to recover apostolic practices for the operation of the Edinburgh Tabernacle Church, he was led to question the scriptural authority for infant baptism. By the start of 1808, he found that he could not conscientiously baptize children, and, in April, he became a Baptist, followed within the year by his brother. The result was to split the Haldane movement, and halt the expansion which had taken the number of Congregational churches in Scotland from fourteen in 1800 to eighty-five in 1807.[69] The Congregational movement, whose foundation in Scotland is to be traced to the work and philanthropy of the Haldanes, continued under paedobaptists, whose refusal to retain any 'visible or church fellowship' with the brothers in effect created the Baptists as a denomination north of the Border.[70]

The year 1808 was a watershed in the career of Robert Haldane. A bruising quarrel with a once close colleague about property rights over the Glasgow Tabernacle (built by Robert at a cost of £3,000) exacerbated feelings of frustration over ecclesiastical disagreements with past associates whom he had been accustomed to lead. The debate over baptism had also demonstrated the importance of further research into the scriptures. Hitherto, much of the Haldanes' theological work had devolved upon James. It is true that Robert had participated in preaching, but he lacked his brother's strong voice and skill in modulating it, and, on one occasion, burst a blood vessel when addressing an open-air

68. Ibid., pp. 242–51, 257–69, 280–82; A.L. Drummond & J. Bulloch, *The Church in Victorian Scotland 1843–1874* (Edinburgh, 1975), p. 55.
69. *Lives*, pp. 334–6; H. Escott, *A History of Scottish Congregationalism* (Glasgow, 1960), p. 82; Drummond & Bulloch, *Church in Victorian Scotland*, p.53.
70. Ibid.; Ferguson, *Scotland 1689 to the Present*, p. 231.

gathering.[71] His major contribution had been in printing and circulating thousands of Bibles and myriads of tracts, in funding and supervising the establishment of Sunday schools, the erection of tabernacles, the education of preachers and catechists, and the dispatch of hundreds of missionaries. 'There is,' wrote his nephew Alexander, 'hardly an object to which he at first devoted his individual energies, for which there has not since been established a special Society.'[72]

In 1809, Robert evidently felt the need for refreshment. His chosen remedy revealed how great a sacrifice the abandonment of Airthrey had, in fact, been. From funds raised by selling those farms on his old estate which he had retained, as well as his lands in Forfarshire, he purchased 2,400 acres of wild and bleak moorland at Auchengray near Airdrie, east of Glasgow. The challenge of the site may have been one inducement for its selection; another was unquestionably the Hillend reservoir, a sheet of water two miles in length, on the eastern end of which Robert built a house, less flamboyant than Airthrey, but with an echo of his previous house in a central flight of steps leading down to the lawn. The wilderness was transformed by the drainage of moss, the planting of hundreds of acres with trees, and the improvement of many more, on which he erected new homesteads.[73]

Here, and at his Edinburgh house, 10 Duke Street (to which he had moved from the west end of Princes Street, where he had lived in the 1790s), Robert devoted himself to writing *The Evidence and Authority of Divine Revelation*. He felt it imperative to counter the influence of German textual criticism and scholastic emphasis on the nuances of Hellenistic Greek, which had produced among contemporary theologians an analytical approach to biblical texts, allowing that their sense came from God, but asserting that their words were the work of men. So far as Robert could see, such academic analysis bred nothing but scepticism and 'assumed the possibility that Christianity might prove a

---

71.   *Lives*, pp. 276–8.
72.   Ibid., p. 357.
73.   Ibid., pp. 358–61. Burnt down in 1937, Auchengray House is now (2016) a roofless ruin at risk of collapse.

fable'.[74] He countered with a robust declaration that every word in the Bible was divinely inspired. Humans could not pick and choose what to accept or reject, but should 'receive with adoring faith and love what they could not comprehend'. The scriptures were infallible and perfect, and those who thought there may be different degrees of divine inspiration were guilty of sophistry.[75] According to two leading historians of the Scottish church, 'so far as Scotland is concerned [Robert Haldane] has a good claim to be called the Founding Father of Fundamentalism'.[76]

After seeing his book through the press, Robert, with his wife Katherine, took advantage of the peace which had followed the battle of Waterloo to visit France and Switzerland. At the close of 1816, they took up residence in Geneva, the city of Calvin. Robert found its religious life in the grip of those very attitudes which his book sought to refute. Students were more familiar with the teachings of Plato and Socrates than of Christ and the apostles. With the recent French occupation, moreover, had arrived French manners, and he was dismayed to find theatres open on Sunday evenings.[77] In February 1817, he began a series of seminars, which were to provide the foundation for his second major theological work, *Exposition of the Epistle to the Romans*. They were regularly attended by between twenty and thirty Protestant students, who responded with enthusiasm and respect for 'this gentleman of the *ancien régime* with his old fashioned powdered hair'. 'What a man!' declared Merle d'Aubigné, the future ecclesiastical historian, 'Such strength in the Scriptures! Such faith! Such Christianity! His religion is something quite different from what we had been taught.' Years later, another Swiss pupil could still envisage 'his tall and manly figure, surrounded by the students, his English Bible in his hand ... a

74. Drummond & Bulloch, *Church in Victorian Scotland*, pp. 250–1; D.W. Bebbington, *Evangelicalism in Modern Britain: A History from the 1730s to the 1980s* (London, 2003), p. 86; *Lives*, p. 361.
75. Ibid., p. 412; Bebbington, *Evangelicalism*, p. 87; R. Haldane, *The Evidence and Authority of Divine Revelation* (Edinburgh, 1816), pp. 134–7.
76. Drummond & Bulloch, *Church in Victorian Scotland*, p. 251.
77. *Lives*, p. 396.

living concordance'.[78] Robert spent one year in Geneva and two at the Protestant seminary in Montauban, during which time he became a central and vital figure in the Continental *Réveil*, 'a disastrous meteor to the careless, card-playing, and Sabbath-breaking pastors'.[79]

While abroad, Robert engaged energetically in theological controversy, directing pamphlets against rationalist clergy in both Switzerland and Germany. After returning home, his target became the British and Foreign Bible Society, a body which, since its creation in 1804 had played an essential part in the evangelical revival and received support from all quarters for its simple declared intention of disseminating the scriptures. Robert himself had been a benefactor, but, in 1821, quite by chance, he discovered that, for the last two years, the Apocrypha had been included in Bibles destined for members of the Roman and Greek churches. Following three years of amicable but inconclusive private negotiation, Robert devoted his formidable energies to a public campaign, castigating the London committee of the Society for agreeing to publish 'as the Bible whatever shall be considered to be the Bible, whether in Christian, Mahometan, or Pagan countries'.[80] He attracted considerable support, but his opponents were resilient, and the controversy blazed for some twelve years, in the course of which his views on the Bible's divine inspiration gained more publicity than they had previously received. At the end of his life, Robert considered that the stand he had taken against the Bible Society constituted his most important work.[81]

The Apocrypha controversy, during which he published no fewer than fifteen weighty tracts, did not exhaust Robert's combativeness. In 1837, he caused a sensation by accusing the Revd Dr John Brown of rebellion against Christ for offering to go to prison rather than support a state church by paying the Edinburgh annuity tax, which maintained the

78. Stunt, *From Awakening to Secession*, p. 34; *Lives*, p. 403.
79. Stunt, *From Awakening to Secession*, p. 33; *Lives*, pp. 387–460, quotation at p. 453.
80. R. Haldane, *Review of the Conduct of the Directors of the British and Foreign Bible Society* (Edinburgh, 1825), pp. 35–6; Lovegrove, 'Unity & Separation', pp. 158–9.
81. Bebbington, *Evangelicalism*, pp. 87–8; *Lives*, p. 481.

city's established clergy. Robert also disapproved of establishment, but, from the very outset of his evangelical mission, he had based his attitude to civil authority on the Epistle to the Romans, which left no room for doubt that a refusal to pay lawfully required tribute was a violation of divine law.[82] Finally, in June 1842, six months before his death, he wrote two tracts upbraiding the Edinburgh and Glasgow Railway Company for running trains on the Lord's day.[83]

Robert died in Edinburgh on 12 December 1842, two months short of his seventy-ninth birthday. In 1836, he had moved west from 10 Duke Street, which had been his family's home since the start of the century, and taken up residence at 6 Randolph Crescent; finally, a move of some 400 yards had been made to 18 Walker Street. The inventory to Robert's testament shows that he also owned 78 Queen Street and commercial property in Greenside Place; also in Greenside was the Tabernacle, in which his brother James was left a life interest; the house in Queen Street was bequeathed to his daughter Margaret, who, since 1805, had been married to James Farquhar Gordon; Auchengray was left to his widow, to be held in trust for their daughter. Arrears of rent from tenants both in Edinburgh and on the Auchengray estate amounted to £928; the contents of Walker Street and Auchengray were valued at £800; altogether his personal estate amounted to £5,383 13s. 2d., which was conveyed in trust to his nine grandchildren.[84] His widow Katherine survived him for only six months; both lie buried in the cathedral of St Mungo at Glasgow.[85]

No portrait of Robert was ever painted: he refused to sit for one, although in Geneva Dr César Malan sketched his profile. It is known that he was two inches taller than his brother, whom he resembled, although his features were sharper. During his last illness, he spent much time attired in a dressing-gown, reclining upon a sofa in his drawing room, but with his hair 'as carefully powdered as when in health'. In health, he

82. Romans 13:1–7; *Lives*, pp. 568–9; above, p. 205.
83. *Lives*, p. 581.
84. NRS, SC70/1/64, inv. 1843 Robert Haldane; *HG*, pp. 209–11 for the grandchildren.
85. *Lives*, p. 591; *HG*, pp. 208–9.

was remembered as a man of 'majestic form, earnest manners, playful urbanity, gentlemanlike bearing, and heavenly-minded conversation'.[86]

James Alexander was in his seventy-fourth year when he succeeded his brother as head of the Haldanes. He had made his last preaching tour – to the north of Scotland – in the summer of 1830, no longer speaking in the open air after losing his voice during a tour of Ayrshire the previous year.[87] His magnetism, however, remained undiminished. His adoption of a plural eldership at the Edinburgh Tabernacle had little practical effect, since congregations fell away dramatically when his place was taken by a colleague. This experiment exemplified his determination to apply apostolic practices to worship, which also led him to adopt weekly communion, mutual exhortation, and salutation.[88] His Bible-searching quest for purity seemed inexhaustible. While he was less combative than his brother, his literary contribution to the religious controversies of the day was as large.[89] He was anxious not to be thought partisan, for 'I heartily rejoice in the number of faithful ministers of any denomination being increased.... But I am Christ's servant: I observe his ordinances in faith, and I cannot be satisfied that I am right without an equal conviction that those who are otherwise minded are wrong.'[90]

James died in his eighty-third year on 8 February 1851 at his Edinburgh house, 34 Drummond Place, which he had bought in 1826. His wife, Mary Joass, had died in 1819, having given birth to nine children, of whom one daughter, Catherine, had died in 1802 at the age of seven, the eldest son, James, was to die unmarried in 1831, a few weeks before his thirty-second birthday, and Elizabeth, a spinster, in 1843 aged forty-nine. On 23 April 1822, James married again. His second wife, Margaret, was the daughter of the late Daniel Rutherford, physician and chemist, professor of botany at Edinburgh University, the discoverer of nitrogen, and an uncle of Sir Walter Scott, who considered him 'more

86. *Lives*, pp. 545, 585, 590.
87. Ibid., p. 553.
88. Lovegrove, 'Unity & Separation', pp. 174–6.
89. *Lives*, p. 549.
90. Ibid., p. 615.

of a gentleman than his profession usually are'. She bore six children, of whom George died before his second birthday in 1831. Margaret survived her husband for nearly sixteen years before joining him and his first wife in the churchyard of Edinburgh's West Church.[91]

James's personal estate amounted to £4,372, of which £2,032 derived from investments in the stock of English railway companies, and £1,485 from the stock of two Scottish railway companies, neither of which was that castigated by Robert for scheduling a Sunday service. He also drew an annual rental income of £220 from property in Edinburgh: in India Place, William Street, Bedford Street, Greenside Place, and Hercules Street (between the Pleasance and Holyrood Park, now demolished), most of which had been acquired in 1824 and 1825. By his first marriage contract James was bound to give £16,000 to the children of that marriage, and had already disbursed £6,000; the children of his second marriage were to have £2,000 each; to his widow was left the liferent of his properties, as well as all furniture, linen, and plate, except that with the Joass arms, which should pass to the two surviving unmarried daughters of his first marriage. James doubted not 'that both families will live together as they have always done'.[92]

The power of the pen: Alexander Haldane, 1800–82

James's successor as head of the Haldane family was Alexander, the elder surviving son of his first marriage.[93] Born in Edinburgh on 15 October 1800, Alexander had been educated in that city, like all his brothers and half-brothers, at the High Scool and then at the University. Before entering the latter, however, he had joined his elder brother James (b.1799)

---

91. *HG*, pp. 219–20; for Daniel Rutherford, see B.B. Woodward, rev. by A.M. Lord, 'Rutherford, Daniel (1749–1819)', *ODNB*; *The Letters of Sir Walter Scott*, ed. H.J.C. Grierson et al. (12 vols, 1932–79), vi. 52–3.
92. NRS, SC70/1/73, 4/16, inv., wills, 1851 Haldane, James Alexander.
93. What follows is based on *HG*, pp. 257–9; J. Wolffe, 'Haldane, Alexander (1800–1882)', *ODNB* (2004); idem, 'Recordites (*act.* 1828–c.1860)', *ODNB* (2015); J.L. Altholz, 'Alexander Haldane, *The Record*, and religious journalism', *Victorian Periodicals Review*, xx (1987), 23–31.

at Winteringham on the Lincolnshire bank of the Humber, where they boarded with the curate Lorenzo Grainger, a widely respected and successful classics tutor.[94] After their mother's death in February 1819, the brothers journeyed both north and south of the border. James died in Scotland, unmarried, in 1831, but Alexander chose to spend his life in England. In 1820, he entered the Inner Temple. Two years later, he married Emma Hardcastle, with whom he had been in love since their first meeting in Edinburgh in 1819. The pair went to live with her widowed mother and unmarried elder sister at Hatcham House in New Cross, on the Surrey–Kent border near Deptford.[95]

During the life of Emma's father, Joseph Hardcastle, Hatcham House had become the resort of a broad cross-section of prominent evangelicals. Joseph, who died in 1819, had been a prosperous London merchant, philanthropist, and nonconformist evangelical. He was a founder of the interdenominational London Missionary Society, and his friendship had been highly valued by Alexander's father and uncle.[96] The personal commitment of Alexander and Emma to the evangelicalism in which they had each been raised was profound. Alexander's career at the bar, where he limited himself to conveyancing law, was, for a while, a necessary source of income, but it inspired neither him nor others. The inspiration which fired his formidable energy and intellect derived from a perceived need to defend biblical infallibility, and protect the nation from decadence.

Alexander's chosen arena was that of the written word, in whose use he displayed a talent for controversy and polemic. His weapon was *The*

94. For Grainger, see *The Life and Remains of Henry Kirke White* (London, 1825), p. 213; W. Andrew, *The History of Winterton and the adjoining Villages* (Hull, 1836), p. 109.

95. 'A biographical sketch of Alexander Haldane', *The Record*, 28 July 1882 (off-print, pp. 7–9); for Hatcham, see B. Weinreb & C. Hibbert, *The London Encyclopaedia* (London, 1983), p. 539.

96. *Lives*, p. 616; S, Gregory, 'Hardcastle, Joseph (1752–819)', *ODNB* (2004); J. Morison, *The Fathers and Founders of the London Missionary Society* (new edn, London, 1844), pp. 71–2, 100. Emma wrote a pious biography of her father: E.C. Haldane, *Memoir of Joseph Hardcastle* (1860; preface 1869); see pp. 310–12.

Record, a bi-weekly religious newspaper, viewing public affairs from an evangelical standpoint, which had run into financial difficulty within six months of its launch in January 1828. Alexander's ability to participate in its rescue in July, and emerge by November as its chief proprietor and, in effect if not in name, editor, was assisted by his wife's inheritance of £3,000 on the death of her mother the previous year.[97] The first issue of *The Record* under Alexander's control was careful to explain that Monday publication could be achieved without Sunday labour since printers could do the necessary work on Monday morning. Fanatical sabbatarianism, vitriolic ant-Catholicism, premillenarianism, biblical literalism, and a dour Calvinism at times brought *The Record* close to caricature. The Great Exhibition of 1851, for example, was castigated in its pages for displaying nude statues, which were 'polluting to morals and unworthy of men'. Alexander was remembered by an English historian of Anglican evangelicalism as 'a man of deep and genuine piety, but a true son of that uncompromising land beyond the Tweed, where toleration is deemed to be the eighth of the deadly sins'.[98]

Nevertheless, Alexander Haldane was taken seriously. The confrontational posture of *The Record* and violence of its language may have been distasteful to many, but they ensured that it was noticed. In 1834, for example, after reading Alexander's leading article denouncing the cabinet's profanation of the Sabbath by arranging the coming week's business at dinner on Sundays during the parliamentary session, the prime minister abandoned the custom. Alexander also claimed that some credit should be given *The Record* for the improved character of the clergy noticeable since the early days when it published lists, culled from

97. By the terms of Joseph Hardcastle's will and the marriage settlement (PROB11/1617/168; marriage settlement 1822, at Gleneagles), Emma received £7,000 on the day of her marriage, plus £4,000 in trust (whereas Alexander brought only £2,000 to the altar: SC70/4/16, wills 1851, Haldane, James Alexander), and was to receive a further £3,000 on her mother's death; Mrs Hardcastle died on 1 July 1827: Haldane, *Memoir of Joseph Hardcastle*, p. 343.

98. G.R. Balleine, *A History of the Evangelical Party in the Church of England* (London, 1908), p. 206.

local newspapers, of those members of the cloth attending county balls, 'a race now wellnigh extinct'; greater decorum was also observed on the turf and hunting-field.[99] With a wide circulation among the middle and upper classes, the journal became tri-weekly in 1855. Alexander had transferred editorial control in 1854 to his friend, the Revd Edward Garbett, but continued to contribute leading articles, and, since he had by now become sole proprietor, his influence remained predominant.

Preparation for the premillennial second advent of Christ led Alexander and others who shared his belief to examine ways of improving the condition of the poor. Among those in whose company he found himself on committees and public platforms was Lord Ashley, who became seventh earl of Shaftesbury in 1855, after achieving, during his time in the House of Commons, significant reforms of the conditions of labour in factories and coal mines. Almost exact contemporaries, the two men struck up a rapport in 1847 and remained intimate friends until separated by death. From the time that his friend became a peer, 'Mr Haldane was so constant an attendant to the House of Lords that he acquired a prescriptive right to a certain place which was always reserved for him.'[100] Both were Low Church Tories, opposed to the advance of rationalism and ritualism in the Anglican church. When the pragmatic Lord Palmerston became prime minister in 1855, it was to his son-in-law, Lord Shaftesbury, that he turned for advice on church appointments, and the earl in his turn 'was greatly assisted in his labours by Mr Haldane', who had become his principal 'counsellor and friend', scarcely a day passing when the earl was in London which did not find them in each other's company. For almost a decade, Alexander Haldane was an *éminence grise* behind clerical advancement to bishoprics, deaneries, and canonries, opening such appointments to clergy of evangelical principles, who had hitherto been excluded. At the end of his life, he rejoiced that it was 'now almost impossible to go back to the old system of nepotism, or of rewarding domestic tutors and editors of Greek plays

99. *Record*, 27 March 1882.
100. E. Hodder, *The Life and Work of the Seventh Earl of Shaftesbury, KG* (3 vols, London, 1887), ii. 401 note.

with the lucrative dignities provided by the state for the chief pastors of the church.'[101]

Alexander and his wife had moved from Hatcham House on the death of Emma's spinster sister in 1846. The advance of suburban villas had already altered the locality, and plans for a major development had been announced by the Haberdasher's Company, who owned the manor. The family moved across the Thames to the Manor House in East Ham, which was still an agricultural village,[102] but so much of Alexander's time was now spent in the metropolis that, in 1852, as soon as he had completed his memoir of the lives of his father and uncle, a final move was made to 118 Westbourne Terrace in 'Tyburnia', from which a short walk would take him to Lord Shaftesbury's house in Grosvenor Square. The relationship between the two men cooled in 1878, when Alexander begged his friend to reconsider resigning from the Society for the Propagation of Christian Knowledge in reaction to its publication of a sceptical critique of methods used to assess evidence for the literal fulfilment of biblical prophesies, and the rift widened the following year, when Alexander's articles in *The Record*, supporting the recent invasion of Afghanistan, contrasted with his privately expressed admiration for Shaftesbury's speeches in the House of Lords castigating it as sinful aggression. The earl felt that he could never again trust the sincerity of 'that feeble and double-faced man'.[103] He perhaps never understood how Haldane the journalist could paint with a broader brush than Haldane the private man, but the quarrel ended in forgiveness and restored cordiality. On 16 June 1882, after falling in the street while running the previous day, the 81-year-old Alexander took to his bed; on 9 July, his son arrived at Westbourne Terrace from Scotland, to find his father very

101. Ibid., iii. 200, 448; G.B.A.M. Finlayson, *The Seventh Earl of Shaftesbury 1801–1885* (London, 1981), p. 320; G. Battiscombe, *Shaftesbury: A Biography of the Seventh Earl 1801–1885* (London, 1974), pp. 217–18; *Record* 27 March 1882; for Palmerston's attitude, see D. Brown, *Palmerston: A Biography* (New Haven & London, 2010), pp. 416–19.

102. *Lives*, p. 620; Weinreb & Hibbert, *London Encyclopaedia*, pp. 249, 539. Haldane Road in East Ham is close to the site of Manor House.

103. Battiscombe, *Shaftesbury*, pp. 320–1.

weak; three days later, he was visited by Lord Shaftesbury; on the seventeenth, he repeated the Lord's Prayer after his son, who thought it was 'the last conscious act of his life'; the following day, Lord Shaftesbury returned, but Alexander 'did not notice him'; the peer 'looked very sad, and said: "This will make a terrible blank in my life". On 19 July, with his son in constant attendance, 'he again and again put his hands together in attitude of prayer. Lord Shaftesbury came twice, and sat a long time by his bedside in much sorrow. All was over at about 6.30.' Alexander died fifteen years after his beloved wife. Like her, he was buried in Paddington Cemetery, on a wet and stormy day, with an inconsolable Lord Shaftesbury refusing to cover his head and resisting the efforts of Alexander's son to protect him from the elements, saying that 'it did not matter what happened to him now'.[104]

The earl remembered his friend's life as 'one less of personal activity than of religious intellectualism, devoted to the advancement of Christ's kingdom and the temporal and eternal welfare of the human race'. Shaftesbury's biographer, who also knew Alexander, added that he possessed 'a strong sense of humour and an inexhaustible fund of anecdote', while the obituary in *The Record* paid tribute to its late proprietor's 'warmth of heart'.[105] Neither humour nor warmth is to be detected in Alexander's journalism; armed with pen, ink, and paper, he put geniality to one side as he smote hip and thigh in his battle to ensure that his compatriots did not fall into the errors bred by the development of scientific thought and ritualist practice as they read their Bibles at home and listened to sermons in church. His son's movement towards the opposite spectrum of the Anglican church to his own, however, never seems to have weakened the loving relationship which subsisted between the two.

Alexander was survived by all his children. The eldest, Anne (b.1823), who in 1845 married John Corsbie, a barrister of the Middle Temple and member of an East Anglian family prominent in Bury St Edmunds and its environs, died in Brighton in 1898 after twenty-seven years of

104. Hodder, *Earl of Shaftesbury*, iii. 450; for Alexander's last days and deathbed, see his son's diary for 9–19 July 1882 (at Gleneagles).
105. Ibid., ii. 400; *The Record*, 28 July 1882, p. 481.

widowhood. Her birth had been followed by that of four daughters, all of whom remained spinsters, Mary Alexina (b.1826) dying in 1911, Selina (b.1828) in 1904, Emma (b.1832) in 1896, and Henrietta (b.1837) in 1906. Alexander's male heir did not arrive until 14 August 1842, when his wife gave birth to James Robert Alexander Hardcastle, her last child.[106]

Alexander's own generation of Haldanes comprised four surviving full sisters (his father's daughters by Mary Joass), two of whom remained unmarried: Margaret (1803–89), who died in London, and Henrietta (1797–1885), the eldest, whose adult life was spent in Edinburgh at 14 Stafford Street, earning admiration for her charitable and pious works, notably in founding and maintaining a school for poor children at Greenside, and in missionary activity in the coalmining village of Kennet on the Bruce estate in Clackmannanshire. Marriage took his other two sisters to a military environment in India: Mary (1801–57) as the second wife of James Eckford, who rose to the rank of lieutenant-general, and Catharine (1806–97) as the wife of her sister's stepson, George Eckford.[107]

Alexander's younger full brother, Robert (1805–77), enjoyed a successful legal career in Edinburgh as a Writer to the Signet. During the 1840s he acted as Lord Camperdown's factor for the Gleneagles estate and, in 1852, strengthened the Haldane presence in the neighbourhood by buying the small estate of Cloan (three miles north-east of Gleneagles), where, some thirteen years later, he transformed the two-storey farmhouse into a castellated mansion. His first marriage, to Jane Makgill, ended in 1851, in its tenth year, with her death in childbed. Two years later, he married Mary Burdon-Sanderson, the sister of Richard Burdon-Sanderson, the Northumbrian landowner and botanist, who, in 1848, had married Robert's half-sister Isabella (1823–92).[108]

---

106. *HG*, pp. 259, 261. Henrietta's year of birth is taken from the census of 1871, and Anne's date of marriage from the register of St Paul's, Deptford. Alexander dropped 'Hardcastle' from his forenames in the late 1860s.

107. *HG*, pp. 239–40, 246–7.

108. *HG*, pp. 221–6; for his courtship of Mary, see E.S. Haldane (ed.), *Mary Elizabeth Haldane: A Record of a Hundred Years (1825–1925)* (London, 1926), pp. 96–8.

Isabella was the eldest of Alexander's father's three daughters by Margaret Rutherford. Her sister Adamina (1826–98) spent her life in Edinburgh as a spinster, while Helen (1828–73), whose husband, Horatio Peile, was the duke of Montrose's factor, went to live at Catter House near Drymen, on ground whose superiority had, until 1816, belonged to the lairds of Gleneagles.[109]

Each of Alexander's surviving half-brothers rose to the top of his chosen profession in Edinburgh. The elder, Daniel Rutherford Haldane (1824–87) followed the path trodden by his maternal grandfather, as consulting physician and pathologist at the Infirmary, and as a popular and influential lecturer in the medical school at Surgeons' Hall, esteemed by his peers for his service as secretary and then president of the Royal College of Physicians in Edinbugh, and as its representative on the General Medical Council, and 'for his kindly, unostentatious disposition'. His wife, Charlotte (née Lowthorpe), born into the gentry of East Yorkshire, survived him for twenty-one years.[110] Rutherford was the first Haldane known to have entered the medical profession. His younger brother James (1831–1906) was the first to enter that of accountancy. In 1858, after two years in the office of his half-brother Robert, acquiring the legal grounding which he wisely saw as advantageous in his chosen field, James joined the accountants Lindsay and Jamieson. By the end of the century, Lindsay, Jamieson and Haldane was the largest and most influential chartered accountancy firm in Scotland. Based at offices in St Andrew Square, but also with a branch in Austin Friars, London, in 1860 it employed twelve clerks; in 1890 that number had risen to sixty; in 1860 fees from its client base totalled £4,761; in 1890 that figure had quadrupled. James's particular value, to colleagues and clients alike, lay in his ability to identify the essence of a problem, to express himself simply and economically, and to act with precision, thoroughness, and determination. He offered his services to the Edinburgh Infirmary, and

109. *HG*, pp. 254–5; for Peile, who ended his career as factor on the Greenock estate of Sir Michael Shaw-Stewart, see NRS, GD220/6/571, 573–5 (Montrose Muniments).

110. *HG*, pp. 249–50; P. Wallis, 'Haldane, Daniel Rutherford (1824–1887)', *ODNB*; *British Medical Journal*, 16 April 1887, p. 854.

to the Scottish Episcopal Church, in whose affairs he took a deep interest. He was also a founder of the Scottish Conservative Club. He died on 30 October 1906, and his wife, Emily (née Grove), the daughter of a naval officer, followed him within seven months to the grave.[111]

Romance, riches, and Episcopalianism: Alexander Chinnery-Haldane, bishop of Argyll and the Isles, 1842–1906

James Robert Alexander Haldane, the youngest child and only son of Alexander and Emma, did not use the names of his celebrated grandfather and great-uncle, but was known to the world as Alexander and to his family and friends as Alick or Aleck.[112] Born on 14 August 1842, he was educated at home until he was fifteen, when it was evidently felt that he needed a more testing régime. Reports arrived at Westbourne Terrace from his married sister in Suffolk praising the achievements of Albert Wratislaw, who had recently arrived at Bury St Edmunds as headmaster of King Edward VI Grammar School, whose decline he had immediately arrested. Wratislaw was a Czech scholar with expertise in many subjects and a reverence for his country's Protestant past, which would have commended him to Alick's parents. In 1857, the boy was duly dispatched to Bury, where he resided with his sister's family but had a miserable time at school. As an adult, he never enjoyed the company of boys, nor did he, it would seem, when he was one himself. Although enthusiastically athletic, he disliked competitive sports (except rowing), and exposure to academic competition would also have distressed him, for even his panegyrical biographer remarked upon 'the extreme slowness with which his mind worked'. Alick remained at school until

111. *HG*, pp. 252–3; S.P. Walker, 'Anatomy of a Scottish CA Practice: Lindsay, Jamieson & Haldane 1818–1918', *Accounting, Business, and Financial History*, iii.2 (1993), pp. 127–54; T.A. Lee (ed.), *Shaping the Accountancy Profession* (London, 1996), pp. 13–14.
112. For 'Aleck' or 'Alec', see T.I. Ball, *A Pastoral Bishop: a Memoir of Alexander Chinnery-Haldane, D.D.* (London, 1907), p. 53; Lord Camperdown to Alec Haldane, 31 Oct. 1905; Selina Haldane to Alec, 25 May 1890 (at Gleneagles); 'Alick' is used in all correspondence by his mother and father.

his nineteenth year, before going up to Trinity College, Cambridge, to read law, as a first step in following his father's plan for him to become a barrister.[113]

His family's move to 118 Westbourne Terrace introduced Alick to other denizens of Tyburnia, the name given to a residential development intended to attract the fashionable world as a northern counterpart of Belgravia. In nearby Hyde Park Square, at number 18, the Revd Sir Nicholas Chinnery, Bt, initially welcomed the proximity of the proprietor of *The Record*, with whose evangelical, Low Church opinions he found himself reassuringly in agreement. On New Year's Day 1863, he sent seasonal greetings to Mr Haldane and his family, as well as thanking Alexander for the gift of a theological work by his father James and promising him a copy of his own *Anglican Formalism*, a sermon still at the printers, which he had recently delivered at Trinity Chapel, Conduit Street, where he had served as chaplain since 1856.[114]

Born in 1804, in holy orders since 1829, Nicholas had succeeded his father Brodrick in 1840, when he became the third Chinnery baronet and inherited estates centred on Flintfield, Co. Cork, as well as property in Dublin and substantial financial assets. On 27 March 1843, in Dublin, he had married his second cousin, Anne Vernon, and, on 3 July 1844, their only child, Anna Elizabeth Frances Margaretta, was born.[115] Domestic tranquillity, however, became undermined by the theological differences which subsisted between Sir Nicholas and Lady Chinnery. He had hoped that 'thru' Evangelical preaching and teaching [his] beloved A.'s mind [had been] led to see Divine truth more distinctly than before, and she [had been] brought to perceive the ignorance and erroneous view

113. S.H.A. Hervey, *Biographical List of Boys Educated at King Edward VI Free Grammar School, Bury St Edmunds: from 1550 to 1900* (Bury St Edmunds, 1908), p. 173; G. Stone, 'Wratislaw, Albert Henry (1821–92)', *ODNB* (2004); T.I. Ball, *A Pastoral Bishop: A Memoir of Alexander Chinnery-Haldane, D.D.* (London, 1907), pp. 51–3, 76, quotation at p. 4.

114. Sir N. Chinnery to A. Haldane, 1 Jan. 1863 (at Gleneagles, as are all MSS referred to in the following notes to this chapter); *The Observer*, 28 Jan. 1856.

115. *Annual Register 1843*, p. 206; *Gentleman's Magazine*, xxii. 200.

of her mother &c, and especially of her brother'; but, in October 1857, a bad-tempered argument showed that hope to be without foundation. After he had written what he considered to be an affectionate request that she repent 'for the bitter and evil words which she had spoken to me – for her total disregard of dutifulness as my wife – in a word, for being, as I told her this morning, "in rebellion" against her husband, she wrote me a letter worded in the most unkindly style, and replete with rancour, bitterness, and even abuse'. Equally, if not more shattering to his happiness, his adored daughter sided with her mother and the Vernons, a position he ascribed not only to unavoidable feminine solidarity, but also to her 'lack of serious impressions', and sensitivity to 'kindness and natural hilarity'.[116] Sir Nicholas and Lady Chinnery subsquently found a *modus vivendi*, but, by the time his family came into contact with the Haldanes, his emotional well-being depended upon his relationship with his daughter.

Unknown to Sir Nicholas, but with the connivance of his wife, young Anna became a regular visitor at 118 Westbourne Terrace, and, in June 1863, after Alick had been permitted to walk with her during a combined family expedition to the newly opened South Kensington gardens of the Royal Horticultural Society, of which Sir Nicholas was a member, the couple announced their betrothal. This development came as a surprise to Alick's father, and as a deplorable shock to Anna's, who asked Mr Haldane to intervene. Alexander replied that any attempt by him to divert his son from 'the object of his attachment' would be utterly hopeless: 'he considers himself pledged and devoted to your daughter, and could not extinguish if he would the flame which she has inspired'. He appealed to Sir Nicholas's 'calm judgment and feelings as a father to consider if it would be well for either of us to attempt an interference which could only blight the happiness of both of the cherished objects of our parental solicitude'.[117] Sir Nicholas was appalled to discover that his wife had known of the liaison and kept that knowledge secret from him. She protested that, as she had heard him speak highly of Mr and

---

116. Sir N. Chinnery's 'Observations on the occurrences of October 1857'.
117. A. Haldane to N. Chinnery, postscript to missing letter, June 1863.

Mrs Haldane, and indeed 'favourably of the youth', she assumed that he would have approved.[118] She was wrong.

Anna was within a month of her nineteenth birthday, and therefore, as a minor, required her father's permission to marry. This Sir Nicholas refused to give. Not only did he dread the loss of his beloved daughter's company, but he was also keenly alert to the danger of predatory fortune-hunters. Exactly ten years previously, he had rescued his sister Margaretta from a bogus lunatic asylum, to which she had been committed by a husband who had then set about dissipating the £13,000 capital and £400 annuity which she had been left by her father.[119] Even though it must eventually have become clear to Sir Nicholas, as it certainly had to Mr Haldane, that their children were in love, the match was far from approaching the sort of alliance that the baronet hoped his only child would in due course make. The summer passed into autumn without Alick being able to advance his suit, and, in September, his father took him to stay with kinsfolk at Cloan and Camperdown. By the time they returned to England, Sir Nicholas had become alarmed that his daughter's emotional distress would seriously damage her health, and, on 28 October, he opened negotiations. He would withdraw his 'positive opposition' on two conditions: firstly, that an income should be secured to Alexander Haldane's son, proportionate to what he himself would give his daughter, and which jointly would maintain the couple in the 'sphere of life in which she ought to be'; secondly, that young Haldane should change his surname to Haldane-Chinnery.[120]

If Sir Nicholas had hoped that the second condition would prove unacceptable, he was to be disappointed. Alexander told him that he found his wish quite natural, held, as it was, by 'the head of an antient and honorable line', and that his son's attachment to Miss Chinnery was too strong to allow him to hesitate to comply with it. The head of the Haldanes, nevertheless, made certain that the head of the Chinnerys

118. Sir N. Chinnery's 'Impartial review of my wife's conduct, 22 Nov. 1863'.
119. 'The note-book of an Irish barrister: Sir Edward Sugden in Ireland', *The Metropolitan Magazine*, xxxvi (1843), 373.
120. N. Chinnery to A. Haldane, 28 Oct. 1863; Journal of J.R.A. Haldane, September 1863.

(who would have struggled to trace his ancestry beyond the sixteenth century) understood that the Haldane name had 'descended from father to son in uninterrupted succession ever since surnames were known'. Leaving the financial negotiations to another day, he assured Sir Nicholas that 'it has been a comfort to my dear wife and me to remember that we were dealing with a man of God, with one who would not be actuated by mere worldly considerations, but who would seek first for the kingdom of God, and whose own will would submit to the directing influence of the Holy Spirit'; after all, since the alliance had not been arranged by the parents, 'it may form the verification of the old Proverb that marriages are made in Heaven'.[121] The reverend baronet would have none of this: 'I do not admit the truth of the remark that worldly considerations are not to be taken into account. . . . We live in a world in which certain things are wanted for the particular spheres in which we are placed by the Providence of GOD.'[122]

The ensuing correspondence became exclusively worldly and increasingly antagonistic. Sir Nicholas scorned Alexander's offer to settle an annuity of £200 upon his son; should he himself double it, the combined sum (equivalent to about £69,000 in 2016) would be inadequate to maintain his daughter in 'the sphere of life in which she has always moved'; when Alexander took this hypothesis as a promise to give £400 a year, Sir Nicholas confided to his notebook that 'the whole of Haldane's proceeding is artful, and thus is the most urgent cause for my caution'; when Alexander (himself, of course, a lawyer) asked that his son's prospective earnings at the bar should be considered, the baronet told the barrister that he had certainly not contemplated 'that my daughter should marry anyone who should spend his days from morning to afternoon or evening in Chambers or in an Office'. In reaction to Alexander's lyricism about the couple's devotion to each other, Sir Nicholas observed that 'faithful feelings and tender sentiments may be all very amiable, but they must not lead our judgment. It is not with poetry but with prose we have to do.'[123] Alick himself sought to calm

---

121. A. Haldane to N. Chinnery, 30 Oct. 1863.
122. N. Chinnery to A. Haldane, 7 Nov. 1863 (letter-book, p. 8).
123. Ibid., pp. 7–8; N. Chinnery's memorandum, 12 July 1864.

matters by writing an apology to Anna's father and promising to do all he could to make amends, but the response from Sir Nicholas to his 'dear young friend' was a chilly reminder that he should have requested an interview with him 'before a word was uttered to his daughter', while, as for amends: 'What amends can you make to remedy what has been done? – to restore the satisfaction and comfort which I had once with my child?'[124]

An impasse had been reached by the middle of November 1863, with Sir Nicholas suggesting that progress could not be made until the undergraduate had completed his university course. His father was able to report on 21 June 1864 that Alick had successfully taken his Ll.B.[125] The fathers now embarked upon two months of hard-nosed bargaining, with Messrs. Bridges, Chinnery's lawyers, providing a buffer between them. 'My trial,' complained the sad and lonely Sir Nicholas, 'is that I have no wife to consult, no-one with whom to confer except the Bridges.'[126] At last, on 20 August 1864, the marriage settlement was signed, and Nathaniel Bridges left his office for three weeks' well-earned holiday. Alexander Haldane transferred to trustees £4,000 worth of railway stock to provide his son with £200 a year, and Sir Nicholas Chinnery transferred £8,000 worth of East India stock to secure an income for his daughter of £400 a year.[127] On 29 July, a royal licence had been granted for Alick's change of surname; on 20 August, Lancaster Herald had informed Sir Nicholas that the new name should be hyphenated, which the baronet considered 'a disfigurement'; he had doubtless hoped that, without a hyphen, 'Haldane' would have fallen into disuse. He had also wanted the change of name to be announced before the wedding, but Alexander resisted, and it was gazetted on the same day.[128] The wedding

---

124. N. Chinnery to J.A. Haldane, 11 & 16 Nov. 1863 (letter-book, pp. 10, 14).
125. Ibid., pp. 8–9 (7 Nov. 1863); A. Haldane to N. Chinnery, 21 June 1864.
126. N. Chinnery's memorandum, 12 July 1864.
127. Copy Settlement on the Marriage of J.R.A. Haldane Esq[re] with Miss Chinnery; Bridges' correspondence with Chinnery and Haldane is at Gleneagles; for Nathaniel's holiday, see his letter to Chinnery, 15 August 1864.
128. Lancaster Herald to N. Chinnery, 20 Aug. 1864; *London Gazette 1864*, p. 4124; the licence is at Gleneagles.

took place on Sunday, 23 August, at St John's Church, Paddington, after the morning daily service, and with the Revd Sir Nicholas Chinnery officiating. He had stipulated that the ceremony 'be in as private a way as possible, and the fewer persons present, the better'.[129]

Mr and Mrs Haldane-Chinnery set off on an extended honeymoon, visiting friends and relations in England and Scotland, and exploring parts of the country that engaged their interest. From 3 March to 24 April 1865, they were to be found in Malvern, doing a great deal of walking; thence they decamped to a hotel in Henley-on-Thames, where Alick indulged his passion for rowing, and the pregnant Anna rested. On 20 May, Alick entered in his journal: 'Early this morning Anna's baby, a boy, was born, but alas without life'. The couple stayed at Henley for another month to allow Anna to recuperate, before returning to London to take up lodgings at 74 Cambridge Terrace in Regent's Park. Apart from spending three days with his father in early May, dining at the Inns of Court, Alick had made no progress in his legal career. On 25 July, after looking at houses in the Home Counties, he and his wife left for Ireland to show themselves to the Flintfield tenantry and visit Anna's Vernon relations, whose theological opinions her father had found so objectionable. Religion must have pervaded their thoughts and conversation, for, by the time the couple returned to England on 12 September, Alick had decided to take holy orders.[130]

It is not known what reaction was produced when knowledge of this decision reached Westbourne Terrace and Hyde Park Square. It must have dominated the four talks which Alick had with his father-in-law in the first week of December 1865. His own father approved of the change of direction, possibly bearing in mind the influence he and his friend Lord Shaftesbury had recently exercised, and might again exercise, over clerical promotions. In the event, however, neither he nor Lord Shaftesbury was to have any influence on the course that Alick's career took.[131]

129. N. Chinnery to A. Haldane, 16 Aug. 1864 (letter-book, p. 20).
130. The above is drawn from Alick's journal for 1865; cf. Ball, *Pastoral Bishop*, p. 59.
131. Ibid., pp. 59–60; Journal of J.R.A. Haldane-Chinnery, 1–6 Dec. 1865.

In 1866, Alick returned to Cambridge to prepare for ordination. This he did under the guidance of a friend of his old headmaster, Charles Swainson, the Norrisian professor of divinity, a kindly, generous scholar, not unfriendly to the revival of ritualist ceremonial for which Cambridge was providing a cradle. He kindled in his charge an interest in ecclesiology and suggested that he consider a curacy at Calne (Wiltshire) in the diocese of Salisbury, whose vicar, John Duncan, was an old pupil, and also a Scot. Alick spent the night prior to his ordination in April 1866 fasting and praying until dawn amid the megaliths of Stonehenge, than which he had thought 'nothing could be more wonderful', when first seeing them nine years earlier.[132]

Both his bishop and his vicar were associated with the Tractarian movement, which aimed to revive the doctrine of apostolical succession and insisted on sacramental rites which the Anglican Church had long represented as Roman errors. That Professor Swainson thought Alick's clerical career should be launched under their aegis indicates how far the young man had already distanced himself from the Low Church evangelicalism into which he had been born, and was moving towards the Anglo-Catholicism which his father and Lord Shaftesbury, and also his father-in-law, sought to eradicate. As a fourteen-year-old, he had rejoiced in Glasgow cathedral's escape from the sixteenth-century reformers' 'fury', and, three years later, on one of many visits to the ultra High Church St Paul's in West Street, Brighton, he noted with approval that the communion table was covered with black, and had candles on and around it; that the chancel was divided from the rest of the church by a screen, and was used only by the priests and choristers. These were the very practices that Sir Nicholas Chinnery and others itemized in a memorandum of complaints about Romish influence in church services, delivered to the archbishop of Canterbury in June 1866.[133]

132. H.G. Matthew, 'Swainson, Charles Anthony (1820–87)', *ODNB* (2004); Ball, *Pastoral Bishop*, pp. 62–4; Journal of J.R.A. Haldane, 11 April 1857.
133. Ibid., 23 August 1856, 1 March 1859; *Morning Post*, 22 June 1866, issue 28,870.

Alick's father was well aware of the Tractarian tendencies of Bishop Hamilton of Salisbury, and also knew that a large number of Low Church parishioners had found John Duncan's ministry, since his arrival in 1865, so objectionable that they had decamped to Calne town hall for their services while a new 'Free Church' was being built. He wrote to Professor Swainson with his misgivings, but was unpersuaded by the don's assurance that he need have no fear of the influence of Bishop Hamilton ('a good and pious man, strong-willed it may be, but not strong-minded'), unconvinced by his judgement that Duncan was 'a wonderful man, high-toned, making everything subordinate to winning souls to Christ', and also unimpressed by the professor's gnomic statement that, of the few men he would introduce to Duncan, Alick was one. Alexander wrote to his son on 8 April 1866, urging that he decline the curacy, but he was too late. Alick told him that he had definitely accepted the offer on 28 March, and that 'Calne has everything to attract me'. His father's letter had perplexed him greatly. 'I shall have but little to do with the Bishop, & I shall <u>never</u>, if I can trust myself, be found identified with the High Church party – though I may not be quite able to take the views of the Low. I seldom open a High Church paper without finding much that disgusts me. But Mr Duncan is not such. Though not a Low Churchman, he is certainly an Evangelical in the truest sense. He says his one object is to preach Christ crucified, and to convert men to Him; and in this work I should humbly endeavour to follow. It has been my frequent prayer that I might turn out to your satisfaction, & I trust that at Calne you would not find me disappoint you.' Alick's evangelical upbringing had given him a passionate belief in the divinity of Christ, and the truth of the Gospels as God's word; controversies such as those about transubstantiation or justification by faith did not greatly interest him; he simply knew and rejoiced that Christ was present when the Holy Eucharist was celebrated, and felt that his presence should be recognized with elaborate ceremonial. Like Alexander Mackonochie, the curate at St Alban the Martyr, Holborn, with whom he had begun a lifelong friendship, he regarded ritual as 'the outward clothing of a sound faith', and, like Mackonochie, he believed that it brightened the drab lives of the poor, whom he felt should be the chief focus of his ministry.[134] He was also tolerant. 'I love all Evangelical Protestants,' he told his father, 'though they do not love us,' and, as for the Established, the Free, and the United Presbyterian churches, he hated the sects, but loved the men. Different liturgical practices interested rather than offended him, and he hoped 'that all those who believe in Jesus and His Gospel will form <u>one party</u> ere long'. His father, however, never ceased to pray that his son and daughter-in-law 'may be delivered from all heresies on the right hand and on the left in these perilous times'. In 1877, in response to Alick's gift of his book, *The Scottish Communicant*, Alexander warned that it approached 'too near the confines of idolatry' in its discussion of the Eucharist, and that, by enjoining people always to kneel at prayer, and to repeat the Lord's Prayer more than once, it was in danger of reducing prayer to 'a form'. He had also been distressed to find his son's name printed by Mr Mackonochie as an adherent, for he thought him 'a shuffler with his conscience' and his followers 'a very low set'. So far as Alick was concerned, it was 'the Catholic party in the Church of England' that was endangered and 'under formidable attack', and he placed himself among that party. But this he confided to his diary, not his father, with whom his relationship remained loving and close. He was, however, sensitive about their divergence of opinion: a parishioner in Calne, who used Alexander Haldane's name when censuring Alick for not being Calvinistic, was treated to a stiff bow and the curate's abrupt departure.[135]

134. W.A Greenhill, rev. H.C.G. Matthew, 'Hamilton, Walter Kerr (1808–69), bishop of Salisbury', *ODNB* (2004); A.E.W. Marsh, *A History of the Borough and Town of Calne* (Calne, 1903), p. 148; D.A. Crowley (ed.), *VCH Wiltshire*, xvii (London, 2002), pp. 109–11; C.A. Swainson to Alexander Haldane, 26 March 1866; J.R.A. Haldane-Chinnery to his father, 9 April 1866; his journal, 24 Nov. 1868; R. Mitchell, 'Mackonochie, Alexander Heriot (1825–87)', *ODNB* (2004); Ball, *Pastoral Bishop*, pp. 14–34, 67.

135. Alexander Haldane to his son, 1 May 1873 (*bis*), 17 June 1877, 10 May 1879; Alick to his father, 10 March, 18 Aug. 1974; Alick to George Standen, 20 April 1900; J.R.A. Haldane-Chinnery, Journal, 17 May 1874; idem, *The Scottish Communicant, to which is annexed The Order for the Celebration of the Holy Eucharist* (1877; later editions under the name Chinnery-Haldane); Ball, *Pastoral Bishop*, p. 67.

Alick was appointed to serve the little church of the Holy Trinity, recently built to meet the needs of the largely working-class community of Calne's eastern suburb of Quemerford and also to act as a chapel of ease for a new parish graveyard. It was here that he and Anna buried their two-month-old daughter, Agnes Elizabeth, who died on 5 July 1866. Anna responded to this heavy blow by involving herself enthusiastically in her husband's work, and, during the course of 1867, they contributed towards the establishment of the Holy Trinity School in Quemerford. At the same time, Anna's relations with her father deteriorated. Although he never visited Calne, not even for the funeral of his granddaughter, Sir Nicholas knew enough about Bishop Hamilton and the Revd John Duncan to fear for Anna's doctrinal safety. Whether as the consequence of a bitter argument, or of an unwelcome discovery, he filled one page of a notepad on 2 June 1867 with the anguished cry: 'My child is gone!'[136]

At some stage in the ensuing months, it seems that Sir Nicholas used the threat of altering his will to persuade Anna to leave Calne. In May 1868, she and her husband took lodgings in Charlotte Street, Edinburgh. She was in the last two months of another pregnancy, and a desire to be close to the medical advice of Alick's uncle, Dr Rutherford Haldane, probably explains the choice of residence. On 24 July, a son was born, and, a week later, he was baptized, and given the Haldane name of James and the Chinnery name of Brodrick, by which he was to be known. Alick soon felt secure enough about the health of his wife and son to return to Calne, for he had not resigned his curacy. On arrival, he found that enquiries had been made by his father-in-law. A local report which had come to his notice made Sir Nicholas frantic about his daughter's continued 'most grievous connection with the teaching in the parish church at Calne'. He evidently feared that, albeit at a distance, she was helping to finance ritualist practice. On 8 August 1868, this disconsolate, friendless man poured out his concern in a letter verging on incoherence, sent via Calne's postmaster to a person he had never met and whose name he did not know. The addressee was the church's treasurer, who was asked by the baronet for 'some account of the proceedings and

136. Ibid., p. 64; *VCH Wilts*, xvii. 109–11; N. Chinnery's 'Observations on the occurrences of October 1857 & the subsequent circumstances'.

doctrines which are going on'. Sir Nicholas was not optimistic. 'That the incumbent is a protégé of the Bishop of Salisbury speaks enough. Is Ritualism set up in the Church? I have heard not – but is this true? Are things getting worse than they were? I take for granted your zeal for sound Evangelical truth in contrast to what is called Sacerdotalism – High Churchism – Ritualism alias Broad Churchism.' He prayed that his daughter should be 'brought back to the reception and love of those precious truths of the Gospel, ... but alas! Circumstances have led to this present state of things, for which I mourn! ... Nothing but absolute necessity has led to this step of withdrawing [her] from the place where error is to be heard.'[137]

Should Sir Nicholas have become convinced that Anna would use her fortune to promote the cause of ritualism, then the possibility that he would indeed change the terms of his will to cut out his daughter became a probability. In August 1868, Sir Nicholas and Lady Chinnery set out from London for Ireland, breaking their journey at Chester, where, on 20 August, they boarded the Irish Mail train, bound for Holyhead. As it steamed along the north coast of Wales, its engine was struck at Abergele by two wagons filled with barrels of petroleum, which had broken loose in a siding on a slope above the main line; the resultant conflagration engulfed the first passenger carriage, burning all its occupants to death; among them were Sir Nicholas and Lady Chinnery. As soon as Anna felt strong enough, she and Alick travelled to Dublin to unpack her parents' luggage, which had been stowed at the back of the train and so escaped the flames. In it they found Sir Nicholas's will; it was unaltered; Anna was the chief beneficiary.[138]

During his extended visit to Edinburgh prior to his wife's safe delivery of their son, Alick had given assistance to any of the city's Episcopal churches and chapels that stood in need of a temporary chaplain. That

137. N. Chinnery to the treasurer of the church at Calne, 8 August 1868 (at Gleneagles); for a detailed account of his son's baptism, attended by Dr Rutherford Haldane, see Alick's journal for 31 July 1868.

138. For rumour that the will was to be changed, and the journey to Dublin, see Alick's journal for August 1868, where his grandson has written a note based on letters now missing.

PLATE 22. (Left) Brodrick Chinnery-Haldane, aged about 19, with penny-farthing, *c.* 1887.

PLATE 23. (Below left) Alexander Chinnery-Haldane (born 1907) and James Haldane (born 1975) in 1980 upon the laird's Triumph Thunderbird.

PLATE 24. (Below) Katherine Chinnery-Haldane (1878–1957), the lady of the glen.

PLATE 25. (Right)
Alexander Chinnery-Haldane
(laird 1937–94), a surprising
warrior; a painting by
Julian Barrow, 1993.

PLATE 26. (Below)
Viscount Haldane of Cloan
(1856–1928), and Albert
Einstein, 1921.

PLATE 27. (Bottom)
'Evidence that geniality can
flourish in the company of
scientific knowledge:' Albert
Einstein's description of his
meeting with Viscount
Haldane of Cloan. Einstein
evidently assumed that Lord
Haldane's sister and
companion, Elizabeth, was
his wife, and addressed his
remarks to an imagined
'Lady Haldane'.

PLATE 28. (Above left) Sir William Haldane (1864–1951), keeper of family secrets.

PLATE 29. (Above right) General Sir Aylmer Haldane (1862–1950), the family historian.

PLATE 30. (Left) James Haldane (1831–1906), a pioneering chartered accountant; the present laird's great-grandfather.

PLATE 31. The *Haeslingfield* before the typhoon, 1743, from a punch bowl of c.1744.

PLATE 32. The *Haeslingfield* after the typhoon, 1743, from the same.

PLATE 33. The Haldane arms transferred in China without modification from a bookplate to an achette, *c.* 1732.

PLATE 34. The impaled arms of Haldane and Wemyss on a wooden pediment, probably from Gleneagles Castle, celebrating a marriage in 1624.

PLATE 35. Gleneagles before the roof was raised, c. 1885, with a veranda linking the two pavilions in place of the planned but unbuilt central block.

PLATE 36. Gleneagles today.

PLATE 37. Interior of Gleneagles Castle, 1928.

PLATE 38. St Mungo's Chapel, Gleneagles; a painting by Petronella Haldane, 2000.

PLATE 39. Brodrick Chinnery-Haldane(laird 1918–37) with his wife Katherine on the right, Alexander in the centre, and Agnes and Brodrick Vernon on the left, before Gleneagles Castle, 1928.

PLATE 40. Martin Haldane (laird since 1994) with his wife, Petronella, 2017.

PLATE 41. Rachel Buxton, James Haldane, younger of Gleneagles, and Anna Blakey.

which made the deepest impression upon him was All Saints' Church in Brougham Street, Tollcross, and indeed it was there that his son was baptized. All Saints' had originated in this deprived neighbourhood as a mission from the sedate St John's, and its building began in the 1850s to provide for those with whom the congregation of the mother church were reluctant to rub shoulders. Its incumbent, Mr Murdoch, proved too High Church for the taste of the St John's establishment; financial backing had been withdrawn, and its congregation had dwindled. Like its neighbourhood, it was half-built and its appearance forlorn.[139] Its need was urgent, its location was in the land of his ancestors, and Alick agreed to place himself at Mr Murdoch's disposal in the late autumn of 1869.

In the meantime, the Haldane-Chinnerys had business both in Calne, where Alick resigned his curacy in November 1868, but promised the vicar a contribution of £500 towards his foundation of St Mary's Anglican School for girls, and in London, where the affairs of Anna's late parents had to be wound up. They moved into 18 Hyde Park Square, which was now theirs, dined frequently with Alick's father (who had been widowed in April the previous year), travelled on the underground railway, visited the waxworks in Baker Street, which they thought more lifelike when viewed by gaslight, and, on 7 December, took baby Brodrick with his nurse to a Miss Oak's establishment in Brompton, where he was to remain for nearly four months; on 14 December, the Chinnery silver was deposited in the London and Westminster Bank, and the next day the couple set off for Folkestone, en route for France and Spain, returning on 29 March 1869 to Hyde Park Square, where they were met 'by the bonnie bairn, who was well and thriving, thanks be to God.'[140]

An immediate visit to Edinburgh to find a house lasted three weeks, but the summer was spent mostly in London, where Alick frequently

139. Ball, *Pastoral Bishop*, pp. 82–3.
140. Journal of J.R.A. Haldane-Chinnery, 2 & 12 Nov., 7, 14–31 Dec. 1868; 1 January–29 March 1869, quotation at 29 March. I am grateful to Elizabeth Christie of St Mary's School for providing details of the Duncan Haldane-Chinnery endowment.

officiated at St Mary's Paddington. Not until the end of October did Alick return to Edinburgh to concentrate his attention on All Saints' and minister to poor people in various parts of the old town. On 13 November, with 18 Hyde Park Square being prepared for sale, and its furniture sent north, the Haldane-Chinnery family moved into their new house. A short distance south of All Saints' Church, on the edge of Bruntsfield Links, stood Bishopscourt, a seventeenth-century tower house once called Greenhill, which had been bought by the Episcopal Church as a residence for bishops of Edinburgh, but, proving inconveniently far from the city centre, was now let to Alick and Anna at an annual rent of £260. They subsequently bought it for £7,000. 'Bishopscourt' was not a suitable designation for the residence of a curate, and, perhaps with a nod to a hymn popular in High Church circles, the name reverted to Greenhill House.[141]

Here, with their family increased on 15 February 1870 by the birth of Patrick Vernon (to be known as Vernie), the Haldane-Chinnerys lived in some style. Their footmen were recruited in London, and their carriage turned heads in Princes Street. For Anna's use on informal jaunts in fine weather, and doubtless to remind her of Dublin, a two-wheeled, open 'Irish car' was also acquired in 1874. When engaged on pastoral work, however, Alick himself usually travelled on foot, walking the length and breadth of the city, as well as out to Craiglockhart on his regular visits to the poorhouse.[142] The importance with which he viewed his task was made clear in 1873 in one of his rare speeches at a diocesan synod. He told his hearers that 'during nearly five years, he had had an opportunity

141. Ibid., 30 March–13 November 1869; the rent is noted on the flyleaf of the journal for 1880; for the hymn, cf. E.J. Lovell, *A Green Hill Far Away: The Life of Mrs C.F. Alexander* (Dublin & London, 1870). Greenhill House was demolished in 1884, and its site and grounds built over; a carving depicting it may be seen on the wall of a tenement at the corner of Bruntsfield Place and Bruntsfield Gardens.

142. Ball, *Pastoral Bishop*, pp. 84, 86–7; J.R.A. Haldane-Chinnery's Journal, 27 July 1871, 6 June 1874; for an appreciation of his work among the poor, see S. Mumm, *All Saints Sisters of the Poor: An Anglican Sisterhood in the Nineteenth Century* (Ch. of England Rec. Soc., 2001), pp. 18–19.

of seeing a good deal of the lower classes, especially in Old Town, and he must say that Scotland – at least as far as Edinburgh was concerned – was an unbaptized country. Presbyterianism had certainly, either through fault or misfortune, failed to carry out our Lord's divine command both as to preaching the Gospel to the poor, and the baptism of children.'[143] While the curate cared assiduously for his flock, his wife opened her purse to complete the building of All Saints' Church and contribute to that of schools, parsonage, and convent.[144]

Dividends payable on investments were producing for the Haldane-Chinnerys an annual income of £3,428 in the mid 1870s (roughly equivalent to £350,000 in 2016), but their expenditure was such that, on 1 May 1873, Alick's father told him that 'it is really a shame that with your income there should not be a surplus instead of a deficiency'. He was convinced that his son was being 'plundered by people practising on your charity'; John Duncan's conduct at Calne (where his new girls' school had just opened with the help of the Duncan Haldane-Chinnery Endowment) had made him to Alexander 'an object of contempt', and he feared that 'your present position at All Saints makes you regarded as one who allows himself to be "plucked"'. He begged Alick 'to withstand temptations to squander either on the church or its objects so as to harass and embarrass you'.[145]

It was not only All Saints' in Edinburgh, but the Scottish Episcopal Church as a whole that was impoverished. The Episcopalians' eviction from the established church in 1689 led to a decline which was accelerated by their association with Jacobitism in the eighteenth century. The toleration accorded them after the death of the Young Pretender in 1788 opened the way for the now legal Episcopal Church to emerge from the barns and tents in which many of its services had been held, and embark on a building programme, for which it desperately needed patrons of independent means. The arrival of the Haldane-Chinnerys, therefore, was bound to excite the keenest interest beyond the bounds

143. Haldane-Chinnery's Journal, 8 May 1873.
144. Ball, *Pastoral Bishop*, p. 92.
145. Mrs Haldane-Chinnery's list of dividends (at Gleneagles); A. Haldane to his son, 1 May 1873; Ball, *Pastoral Bishop*, p. 73.

of Edinburgh. In August 1872, on the other side of Scotland Bishop Ewing of Argyll and the Isles delivered an address at Ballachulish, where he resided, promising that 'should it come into the head of any wealthy churchman to give himself to the restoration of this church and people, and to make himself a home in this place, he would find a noble work and a hearty welcome awaiting him'.[146]

In March 1873, the bishop's wife, Lady Alice Ewing, called at Greenhill House, a visit the Haldane-Chinnerys reciprocated the following year, staying with the now widowed Lady Alice and doubtless discussing her late husband's vision. Alltshellach, her house at Ballachulish, was on the northern shore of Loch Leven, where it opens through often turbulent narrows into Loch Linnhe. Set amid spectacular scenery in Lochaber (Cameron country), approached from the south-east through the gloomy majesty of Glencoe, the locality had enchanted Alick when he first saw it during a Highland tour with his father in 1856. Twenty years later, he and his wife decided to live here during the summer, bought Alltshellach, and moved in on 17 May 1876. Alick at once began ministering to the congregation of St Bride's Church, newly built by Lady Alice to serve the Episcopalians of Onich, Ballachulish's northern neighbour. The experiment was successful, and at the end of December, on the understanding that he would have leave of absence for 'the winter half of each year', he accepted his appointment as its first incumbent. For the next two years, he apportioned his time between St Bride's, Onich, in the summer and autumn, and All Saints', Edinburgh, in the winter and spring, but Bishop Mackarness, the new bishop of Argyll and the Isles, recognized the importance for his diocese of securing Alick's undivided attention. He was able to offer him scope for his pastoral talents and charitable impulses which could not be matched in Edinburgh, and the link with All Saints' was officially severed in 1878.[147]

In the same year, as if to punctuate his career, Alick reversed his surname. Whereas Sir Nicholas Chinnery had made his consent to

146. A.J. Ross, *Memoir of Alexander Ewing, D.C.L., Bishop of Argyll and the Isles* (London, 1877), p. 589.

147. For the above, see Alick's journal for 29 August 1856, 3 March 1873, 17 May 1876; Alick to his father, 10 Oct. 1976; Ball, *Pastoral Bishop*, p. 93.

his daughter's marriage conditional on Alick adopting the name of Haldane-Chinnery, his will simply stipulated that successors to his estate should bear the Chinnery arms and name along with their own. With a deep interest in heraldry and genealogy, Alick was keenly aware of his position as heir to the seniority of the Haldane family of Gleneagles, and, with Anna's 'most loving consent', sought a licence, which was duly granted, to change their name to Chinnery-Haldane.[148]

In 1879, he became rector of St John's Ballachulish, on the southern bank of Loch Leven, and the following year added a third congregation to his flock when he built the church of St Mary to serve the people of Glencoe. In 1881 he was appointed dean of the diocese. Bishop Mackarness of Argyll and the Isles died on 20 April 1883, and in the subsequent election Alexander Chinnery-Haldane was unanimously chosen to succeed him. Before confirming his appointment, the Primus (the bishop of Moray and Ross) suggested that he avoid partisanship by resigning his membership of the Society of the Holy Cross and the Confraternity of the Blessed Sacrament. Alick answered: 'Were I now to withdraw from either, I think I should never again deserve the respect or confidence of my fellow men, ... and with regard to the Confraternity I feel that by now forsaking it I should be guilty of an act of disloyalty towards JESUS Christ My King and My God.' No more was heard of the matter.[149]

As the first ritualist to be elected to a British bishopric, he was bound to be viewed with apprehension in some quarters of the Episcopal Church. Ballachulish itself was at the centre of a region where traditional Scottish episcopacy remained strong. The largely Gaelic-speaking population needed to be reassured that its new bishop was no harbinger of Anglican hegemony.[150] Alick had, in fact, started taking Gaelic lessons within two months of his arrival at Ballachulish in 1876, but he was no linguist, and initial attempts to use the language when officiating were

148. A. Haldane-Chinnery to his father, 1 August 1878; [A. Haldane], *Memoranda re Haldanes of Gleneagles*, p. 10.
149. Ball, *Pastoral Bishop*, pp. 96–7, 101, 104–5; Alick to Primus, 2 July 1883.
150. Cf. R. Strong, *Episcopalianism in Nineteenth-Century Scotland: Religious Responses to a Modernizing Society* (Oxford, 2002), p. 137.

not encouraging, so colleagues who had 'the Gaelic' were engaged to take those services or parts of services which were conducted in that tongue.[151] But, if the language of the Highlands escaped him, he could still embrace its customs. He relished the challenges and advantages of the landscape and climate, bathing in the loch before breakfast and fishing in it later, rowing in rough waters and hiking long distances over difficult terrain in all conditions, for Ballachulish was frequently cut off by storms and snow. Its weather could be deadly: on 15 December 1887, Alick's friend Mackonochie failed to return to Alltshellach from a morning walk and was found on the seventeenth frozen to death in the hills north of the loch. The bishop's hospitality was partly modelled on that of a Highland chief, with his butler and footmen supplemented by his piper, Angus Cameron. This assumption of local ways elicited a cynical response from Cameron of Lochiel, from whom Alltshellach was feued and with whom relations were not always cordial; at a dinner given for him at Alltshellach in January 1889, with the piper playing a Cameron air, Lochiel appeared clad in trousers, which sadly shocked the bishop's kilted son, Brodrick.[152]

Lochiel's mood was clouded by his disapproval of the bishop's plan to enlarge Ballachulish's Loch Leven Hotel, which he leased. It was but a small item in a programme which saw very large sums of money pass from the Chinnery-Haldanes to architects, masons, builders, joiners, decorators, and gardeners. Apart from raising St Mary's and its parsonage from their foundations, adding a chancel to St Bride's, and building schools and teachers' houses in Ballachulish and Glencoe, they rebuilt and aggrandized Alltshellach, so that it eventually comprised a chapel, some thirty-five rooms (including domestic offices and servants' quarters), and separate staff cottages, while, between 1901 and 1903, a substantial house (Dunbeg) was built nearby for Brodrick.[153] Beyond the area of Loch Leven, the bishop provided a house and chapel on the isle of Iona for clerical retreats, which he had greatly valued since first

151. Journal, 5, 12, 14 July 1876; Ball, *Pastoral Bishop*, p. 118.

152. Bishop's journal, 7 Jan. 1889; Brodrick's diary, 7 Jan. 1889; for Mackonochie's death, see Ball, *Pastoral Bishop*, pp. 138–44.

153. Brodrick's diary, 7, 9, 14 Jan. 1889; Alltshellach inventory, 1907.

making Greenhill House available for such a purpose in 1870. When the future of the college buildings built by Lord Glasgow for Episcopalians on Cumbrae was imperilled by their founder's financial crash in 1885, the bishop accepted responsibility for the costs involved in retaining them and subsequently made them available for retreats, the expenses for which, here as on Iona, he bore himself.[154] After consulting the relevant bishops, he also organized, and paid for, Gaelic ministrations outside his diocese, in Cullipool, Ardchattan, Glasgow, and Aberfoyle.[155]

Expenditure on such a scale strained the resources even of Anna Chinnery-Haldane. In 1875, against the advice of Uncle James, the family accountant and general source of wisdom, she mortgaged part of her Irish property, and, in 1878, began negotiations with Lord Lisle of Mountnorth which ended in the sale of the Flintfield estate. Finally, in 1881, the sale of Greenhill House and its extensive grounds to Edinburgh property developers for £22,200 (roughly equivalent to £2,500,000 in 2016) provided funds to be used exclusively for ecclesiastical and educational purposes.[156]

The bishop lacked any business capacity. His failure to grasp the value of money was engrained; once, as a schoolboy, he had rung for the butler, and said: 'Bring me some money, please.'[157] It was his good fortune, and that of the objects of his philanthropy, that the butler was replaced by his wife. It should be emphasized that Anna was in no way a reluctant collaborator, and their marriage seems to have been a happy one. Both enjoyed travel; between 1868 and 1898, they spent over thirty months on foreign tours, most lasting about eight weeks, in France, the Low Countries, Germany, Switzerland, Italy, Spain, North Africa and the Holy Land, Turkey, Greece, Hungary, Austria, Russia, Finland, and Sweden, where few art galleries and fewer churches escaped their notice.

---

154. J.R.A. Haldane-Chinnery's Journal, 21–26 Nov. 1870; Ball, *Pastoral Bishop*, pp. 129–33.
155. J.B. Craven (ed.), *Records of the Dioceses of Argyll and the Isles 1560–1860* (Kirkwall, 1907), p. 288.
156. J.R.A. Haldane-Chinnery & Chinnery-Haldane's journals, 29 Sept. 1875, 26 Feb. 1878, 14 Dec. 1881; cf. Ball, *Pastoral Bishop*, p. 94.
157. Ibid., p. 12.

Alick also liked the theatre, enjoyed playing whist, although he did not play it well, and was habitually cheerful.[158] He was also a teetotaller and an enthusiastic supporter of the temperance movement, an enthusiasm not shared by his wife, who, in later life, found that wine relieved the strain of 'marriage to a saint' and imported bottles to Alltshellach concealed in book boxes.[159]

Alick's favourite recreational pastimes were athletic: rowing, hiking, and running; ten days after his fifty-fourth birthday, he ran three miles in thirty-one minutes.[160] He was slow to take up the new craze of bicycling, which his son Brodrick had introduced to Alltshellach in June 1891, and at which Anna had become 'quite at home' in June 1897; not for another two years did the bishop take to the high road on two wheels, but thereafter it became his favourite means of locomotion.[161] His least favourite activity was attention to business, whether of his diocese or of his small estate. The latter he left increasingly to Brodrick, but the former he transacted with meticulous and painstaking care, which, given his ponderous deliberation and congenital unawareness of the passage of time, frequently left only two or three hours for sleep. This regime began to affect his health. Years of testing his body against the harsh conditions of Scotland's west coast resulted from 1899 in attacks of lumbago which became increasingly debilitating. Years of smoking took a harsher toll. In 1902, a mystery illness persuaded him to visit a consultant in Wimpole Street, but nothing more alarming was diagnosed than 'natural deterioration'; he was told that writing at night was bad and that he should employ a secretary. Illness returned in June 1905; his diary's last reference to rowing is on 20 August and to cycling on 9 September. After nearly fainting while celebrating in his family chapel on 1 October,

158. Ibid., pp. 9–10, 167–86; Alick's journal, *passim*.

159. Alick's Journal, 10 Dec. 1879, 9 Jan. & 29 Oct., 1883; B. Haldane & R. Martine, *Time Exposure: The Life of Brodrick Haldane, Photographer 1912–1996* (London, 1999), p. 5. Loch Leven was a temperance hotel during the bishop's leasehold.

160. Journal, 24 August 1896.

161. On 10 April 1901, he cycled 46 miles 'on hilly roads': J.B. Chinnery-Haldane, Diary, 19 June 1891; Bishop's Journal, 23 June 1897, 26 June 1899; 10 April 1901.

he saw doctors first in Edinburgh, then in London. On 9 October, he and Anna went to the theatre to see Beerbohm Tree's 'Oliver Twist', but 'at this I was unfortunately faint and had to go home'.[162]

Lung cancer was diagnosed on 22 October, when the bishop was told that he had no more than a fortnight to live. Lord Camperdown offered him the graveyard at Gleneagles as his final resting-place, knowing how much his ancestral home meant to him. Alick replied 'with my dying hand, for I suppose I am dying, though I don't feel like it', thanking his kinsman 'for the greatest kindness you could have conferred on me', but confessing 'that there are things and places I love even more than Gleneagles', and declaring that he wished to be buried at St Bride's, 'the poor little church where I and my poor little Highland flock have so often (during the last 30 years) met with our Lord JESUS Christ at his Holy Table'. He returned by train from London to Edinburgh, instructing his nurse to wake him as they crossed the border into Scotland. In Edinburgh, he was installed first in a nursing home and then in the Roxburghe Hotel. Lord Camperdown had warned Anna that her 'misery may be more prolonged than the doctors think', and so it proved. On 13 November, Alick returned to Alltshellach, where a bed had been prepared for him in the library, overlooking the loch and the mountains beyond it. There he died, in his sixty-fourth year, on 16 February 1906.[163] He had sent 'a dying charge from a dying friend' to his diocese, pleading that 'you shut your ears against anything said about my goodness', and had instructed those organizing his funeral to 'be very careful to keep out from the newspaper-notice anything boastful about pedigree or family'. About 1,000 people attended the funeral at St Bride's on 21 February, a clear, frosty day, with 'the place looking perfect' and a tearful Angus Cameron piping 'Lochaber no more'.[164]

162. Bishop's Journal, 23 May 1902; 21, 26 June, 20 Aug., 9 Sept., 1, 3, 5, 9, 11 Oct. 1905; Ball, *Pastoral Bishop*, pp. 6–7.

163. Ibid., pp. 194–206; Lord Camperdown to Mrs Chinnery-Haldane, 29 & 31 Oct. 1905; idem to Alec Haldane, 31 Oct. 1905; copy letter, Bishop to Lord Camperdown, 30 Oct. 1905.

164. Alick to diocese (n.d.), and pencilled note written before leaving Edinburgh; J.B. Chinnery-Haldane, Diary 21 Feb., 1906; Ball, *Pastoral Bishop*, pp. 206–9.

Gleneagles Regained

(James) Brodrick Chinnery-Haldane, 1868–1941; laird 1918–37

The seniority of the Haldanes passed on the bishop's death to his elder son. At the age of thirty-seven, Brodrick's experience had been circumscribed by the muscular Christianity of his schooldays at Loretto in Musselburgh, by a somewhat earnest undergraduate career at Oxford, and by life, latterly as a married man, in the remote environment of Alltshellach – sometimes idyllic, often claustrophobic, and always challenging.

Prompted by the fact that its headmaster and proprietor was a lay member of the Episcopal Church, Brodrick's father had inspected Loretto in May 1878 and approved of what he found: a system based on physical exercise in all weathers, numbers limited to 150 boys, ruled by persuasion rather than threat.[1] Brodrick was enrolled in October 1879 and thrived. He swam, played cricket, fives, golf, and, above all, rugby – at Loretto an almost sacred activity. He became captain of the first fifteen and then head of the school in 1887. His headmaster, Dr Almond, came to rely on him in much the same way as his father was to do, even requiring his company when doctors advised a week's holiday to avert a mental and physical collapse. Brodrick's final service on his behalf was to negotiate between the police and his schoolfellows, when the latter

1. M.C. Curthays, 'Almond, Hely Hutchinson (1832–1903)', *ODNB* (2004).

proved reluctant to comply with Musselburgh Town Council's enactment that they should wear bathing drawers when swimming in the river Esk.[2]

Loretto's lack of pretension to academic prowess suited Brodrick. The promise of a place at Christ Church was secured through his father's influence, and he had 'a splendid time' in Oxford in March 1888 to sit (and pass) an undemanding entrance examination, noting in his diary after three days that he was 'awfully happy here'. He went up to read classics, but, after three terms, decided to switch to modern history, being 'tired and sick of turning over the pages of Latin and Greek authors; a thing in one's own tongue will be more in my line'. At first, his undergraduate life revolved around rugby and rowing, whose training regime suited him 'admirably'; he tried lawn tennis, but found that 'the tennis club seems to contain most uninteresting men', and eventually he gave up college rugby, because 'nobody seemed to care'. Throughout his life, his commitment to the tasks he undertook was total. His peers at Christ Church, like his father and headmaster, recognized in Brodrick the qualities of a willing and reliable workhorse, and elected him secretary of the Junior Common Room. At the end of his first term in the post, he noted that his official duties had so fully occupied him that not only his studies but even his rowing was adversely affected.[3]

From the beginning of 1890, Brodrick was also considerably distracted by the presence in Oxford of his twenty-year-old brother Vernon. An idyllic childhood and early youth had ended for Vernie (as he was always known) on 27 August 1886, when he stumbled on clambering into a boat while shooting duck; his gun became entangled in his clothing and shot him in the right elbow; he endured seven weeks of agony and mortal danger before an incompetent attempt to save his arm was abandoned and the mangled limb was amputated (and buried after

2. Brodrick to his mother, 2 June 1886; J.B. Chinnery-Haldane, Diary, 19, 25–6 June 1888 (at Gleneagles, as are all MSS referred to in subsequent notes to this chapter, unless otherwise stated).

3. Ibid., 7–13 March 1888; 2 Feb. 1889; 3 May 1889; 7 Nov. 1890; 27 Feb. 1891; 18 June 1890; 2, 4 Dec. 1890; Brodrick to his mother, 22 June 1889.

dark in St Bride's churchyard).[4] That Christmas, when Brodrick saw his brother for the first time since the accident, he found him managing 'wonderfully well' with his one hand, being 'very jolly, full of humbug'. On 18 January 1890, Vernie appeared in Oxford to be coached for entry to Pembroke College, where a provisional place had been promised him; hardly a day of that term passed when he was not in his brother's company. Despite leaving his Latin grammar paper with nothing written upon it other than his name, Vernie was admitted to Pembroke, whose situation proved dangerously close to Christ Church. One night after dinner at the end of Hilary Term 1891, Brodrick's rooms were invaded by a drunken brother, who was 'very rowdy', broke several things, and on departure smashed a window with his hook, 'which was all over the place'. The next morning found Vernie neither any the worse nor notably repentant.[5]

Brodrick missed the following Michaelmas Term, for his assistance in running his father's estate was deemed necessary at Alltshellach. Already, in February 1889, he had spent hours in his college study going over papers regarding the lease of the Loch Leven Hotel, and the following month in corresponding with the bailiff about livestock purchases and 'a kind of league among estate workers to ask more wages'. On his return to Oxford in the middle of Hilary Term 1892, he engaged a don at Wadham College to coach him for the final examinations which loomed in June; accepting his tutor's advice to stay up during the spring vacation, he did 'some good work', limiting his recreation to a lot of bicycling (for which his enthusiasm had been born at Loretto) and teaching others how to ride. Vernie was less in evidence, although his stick came through his brother's windows one morning in May; Brodrick told his mother that, as 'Vernie lives in an atmosphere of eucalyptus, I really bar him coming into my rooms; he is like a walking pot of furniture polish'. Brodrick sat his finals in a heat wave and was awarded a third-class degree after a 'very decent' viva.[6]

4.   Bishop's Journal, 27 August–14 Oct. 1886.
5.   J.B. Chinnery-Haldane, Diary, 23 Dec. 1886; 12–13 March 1891.
6.   Ibid., 3 Feb. 1889; 14 March 1889; 21–2 May, 8, 19 June 1891; 10 May 1892; 11, 25 July 1892; Brodrick to his mother, 9 Feb. 1892.

Back at Alltshellach, Brodrick's days were filled with estate business, as well as so much rowing of people to and from the house that, to his mounting irritation, 'excursionists' mistook him for the ferryman. A typical evening comprised dinner, whist, prayers (taken by Brodrick during the bishop's frequent absences), smoking, and bed. The Loch Leven Hotel required a frustrating degree of attention, with Brodrick, for example, needing to pacify the manageress, 'in a great state because the new tablemaid is utterly useless: stupid and also deaf'; and, for one dramatic week, having to sleep at the hotel while trying to control a maid who had become 'perfectly raging mad'. Her husband was summoned from Glasgow, but he remained obstinately drunk; the local policeman arrived to take her away, but was deterred by her singing at the top of her voice and then fainting; the doctor was called, and prescribed brandy and eggs, but as a result the woman was 'now drunk as well as mad'. Defeated by the strain of maintaining an adequate level of intoxication in a temperance hotel, the husband left after four days; 'he said goodbye to his wife, who was lying with her legs up in the air, singing "Tommy make room for your uncle"'. The doctor now prescribed 'an enormous dose of castor oil', but she was still singing when two doctors and two nurses arrived to take her away to Fort William, and Brodrick was able to return to his own bed. The lease of the hotel was surrendered some ten weeks later, in May 1896.[7]

Life was rarely so sensational, but acquired a new dimension on 1 May 1894, when Brodrick took possession of the steam launch *Rona*, a gift from his mother, and, with the sea being the main highway, as much a convenience as a luxury. The dominance of bicycle maintenance and weather reports in Brodrick's diary is now challenged by the scraping and varnishing of his vessel. The *Rona* also enhanced his social life, which may have been part of his mother's intention. Before the end of May, she invited the eighteen-year-old Rebecca (Rébé) Monteith to stay at Alltshellach. Rébé was the daughter of a deceased fleet surgeon, whom her mother Clara had divorced in 1884, and had been brought to the west of Scotland in 1890, when Clara became the second wife of

7. J.B. Chinnery-Haldane, Diary, 3 Aug. 1893; 27 Feb.–6 March, 26–8 May 1896.

Archibald Maclean of Pennycross in the Isle of Mull.[8] Brodrick and Rébé established a rapport. He met her stepfather at his Oban residence on 17 September, and the young couple spent the following 'very jolly' days sailing, hill-walking, and simply talking. On the twenty-sixth, however, Vernie arrived home from Oban, where he was working in a lawyer's office (having left Oxford without a degree), and where, it seems, he had already made Rébé's acquaintance. Her attentions immediately switched to him. On 3 October, when she sang after dinner, it was Vernie who turned over her music. The signs could scarcely have been clearer. Brodrick stiffened his upper lip, recording in his journal: 'Mater spoke hoping I did not mind how things were going. Why should I mind?' He spent the next day cleaning his bicycle, while the others went on the *Rona*. That afternoon, he told his brother: 'Don't let me stand in your light', and that evening he went to Rébé, and 'heard the expected; really glad, but it is awfully sudden; after dinner went off to bed feeling about done in'. The following day, 'Vernie and Rébé are awfully good to me. Poor things, they are wretched about me, and can't understand me; no wonder, when I can't understand myself.' Apparently oblivious to his elder son's disappointment, the bishop was 'simply delighted with things', but his wife felt that some form of consolation was called for, and, before the end of the month, Brodrick found himself the possessor of the steam yacht *Malvina*, for which his mother had paid £1,000, with the *Rona* (valued at £500) added in part exchange (a total outlay equivalent in 2016 to approximately £174,000).[9]

The wedding of Vernie and Rébé took place in Oban on 16 January 1895. Brodrick's suppressed emotions allowed him not only to serve as best man, but also to organize the bonfires and fireworks which celebrated the event in Ballachulish, and to help 'sort out the confusion' at the couple's house in Oban.[10] In 1898, Vernie moved closer to Alltshellach, when his mother bought him Acharra (near Kentallen), but, in 1906, Rébé left him. In 1907, he set off to try his luck in the West Indies,

8.   Rébé's origins recovered from TNA, J77/311/9273; *Morning Post*, 7 Jan. 1895, issue 38245; *Aberdeen Weekly Jnl.*, 23 Jan. 1895, iss. 12475.
9.   J.B. Chinnery-Haldane, Diary, 3–6, 26, 30 Oct. 1894.
10. Ibid., 11, 17 Jan., 16 April–7 May 1895.

leaving Brodrick to oversee the auction of his effects at Acharra, which was subsequently sold. Vernie returned after only five months, and, in 1908, used part of his legacy from his mother to buy Cameron House in Onich, which he rebuilt and renamed Dal Bhan.[11] For long, the constant in Vernie's often unstable life was the support of his elder brother, but, as politics became polarized in the early years of the twentieth century, and an industrial dispute in the quarries brought Keir Hardie to Ballachulish in 1902, the two found themselves in opposite corners. They had a 'great discussion on socialism' in April 1909, and when, in the general election of January the next year, following the Lords' rejection of Lloyd George's budget, Vernie took the chair at a meeting in Onich on behalf of the radical Liberal MP and philanthropist, Sir John Dewar, the Unionist Brodrick was reduced to confiding a shocked monosyllable to his diary: 'Oh!!' Nevertheless, relations between the brothers remained warm, until 1930, when Vernie converted to Roman Catholicism, with 'never a word' to Brodrick. The latter was appalled, and henceforth rarely mentions Vernie in his diary.[12]

In September 1897, Brodrick started to socialize with the nineteen-year-old Katherine Annie Napier, whose mother had been widowed three years previously on the death of her father William, a distinguished retired railway engineer, whose career had been spent mostly in Canada. The courtship between Brodrick and Katherine (or Annie, as she was then known) was lengthy, it not being until 23 July 1901 that they were

11. Ibid., 22, 27 March, 2, 12 May, 14, 31 Aug., 1907; 20 Jan., 12 March 1908. Rébé took with her the two children of the marriage, Dorothy (Dolly) and Kathleen, but regularly brought them to see their father; having lived modestly in Bournemouth under her unmarried name, she died in 1925 (NRS, Wills & Testaments, SC29/44/67, Rebecca Monteith or Chinnery-Haldane). Dorothy married Ivan Parnell and brought up their two sons in Dal Bhan, while Vernie temporarily moved to Bayside in North Ballachulish. Kathleen, who had two sons and a daughter by her husband Ian Duff, committed suicide in 1932.

12. J.B. Chinnery-Haldane, Diary, 14 Sept. 1902; 11 April 1909; 6 Jan. 1910; 18, 20, 25, 27 July 1930; Haldane & Martine, *Time Exposure*, p. 6; N. Kirk, *Custom & Conflict in 'the Land of the Gael': Ballachulish 1900–1910* (London, 2007).

engaged. The bishop noted in his journal that his son was 'jubilant' and immediately made plans to build a house for the couple a little to the east of Alltshellach. The wedding took place in London on 23 April 1902, with Lochiel's younger son, Ewen Cameron, as best man. That evening, the couple visited Wyndham's Theatre to see *The End of a Story*, a curious title to attract newly-weds, and Katherine doubtless took heed that, after dinner at the end of the second day of their married life, her husband spent his time in examining the wedding accounts and associated expenses.[13] On 30 April 1903, they slept for the first time in their new house, named Dunbeg and resembling a Swiss chalet, romantically sited by the lochside. On 25 June, their first child, Marjorie, was born in Edinburgh; she was joined by a sister, Agnes, whose birth in London on 22 June 1905 left 'most of us disappointed, and especially poor Katherine herself'. It was not until 17 June 1907 that 'our long-hoped-for son' arrived, when the bonfires and fireworks of Ballachulish could be lit to celebrate the arrival in Edinburgh of Alexander Napier Chinnery-Haldane.[14]

On the bishop's death sixteen months earlier, Brodrick had succeeded to the headship of the Haldanes and also to responsibility for his mother, who retired into alcoholic seclusion. His diary for 1906 is strewn with references to 'the very unsatisfactory state of things' at Alltshellach: 'mater very feeble'; 'mater invisible'; 'mater not well'; 'mater's usual state'; 'mater in deplorable state'; 'mater says influenza!'; 'mater hopeless again'; 'mater again!'; or simply, despairingly, 'mater!!'.[15] In the second half of 1907, Anna's health, which had been frail since the turn of the century, broke down completely. She had cooled towards Brodrick, complaining that 'he grudges me every penny I spend because he thinks when I die, as I shall shortly, he will have all the more: but he is quite mistaken'. She died on 30 November 1907, and Brodrick's inheritance was indeed neither as large nor as untrammelled as he may have expected. Of the

13. Bishop's Journal, 27–8 July 1901; J.B. Chinnery-Haldane, Diary, 23–4 April 1902.
14. Ibid., 30 April, 25 June 1903; 22 June 1905; 17 June 1907; Haldane & Martine, *Time Exposure*, p. 7.
15. J.B. Chinnery-Haldane, Diary 6 July–11 Dec. 1906.

Irish lands in her father's trust estate, Anna allocated Rhaduane, with an annual rental of £460, to Vernie, and the remainder, producing about £1,440 a year, to Brodrick, while the brothers were left equal shares of the £15,660 realized by a recent sale of land. Of Anna's personal estate, valued at £43,393 15s. 8d. (about £4.75 million in 2016 values), £17,000 (the profit from the sale of Greenhill House in 1881) was left to the bishopric of Argyll and the Isles 'to be applied for the purpose of religious education according to the principles of the Episcopal Church'; a capital sum was to be set aside to pay the stipends of the provost of Cumbrae Cathedral and the bishop's old friend, John Weddderburn, incumbent of St Bride's; legacies to a few friends and servants amounted to about £2,000; while Vernie was to receive, not only £5,000 as well as the freehold of Acharra (which Anna had bought for £4,800), but also half the residue of her estate. The other half went to Brodrick, but Alltshellach and Dunbeg were to go to him only should he choose to buy them, the former for £5,000, the latter for £750. His mother explained that Vernie's preferential treatment was because 'Brodrick will probably benefit under other family settlements'.[16]

The most significant probability was succession to Gleneagles, which had never been absent from the thought-world inhabited by the senior descendants of Colonel James Haldane. In 1863, Alexander Haldane had acknowledged that there was 'no great probability' of the contingency occurring, but, as the years passed, and neither the third earl of Camperdown nor his brother produced children, the remoteness of the chance diminished. Alexander was contemplating the contingency in 1878, when he matriculated his arms and obtained confirmation that the Lyon Office accepted the validity of his great-grandfather's marriage to Margaret Pye. In the same year, his son, the future bishop, emphasized his Haldane credentials by reversing the order of his surname, an achievement he considered 'a cause for humble thankfulness to

16.   Ibid., 29 June 1907; Bishop's Journal, 8 Jan. 1900; 16 Jan. 1902; 14 Dec. 1904; NRS, Wills & Testaments, SC29/44/50, Anna Chinnery-Haldane, 16 Jan. 1908 (will signed 6 June 1906); 'Estates held by trustees of Sir N. Chinnery, 1906'; 'Memorandum as to deeds executed by Mrs Chinnery-Haldane re Sir N. Chinnery's trust estate, 1906'.

Him in whose sight nothing is small'; in congratulating him, a cousin wished that he could add 'of Gleneagles', a wish implicit in his own gift to his father of a watercolour of Gleneagles by Clelland and trans-mitted to his ten-year-old son Brodrick, who was 'full of Gleneagles and "the old Haldanes"'. The third earl remained a bachelor, and, although George Haldane-Duncan, his brother and heir presumptive, did marry in 1888 at the age of forty-three, he was still childless when the bishop fell ill in 1905. Once the imminence of his father's death became apparent, Brodrick immersed himself in the study of Haldane genealogy, for it was now almost certain that the Camperdown peerage was close to extinction and that the Gleneagles entail would open to the senior lineal descendant of the Entailer's eldest brother, Brodrick's great-great-great-grandfather, Colonel James Haldane, and his wife, Margaret Pye.[17]

In 1912, two years after the childless George Haldane-Duncan had become a widower, his elder brother decided to recoup some of the outlay incurred by his family in maintaining the Gleneagles estate by selling Aberuthven, for which permission was granted by the Court of Session. The price was £27,400 (about twenty-five times the annual rental); the purchaser was Brodrick. The first step had been made towards the senior Haldanes' return to their ancestral acres. The second took place in London on 15 August 1916, when Brodrick met George Haldane-Duncan, and the latter, 'after tea and a pleasant chat', signed a deed transferring to Brodrick, 'without reserve', his rights as heir to Gleneagles.[18]

Considered by his cousin, Adamina Anstruther-Duncan, to be 'one in a million', the 71-year-old George had persuaded his brother to exclude him entirely 'from benefiting even to the value of one shilling' under his will. 'Material things', he had explained, 'do not count with me at

17. Alexander Haldane to Sir N. Chinnery, 30 Oct. 1863; Bishop's Journal, prefatory notes & 6, 29 May 1878; above, cap. VI, n. 17; Alick Chinnery-Haldane to his father, 10 & 14 Aug., 16 Oct. 1878; 13 June 1879; J.B. Chinnery-Haldane, Diary, 17 Dec. 1905.

18. Press cutting of April 1912, interleaved in 1914 pages of Brodrick's diary; J.B. Chinnery-Haldane, Diary, 15 Aug. 1916.

all, being possessed of ample independent means.' He was convinced that 'it would be a great misfortune for any estate, and for the people on it, to have a life so far on in years intervene in the succession', not only because of the probably rapid double imposition of death and land-value duties, but also because of the double break in administrative continuity. Moreover, George thought it essential for the viability of the Camperdown and Gleneagles estates, and the well-being of their tenants, that their future owners should have adequate capital resources to withstand fluctuations in the economic climate without resort to short-term strategems or passive inertia. For this reason, he earnestly advised his brother to transfer 'a just portion' of his substantial capital, not to himself, but to the next heirs of entail, and begged him 'not to allow personal prejudice to override [his] high sense of justice and right' in this matter.[19]

Even had George not been obliged to return to Boston to attend to his charitable work, it is unlikely that he could, in fact, have overcome Earl Robert's prejudices. The earl felt no antipathy towards his cousin Georgiana, countess of Buckinghamshire, who was heir to the Camperdown and Lundie estates, but he recoiled at the thought that they should pass under the control of her husband, who, in 1894, had deserted the Conservative for the Liberal Party, thus helping Gladstone return to power and introduce the Second Irish Home Rule Bill; it had been over the First that Robert himself had left the Liberals. Similarly, he had no objection to the Gleneagles heir, whose political position was close to his own, but, when it came to disposing of his personal assets, he could not forget that Brodrick's close kinsman was Richard Haldane, a man with whom he had 'got off on the wrong foot and never recovered', a cabinet member in a government he had abhorred and whose own record he deprecated. The third earl of Camperdown died at Weston Park on 7 June 1918. On 11 June, Brodrick travelled to Worcestershire for the funeral at Long Compton and the reading of the will at Weston. Its

---

19. Ada Anstruther-Duncan to Brodrick Chinnery-Haldane, 24 Sept. 1916; George Haldane-Duncan to Lord Camperdown, 1 Aug. 1916, & to Brodrick Chinnery-Haldane, 7 Aug. 1916; above, pp. 179–80.

contents, when transmitted to the fourth earl in America, caused him deep distress.[20]

George had already been disappointed in the hope of avoiding taxes by his resignation, an outcome dependent on his brother's living beyond three years from the date of the deed, which his brother had failed to do. Reluctantly, he felt obliged to accede to the offers made by Brodrick and Lady Buckinghamshire to shoulder his liability for their entailed estates. His reluctance was the deeper because his late brother had completely ignored his plea that capital endowments should underpin each ancestral estate. More than that, at Camperdown he had left the contents of the house, including the memorabilia of the great admiral, to his friend and political ally, Sir John Seymour Lloyd, and his English agent, Henry Warriner, from whom Lady Buckinghamshire would have to buy them back. At Gleneagles, at least Brodrick was left the house's contents, but, as the third earl had been well aware, those contents had been significantly reduced when his sister and companion, Lady Abercromby, removed much of value, including most family portraits, to the drier environment of Camperdown, where they duly passed into the hands of Lloyd and Warriner. These two gentlemen were also the deceased's executors and divided between themselves half the residue of his personal estate, while Warriner was left the whole of Weston – house, contents, and land.[21]

The executors' initial response to Brodrick's request to buy the Haldane pictures at Camperdown gave him grounds for optimism that the matter would be handled sympathetically, but, within three weeks, Mr Warriner was alluding to 'the considerable value' of some of the portraits and recalling that the late earl 'had not been very anxious that Mr Haldane should have them'; rather, he had hoped that they would 'help with succession duty' at Camperdown; in any case, nothing

20. Above, pp. 178–9; *Complete Peerage*, ii. 405; B. Chinnery-Haldane to Lord Camperdown, 13 Aug. 1918; Lord Camperdown to B. Chinnery-Haldane, 17 Sept. 1918 (for the quotation); J.B. Chinnery-Haldane, Diary, 7, 11 June 1918.

21. Lord Camperdown to Lindsay Howe, 13 June 1918; Brodrick to Lord Camperdown, 17 June 1918; Warriner to Lord Camperdown, 15 July 1918; above, p. 180.

could be done until a professional valuation had been made. In vain Brodrick argued that the portraits removed from Gleneagles 'morally' belonged to the house from which they were taken, and that he was requesting them not for himself but for the Haldanes in perpetuity. In the event, they were included in the Camperdown contents sold to Lady Buckinghamshire, with whom Brodrick had established friendly relations and who offered to pass on to him the fifteen pictures he wanted at the price she had had to pay (£4,972 5s.). Gleneagles heirlooms also found their way into the contents of the earl's London house in Charles Street, which were auctioned in September 1918, when Brodrick paid £850 for the Haselingfield silver salver presented to Captain Robert Haldane in 1743. Mr Warriner and his wife sat beside the auctioneer, which Brodrick thought displayed thoroughly bad form.[22]

Both Brodrick and Lady Buckinghamshire wished that the new earl could have been on their side of the Atlantic, but acknowledged that the risk of being torpedoed by German U-boats was too great. Nevertheless, Brodrick wrote to him bemoaning the lack of someone in authority 'with more feeling for old things than a man like Warriner and a stranger like Lloyd'. By the time the war ended, it was too late, and the earl could only commiserate, owning that he was 'particularly sorry about Warriner – for it seems as if he had temporarily lost his better judgment through having suddenly inherited more than he ever dreamed of'. He also urged Brodrick to prompt his cousin and lawyer, Sir William Haldane, to send him the instrument to break the Gleneagles entail as soon as possible, for he would have to survive for three years after signing it to ensure that the estate escaped another succession duty; his first attempt at resignation had been frustrated, and he was anxious that his second should not be. In the event, the fourth and last earl of Camperdown lived into his eighty-eighth year, dying in Boston on 1 December 1933, and no one could have been more relieved at his longevity than Brodrick,

22. Brodrick to Warriner, 15 June & 8 July 1918; idem to Seymour Lloyd, 15 June 1918; idem to Lord Camperdown, 28 Sept. 1918; Warriner to Brodrick, 19 June, 6 & 15 July 1918; idem to Lord Camperdown, 6 July 1918; Lady Buckinghamshire to Brodrick, 29 Oct. 1918; Lord Buckinghamshire to Brodrick, 30 & 31 Dec. 1918.

who told Cousin Willie: 'Really, coming into Gleneagles is a costly business.'[23]

No one knew more about the finances of members of the Haldane family than Sir William Haldane, who considered it 'rather too heavy a burden' for Brodrick alone to meet the cost of recovering the Gleneagles portraits. Sure that 'everyone would like to help as they can', and backed by his brother, Lord Haldane, and his cousin, the chartered accountant Herbert Haldane, he called a family council, which established 'the Gleneagles syndicate' to buy the pictures. The question then arose of where to hang them. Since Gleneagles was 'certainly damp' and anyway incapable 'in its present condition' of showing them to advantage, Brodrick asked Lord Buckinghamshire if they might remain for the time being *in situ* at Camperdown. The expert from Scotland's National Gallery, brought in by Sir William for an insurance valuation, reported that they had been 'grossly overvalued' by the third earl's executors. 'There is, I fear,' wrote Brodrick to Willie, 'nothing to be done but try to look cheerful. We are getting plenty of practice at this game.' In June 1920, the pictures were moved to Alltshellach, as Brodrick feared that proximity to Dundee made 'a house like Camperdown quite a tempting place for Bill Sykes'.[24]

There remained at Camperdown one other picture which, according to Brodrick's information, belonged to Gleneagles: a double portrait on panel of unidentified gentlemen, dateable to about 1610. For reasons now unclear, Brodrick did not mention this to Lady Buckinghamshire until 1923, nor ask to buy it from her until 29 August 1925. At the same time, he revived his request (last made in 1918) for the ancient key, presumed to be that for Gleneagles Castle, where it had been found by his father and the future third earl when playing as boys. He evidently asked at the

23. Lady Buckinghamshire to Brodrick, 19 Dec. 1918; Brodrick to Lord Camperdown, 18 Aug. 1918; idem to Wm Haldane, 2 Nov. 1918; Lord Camperdown to Brodrick, 18 July, 17 Sept. & 19 Nov. 1918.
24. Wm Haldane to Brodrick, 9 Nov. 1918; Brodrick to Lady Buckinghamshire, 3 Jan. 1919; idem to Lord Buckinghamshire, 5 April 1919; idem to Wm Haldane, 31 Oct. 1919; idem to Francis Haldane, 5 June 1920; Francis Haldane to Brodrick, 2 June 1920.

wrong time, when the Buckinghamshires had been angered by a demand from one of the executors for a cheval glass and had resolved 'not to part with anything more from Camperdown House'. A dusty reply from Lord Buckinghamshire added that the present Lord Camperdown also thought that the key ought to remain where it was. It was not until July 1941, after the death of Lady Buckingamshire, when Brodrick's widow, aided by his cousin Sir Aylmer Haldane, was able to buy them, that both panel picture and castle key returned to Gleneagles.[25]

For all its attendant tribulations, the return of the Gleneagles barony to Brodrick as the senior representative of the Haldane family was a source of inestimable satisfaction and pride. For him, as it had been for his father, 'the association of Gleneagles was almost a religious feeling'. In 1930, plunged into pessimism by life under the second Labour government, he envisaged a time when 'it will be necessary to sell part of Gleneagles, but, so long as the family own the ground with the old chapel, house and castle, that is the old place, unless nobody is allowed any property at all, our descendants would surely have the house and the immediate ground as a smallholding, and keep cattle right up to the house in order to hold on to the old name'. The house itself, however, was barely habitable except as a shooting-lodge. The late Lord Camperdown had introduced running water and made some structural alterations, but Brodrick found that much that had been done 'would have been better not done'. Major improvements were needed to make it acceptable as a permanent residence, but, until Brodrick could contemplate the expense with equanimity, Gleneagles would be let to game-tenants, and, outside the season, occasionally used by Brodrick or made available for holidays to family members based in Edinburgh. General Sir Aylmer Haldane provided the inspiration and the funds for the restoration of the chapel, which began in 1925, and for the preservation of the castle's ruins, excavation of which started the following year. In

25. *HG*, p. 311 & n.; Brodrick to Warriner, 8 July 1918; idem to Lady Buckinghamshire, 2 Nov. 1918; Warriner to Brodrick, 15 July 1918; Ada Anstruther-Duncan to Brodrick, 30 Jan. 1926; Lord Buckinghamshire to Brodrick, 1 Sept. 1925 (copy in 'Notes', ii. 554); Wm Haldane to Alex[r] Chinnery-Haldane, 1 Oct. 1941.

June 1926, the decision was taken to let Alltshellach, and for the family to move east, squeezing into the Kinnaker (the old North Mains), until the big house was ready for them. After a prolonged lawsuit to remove the sitting tenant, followed by some mediocre alterations to a house which 'all feel is rather dreadful', the Kinnaker became the family's base on 30 July 1927, and remained such until they moved into Gleneagles itself on 8 December 1928. It took Brodrick's daughter Agnes three days to decide on a bedroom which she did not find too cold; even her father admitted that 'the draughts in this house are too awful for words, and come from everywhere'. After five months, when he returned to Alltshellach to settle details of its lease to the Holiday Fellowship, Brodrick found 'the whole thing horrid, and the place looking lovely – the house so bright and cheerful after Gleneagles'.[26]

Although the late Lord Camperdown had not left the Haldanes' house as comfortable as his successor might have wished, pipes could be defrosted and draughts reduced, and, after all, the place was 'just as nice in summer as nasty in winter'.[27] By default, the third earl had bequeathed a far more intractable problem, which drove Brodrick to the verge of distraction. In 1910, while travelling in Strathearn, the general manager of the Caledonian Railway Company, Donald Matheson, conceived a scheme for a palatial golfing resort readily accessible from the railway. A suitable site was the West Muir of Auchterarder; a suitable station was Crieff Junction, where carriages destined for Crieff left the main line; a suitable name was that of the glen at the head of which stood the ruins of Gleneagles Castle, a mile south of the station, and the seat of the Haldane barony of Gleneagles. On 1 April 1912, Crieff Junction was renamed 'Gleneagles'. At this point, Lord Camperdown could have intervened: had his permission been sought, he may have refused it; had it not been sought, he could publicly have expressed disapproval; there was no copyright on the name, but the hostility of a distinguished

26. Brodrick to George Haldane-Duncan, 16 August 1916; idem to Sir Aylmer Haldane, 22 June 1925; idem to his son Alex, 5 Feb. 1930; J.B. Chinnery-Haldane, Diary, 22 April 1921, 6 April 1923, 19 April 1927, 13 Dec. 1928, 15 May 1929.
27. J.B. Chinnery-Haldane, Diary, 13 June 1926.

and near neighbour would probably have been avoided by the sponsors of the project. Whatever his involvement, it is, in fact, unlikely that he saw anything but convenience, and perhaps even a modest cachet, in the attachment of the name of his property to a nearby railway station. In 1913, however, the company formed to construct and operate the hotel and golf courses showed its hand by taking the name 'Gleneagles Ltd'. Interrupted by the outbreak of war, the hotel's construction was resumed in 1922, three years after the opening of the King's Course in 1919, when *The Times* declared that 'a new golf course at Gleneagles would challenge comparison with any in the British Isles'.[28] The hotel itself opened in 1924, now owned by the London, Midland, & Scottish Railway Company (LMS), with which the Caledonian had recently amalgamated. Like the golf course, it was given the name of the railway station: 'Gleneagles'.

Post intended for the hotel began to arrive at Gleneagles, and that addressed to Brodrick at the hotel. He contacted the Post Office surveyor, who gave an undertaking that, unless the word 'hotel' was included in the address, all mail sent to 'Gleneagles' would be delivered to the house. This, of course, left Brodrick the problem of unwanted mail, which he returned either to the sender or to the Post Office, but his time was being wasted and his temper tested. Confusion was unquestionably encouraged by the company's major advertising campaign, which frequently suggested that the hotel *was* Gleneagles; that it stood on an estate of its own, from which it took its name, and from which it was supplied with provisions. Warned by cousins that he could not do much, Brodrick told his wife: 'I expect to do more than they think. It merely wants someone with some tact and firmness to get things right. If I fail, we shall be no worse off than before, and I am not going to fail.'[29]

In 1927, through dogged persistence, Brodrick extracted from the LMS president a promise that the word 'hotel' would be used in all future advertising of the establishment and its sporting facilities, but he knew that this was only a preliminary step. Newspapers had to be taught

28. *The Times*, 23 Sept. 1919, issue 42212.
29. J.B. Chinnery-Haldane, Diary, 13 June 1926.

that 'Gleneagles' without the qualification 'hotel' referred only to an ancient barony, on not one inch of whose ground stood any part of the misnamed railway station or of the railway hotel and its golf courses. A press cutting agency supplied the laird with evidence of the transgressions of journalists throughout the British Isles, when they wrote of 'Gleneagles' golf tournaments, 'Gleneagles' tennis championships, or, worse, of people staying at 'Gleneagles'. When *The Times*, in reporting a divorce case, captioned a paragraph 'VISIT TO GLENEAGLES', and proceeded to describe how a violent baronet had offered his wife £1,000 to throw herself out of one of its windows, Brodrick raged against the 'disgusting' and 'scandalous' imputation that he would wish to have such people under his roof.[30] He spoke darkly of a railway hotel 'and all that such a place implies' and once, in 1931, when in correspondence with the editor of *The Spectator*, became almost libellous: 'The hotel is in plain language an immoral hole, and a trap for many a young man or girl. No decent local parent will allow her girl to go there as a servant if she can help it. . . . And it is because the wretched place has such a reputation that I so strongly object to our name being mixed up with it.'[31]

With his terrier-like absorption in the task in hand Brodrick had begun to lose his composure and sense of proportion, but when, in 1936, he quite reasonably repeated the request he had made since 1930, that the hotel cease providing guests with writing paper headed 'Gleneagles Hotel, Gleneagles, Scotland', and replace it with paper headed 'Gleneagles Hotel, Auchterarder, Perthshire', the Controller of LMS Hotel Services himself abandoned common sense in stating that 'it would be belittling the hotel to put the name of the post town on the heading'. Lord Younger, a member of the LMS board, made the unhelpful suggestion that the laird should revert to the old Gaelic name for his house, but this was wisely not transmitted to Brodrick. In 1937, the LMS chairman summed up: 'There is only one remedy, and that is an alteration in the name of the hotel, and this cannot be done. I really do not think that, short of repetition, there is anything further which can be said on the subject.' Brodrick withdrew into temporary silence, and,

30.   *The Times*, 17 Feb. 1933, iss. 46371; Brodrick to *Times* editor, 18 Feb. 1933.
31.   Brodrick to *Spectator* editor, 1 June & 25 Sept. 1931.

towards the end of the year, the LMS office in Glasgow rejoiced that 'the geyser is quiescent just now'.[32]

Brodrick would visit the hotel only in order to confront the manager with a complaint, but his family's commitment to his crusade stopped short of denying themselves the facilities offered by the offending establishment. During 1928, his wife, younger daughter, and younger son often escaped from their cramped quarters in the Kinnaker to play golf or tennis, or take tea at the hotel, and, after moving into the big house, Katherine made regular use of the hotel's hairdresser, while Marjorie, the elder daughter, and her husband actually stayed overnight on occasional visits from the west. Even Alex, his father's most committed fellow crusader, might be spotted on one of the golf courses or waiting on the premises for his car to be washed. His younger brother, Brodrick Vernon, frequently accompanied their mother to the hairdresser, and, in late summer 1937, spent a number of nights in the hotel gratis, in return for photographing guests for society magazines.[33]

The birth of Brodrick Vernon (known in the family as 'BV', or by his father occasionally as 'Number 4'), on 12 June 1912, came five years after that of his brother Alex. In the interim their parents' marriage had deteriorated. The move into Alltshellach in July 1909, after extensive alterations and improvements (including the installation of electric light and of mantelpieces from the Chinnery house in Dublin), imposed a financial strain on Brodrick, not appreciated by Katherine, who wished him to maintain the same staffing levels as had his mother with over double the income available to him. There is no mention of his fourth child's birth in Brodrick's diary; in fact, there are very few entries on any subject between March 1912 and December 1914, and, in later years, his elder son speculated that his father was too worried and unhappy to record the period: 'we [children] witnessed much bickering between our parents, which at times became serious, and we felt they might part company'.[34]

32. NRS, BR/LMS/4/177, *passim*.
33. J.B. Chinnery-Haldane, Diary, 1928 *passim*; 31 Aug. 1930; 18 Aug. 1931, 20–21 Aug., 4 Sept. 1937.
34. Ibid., 8 Jan., 11 April, 9, 13 July, 24 Aug. 1908; 5 March, 22 July 1909; Alexander's note to Dec. 1914.

A warning sign had been posted in spring 1909, when Brodrick showed Katherine an advertisement in the *Westminster Gazette*, recommending 'to all but the superior' a book entitled *Ideas of a Plain Country-Woman*. This may have been partly a joke, but there was no room for humour in the relationship on 20 January 1915, when Katherine got hold of her husband's diary, and, affecting his identity, followed his own entry about 'doing house accounts' with the following: 'Made Katherine as miserable as I could in the morning – quite surprised that she still has some feelings for me to hurt'.[35] At the end of the month, Brodrick suggested closing Alltshellach and returning to Dunbeg, but was persuaded that the family would not fit, and therefore decided to shut up part of the house and reduce the servants, while Dunbeg was to be let. A house in Eastbourne, which Brodrick had inherited on the death of the last of the bishop's sisters in 1911, and which had served as a regular holiday home, was also let in 1918. The *Malvina* was commandeered by the navy at the start of the Great War, and Brodrick's waterborne activity was restricted to a motorboat. By the end of the war, the butler, footman, one gardener, and one undergardener had gone, the male staff at Alltshellach being reduced to a single gardener. In 1927, in an exceptionally dark mood, Brodrick looked back on Alltshellach as associated with 'so much misery and unhappiness that I would not care if I never saw the place again'.[36]

Although often coexisting under the same roof, Brodrick and Katherine were in effect living separate lives when they moved to Perthshire. Even when visiting Edinburgh together, Katherine would stay at her club in Charlotte Square, and Brodrick at the Tartan Hotel in Rothesay Place. The difficulties of the move once more exposed the fault-line in their marriage. Brodrick complained of her 'appalling accounts', while her son BV empathetically described her as 'extremely sociable, and always extravagant'. Her husband was neither: he would

35. Ibid., 6 March 1909; 20 Jan. 1915.
36. Ibid., 5 Feb., 1915; 29 June, 18 July 1916; 1 Jan. 1918; tax returns copied into 1915 & 1918 volumes (only male staff incurred tax); Brodrick to Alex, 15 May 1927. The sisters bought the freehold of 4 West Cliff, Eastbourne, in 1898, the lease having been held since at least 1884: Bishop's Journal, 11 Nov. 1884, 16 March 1898.

contentedly drive Katherine and Agnes to a dance, go home, and then back to wait until they were ready to be collected in the early hours of the morning; after seeing his wife and children off to the Crieff Games in August 1928, or to meet the queen at the Holyrood Garden Party in July 1931, he cheerfully set about cleaning bee-frames and melting wax. When Katherine took the three unmarried children to Switzerland in the winter of 1925–26, he spent Christmas and the New Year alone at Gleneagles, but he was never at a loss for a satisfying solitary occupation: beekeeping, bicycle repair, motor car maintenance, and the myriad tasks about the house and its policies which a laird might be expected to delegate to an odd-job man. His wife did not enjoy sharing meals with a man whose face was often swollen with bee stings and clothes spattered with grease or paint, and who was impatient to return to his labours. He chafed under a regime such as that of his cousin William at Foswell, where everyone 'sat in the drawing-room after dinner in the usual aimless way'.[37]

Beekeeping had been a passion with Brodrick since 1898, when he began it at Alltshellach, and hives were positioned in all his properties: Eastbourne in 1912, Aberuthven in 1915, and Gleneagles in 1918, when bees were lodged in the west pavilion ('the ruin') and tenants come to the house to pay their rents left with hives to place on their tenancies. He was not a proud man, but he recorded his continued re-election as president of the Perthshire Beekeepers Association with evident gratification, especially in 1937, when he should have retired – 'so quite against the rules'. Rivalling his enthusiasm for apiary was that for bicycles, which had begun at school in the 1880s; cleaning and overhauling Katherine's machine had been part of Brodrick's courtship display in November 1900. Bicycles were eclipsed by motor cars, the first of which, acquired in 1911, he retained until 1930, when it merited an affectionate farewell in his diary. He kept two cars, became a competent motor mechanic, resented speed limits, and thought speed traps 'ridiculous' and 'absurd': fined for exceeding 10 m.p.h. on an empty road in Bridge of Allan in 1926, he told

37. The above is based on entries in Brodrick's diary for 1924–26, 1928, 1931, and Haldane & Martine, *Time Exposure*, p. 50.

the sheriff what he thought 'of such a foolish charge, so got something for my money'. Mechanical novelties were always received by Brodrick with eager enthusiasm: a vacuum cleaner ('the carpet machine') in 1909, a typewriter in 1916, a wireless in 1923. Developments in the cinema, however, did not impress: a visit to the Rutland Cinema in Edinburgh in 1934 bored him with 'the usual rot'.[38]

Brodrick would have considered his life incomplete had he not undertaken public duties of some sort. During his father's episcopate, he was kept fully busy acting in effect as the bishop's secretary and the diocese's accountant, and, after his father's death, diocesan affairs continued to occupy much of his time, while, after the move to Perthshire, he became a stalwart of St Kessog's, the Episcopalian church in Auchterarder, his services as a lay preacher being frequently called upon both there and at Muthill. His sense of duty, however, required service in the political world as well. In 1898, at the age of thirty, he had sought election to the Inverness-shire County Council, but, despite energetic campaigning (during which, on one day, he tramped forty-two miles in heavy snow) he lost by six votes, largely owing to open opposition from Presbyterian ministers, combined with covert opposition from Cameron of Lochiel, who felt that the influence in his territory of the newly arrived Chinnery-Haldanes had already reached its acceptable limit. Salt was rubbed in his wound by the bishop's 'fury' that two servants had been absent for a whole day canvassing for his son without his permission. It was not until after the death of Lochiel in December 1905, and of the bishop in the following February, that Brodrick renewed his attempt to participate in local government. In April 1906, he was elected to the Lochaber School Board, to which he was consistently returned until the boards were replaced in 1919 by Education Authorities. That for Lochaber was a widely scattered district, including some of the islands, but he was equal to its challenges, and was re-elected. After coming into Gleneagles, he accepted almost automatic election to Blackford's Parish Council, and sought and won election to the Perthshire County

38. See Brodrick's diary for 1891, 1898, 1900, 1909, 1911–12, 1915–16, 1918, 1923, 1926, 1930, 1934, 1937.

Council, where he was active on the Housing and Public Health committees.[39]

Brodrick's work in education had introduced him to the duchess of Atholl, a member of the Association of Education Authorities in Scotland, and, after his move from Lochaber to Perthshire, a political relationship developed between the two. She had narrowly won the parliamentary seat of Kinross and West Perth for the Unionists (i.e. Conservatives) in 1923; by the time she was re-elected in 1929 with a much increased majority, Brodrick was a member of the party's local executive committee. He had occupied a similar position in the west since 1907. Since the Atholls' lack of financial muscle gave the county gentry and professional and commercial classes of the constituency a dominant influence in local Conservative politics, Brodrick became a valued and loyal ally as the duchess deviated with increasing frequency from the party line: in 1934, denouncing the coalition government's proposed Indian constitution as premature; in 1935, opposing its policy on unemployment benefit as 'more appropriate to a socialist government'; and splitting her supporters in 1937 by unexpectedly castigating the Conservative government for its failure to deter Germany and Italy from giving Franco armed support in the Spanish civil war. Her attitude was criticized at a special meeting of the Perthshire executive, which Brodrick found 'painful'. Losing the whip in 1938 through her opposition to appeasement, she resigned to force a by-election in November, when she stood as an Independent and was narrowly defeated after an ill-tempered contest which some of Brodrick's fellow lairds brazenly sought to influence by promising rent reductions should the duchess lose. Having worked tirelessly on her behalf, Brodrick himself thought that the surprise result reflected women voters' preference for 'what they thought was the safe thing' – appeasement.[40]

39. Ibid., 9, 19, 23, 29 Nov., & 6–7, 14 Dec. 1898; 18 April 1906; 1931 *passim*; 18 Nov. 1932.

40. Ibid., 19 April 1907; 21, 28 Oct. 1935; 2 June 1937; 1, 11, 31 Aug. & 21–2 Dec. 1938; 6 May 1939; S. Ball, 'The politics of appeasement: the fall of the duchess of Atholl and the Kinross and West Perth by-election, December 1938', *Scot. Hist. Rev.*, lxix (1990), 51–3, 57, 76 & n. 4; D. Sutherland, 'Murray, Katharine Marjory Stewart-, duchess of Atholl (1874–1960)', *ODNB*.

One woman who did not support appeasement was Brodrick's wife. The duchess's campaign in 1938 provided a rare opportunity for Brodrick and Katherine to share a common interest, with Katherine becoming a committee member of the Blackford Conservatives and helping to bring them behind the duchess. Determined to capitalize on the improved relations, Brodrick proposed a motoring trip to the north of Scotland, and Katherine agreed. They set off on 6 July 1939, Katherine equipped with 'a Dunlop map which she swears by, but it is all wrong and out of date'. Her obstinate reliance on this map gave ample scope for discord, which Brodrick evaded with weary resignation, but the violence of her rage when they were delayed on a narrow road by a broken-down lorry produced a *cri de coeur* to his son Alex: 'From the time we left Gleneagles I have simply done all I could to make her enjoy herself, and on the whole have succeeded better than I expected, but she is at times almost hopeless to deal with. I want the tour more for her sake than my own, but at times I have had much to contend with, and all so needless.'[41]

After a week, the couple were back in Gleneagles, where gas masks had been delivered. BV arrived on 30 August from Aix-les-Bains; on 1 September, critical of the absence of organization, Brodrick helped deliver evacuated Glasgow children to local farms; on the second, Alex arrived from London; on the third, war was declared. While Katherine set about draping the house in blackout material, Brodrick and the chauffeur gave the cars their coats of regulation paint and fixed shades to the lamps, so that it became 'impossible to go at more than walking pace at night'. BV's contribution was to create 'a scene' about a friend he wished to invite to stay. 'He had a sudden terrible outburst,' his bewildered father told his diary, 'and quite lost himself, as a result of which poor Katherine was utterly overcome and lay prostrate on the dining room floor. He remained in a state of hysterical rage. It is not clear what the trouble is about, but [it is] connected with his friend Victor. The poor fellow is under great delusions as to our feelings for him.' Domestic peace was achieved by inviting BV's friend, and sending the pair, with Katherine and the servants, to Dunbeg. Brodrick and his elder son spent

41. J.B. Chinnery-Haldane, Diary, 12 Dec. 1938; Brodrick to Alex, 6 & 8 July 1939, interleaved in Diary.

Christmas alone at Gleneagles, and saw in the new year regaled by 'a dreadful drawl by a Presbyterian minister' on the wireless.[42]

In February 1940, BV went as a gunner to serve in an anti-aircraft battery in Kent, where he managed to display ineptitude of an order high enough to be given office work for the rest of the war. His brother Alex had been commissioned into the Royal Scots and joined the British Expeditionary Force in France. Meanwhile, at Gleneagles Brodrick was dealing with attempts by army officers to find billets and diverting them to Cloan and Millearn. On 11 April 1941, he was asked about the possibility of converting Alltshellach and Dunbeg into hospitals; they had been earmarked for an evacuee school, but, with Brodrick's agreement, Alltshellach became a hospital for commandos, with Dunbeg supplying accommodation for nurses.[43]

Later that month, on 22 April, Brodrick suffered 'a horrid pain' in his chest, which he diagnosed as indigestion. It was accompanied by a pain in his right upper arm, which he thought was rheumatic. He had been plagued for many years with cardiovascular problems, as well as arthritis in his neck; a mysterious ailment in 1932 had laid him low for nearly six months, most of which he spent in a nursing home in Bridge of Allan. His doctor called at Gleneagles on 23 April, 'but could not do much'. The next day, Brodrick insisted on driving Katherine to a meeting in Perth, where he had his car greased, and 'there was a dispute at the Garage whether I was two thirds or three quarters dead'. The trip to Perth was the last occasion he left Gleneagles. On his return, he retired to his bed. On the twenty-eighth, he wrote a cheerful letter to Alex, describing how he had 'got a wonderful lot of fun' out of the attentions of friends and staff, and how he had tried to fool his doctor by scraping some rust off a razor blade into a sample of sputum. That was the last letter he wrote, and he died, with his wife by his side, in the early hours of 2 May 1941, in his seventy-third year. He had successfully protected his heir from estate duty on Gleneagles by transferring the barony to Alex on 14 June 1937 and surviving for the requisite period of three years. It

42. J.B. Chinnery-Haldane, Diary, 2, 9, 11, 18 Sept. & 31 Dec. 1939.
43. Ibid., 22 Jan., 9, 26 March, 20 June, 2 July 1940; 11 April, 1941; Haldane & Martine, *Time Exposure*, pp. 81–6.

was, therefore, as J. Brodrick Chinnery-Haldane of Aberuthven that he drew up his will, dividing his capital (£46,620) between all his children except Marjorie, whose late husband had left her fully provided for; his widow had the liferent of Dunbeg and other real estate, while trustees were empowered to hold Aberuthven in reserve for emergencies. His funeral was conducted in the family chapel, and his burial, the first of a laird of Gleneagles since 1768, took place in the adjacent graveyard.[44]

Brodrick's body was laid at the opposite side of the enclosure to that of his cousin, Richard, Viscount Haldane of Cloan. Above Richard's grave rose an obelisk memorializing his achievements. Plans for its erection had not been welcomed by Brodrick, but, when it was put in place in January 1930, he saw that it was 'fairly well hidden, and perhaps less objectionable than I feared'.[45] His doubts may have been entirely aesthetic, but it would be understandable had they been mixed with a reluctance to allow the Haldanes of Cloan as prominent a position in the chapel yard at Gleneagles as they occupied in the life of Perthshire and beyond. Regular visitors to Cloan included leading figures in the political, religious, literary, legal, financial, and academic worlds, a flow which did not cease with Lord Haldane's death but continued during the life of his sister Elizabeth (1862–1937). Affectionately known as 'the queen of Perthshire', she had acted as hostess for her bachelor brother both at Cloan and at his London residence in Queen Anne's Gate, but also had her own career, being appointed the first female JP in Scotland, writing on Hegel and Descartes, promoting the cause of women in medicine and education, and of the socially deprived in Edinburgh, and, in 1918, created a Companion of Honour in recognition of her work in nursing during the Great War.[46]

44. J.B. Chinnery-Haldane, Diary, 24 March–16 Sept 1932; 18 March 1937; 22–24 April 1941; Brodrick to Alex, 28 April 1941; NRS, Inv. SC49/31/276, pp. 529–35; Will SC49/32/71, pp. 221–32; Gleneagles records at Turcan Connell, Edinburgh.

45. J.B. Chinnery-Haldane, Diary, 24 Jan. 1930.

46. *Times*, 28 & 31 Dec. 1937, issues 47877, 47880; L.A. Ritchie, 'Haldane, Elizabeth Sanderson (1862–1937)', *ODNB* (2004). Elizabeth's ashes were placed in Richard's grave: J.B. Chinnery-Haldane, Diary, 25 Dec. 1937.

The strength of the family bond had ensured that Richard and Elizabeth at Cloan and their youngest brother, Sir William Haldane, at Foswell (each within three miles of Gleneagles), welcomed their Conservative and Episcopalian cousin as a neighbour, and made their houses available to him during his frequent visits to the vicinity after his purchase of Aberuthven in 1915 and prior to his move to Gleneagles in 1927. Socializing, however, was limited, for William was a Liberal and a Baptist, Elizabeth a Liberal suffragist and a member of the United Free Church, and Richard had been a Liberal but in 1918 was moving in Labour circles, while his religious position was unchanged from his declaration at the age of eighteen, when he had risen dripping from the baptismal font to announce that he had 'no connection with the [Baptist] church, or its teaching, or with any other church', although, when at Cloan, he worshipped in St Andrew's United Free Church in Auchterarder.[47] To avoid exposure to Anglican influence neither brother had been educated in England, but both at Edinburgh Academy and Edinburgh University, while Richard also spent four months in Germany at Göttingen.

Of the brothers, it was William whom Brodrick saw most often. William (1864–1951) had been admitted Writer to the Signet in 1880, established his own firm with his cousin Frank (W. & F. Haldane) in the early 1890s, built up a wide and important clientèle, and in 1897 bought Foswell with 1,100 acres bordering Cloan. In 1905, he was appointed Crown Agent for Scotland, and in 1912 rewarded with a knighthood for the efficiency with which he discharged the multifarious duties of that office. A large part of the work of a Writer to the Signet concerned estate management and the oversight of clients' expenditure in that management. William applied his analytical brain to a deep study of agriculture, and particularly of forestry, for which he established a research centre. Like almost every member of the extended Haldane family, Brodrick depended on 'Willie' for legal and financial advice, and, after inheriting Gleneagles, for detailed guidance in the management of his estate; within four months of Lord Camperdown's death, Brodrick was 'going

47. R.B. Haldane, *An Autobiography* (London, 1929), pp. 22–3.

round woods with Willie with a view to planting'.[48] William also gave Brodrick an opportunity to diversify his resources by bringing him on to the board of a new company he had formed to revive the slate quarries at Ballachulish; the Liberal William's readiness to hear the opinions of the workforce brought the board face to face with industrial discontent, and Brodrick did not share his cousin's tolerance of '90 minutes of socialist nonsense' at one meeting with 'the men's directors', and 'socialism from 1.40 till 4.30' at another.[49]

William's attitude was in harmony with that of his eldest brother. Richard Haldane (1856–1928) was an intellectual dynamo. With a first in philosophy, a mastery of jurisprudence (having been called to the bar in 1879), the physical resources of a massive frame, an ability to devise grand schemes and a command of detail which made his advocacy of them the more powerful, he was a realistic visionary, who looked upon life as a journey towards the betterment of society. This view led him into Liberal politics (being elected MP for East Lothian in 1885), but not to the exclusion of other contacts: he was friendly with Fabians like the Webbs and Conservatives like Balfour, and excelled as a go-between, building temporary alliances to further causes he championed. Chief among such causes was the expansion of higher education, an area in which he derived inspiration from Germany. To the development of technical and adult education he devoted a missionary zeal reminiscent of his grandfather and great-uncle, James and Robert Haldane. The remodelling of the University of London, the funding of Imperial College, the pioneering of what became known as the Redbrick movement, the provision of extramural education: all depended on the work of Richard Haldane, work recognized in 1902 by his admittance to the Privy Council before ever holding government office.

He himself wished to be remembered above all for his services to education, but the inscription on his tombstone puts equal emphasis on his reform of the Army. As Secretary for War from 1905 to 1912, he applied his talents to the creation of a 'scientific army', in which economy

48. J.B. Chinnery-Haldane, Diary, 12 Oct. 1918. For William, see *Times*, 8 Nov. 1951, iss. 52153.
49. J.B. Chinnery-Haldane, Diary, 26 July 1930; 7 Nov. 1931.

and efficiency coexisted. He began his reform with the introduction of a General Staff, another idea imported from Germany; he dared to confront entrenched institutions of country life like the yeomanry by remodelling the non-professional reserve into the Territorial Army; and he devised secret plans for an expeditionary force which were used with hardly any modification in August 1914. Field-Marshal Haig called him 'the greatest Secretary of State for War England has ever had'.[50]

An attempt in 1956 to recognize 'the debt owed by the country to so great a man' by erecting a statue to his memory failed to receive government support, despite professions of shared admiration.[51] The reason for the eclipse of Haldane's reputation is to be traced to a press campaign in 1915 of unparalleled and venomous scurrility, smearing him as pro-German. Among the accusations hurled at him, which included statements that he invested in German armaments, that he had a German wife, that he was the Kaiser's illegitimate half-brother, the least fanciful were that he had said that Germany was his spiritual home; that he had visited Germany in 1912, and must have returned aware that the Kaiser intended war, but said nothing; that he had wanted to keep the expeditionary force at home in 1914. In fact, it was the classroom of his old teacher at Göttingen that he had said was his spiritual home; his 1912 visit to seek a compromise on naval expansion failed because the Germans insisted on a British guarantee of neutrality, which he faithfully reported on his return; and the dispatch of four divisions of the expeditionary force in 1914 was indeed against his advice: he had urged the dispatch of six.[52] Nevertheless, when the Conservatives made the exclusion of Haldane a condition of their joining Asquith in a coalition, Asquith consented. Go-betweens lack power bases, and Haldane was easy prey for the populist predators of the contemporary press.

50. D. Sommer, *Haldane of Cloan* (London, 1960), pp. 367–70. For Lord Haldane, see H.C.G. Matthew, 'Haldane, Richard Burdon, Viscount Haldane (1856–1928)', *ODNB* (2004) & works cited.

51. Lord Wigg, *George Wigg* (London, 1972), p. 53, a reference for which I am endebted to Tam Dalyell of the Binns.

52. Sommer, *Haldane*, pp. 314–21; S.E. Koss, *Lord Haldane: Scapegoat for Liberalism* (New York & London, 1969).

Richard had been ennobled as Viscount Haldane of Cloan in 1911 in order to lead the Liberals in the House of Lords in the year of the Parliament Bill, and in 1912 became Lord Chancellor. After his removal from government in 1915, he joined no party organization, but moved closer to Fabian and Labour circles, and, when the first Labour government was formed in January 1924, he became Lord Chancellor 'to help them out'.[53] He left office for the last time in October 1924, when that government fell. He died on 19 August 1928, and, four days later, as an indication of the importance the home of his ancestors held for this most unsentimental of men, his body was carried from Cloan through Auchterarder for burial at Gleneagles.[54]

The magnetism of Gleneagles was also felt by Richard's younger brother, John Scott Haldane (1860–1936), a physiologist and biologist of great distinction and originality, who had lived in Oxford since 1887. There he died, but it was at Gleneagles, in his brother's grave, that his ashes were interred. John had pioneered the engagement of 'pure' science with the needs of the workplace outside academia. His ground-breaking researches into human respiration led to major reforms in industrial practices, none more important than in improving safety in collieries; it was to him that the government turned to produce countermeasures to the use of chemical weapons; and, in 1928, he was appointed a Companion of Honour for his work on public health and hygiene. Much of the experimentation necessary for his research was conducted upon himself and (from the age of three) upon his son, John Burdon Sanderson Haldane, who grew up to be a geneticist and biochemist of equal brilliance. He similarly used himself as a guinea pig, once remarking, after piercing an eardrum, that it would probably heal, but, should it not, the ability to exhale cigarette smoke from the ear would be a useful social attribute.[55]

53. Sommer, *Haldane*, p. 393.
54. *Times*, 24 Aug. 1928, iss. 44980; for the opening of the grave by 'a religious maniac', see J.B. Chinnery-Haldane, Diary, 23–24 Aug. 1928.
55. For J.S. Haldane, see *Times*, 16 March 1936, iss. 47324; S. Sturdy, 'Haldane, John Scott (1860–1936)', *ODNB* (2004); idem 'The meanings of "life":

The request that Professor J.S. Haldane's ashes be buried at Gleneagles disconcerted Brodrick. He could not refuse it, but it is unlikely that he relished the prospect of conversing with the deceased's immediate family. His son, Professor J.B.S. Haldane, was not only preposterously clever but he was also an atheist and an outspoken man of the left, on the cusp of joining the Communist party, while his sister, Naomi Mitchison, also dauntingly erudite and acquiring fame as a novelist, was a confident feminist married to a socialist politician. Their mother was reassuringly sound politically, being a Tory imperialist, but, should conversation turn to religion, it was her stated view that Christianity was suitable only for servants. To ensure Brodrick's discomfort, the officiating clergyman was a minister of the United Free Church. Cousins more congenial to Brodrick were present: descendants of James Haldane's second marriage (to Margaret Rutherford) were represented by the chartered accountants Herbert Haldane and his son James, both Episcopalians and Conservatives, but the occasion received not the baldest notice in Brodrick's diary, although *The Times* newspaper recorded that he was there.[56]

An absentee was General Sir (James) Aylmer Haldane (1862–1950), a Rutherford cousin profoundly attached to Gleneagles, who devoted much of his retirement to the study of Haldane history and genealogy, and financed the restoration of the chapel and excavation of the castle. The only boy among the six children of Dr Rutherford Haldane, he entered Sandhurst, for which he had been prepared at Wimbledon School after leaving Edinburgh Academy. What proved to be a highly distinguished military career was almost blighted by an indiscretion in 1888 when serving in Ireland as a young subaltern with the second Gordon Highlanders. Persuaded by a 22-year-old barmaid that he had

biology and biography in the work of J.S. Haldane (1960–1936)', *Trans. Royal Hist. Soc.*, 6th ser., xxi (2011), 171–91. For J.B.S. Haldane, see R. Clark, *JBS: The Life and Work of JBS Haldane* (London, 1968); V.M. Quirke, 'Haldane, John Burdon Sanderson (1892–1964)', *ODNB* (2004), & works cited.

56. *Times*, 19 March 1936, iss. 47327; cf. J.B. Chinnery-Haldane, Diary, 15 March 1936 ('They want the ashes put in Richard's grave!').

made her pregnant, he agreed to a civil marriage. Her partnership would effectively have stunted his social progress within the Army, and, in an attempt to minimize its publicity, the pair crossed the Irish Sea to Old Greenock, where, in the presence of a law student and a maid, their cohabitation or 'irregular marriage' was regularized by sheriff's warrant, which 'acclaimed' the marriage of 'James Haldane gentleman' to Kate Stuart, who thereupon went their separate ways. Aylmer agreed to pay his wife an allowance on condition that she never called herself by his name, but, after it became clear that she was not pregnant and that he had been deluded, he consulted the family lawyer. William Haldane put a private detective onto the case to seek evidence of Kate Stuart's suspected adultery, but none was established, and it was not until 1901 that she was induced to obtain a divorce on the grounds of desertion, which Aylmer did not, of course, contest.[57]

During the unhappy period of his concealed marriage, he was on active service in India and South Africa. Twice seriously wounded, and captured by the Boers, he was nursed by 'a war correspondent, Mr Churchill', a fellow prisoner to whom he confided an escape plan which was promptly appropriated and successfully employed by the future statesman, who thus extended Aylmer's captivity in Pretoria until another scheme could be devised. Invalided home, he joined the intelligence section of the War Office under Sir Henry Trotter, commanding the Home District, and, by the end of 1902, had risen to the brevet rank of lieutenant-colonel. He had also become a Christian Scientist, much to the dismay of Brodrick's father, who had baptized him. The bishop felt compelled to write to Sir Henry 'as an old friend', alerting him to the possibility that people 'might tell you that [Aylmer] was a fast man who had married his mistress, and had been divorced for deserting her', placing the true facts before him, but nevertheless fearing 'that he may get out of touch with what is good'. 'From this,' he told the general, 'you may be able to save him. You may be able to give him a helping hand, morally I mean, and above all religiously.' Whatever Sir Henry's

57. Statutory register, marriages, 564/03/0155 (Greenock, Old or West, 30 July 1888); correspondence between Aylmer and William Haldane, 14 Feb.–13 Nov. 1892 (at Gleneagles).

response, it did not weaken Aylmer's attachment to his new religion. On 17 November 1902, he told the bishop: 'I can honestly claim that what is known as Christian Science has done more for me in the few months during which I have studied it than all the years that I have passed in alternate sin and repentance. You have always taken such a lively interest in my spiritual well-being and have so consistently stood by me in the unfortunate episode of my life, which was closed scarcely a year ago, that I should not like you to think that I had not given your appeal in the present matter full weight and consideration.'[58]

When the Russo-Japanese war broke out in 1904, Aylmer was sent to Manchuria as a military attaché with the Japanese army, on whose fighting qualities he reported favourably. At the outbreak of the Great War in 1914, he was a brigadier-general; when it ended, he was a lieutenant-general and a knight, having commanded the Tenth Infantry Brigade, the Third Division, and the Sixth Corps, seeing action on the western front throughout the war, and employing the technocratic skills which ultimately gave the allies victory. In December 1919, he was dispatched to Mesopotamia (soon to be Iraq) to oversee the reduction of the British garrison, and, in the event, put down an Arab rising which had united both Sunni and Shi'a tribes, disrupted the civil administration, and threatened to overwhelm the forces at his command. He lived on bluff until reinforcements arrived from India, suppressed the revolt, and facilitated the enthronement of King Feisal, whom, in March 1922, he left in Baghdad at the head of the local militia which Aylmer had organized to replace the British military presence. Promoted full general, he retired in 1925, and died in 1950, having requested a private funeral with no flowers or mourning; 'if the king's intention to be represented is expressed, it is to be respectfully declined.'[59]

58. Bishop to Sir Henry Trotter, undated copy, probably late 1902; Aylmer to bishop, 17 Nov. 1902; Selina Haldane to Evelyn Hardcastle, 1 Dec. 1899 (for reference to Churchill's nursing).

59. For his career, see *HG*, pp. 250–1; A. Simpson, 'Haldane, Sir (James) Aylmer Lowthorpe (1862–1950)', *ODNB* (2008), & works cited; a copy of his will is at Gleneagles.

Aylmer's published opus consists almost entirely of accounts of his military campaigns and exploits. The exception is his history of the Haldanes of Gleneagles, a work for which he enlisted the scholarly assistance of Henry Paton of the Register House and of the jurist Thomas Miller, who assembled (and sometimes interpreted) a mass of documentary evidence, which he marshalled and presented to the public in 1929. The book contains a chapter which Aylmer had requested from Professor J.S. Haldane on 'the heredity of the Gleneagles family', in which the physiologist argued that inherited land was on loan from the community, held in return for rent in the form of service or financial dues, and, should its holders fail to keep apace with developments in that community by accumulating resources from successful involvement in occupations beyond the borders of their estate, they would fail to resist the erosion of their inheritance through taxation and death duties, 'and the direct family line suffers disaster'.[60] This essay was read carefully by Brodrick, who underlined some of its passages in red ink. As he attended the interment of its author's ashes in 1936, in the company of cousins who had achieved notable success in their chosen fields of endeavour, he may have wondered what contribution his own progeny would make to the history of the Gleneagles inheritance.

Brodrick was survived by his four children and two grandchildren, John and Alaisdhair, the sons of his elder daughter Marjorie. In 1922, Marjorie had married a rich neighbour, Guy Bullough of Fasnacloich (in Appin, south of Ballachulish), and they had taken up residence in Dunbeg. There, in 1926, their second son was secretly baptized by a Presbyterian minister, in the presence of Marjorie's mother-in-law, but without a word to either of her own parents. The betrayal was acutely felt, but not allowed to blunt their solicitude for Marjorie when she tried to rescue her marriage from the consequences of Guy's infidelity and alcoholism. Apart from a brief separation in 1930, when he was cited in an Edinburgh divorce case, Marjorie offered him what support she could before his death in 1934. She resided for some years in Belgravia

---

60. *HG*, pp. 269–72, quotation at p. 269; Sturdy, 'The meanings of "life"', pp. 181–3.

before returning to the west of Scotland to live in one of the cottages at Alltshellach until her death at the age of sixty-eight in 1971.[61]

Marjorie's younger sister Agnes was twenty-two when she announced her engagement in 1927 to Hugh Harris, an Old Harrovian friend of her brother Alex, and the second son of an English landowner based at Brackenburgh Tower near Carlisle. The marriage was delayed until 1929, when Hugh was given an opportunity to farm in Kenya; the couple set off for the colony in May, but returned a little over a year later, having found everything there to be 'in a grim way'. Brodrick leased them the Kinnaker, where Hugh established a poultry farm; in 1933, he was also given the lease of Glenhead as a base for farming sheep. By the time war broke out, he had branched into trade by opening a petrol station at Loaninghead, and the Gleneagles estate was in effect being run by a triumvirate of him, Alex, and Brodrick.[62]

The lowering of social barriers since the beginning of the century had opened occupations previously favoured by the younger sons of landed families to increased competition. The response of Agnes's husband had been to try his luck in an African colony. That of her younger brother, Brodrick Vernon, was to remain in Britain and follow his instinct into the newly emerging world of celebrity. His options were limited by a complete lack of scholastic achievement: Stowe and Harrow had been closed to him after his failure to pass the common entrance examination, and, by his own account, his acceptance at Lancing had been thanks entirely to an assurance by his preparatory school's headmaster that he would prove an amenable and amusing ornament.[63] Leaving school without qualifications, his ability to amuse ensured a regular flow of invitations to London parties and country house weekends. Using the advantage of his name to gain entrées denied to rivals, BV became a society photographer and has been acclaimed as 'the first of the paparazzi', with his work praised for its vitality and invention. His success in recording private moments of the glitterati, whether aristocrats or film stars,

61. J.B. Chinnery-Haldane, Diary, 18 Jan. 1922; 6 May 1926; 4 March, 17–18 April, June–July 1930; 5 May, 2 July 1934.
62. Ibid., 3–4, 22 Aug. 1930; 19 March, 13 July 1933; 26 Aug. 1938.
63. Ibid., 20 March, 21 July 1926; Haldane & Martine, *Time Exposure*, pp. 38–9.

did not, however, impress his father, who considered most films likely to be 'rot', found it 'horrible' that publicity should be given to an individual's private life, and shuddered at the thought that the public might be led to believe that the sort of people BV photographed at the Gleneagles Hotel were enjoying the hospitality of the true Gleneagles.[64]

Alexander Napier Chinnery-Haldane, 1907–94; laird 1937–94

His elder son, however, with whom Brodrick had a much closer rapport, never lost his admiration for his brother's achievement in breaking new ground. Alex's own attempts to embark on a career had all stalled. His education had not been as undistinguished as BV's, but success in crucial examinations required more than one attempt, and the insistence of a growing number of Oxford colleges upon such success as a qualification for admission meant that he went up to Wadham rather than follow his father into Christ Church. Shy but transparently good-natured, he had been happy enough at Warren Hill, his preparatory school in Eastbourne, and at Harrow, but the occasional obligation to produce an essay and sit an examination made his time at Oxford more a penance than a privilege. In later life, he readily admitted to the slowness with which he read and wrote and laboured to grasp an argument, characteristics evidently inherited from his grandfather, the bishop. A burst appendix, necessitating a month's convalescence in a nursing home in April–May 1929, made it pointless for Alex to undergo the trauma of sitting his Oxford finals that summer, and he left the university without a degree.[65]

Ever since the age of nine, when he had been taken by his father 'to watch flying machines' at an aerodrome in Eastbourne, aviation held a fascination for him. Alex had joined the Air Squadron at Oxford, made his first solo flight in July 1928, and, after going down, spent time at its training camp at Manston in Kent. His enquiries at an aeroplane rally at the Gleneagles Hotel in 1929, however, found 'nothing doing among the flying folk'. It had already been decided by his father and cousin, General

64. J.B. Chinnery-Haldane, Diary, 21 Feb. 1929.
65. Ibid., April–May 1929; letters from Alex to his father during 1940.

Sir Aylmer Haldane, that the Army was 'out of the question except as a soldier', since the five-foot-eight-inch Alex was 'not built for the social part of it'.[66] Towards the end of 1929, Alex went to London on a fruitless search for an opening in the Lloyds insurance market. Participation in an Alpine tour testing motor cars and work for the Association for the Protection of Rural Scotland helped pass the time, but neither provided the springboard for a career. In conversation with his cousin Sir William Haldane, he explained that 'the only thing he could do any good in is the Air, of which he has some knowledge and is keen on; he has no education fitting him for commercial or almost any other line he could try for with the slightest hope of making good; he would not mind a bit roughing it in however humble an effort to develop himself, but his father has always urged on him that he could not earn enough to keep himself, and that he could not afford to help in this.' In fact, as Sir William rightly divined, Brodrick dreaded the prospect of Alex leaving him, as he was 'the only one of the family he can confide in'. Just as his own father, the bishop, had discouraged his own independence, so Brodrick unconsciously undermined what self-confidence his elder son possessed, while Alex's deep filial devotion supplied the decisive factor in determining that his life was to be spent almost entirely at Gleneagles.[67]

The outbreak of the Second World War determined that this scenario was to require temporary adjustment. On 22 January 1940, Alex was called up and posted as a lieutenant to the Royal Scots, who disembarked at Cherbourg on 5 March as part of the British Expeditionary Force sent to support the French and protect the Low Countries against German invasion. They had reached Wavre, a few miles from Brussels, when news arrived on 14 May that they had been cut off by the enemy break-through at Sedan. In the consequent retreat into France Alex survived aerial bombardment, shelling, sniping, sleepless nights, ten-hour marches, and an unsuccessful attempt to milk a cow, before his company took up 'a nasty position' in an old quarry at Calonne-sur-la-Lys. Here

66. J.B. Chinnery-Haldane, Diary, 5 May 1916; 8, 21 July 1928; 12 May, 9 July 1929; Brodrick to Katherine, 13 June 1926, interleaved in Diary.
67. Sir William Haldane to Sir Aylmer Haldane, 4 Dec. 1938.

they saw close action on 20 and 21 May: 'heavy losses and much horror; continual casualties and not enough stretchers; many narrow escapes, but managed to inflict some 20 casualties myself'. On 23 May, he was taken out of the fighting line to become ADC to General Irwin, an appointment which he guessed may have saved his life, for the Royal Scots lost 66 per cent of their officers and 75 per cent of their men. 'But even behind the line,' he told his brother, 'we were bombed and machine-gunned and shelled. I had many near ones, but the only trouble caused was a shell burst my sock suspender.' On 28 May, orders came to destroy vehicles, 'dump everything except what carried', and make for Dunkirk, forty miles away, which Alex reached at four o'clock the next morning. After waiting for most of 30 May, under bombardment from the sky and shelling from the east, Alex got onto the breakwater at 9.30 p.m., where he huddled for six hours before boarding the destroyer HMS *Malcolm*, from which he disembarked at Dover in time for breakfast on 31 May.[68]

Given the acting rank of captain, Alex spent the remainder of the war in charge of a company of 150 Royal Scots, 'a quarter of whom are most troublesome ruffians,' preparing the defence of vulnerable parts of the British coastline and undergoing exacting training exercises. He soon discovered that 'soldiering is so utterly against the grain with me that it is a big strain keeping going – one has to be so hardhearted that I almost weep sometimes'. Nevertheless, he performed his duties with painstaking diligence, being warned by his commanding officer that he worked too hard, spent too many late hours in his office, and should delegate more, all of which he took as a compliment.[69]

Demobilized at the end of the war in 1945, Alex returned home to preside over a shrunken estate. Although the transfer of the barony to him in 1937 had taken Gleneagles out of the taxman's net, Alex had still been obliged, in 1944, to sell Aberuthven to help meet the death duties payable on his father's remaining assets. In 1946, he renewed the Holiday Fellowship's lease of Alltshellach House for ten years at £200 p.a.,

---

68. Paragraph drawn from Alex's pocket diary for 1940, his letter to his brother of 13 June 1940, and his annotations in his father's diary 19 May–2 June 1940.

69. Alex to his father, 4 Aug., 3 Nov. 1940; 23 Feb. 1941.

but five years later sold it outright to the same organization for the surprisingly modest sum of £650 (equivalent to about £18,400 in 2015). He also sold two of Alltshellach's five staff cottages to descendants of old servants, a generous but commercially unwise gesture which broke up a potentially valuable site for development. He did not, in fact, have a coherent management policy. Providing a genial but almost invisible presence within his estate, he rarely moved around it in daylight lest he should see things that needed attention; when he did, it was astride his Triumph motorcycle, not on tours of inspection, but on thunderous and express circuits designed to satisfy his somewhat incongruous love of speed; in his later years, he regularly slept through estate meetings which he chaired. By contrast, after the hotel reopened in 1947, he was almost unrecognizably energized in detecting failure on the part of journalists 'to enlighten the public that the Gleneagles Hotel is not Gleneagles, and avoid misleading them into thinking otherwise'. For Alex the continuation of his father's campaign was an almost sacred trust: 'as the present Haldane of Gleneagles,' he told the editor of *The Scotsman* in 1963, 'I would be failing in my duty to my forebears and to those who come after me by allowing the name of our ancient family property to be misapplied to a golfing hotel.'[70] On occasions when he felt that the hotel management was itself remiss, he would visit the establishment to confront its hapless representative with a hostility that this gentlest of gentlemen had only otherwise displayed when fighting Germans on the retreat to Dunkirk.

In 1950, when arranging for the disposal of the transcripts of sources he had used in writing *The Haldanes of Gleneagles*, Sir Aylmer Haldane requested that they remain in the office of the family lawyers (W. & F. Haldane), since 'it would be of no use to send them to Gleneagles, as the future of that place is uncertain.'[71] The likelihood was remote that Alex would improve his financial position either by marrying money or by earning it outside the estate. He was a reluctant bachelor, but his

70. A. Chinnery-Haldane to editor of *The Scotsman*, 30 July & 8 August 1963.
71. Will of J. Aylmer L. Haldane (at Gleneagles); records of the sale of Aberuthven are at Turcan Connell, Edinburgh; those of Alltshellach at Gleneagles.

confidence in marriage had been undermined by his observation of the unions of his parents, his uncle Vernie, and his sister Marjorie, while his sister Agnes, of whom he saw much, lived a life largely independent of her husband. His lack of confidence in his own ability to succeed where others, notably his admired father, had been seen to fail, left him resigned to the prospect that he would not, in his own words, 'take on a wife'.[72]

Since his brother Brodrick was also a bachelor (and resolute rather than reluctant), Alexander Chinnery-Haldane of Gleneagles faced the problem of selecting a successor. The entail had ended with his father, so in law he had complete freedom of choice. In effect, his freedom was circumscribed by his father's expressed wishes, which he would hesitate to contravene. In a letter of 5 February 1930, which Alex kept in an envelope marked in red ink 'KEEP carefully', Brodrick had told him that 'failing all my own children, I don't want Foswell or Cloan people to have Gleneagles, for reasons on which we all agree'.[73] The unstated reasons can confidently be assumed to have been religious and political. The Haldanes of Foswell and Cloan were radical in their politics and Presbyterian in their religion, positions that Brodrick found hard to understand and impossible to accept as the guiding principles of a future laird. By 1965, however, when the ownership of Gleneagles was converted into a trust, and a list made of potential future beneficiaries from whom an heir would be selected, divisions within the family had softened. Helped doubtless by the presence of Archibald Haldane from Foswell as a legal adviser, candidates were considered from the entire family.

The field was narrowed by its limitation to male lines, and by the decision to rule out all members of his own generation, which, of course, included his brother Brodrick, younger of Gleneagles. Only five of Alex's contemporary male cousins were married, and of them only three had sons: Robert Aylmer (1907–98), whose son (John) Duncan was an Arabist and Islamic scholar; Archibald (1900–82), the lawyer whose deepest interest lay, not in the law, but in the history of Scotland's road

72.   The phrase was used in conversation with the author.
73.   At Gleneagles.

and postal network, and whose son John could be expected to inherit Foswell; and James (1903–90), whose elder son (James) Martin had followed him into chartered accountancy, while his younger son Robert became a London lawyer; Richard, the son of (Thomas) Graeme Haldane at Cloan (1892–1981), being adopted and so not 'of the blood', was excluded from consideration. The decision was delayed until one of the four members of the younger generation should produce a male heir. The first to do so was Martin Haldane in 1975.

In 1968, at the age of twenty-seven, Martin had married Petronella, a daughter of the diplomat Sir Peter Scarlett, and kin to Lord Abinger and the Scarletts of Inverlochy, who had been close friends of Bishop Chinnery-Haldane and his family. On 19 December 1975, she gave birth to James, a brother for Rachel and Anna, who had been born in 1970 and 1973 respectively. Martin was probably already in pole position to be named as Alex's successor: he and his family saw a good deal of the laird; Martin's profession as an Edinburgh chartered accountant, with a number of landowners among his clientèle, made him eminently suitable to direct the future management of the estate; his membership of the Episcopal Church, moreover, satisfied a consideration to which the laird gave great weight. And now he had a son, who was duly declared the future beneficiary of the Gleneagles Trust. In order to avoid the separation of the chieftainship of the Haldane name from the lairdship of Gleneagles which had persisted from 1760 until 1918, the laird executed a deed of tanistry which nominated Martin 'younger of Gleneagles', an act which distressed Brodrick, who had accepted exclusion from the landed inheritance, but, in losing his appellation 'younger', now felt 'as if he had been declared illegitimate'.[74]

Alex invited his young cousins to share the house, and, after some structural alterations, they moved into its larger, eastern half, while he retired into the remainder. Here he devoted almost all his time to the preservation, perusal, arrangement, and occasional annotation of his grandfather's and father's voluminous archive, thus meriting the profound gratitude of future historians. He would speak of retiring to Dunbeg in Ballachulish 'to have some fun', but the realization of this

74. *The Times*, 8 April 1994.

dream was limited to sojourns in his late sister Marjorie's Alltshellach cottage. His social life was lived largely vicariously through his brother, to whom he spoke daily on the telephone, but he responded with genuine pleasure to the increased social activity that came to Gleneagles with the arrival of Martin and Petronella. He delighted in the company of their children, and they in his, and great sadness descended on the family when, on 7 April 1994, in his eighty-sixth year, he was discovered lifeless on his kitchen floor.

(James) Martin Haldane; born in 1941; laird from 1994

The twenty-eighth Haldane of Gleneagles was born on 18 September 1941 to James Haldane and Joanna, daughter of Lieutenant-Colonel William Thorburn of Craigerne, Peeblesshire. Educated, like his father James, at Winchester and Magdalen College, Oxford, he followed not only his parent but also his grandfather and great-grandfather into the profession of chartered accountancy. The family firm of Lindsay, Jamieson, & Haldane had become Haldane, Brown & Co. by 1970, when it merged with Arthur Young, McClelland, Moores, an international company of which Martin remained a partner until it became an even larger conglomerate after its merger with Ernst & Whinney in 1989, when he moved to the long-established but independent Edinburgh house of Chiene & Tait, presiding as its chairman from 1998 until his retirement in 2001. He also sat on the boards of a number of investment and insurance companies, was treasurer of the Royal Company of Archers (the monarch's bodyguard in Scotland), and provided financial advice on the Court of Stirling University, service which was acknowledged in 2006 by the grant of an honorary doctorate.

The success of his professional career has been opportune for the Gleneagles estate, whose gap between income and expenditure was ominously wide when he became active in its management in the 1970s. Since his succession to the lairdship, no funds have been transferred from the estate for personal expenditure; profits have been returned to the land. That profits existed at all was the result of his alertness to the estate's potential in a changing environment. The suitability of Gleneagles ground for the erection of telephone masts and wind turbines, and for providing access to larger wind farms beyond its boundary, has produced rental income at no cost to the estate. Similarly, although less durably and on a smaller scale, the ambition of an ex-director of Highland Spring to rival his erstwhile company by drawing water from the estate, bottling and marketing it as 'Gleneagles Water', provided royalties during the 1990s and early 2000s, while the capital costs were borne by others. The wish of the Gleneagles Hotel to enlarge one of its golf courses resulted in the sale of some acres near Loaninghead, which symbolized the improvement in relations between house and hotel. The strains imposed on the estate by the G8 summit in 2005 were the result of the lack of cooperation, not by the hotel, but by the government, which did nothing to discourage reference to the summit as located 'at Gleneagles', and declined to discuss compensation for the significant expense involved in security and insurance against mob violence and vandalism.

It was Martin's good fortune that the presence in his client list of other landowners brought him into contact with Iain Chalmers, who factored some of their estates and was ready to include Gleneagles in his portfolio. With the benefit of his advice on agricultural, forestry, and sporting matters, the laird was able to put the economy of Gleneagles upon a sound footing. The amalgamation of farms in response to changing agricultural conditions has reduced their number from seven to three, of which only West Mains, the smallest (225 acres), has a resident farmer and retains an arable component. Otherwise, the estate is given over to grazing and forestry. In 2006, 346 acres were planted at Frandy in the largest such scheme undertaken in Scotland that year; essentially a commercial plantation of softwoods, its appearance on the perimeter is broken with hardwoods, while the provision of bridle paths and footpaths will allow riders and walkers to explore the interior. Decisions to plant and fell are taken after full consideration of their impact on the shoot, which offers good, challenging drives, with pheasants and partridges on the low ground, and a few grouse on the hill. The sporting profile of the estate includes fishing on the lower Frandy reservoir. In the 1930s, Martin's predecessor Alex, when younger of Gleneagles, had been obliged to spend nocturnal vigils at Frandy watching for poachers; James, the present younger, has now put the exploitation of fishing rights on a more organized, and secure, commercial foundation, and they are now let within the wider family.[75] James indeed is focusing his entrepreneurial eye on all estate assets, and developments in this respect can be confidently expected.

The amalgamation of farms, and reduction in agricultural manpower, has released a number of houses and cottages onto the rental market. One, The Kinnaker, left vacant since the death in 1983 of both Hugh and Agnes Harris, and subsequently allowed to fall into terminal decay, has been demolished, but this loss to the glen's housing stock was amply compensated when Martin's brother, the English-based solicitor Robert, and his wife Elizabeth decided to enlarge the Old Schoolhouse to make a Scottish residence for them and their three sons, William, Mungo, and Alexander. Meanwhile, the remnants of the Alltshellach estate in Lochaber have been sold: Dunbeg to a Glaswegian businessman whose long-held ambition had been to own it and the cottages to a property developer. In 1930, Brodrick Chinnery-Haldane had told his elder son: 'Our living in Alltshellach was an accident. Perthshire is our proper place, and people in the future will look back to our being in Lochaber as a sort of freak that happened while the family was waiting to return to its old home here.'[76]

That old home is now more comfortable than ever before, and its setting even more enchanting. Petronella Haldane has taken part of the glen, drained it, planted some fifty trees and countless shrubs, transformed a boggy field into a lochan, and created a wild water garden, home to a wide variety of birds, and a restaurant for red squirrels, which are beginning to recolonize this corner of Perthshire. The better to enjoy this setting, a garden room has been added to the south-east corner of the house, providing an early twenty-first century contribution to the architectural diversity of Gleneagles.

Meanwhile, the ambience of the house has been enlivened by the varied interests of its custodians. Both Martin and Petronella give energetic support to the Episcopal church of St Kessog in Auchterarder and to Old St Paul's in Edinburgh. The marriage of their elder daughter

75.   For Alex's vigils, see B. Chinnery-Haldane, Diary, 13 June 1933, 27 July 1937.
76.   B. Chinnery-Haldane to A. Chinnery-Haldane, 3 February 1930.

Rachel to Tim Buxton in 2001 was conducted in Gleneagles chapel by the Primus, Bishop Richard Holloway of Edinburgh, who had reconsecrated the building after the restoration of its roof, while their younger daughter Anna was married in 2006 to Dominic Blakey in St Kessog's, Auchterarder, by Bishop Martin Shaw of Argyll and the Isles, whose predecessor, Bishop Chinnery-Haldane, had laid the church's foundation stone in 1897. Martin's musical interests are reflected in his past chairmanship of the Scottish Philharmonic Society and the Scottish Chamber Orchestra, his support for Scottish Opera, and membership of the D'Oyly Carte Opera Trust, while Petronella is an accomplished artist. The west pavilion, which has failed to shed its nickname of 'the ruin' despite its restoration in the 1990s, is as likely to house a painting workshop or a musical evening as a shooting lunch, while at dinner in the main house an actor may find himself seated opposite a bishop. After its long slumber throughout the nineteenth century and for the greater part of the twentieth, Gleneagles has reawakened.

Appendix I

The Castle, House and Chapel of Gleneagles

The castle

The ruins of Gleneagles Castle occupy the top of an apparently natural, steep-sided mound, with the Ruthven Water flowing past its eastern base and (until it was drained, probably in the mid eighteenth century) a loch protecting its northern and western approaches. Although the site must surely have been fortified long before, the ruins have been dated to no earlier than the late fifteenth century. They comprise the walls, nine feet thick, of the basement and ground floor of a rectangular tower, both storeys vaulted the better to bear the weight of two or even three higher ones, which would have included the main hall, the laird's private chamber, and accommodation for guests and servants, reached by a stair turret rising from the ground floor, by the side of the entrance in the south-east corner. A hole in the surviving jamb was for a draw-bar to secure the door. A cell within the thickness of the wall in the north-east corner was probably a pit prison, where those awaiting the laird's justice might be kept until trial. A privy in the north wall of the first floor was evacuated into an exterior cesspool, which was also the destination for chutes from elsewhere in that wall, and whence waste found its way via a paved drain into the loch. The tower, whose dimensions were about thirty feet north to south, and fifty feet east to west, would have been circled by a wall, enclosing such offices as kitchen, brewhouse, and stables.[1]

1. *HG*, pp. 310–12; J. Gifford, *The Buildings of Scotland: Perth & Kinross* (New Haven, 2007), p. 400.

Writing in 1550 to set the scene for events which took place in 1514, Sir David Lindsay described Gleneagles Castle as a 'triumphant plesand place', whose favoured guests might expect to find themselves sleeping in a 'well-arrayit' chamber. Together with two references in deeds of 1547 to 'the tower or fortalice' of Gleneagles, this is the earliest explicit documentary evidence for the castle.[2] The formula 'with tower and/ or fortalice' became conventional and continued in legal usage late into the eighteenth century, when it can no longer be taken as evidence for the castle's enduring role as a dwelling. In fact, objects unearthed during work to preserve the ruins in 1926–28, and later excavations in 1992, suggest that occupation ceased in the latter part of the seventeenth century.[3]

The castle seems to have been unscathed during royalist raids on the glen in 1645 and 1646, but it is possible that it suffered during the summer of 1654, when General Monck told Cromwell that small parties of the enemy had burnt Castle Campbell (about eight miles to the south) and that their commander had given orders 'to burne all the stronge houses neere the Hills'.[4] Whether or not his castle was in fact damaged at this time, it was chronic insolvency rather than physical discomfort which drove the laird from his home, probably in 1656, and kept him abroad until his death in Poland between 1660 and 1662. His half-brother Mungo was established on his mother's land near Brechin at the time of his succession, and would not appear to have resided at Gleneagles until 1668 at the earliest.[5] When he did return, he seems not to have lived at the castle, but at the Mains.

2. Above, pp. 41–2; NRS, GD198/128; *Exchequer Rolls*, xviii. 411.
3. J.B. Chinnery-Haldane, Diary, 17 Nov. 1927, 19 Sept. 1928; Perth Museum notes, 26 Feb. & 13 March. Finds include the seal on a glass bottle fragment: 'To be sold by James Stewart druggist 1661'.
4. Above, pp. 78–9; C.H. Firth (ed.), *Scotland and the Protectorate: Letters & Papers relating to the Military Government of Scotland 1654–1659* (Scot. Hist. Soc., xxxi, 1899), p. 153.
5. Above, pp. 85–7.

The house

The Mains was the laird's home farm, either exploited directly or leased in part or wholly to tenants, and its farmhouse, dateable to the early years of the seventeenth century, forms the oldest part of the present house of Gleneagles, set to the west of Ruthven Water on the plain about a third of a mile south of the castle. It would seem a reasonable conjecture that the house was adapted during Mungo's absence, reusing certain features of the castle – perhaps some panelling and a wooden pediment carved with the impaled arms of Haldane and Wemyss, and the date 1624, celebrating the first marriage of Mungo's father.

Moving into the converted farmhouse did not bring the laird into the vanguard of fashion, although it must have been less antiquated than the castle, whose only improvement since its construction had been the erection of a porch for the main doorway in the late sixteenth century. Its site was too restricted for any rebuilding in the classical or Palladian style which was now fashionable, and with which Mungo was familiar. His half-sister Jean had married into the Halkett family, who had also provided a wife for the eminent Scottish architect, Sir William Bruce, and Bruce's father-in-law, Sir James Halkett of Pitfarrane, was among the creditors whose financial aid had preserved Mungo's inheritance.[6] It may not be fanciful to suppose that Mungo regarded the move into the Mains farmhouse as a temporary measure before his finances were on a secure enough foundation to build an entirely new house conformable to current taste.

His death in 1685, aged about fifty, left the task to his son John (Union Jack). Among John's acquaintances was Sir John Clerk of Penicuik, with whom he sat on a committee to examine public accounts in 1703.[7] Sir John was a skilled architect, whose plan for the ideal house for 'a man of quality' was so close to that which was begun at Gleneagles, that it bears quoting at length:

---

6. Above, p. 86.
7. J.M. Gray (ed.), *Memoirs of the Life of Sir John Clerk of Penicuik* (Scot. Hist. Soc., xiii, 1892), pp. 50–1.

A good family house should be divided in three parts, viz. the body or main house with a large pavilion on each side.... The main or chief body of the house ought to be at least double the bigness of each pavilion, and may serve chiefly for lodging the master of the family and the better kind of guests who come to visit him. One of the pavilions ought entirely to be appropriated for women and children, and the other ought to contain the kitchen, with apartments for men servants and such like conveniences.[8]

A new house on such a plan was begun immediately to the west of the Mains. It was perhaps in order to speed the family's access to extra accommodation that the east pavilion was actually attached to the existing house and built first. The west pavilion was also erected, with the kitchen occupying most of the ground floor and the interior of the upper floor panelled. The central block was never started. Had the original architectural scheme been completed, the converted farmhouse would certainly have been demolished. The style of the somewhat squat, two-storey, hipped pavilions indicates an origin in the late seventeenth or early eighteenth century, and a reference in 1722 to the Mains being 'the old house of Glenneglis' confirms that by then the eastern pavilion was complete.[9] The Mains's tenant was presumably installed in the easternmost part of the older house, with the laird's family residing in the remainder and having access to the new rooms in the east pavilion. Precisely when the larger scheme was abandoned is not known, but, by the middle of the eighteenth century, Mungo (II) had extended

8.   Cited by R. Mitchison, *Lordship to Patronage: Scotland 1603–1745* (London, 1983), p. 149.
9.   The identification of 'the old house' as the Mains is inferred from the facts that, in 1722, an aged and blind John Haldan resided with Thomas Haldan 'at the old house of Glenneglis', and that a Thomas Haldan had succeeded William Haldan 'in the Mains of Glenegles' in 1688, and was designated 'in the Mains of Glenglis' in 1731: NRS, CC6/12/7, 8 (Dunblane Commissary Court records, Register of Deeds & Protests), abstracted in 'Notes', ii. 570–2; CC6/5/201, test. 1688 William Haldane.

the older house eastwards, inserted in the new north-eastern wall a now indecipherable stone cartouche, carved with three heraldic shields, and placed a date stone for 1750 above it. If, as seems likely, the heraldic stone came from the castle, its removal would suggest that a local tradition, current in the mid nineteenth century, that the fabric of the castle was still substantially intact in the late eighteenth century was not too inaccurate a memory.[10] It is possible that the massive lintel of a fireplace in the hall of the present house also came from the castle. In addition, at much the same time, Mungo erected two decorated gate piers, dated 1749, which were perhaps placed to the north of the house, close to where Bargate Cottage, originally known as Gleneagles Gate, has stood since 1776.[11] At some unknown date, they were removed to the chapel enclosure, before, in 2000, being found a more suitable site where the Gleneagles drive meets the Dunfermline to Crieff road. There was also a gatehouse to the west of the house, supervising access from the drove road along the west side of the glen, but its description in 1812 as 'the old west gate' suggests that the gate itself had by then been dispensed with, and the cottage itself disappears from record after 1851.[12] Mungo evidently never had sufficient funds to undertake the erection of the central block, while the increasing financial embarrassment of his heir

10. Gifford, *Buildings*, pp. 397–9; *HG*, pp. 132 (for datestone), 314 n. 4.
11. For Gleneagles Gate, see 'Rental of Estates of Gleneagles & Aberuthven 1812' (Camperdown MSS at Gleneagles); 1841 census; NRS, SC45/31/20, inv. 1867 Adam Duncan-Haldane; date stone at Bargate. Above another chimneypiece is a marble shield carved with the arms of Haldane impaling Drummond, which could represent either John Haldane's first marriage, to Mary Drummond, in 1677, or George (Cockburn) Haldane's second marriage, to Margaret Drummond, in 1799. The latter is more likely, as the shield was found in the 1840s by Mrs Robert Haldane of Cloan in a house near Greyfriars, Edinburgh, the site of George's tomb, for which the shield was probably intended but either never fitted or subsequently removed; Mrs Haldane presented the shield to Lord Camperdown for Gleneagles: 'Notes', i. 195 (although not the head of the family, being holder of the barony George had no hesitation in his use of the heraldic supporters which appear on this shield).
12. 1812 rental; census returns for 1841–61.

Patrick led to the sale of the barony to their half-brother Robert, whose architectural ambitions had already been fulfilled at Airthrey, where he continued to reside for most of the year. With Camperdown and Lundie at their disposal, his Duncan successors similarly had no need to rebuild Gleneagles, so the scheme prompted by the decommissioning of the castle was never more than partially realized.

Once the whole of the old Mains, incorporating its eastern and western extensions, was retained by the laird, other accommodation was required for lessees of the home farm. The last tenant 'in the Mains' was mentioned in 1742; in 1744, the lease granting the home farm to Neill McKinnon designated his farmhouse as West Mains, which may have been newly built, as this is its earliest documentary reference. East Mains, first recorded in 1768, was the renamed Eastside, mentioned regularly after 1556; North Mains, also called The Kinniker or Kinechar, first appears in 1812.[13]

The inventory of the roup of George (Cockburn) Haldane's possessions in 1799 provides the only evidence available for the interior layout of the house before modern times. (By his own account, he had built a new set of offices in 1779, and, the following year, made 'an addition to the mansion house'.) The inventory lists a dining and a drawing room, Mrs Haldane's room and closet, her eldest daughter's room and closet, 'the Captain's room' (presumably a reference to the Entailer), four other bedrooms, a nursery, a 'woman house' with more beds, a library with two adjoining closets, garrets in both the 'easter' and 'wester' houses; the wester house contained three wine cellars (which must have been above ground), a 'harpsichord room' which seems to have been a bedroom, the butler's pantry, the housekeeper's room, the kitchen and servants' hall, and a dairy; the washhouse and brewhouse were probably outhouses, like the stables; an exterior feature of the eastern wall has suggested the possibility that the coach

13. NRS, CC6/5/25, test. 1743 John Blyad, 1746 Neill McKinnon (p. 255); GD220/1/A/3/6/3 (for Eastside, 1556); CC6/5/19, test. 1686 Mungo Stewart (Eastsyde 1686); CC6/6/29, test. 1784 Robert Haldane (East Mains 1768); 1812 rental; census returns 1841 onwards.

house was incorporated on the ground floor at the easternmost end of the house.[14]

The west pavilion or 'wester house' was connected to its eastern counterpart by a verandah, in whose centre was a water closet, known by polite or amused neighbours as a 'Glennegies', a name-form that was still in local usage in the middle of the eighteenth century, but was obsolete by the 1850s, when the present verandah was built, and when running water was introduced, with water closets and sitz baths installed inside the house by the first Lord Camperdown.[15] The third earl undertook more substantial work, adding ten or eleven rooms by converting the garrets of the 'easter house' and raising the roof of the east pavilion to accommodate an extra floor. Bishop Chinnery-Haldane inspected the alterations in 1888 and thought them 'all for the better', while, six years later, he found many of the rooms 'much improved' and named after farms on the estate: Frandie, East and West Mains, Miss Haldane's Bath (i.e. St Mungo's alias Holywell). On the second visit, he was accompanied by his son Brodrick, who thought 'everything is in very good order and well cared for'.[16] The census returns reflect the enlargement: eighteen rooms in 1871, twenty-nine in 1881.

The chapel

Between the house and the castle stands Gleneagles Chapel, twenty-five feet by eighteen, built *circa* 1520, reusing some material from an earlier building. A boldly carved corbel, invoking Mary's intercession for the souls of the pious and displaying the arms of Haldane impaled with those of Erskine in recognition of a marriage contracted in 1518, is the only survival of interior decoration which would have been swept

14. CC6/5/30, test. 1800 George Haldane (the text has two successive entries headed 'dining room', but the second is clearly a scribal slip for 'drawing room'); Gifford, *Buildings*, p. 399; above, p. 167.
15. Above, p. 20 & n. 81; NRS, CC8/8/114, test. 1753 Neill McKinnon; Camperdown MSS at Gleneagles, 1850s bundles nos. 32, 34, 41.
16. Bishop's Journal, 15 Oct. 1888, 15 Oct. 1894; J.B. Chinnery-Haldane, Diary, 15 Oct. 1894; cf. 5 July 1918; for the roof, see plate 2.

away by the Presbyterian Haldanes of the latter part of the sixteenth century.[17]

In the chapel yard gravestones record the burials in 1686 of M[ungo] S[tewart], servitor (i.e. factor) to Laird Mungo (I), in 1698 of T.H. (possibly Thomas Haldane 'in the Mains of Gleneagles', who appears in 1688), and in 1701 of the 86-year-old David Haldane, who had served as tutor of Gleneagles during the absence of his elder brother, Sir John Haldane, in 1633.[18] In 1742, Union Jack's third surviving son Colonel James Haldane expressed his wish to be buried at Gleneagles, 'the vault of my ancestors', but the first laird for whom evidence survives of burial here was the Entailer, Robert Haldane, in 1768. He had been baptized in the chapel by the Blackford minister in 1705, but his father's request for this dispensation, based on the inclemency of the weather, suggests that such use of the chapel at this time was exceptional.[19]

This situation altered under the third earl of Camperdown, for, in September 1871, the future bishop of Argyll and the Isles was invited to say the morning service in the chapel, and, on a visit twenty-three years later, he examined the holy water basin, just inside the door, with the Haldane arms and supporters upon it.[20] In November 1924, General Sir Aylmer Haldane showed Brodrick Chinnery-Haldane plans for his proposed restoration of the chapel in memory of the bishop, and work started the following spring. On 5 May 1925, Brodrick recorded that 'there seems very little of the walls left'; in July, a man from London arrived to install the stained-glass east window commemorating those family members who fell in the Great War and including a depiction of St Mungo resembling the late bishop. A Madonna commissioned by Aylmer arrived in April 1927, and, two months later, Brodrick was arranging in the chapel a crucifix and 'other things' from Alltshellach.[21]

17. *HG*, pp. 307–10; Gifford, *Buildings*, p. 399.
18. NRS, CC6/5/19, 20, test. 1686 Patrick Haldane, 1686 Mungo Stewart, 1688 William Haldane; *HG*, pp. 74–5.
19. *HG*, pp. 126, 194, 296; 'Notes', i. 7.
20. Bishop's Journal, 15 Sept. 1871, 15 Oct. 1894.
21. *HG*, p. 308; J.B. Chinnery-Haldane, Diary, 27 Nov. 1924, 5 May & 21 July 1925, 18 June 1927.

The chapel's Presbyterian phase had ended. In August 1928, when Lord Haldane of Cloan was buried in the enclosure, the service at the grave-side was conducted by a minister from Auchterarder, but that which took place later in the chapel was conducted by the dean of St Paul's.[22] The roof-timbers had to be replaced in 1996, after which the building was reconsecrated by the Primus, Bishop Holloway of Edinburgh, and, for some five years, was served by Michael Hunt, previous rector of St Kessog's Auchterarder, who lived in part of the house, and said his daily offices in the chapel.

22.   *The Times*, 24 August 1928, issue 44980.

Appendix II

The Later Haldanes of That Ilk

That the Haldanes of Hadden survived as lairds into the seventeenth century was largely the result of their acquisition, at some point in the reign of David II (1329–71), of Broughton in Peeblesshire, a property less exposed to border warfare than Hadden, and one which doubled the value of their landholding.[1] By 1491, however, William Haldane of that ilk was obliged to sell to his powerful neighbour, Kerr of Cessford, the southern, upland part of Hadden known as Lowsilaw, which included superiority over Kirk Yetholm.[2] The attachment of his great-grandson John to unsuccessful factions during the reign of Mary (1542–68) brought upon him financial penalties which accelerated a slide towards the verge of insolvency, and the years between 1579 and 1582 saw Broughton twice apprized for the repayment of debt.[3] In 1625, his descendant and namesake saw no alternative but to sell the barony of

1. W. Robertson, *Index of Records of Charters* (Edinburgh, 1798), p. 59, noting a charter now lost; values of Hadden and Broughton are given in John Haldane's inventory: NRS, CC8/8/64, 1648 John Halden. For the Hadden Haldanes up to 1357, see above pp. 2–11 & 22.
2. *RMS*, ii. 422 (no. 2002).
3. *RMS*, iv. 780 (no. 2838), v. 119 (no. 383); for his political and military activity, see *RMS*, iv. 184 (no. 819); *ATS*, xii. 217, 222; xiii. 383 & p. xiv; *RPCSc*, i. 653; ii. 552.

Hadden to Andrew Kerr, master of Jedburgh, and, nine years later, to sell Broughton to the Murrays of Stanhope.[4]

Still designated 'of that ilk', despite the sale of Hadden, John had established his family south of Broughton at Cardon (between Glenholm and Drumelzier, Peeblesshire) before setting out, in February 1644, to join the Army of the Solemn League and Covenant, which had entered England. He never returned, but was killed in Yorkshire, either in the skirmishing with the royalist army under the marquess of Newcastle that preceded the battle of Marston Moor, or in the battle itself, on 12 July 1644.[5] His younger but only surviving son, Andrew, died in 1673, worth no more than £60, the value of his silver watch and silver-hilted sword, a pair of pistols, a saddle, and his clothes.[6] Two years later, Agnes Haldane (1650–1724), Andrew's first cousin once removed, being a granddaughter of John's brother George, was to marry Patrick Haldane of Lanrick, a cadet of the Gleneagles Haldanes, who were thus reunited with the border family from which they had sprung.[7]

4. *RMS*, viii. 307 (no. 844), 402 (no. 1151); ix. 166 (no. 436).
5. J.W. Buchan & H. Paton, *A History of Peeblesshire* (3 vols, Glasgow, 1925–27), iii. 270; for his will, see NRS, CC8/8/64, 1648 John Halden.
6. CC8/8/79, 1673 Andrew Haddin.
7. *HG*, pp. 278, 281. The male line of the Lanrick Haldanes died out in 1764.

Appendix III

Lairds and Ladies of Gleneagles

(Presumed) Simon de Hauden, 1300x1313–post 1337; m. Matilda de Arnot

(Presumed) Sir Bernard (I) de Hauden, pre 1376–1401

Sir John (I) de Hauden, 1401–56

Bernard (II) Haldane, 1456–59 (resigned; died post 1472); m. Elizabeth

John (II) Haldane, 1459–93 (barony of Gleneagles erected 1483); m. Agnes, dr. of Murdoch Menteith of Rusky

Sir James (I) Haldane, 1493–1503; m. Christian, dr. of William, 2nd Lord Graham

Sir John (III) Haldane, 1503–13 (barony of Haldane erected 1509); m. Marjorie, dr. of Richard Lawson of Humbie

James (II) Haldane, 1513–47; m. Margaret, dr. of Robert, 4th Lord Erskine

John (IV) Haldane, 1547–63; m. Elizabeth, dr. of John Lundie of that ilk

George (I) Haldane, 1563–74; m. Jean Cunningham, dr. of William, 6th earl of Glencairn

John (V) Haldane, 1574–91; m. (1) Isobel, dr. of David Home of Wedderburn (she d.1575), (2) Barbara, dr. of James Johnstone of Elphinstone

James (III) Haldane, 1591–1624; m. Margaret Murray, dr. of John, 1st earl of Tullibardine

Sir John (VI) Haldane, 1624–50; m. (1) Catherine, dr. of Sir John Wemyss of that ilk (she d. before 1634), (2) Margaret Fraser, dr. of Simon, 6th Lord Lovat

John (VII) Haldane, 1650–60 or 62

Mungo (I) Haldane, 1660 or 62–1685; m. (1) Anne, dr. of John Grant of Lurg (she d.1662), (2) Margaret, dr. of Gray of Balgarno

John (VIII) Haldane, 1685–1721 (Union Jack; bought Aberuthven 1686); m. (1) Mary Drummond, dr. of David, 3rd Lord Maderty (she d. 1685), (2) Helen, dr. of Sir Charles Erskine, Bt of Alva

Mungo (II) Haldane, 1721–55

Patrick Haldane, 1755–60 (resigned; died 1769); m. Margaret, dr. of William, 7th Lord Forrester

Robert Haldane, 1760–68 (Entailer); m. Elizabeth, dr. of Sir William Oglander, Bt

George (II) [Cockburn] Haldane, 1768–99; m. (1) Bethia, dr. of Thomas Dundas of Fingask (she d. 1770), (2) Margaret Drummond, dr. of James, 5th Viscount Strathallan

George (III) Augustus Haldane, March–October 1799

Adam Duncan, 1st Viscount Duncan, 1799–1804; m. Henrietta, dr. of Robert Dundas of Arniston

Robert Duncan-Haldane, 2nd Viscount Duncan, 1st earl of Camperdown, 1804–59 (sold barony of Haldane 1815–16); m. Janet, dr. of Sir Hew Dalrymple-Hamilton, Bt of North Berwick

Adam Duncan-Haldane, 2nd earl of Camperdown, 1859–67; m. Juliana, dr. of Sir George Philips, Bt

Robert Haldane-Duncan, 3rd earl of Camperdown, 1867–1918 (sold Aberuthven 1912)

(James) Brodrick Chinnery-Haldane, 1918–37 (resigned; died 1941; bought Aberuthven 1912); m. Katherine Annie, dr. of William Napier

Alexander Chinnery-Haldane, 1937–94 (sold Aberuthven 1944)

(James) Martin Haldane, 1994–; m. Petronella, dr. of Sir Peter Scarlett

Appendix IV

Heads of the Family 1760–1941

Patrick Haldane of Bearcrofts, late of Gleneagles, 1760–69; m. Margaret Forrester

Robert Haldane, sometime of Airthrey, later of Auchengray, 1769–1842; m. Katherine, dr. of George Oswald of Scotstoun

James Alexander Haldane, 1842–51; m. (1) Mary, dr. of Major Alexander Joass (she d. 1819), (2) Margaret, dr. of Prof. Daniel Rutherford

Alexander Haldane, 1851–82; m. Emma, dr. of Joseph Hardcastle

Alexander Chinnery-Haldane, bishop of Argyll and the Isles, 1882–1906; m. Anna, dr. of Sir Nicholas Chinnery, Bt

(James) Brodrick Chinnery-Haldane, 1906–41 (of Aberuthven from 1912; of Gleneagles 1918–37); m. Katherine Napier

SIMPLIFIED TREE TO ILLUSTRATE THE 1768 ENTAIL AND 1994 SUCCESSION.

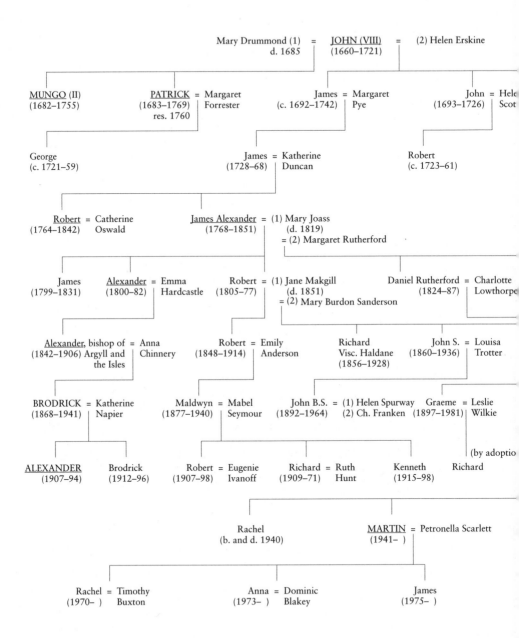

LAIRDS of Gleneagles in capitals.
<u>Chiefs</u> of Haldane name underlined.

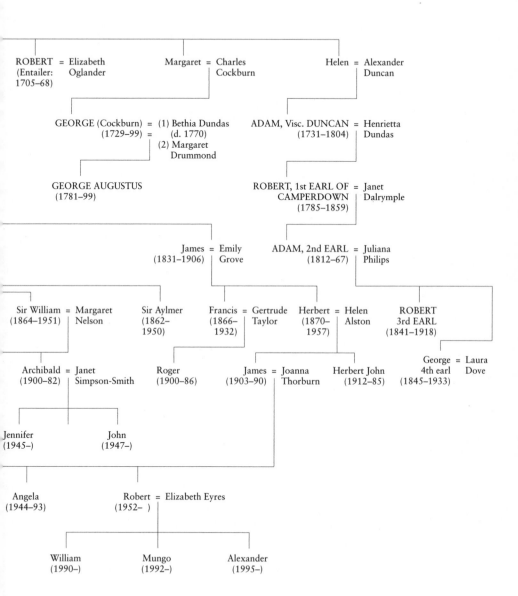

ROBERT = Elizabeth
(Entailer: Oglander
1705–68)

Margaret = Charles
          Cockburn

Helen = Alexander
      Duncan

GEORGE (Cockburn) = (1) Bethia Dundas
(1729–99)   =   (d. 1770)
                  (2) Margaret
                  Drummond

ADAM, Visc. DUNCAN = Henrietta
(1731–1804)   Dundas

GEORGE AUGUSTUS
(1781–99)

ROBERT, 1st EARL OF = Janet
    CAMPERDOWN   Dalrymple
    (1785–1859)

James = Emily
(1831–1906) | Grove

ADAM, 2nd EARL = Juliana
(1812–67)   Philips

Sir William = Margaret
(1864–1951) | Nelson

Sir Aylmer
(1862–
1950)

Francis = Gertrude
(1866–   Taylor
1932)

Herbert = Helen
(1870–   Alston
1957)

ROBERT
3rd EARL
(1841–1918)

Archibald = Janet
(1900–82) | Simpson-Smith

Roger
(1900–86)

James = Joanna
(1903–90) | Thorburn

Herbert John
(1912–85)

George = Laura
4th earl   Dove
(1845–1933)

Jennifer
(1945–)

John
(1947–)

Angela
(1944–93)

Robert = Elizabeth Eyres
(1952–)

William
(1990–)

Mungo
(1992–)

Alexander
(1995–)

Index